OXFORD WORLD'S CLASSICS

THE RISE OF ROME
BOOKS ONE TO FIVE

Titus Livius (Livy), the historian, was born in Patavium (modern Padua) in 64 or 59 BC and died in AD 17 in Patavium, surviving therefore into his late seventies or early eighties. He came to Rome in the 30s BC and began writing his history of Rome by the end of that decade. There is no evidence that he was a senator or held other governmental posts, although he was acquainted with the emperor Augustus and his family, at least by his later years. He appears to have had the means to spend his life largely in writing his huge history of Rome, *Ab Urbe Condita* or 'From the Founding of the City', which filled 142 books and covered the period from Rome's founding to the death of the elder Drusus (753–9 BC). Thirty-five books survive: 1–10 (753–293 BC) and 21–45 (218–167 BC).

T. J. Luce is professor of Classics emeritus at Princeton University. He received his AB degree from Hamilton College in 1954 and his Ph.D. from Princeton University in 1958. He is the author of *Livy: The Composition of his History* (Princeton, 1977) and *The Greek Historians* (Routledge, 1997).

OXFORD WORLD'S CLASSICS

＝

LIVY

The Rise of Rome
Books One to Five

＝

Translated with an Introduction and Notes by
T. J. LUCE

OXFORD
UNIVERSITY PRESS

OXFORD
UNIVERSITY PRESS

Great Clarendon Street, Oxford OX2 6DP

Oxford University Press is a department of the University of Oxford.
It furthers the University's objective of excellence in research, scholarship,
and education by publishing worldwide in

Oxford New York

Athens Auckland Bangkok Bogotá Buenos Aires Calcutta
Cape Town Chennai Dar es Salaam Delhi Florence Hong Kong Istanbul
Karachi Kuala Lumpur Madrid Melbourne Mexico City Mumbai
Nairobi Paris São Paulo Shanghai Singapore Taipei Tokyo Toronto Warsaw

with associated companies in Berlin Ibadan

Oxford is a registered trade mark of Oxford University Press
in the UK and in certain other countries

Published in the United States
by Oxford University Press Inc., New York

First published as an Oxford World's Classics paperback 1998
Reissued 2008

British Library Cataloguing in Publication Data

Data available

Library of Congress Cataloging in Publication Data
Livy.
[Ab urbe condita. Liber 1–5. English]
The rise of Rome : books one to five / Titus Livius (Livy) ;
translated and edited, with an introduction and notes by T. J. Luce.
(Oxford world's classics)
Includes bibliographical references and index.
1. Rome—History—Kings, 753–510 B.C. I. Luce, T. James (Torrey
James), 1932– . II. Title. III. Series: Oxford world's classics
(Oxford University Press).
DG233.L58213 1998 937'.01—dc21 98–11367

ISBN 978–0–19–954004–4

8

Typeset by Ace Filmsetting Ltd., Frome, Somerset
Printed in Great Britain by
Clays Ltd, St Ives plc

For Pat Kane, his progeny and their spouses:
Molly and Curt Bailey, Pete and Alice Kane,
Kate and Mike Buckley, Matt and Chrissie Kane,
Liz and Rick Czerniak

CONTENTS

INTRODUCTION

Livy's Life and Times

Titus Livius was born in 64 or 59 BC, with the former being somewhat more likely; his birthplace was Patavium in north Italy (modern Padua, Padova), then the wealthiest city of the peninsula after Rome and part of the province of Cisalpine Gaul (hence Livy may not have been born a Roman citizen). He is said to have died in Patavium in AD 17, three years after the death of the emperor Augustus, surviving therefore into his late seventies or early eighties. He shows pride in his birthplace in several passages, the first coming in the opening words of his history where he represents Antenor's settlement of the area as coeval with Aeneas' landing near Rome, after both had fled their native Troy when it was captured by the Greeks. In a digression in Book 10 (ch. 2) he describes with satisfaction the defeat that the Patavians dealt the marauding Spartan Cleonymus in 301 BC, and mentions both the beaks of his ships that were still to be seen in the city and a mock naval battle held every year on the anniversary of the victory. In Book 111 he affirmed that an augur known to him personally announced at Patavium Caesar's victory over Pompey at the moment it was taking place at Pharsalus in Greece (48 BC).[1]

The city was well known as a bastion of old-fashioned, conservative values in politics and morality. Ninety years after the historian's death the younger Pliny in a letter of recommendation (14.6) could cite as a significant point in a young man's favour the fact that his maternal aunt came from Patavium: 'You know the high moral character of *that* place.' The statesman and historian Asinius Pollio sneered at Livy's 'patavinity' (*patauinitas*), alleging his Latin exhibited certain provincialisms frowned on at Rome, or at least by Asinius.[2] The remark may also have been an oblique thrust at Livy's somewhat romantic approach to history. (One scholar in the seventeenth century retorted that it was difficult to decide whether there was more patavinity in Livius or more asininity in Asinius.)

The historian's teens coincided with the civil wars that racked

---

[1] Plutarch, *Caesar* 47 = frag. 34.   [2] Quintilian 1.5.56, 8.1.3.

Italy and the Roman world at large during the 40s BC. When Pollio as governor of Cisalpine Gaul tried to bring the city into Antony's camp, the wealthier inhabitants refused to contribute money and arms and went into hiding; Pollio then unsuccessfully attempted to bribe the slaves to betray their masters' whereabouts (43 BC);[3] instead, the townspeople declared their allegiance to conservatism and the senate.[4] Pollio's jibe at Livy's patavinity may have owed as much to his animus against the town for having closed its gates in his face as to his exacting standards for correct latinity (he later quarrelled with Antony, and went on to assume a neutral stance in the struggle between Antony and Octavian, the future Augustus, for supremacy). It is therefore doubtful that the civil wars of the 40s allowed the young Livy to continue his education by taking up residence in Rome or by going on a Grand Tour of Greece, although the dismayed Horace, born in 65 BC, found himself fighting on the side of Brutus and Cassius when the triumvirs came East in 42 BC to avenge Caesar's assassination.

The historian probably came to Rome in the 30s and spent considerable time in the city thereafter, although it may not have been his principal residence. He appears to have held no positions in government, nor was he a senator, as some minor but telling errors concerning senatorial protocol show. His mistakes in military matters, a few quite elementary, indicate he was never a soldier. He enjoyed a thorough education in rhetoric and philosophy, and seems to have had the financial resources to live an independent life devoted largely to writing. We are told he gave recitations, presumably from his history, to small but appreciative audiences,[5] but do not hear of him engaging in the popular pastime of declamation. Nor do we hear of any anecdotes that connect him to other leading literary figures of his time, such as Virgil, Horace, or Ovid. He was, however, known to Augustus and to the imperial family, for a personal acquaintance with the emperor developed, at least by his later years (see below), and he is said to have encouraged the young Claudius, born in 10 BC, in that future emperor's efforts to write history.[6] The historian married and had at least one son and one daughter.

[3] Macrobius 1.11.22.   [4] Cicero, *Philippics* 12.10.
[5] *Suda*, s.v. Kornutos.   [6] Suetonius, *Claudius* 41.

In addition to his history Livy wrote an essay in the form of a literary letter to his son in which he enjoined the young man 'to read Cicero and Demosthenes, and then everyone most like Cicero and Demosthenes'.[7] It may be that this work also contained several strictures on style attributed to him: on orators who use archaic and vulgar words,[8] on the folly of calculated obfuscation,[9] and on the historian Sallust's attempt to adapt an epigram of Thucydides.[10] He also wrote a number of dialogues, doubtless using Cicero as a model. The younger Seneca says that some were as much historical as philosophical, while others were overtly philosophical.[11] If he favoured any one school, it was surely Stoicism. His view of divine providence guiding the course of Rome's history may have a Stoic basis (e.g. 1.4, 5.36, 25.6), as might some other passages in the history, such as that in which Lucretia's male relations declare that the mind alone sins, not the body (1.58), or when Camillus tells the Faliscan schoolmaster that nature has forged a common bond among all men everywhere, whether formal agreements exist among them or not (5.27).

The History of Rome

Livy's history ran to 142 books, one of the longest works known from antiquity. It covered a span of 744 years, beginning with Rome's founding in 753 BC, and came down to the death of Drusus in 9 BC. If it were fully extant, a translation would run to over twenty-five volumes in the present World's Classics series. Its conventional title is *Ab Urbe Condita*, 'From the Founding of the City'. Thirty-five books survive: 1–10 (753–293 BC) and 21–45 (218–167 BC).

It appears that few had the time or endurance to read the whole work despite its fame, and still fewer the resources to have copies made for their personal use. Summaries were written for each book, which survive today and are known as the *Periochae*. They range from several pages for the early books to only a few lines for some of the later ones: clearly the epitomators' industry flagged in face of the daunting task (the summaries for Books 136 and 137 are missing). There were at least two different sets of *Periochae* in circulation, for

---

[7] Quintilian 10.1.39.
[8] Seneca the Elder, *Controuersia* 9.2.26.
[9] Quintilian 8.2.18.
[10] Seneca the Elder, *Controuersia* 9.1.14.
[11] *Letters* 100.9.

we have two for the first book and two for Books 37–40 and 49–55.
An epigram of the poet Martial reads (14.190), 'Huge Livy has been
slimmed down to a few volumes. | My bookcase hasn't room for all
of him.' Possibly Martial refers here to an epitome, although ex-
cerpts are more likely. We hear of a separate collection of Livy's
speeches,[12] and the younger Pliny tells us that as a youth of eighteen, on the day Vesuvius erupted in AD 79, he continued to excerpt
a book of Livy with studious sang-froid amid earth shocks and
collapsing buildings.[13]

When Livy published his first five books, he must have been a
young provincial *arriviste*, unknown in the literary circles in Rome.
His first book can be dated between 27 and 25 BC, since in chapter
19 he calls the emperor Augustus, a title bestowed on 16 January 27
BC; yet, while mentioning at the same time the emperor's closing of
the gates of the temple of Janus in 29 BC to signal the end of civil
wars and the restoration of peace, he says nothing of Augustus'
second closing in 25 after his subjugation of Spain. Although the
first book, which concerns the regal period (753–510 BC), may have
been published separately (Book 2 has its own preface), the first five
books clearly constitute a whole: the preface to Book 6 marks a clear
break with those that precede, while the fifth book hearkens back
frequently to events of Rome's earliest days as described in Book 1,
especially in Camillus' stirring speech at the end, which has all the
marks of summation and closure (5.51–4).

Livy began writing in pentads or groups of pentads (later in
antiquity the work was copied out in decades). The prefaces to
Books 2, 6, 16, 21, and 31 mark the main divisions of the first third
of the work. Thus the first pentad covered Rome's early history
from the city's founding to its sack by the Gauls in 390 BC. The next
decade (Books 6–15) described Rome's conquest of Italy (390–265
BC). The following pentad began with a preface on the founding and
early history of Carthage (*Periocha* 16) and went on to narrate the
First Punic War (coming down to 219 BC). Books 21–30 cover the
Second Punic War in which Rome fought Hannibal, and have their
own preface (218–201 BC). Book 31 introduces Livy's next theme:
Rome's wars in the East (201–167 BC). These fifteen books comprise
three pentads, the first having as its chief theme Rome's war against

---

[12] Suetonius, *Domitian* 10.   [13] *Letters* 6.20.

Philip V of Macedon, the second the war against Antiochus III of Syria, the third the war against King Perseus of Macedon. Book 45 concludes with the fall of the Macedonian monarchy—the end of the dynasty of Philip II and his son Alexander the Great.

Curiously, at just the point where our extant books end the pentad-decade arrangement seems to lose some of its prominence. To be sure, certain major turning-points coincide with later pentads and decades, at least from our modern perspective. But not many: one could cite Book 70 (71 begins with the start of the Social War), 80 (death of Marius), and 90 (death of Sulla, followed by the revolt of Lepidus and Sertorius' rebellion). And Book 120 marked a break (43 BC) since in the superscription to the *Periocha* of Book 121 the last twenty-two books are said to have been published after the death of Augustus. Thus the pentad-decade pattern seems to recede somewhat into the background when viewed through the *Periochae*. As the pace slows and the details increase, the narrative, like a gradually decelerating vehicle, causes landmarks to appear further and further apart. Livy probably began writing *circa* 30 BC; if he wrote at an even pace up to his death, he would have averaged a bit more than three books a year.

Livy as Impartial Recorder

The publication of Books 1–5 attracted attention at once, for Livy tells us that Augustus took exception to the version of events he had given in chapter 19 and the first part of 20 in Book 4 (437 BC). He had described there how Aulus Cornelius Cossus while serving as military tribune was the second after Romulus to slay an enemy commander in personal combat, which entitled him to dedicate the spoils of honour, or *spolia opima*, in the temple of Jupiter Feretrius (cf. 1.10). Yet we hear from another source[14] that when in 29 BC the proconsul of Macedonia, Marcus Licinius Crassus, defeated the Bastarnae in battle and killed their chieftain, Deldo, the emperor rejected Crassus' claim to set up the spoils of honour on the ground that only an independent commander fighting under his own religious auspices was qualified (Augustus was naturally unwilling to have his reputation as a military leader eclipsed by that of Crassus).

---

[14] Dio Cassius 51.24.

The question of Cossus' status then became all important, for a military tribune did not possess his own religious auspices any more than did a proconsul (i.e. one acting in place of a consul). Yet at the end of chapter 20 Livy changes his mind about what precedes: the emperor had recently discovered Cossus was actually consul at the time (which meant he *was* fighting under his own auspices), for, while inspecting the half-ruined temple of Jupiter Feretrius with a view to restoring it, he came upon Cossus' still surviving linen corselet, on which were inscribed his name and his rank: consul. Livy then says that even though all his written authorities agree that Cossus was military tribune in that year, Cossus' own words must carry the day, for he surely would not have lied in the presence of Jupiter and Romulus, and it would be 'well-nigh sacrilegious to disqualify Augustus as a witness to Cossus and his spoils'.

This part of chapter 20 has all the marks of a later insertion into an already completed text (if it was not added later, Augustus cannot have liked seeing his evidence tacked on as a 'corrective', much less finding a few pages later, in chapter 32, Cossus referred to as military tribune when he won the spoils). It is difficult to know how Livy was apprised of Augustus' discovery (the timing and nature of which are deeply suspicious). It may have been direct, through an intermediary, or because of friends, who called his attention to the emperor's public stance on the question. That Livy took the trouble to insert a correction into a text he had completed earlier suggests that his history was in the public eye, that it mattered to Augustus to have the issue set straight, and that Livy was made aware that it mattered. It may even be that what first drew the public's attention to the *Ab Urbe Condita* was just this passage on Cossus, since it gave a version that the emperor had recently taken pains to demonstrate as erroneous. In any event, Livy's resolve to give an equal hearing to the pros and cons of the question is noteworthy. He pays deference to Cossus' trustworthiness and to Augustus' personal testimony, but at the same time emphasizes that all his written sources agree Cossus was military tribune when he won the spoils and that his exploit could not have taken place some years later when Cossus was consul because pestilence prevented Rome from engaging in any military actions whatever in that period.

The same two-edged treatment of Augustus is evident elsewhere. We know that an acquaintance developed between the two men, at least in later years, for a speaker in Tacitus' *Annals*[15] is represented as saying, 'Titus Livius, famed above all for eloquence and truthfulness, praised Gnaeus Pompeius so highly that Augustus used to address him as Pompeianus; yet this did not hurt their friendship.' Pompey, of course, was the rival of Julius Caesar, defeated by Caesar at the Battle of Pharsalus in 48 BC. Augustus here wittily gives Livy what he lacked, a third name or cognomen, the ending -ianus denoting someone adopted into the Livian family but born a Pompeian. (Augustus' wife was a Livia.) Livy's praise of Pompey must have come in Books 109–12, which carried the subtitle of 'The Civil Wars'. That Livy favoured Pompey, who posed as the champion of the senate and the political establishment, is not surprising. And he was an outspoken critic of Caesar, at one point wondering out loud whether the world would have been a better place if he had never been born (this in reference to one who had been deified and was Augustus' great-uncle and adoptive father).[16] And of the Julian family's claim to be descended from Iulus, son of Aeneas and grandson of Venus, he says at the start of the history (1.3), 'Who could establish the truth of something so ancient?' Most striking, however, is the deep and pervasive pessimism of the Preface, where there is no mention of Augustus, of the end of civil war and the restoration of peace, or of hope for the future. On the other hand, when he mentions a little later (1.19) Augustus' closing of the gates of Janus he credits him with having brought peace to the Roman world over land and sea, while in the addendum to the passage on Cossus he describes him as one 'who founded and restored all our temples'.

The conflicting evidence about Augustus is doubtless a mirror of genuine ambivalence on Livy's part. On the one hand, there was much to commend: the establishment of peace, the restoration of the façade of republican government, the sponsorship of moral and religious reform. But there were actions that probably excited his distrust: Augustus' turning his back on the senatorial establishment in 43 BC and joining Antony and Lepidus in the Second Triumvirate, his subsequent determination to place the essential powers of government in his own hands, his attempts over the

---

[15] *Annals* 4.34.
[16] Seneca the Younger, *Natural Questions* 5.18 = frag. 48, assigned to Book 116.

years to put a family member in a position to succeed him. The last twenty-two books are said to have been published after Augustus' death. Did Livy decide to withhold them after discovering that Books 111–20 had given offence? For they contained praise of Pompey, criticism of Caesar, and a description of Augustus' entry into public life as one of the triumvirs, who ordered the proscription of their enemies; the first to die was Antony's *bête noire*, Cicero, one of Livy's heroes. His account of the statesman's murder in Book 120 is preserved to us by Seneca the Elder.[17] It is worth noting that the young Claudius was persuaded by his mother and grandmother not to begin his history with the assassination of Julius Caesar because frankness and truth would not be possible; accordingly, his history started with the establishment of peace at the conclusion of the civil wars.[18]

There is another factor in assessing Livy's attitude toward Augustus that has not received the emphasis it deserves, his obligation as an historian to maintain a stance of independence and even-handedness: whatever his personal opinions, he must appear to speak without fear or favour, especially when referring or alluding to those in power. The passages just discussed show that he did this, as does the failure of scholars to agree among themselves, though using much of the same evidence, some arguing that he was a spokesman for the regime, others that he was a veiled critic. Even when lauding Cicero, he appends this cool appraisal: had their roles been reversed, Cicero would have done to Antony what Antony did to him, and if one were looking to praise Cicero, it would take a Cicero to do it, alluding both to the orator's eloquence and to his penchant for self-praise (which he engaged in, according to the younger Seneca, 'not without reason, but without end').[19]

Livy and his Sources

The period covered in the first pentad lay in the remote past, ending more than three centuries before the historian's birth and almost two centuries before the first Roman historian, Fabius Pictor, wrote

---

[17] Seneca the Elder, *Suasoria* 6.17 = frag. 50.
[18] Suetonius, *Claudius* 41. [19] *On the Brevity of Life* 5.1.

at the end of the third century BC. Scarcely any written sources survived from that distant age; most of the information had been handed down by word of mouth, and much of that lay in the realm of myth and legend. Livy is keenly aware of the unreliability of the material for this early period. In the preface to Book 6 he says that almost all written records—'the only reliable guardian of the remembrance of past events'—were destroyed in the Gallic Sack of Rome in 390 BC. In the same passage he likens events before the Sack to objects seen from a great distance: general shapes alone can be discerned, the details have become lost or blurred. He repeatedly stresses the questionable nature of the evidence, beginning with the Preface, where he says he will not bother to affirm or deny the truth of much that he will write because of the legendary character of the material (compare 5.21: 'In matters so ancient, I am satisfied to accept as true what has the appearance of truth'). At 2.10 he tells the famous story of how Horatius Cocles single-handedly repelled an Etruscan invasion by standing his ground on the sole bridge spanning the Tiber until it could be cut down; as it fell, he plunged into the waters in full armour and swam safely to his cheering comrades on shore, a feat, Livy adds, 'that posterity was to find more praiseworthy than credible'.

Livy's scepticism contrasts sharply with the attitude evinced by Dionysius of Halicarnassus, a younger contemporary resident in Rome and writing in Greek, who covered the same period in his *Roman Antiquities*. Dionysius repeatedly affirms the truth of what he reports and nowhere admits to any doubts or to the possibility that the evidence might be unreliable. Of course, it was the job of the ancient historian to recreate the actions and words of his historical characters, whether they be contemporaries or characters of myth and legend. But Livy considered the addition of extraneous and punctilious details to an imaginative reconstruction of the distant past to be misguided, for they suggested a bogus precision that was untrue to the spirit and nature of the material. Exact casualty figures he found particularly out of place for early battles, and criticizes one of his authorities, Valerius Antias, on this score (3.5, cf. 3.8). Dionysius was fond of including fussy and implausible details, such as that among the many wounds that Horatius Cocles received the most serious was located precisely 'through one buttock above the top of the thigh bone' (5.24). For Livy, what mattered was the spirit that lay within the stories, however indistinct their outward shapes, and it was the historian's task to bring out this spirit in a manner consistent with the nature of the evidence. Hence he gives a poetic, even fairy-tale, colouring to some of the material, as in his account of Hercules and Cacus (1.7) or in his lengthy narrative of the Gallic Sack (5.32–55). In the latter, the collapse of Roman morale and principles before the defeat at the Allia is total, affecting all elements of society: magistrates, senate, and people. No reason is given for their wrong-headed and at times senseless behaviour; instead, the inscrutable workings of fate are invoked (5.33, 36, 37). When Roman fortunes reach their nadir, everything is suddenly reversed, literally overnight, which again goes unexplained (5.39). Livy's aim, of course, is to create the strongest contrast possible and to make the reversal, or peripeteia, dramatic and powerful. The final scene in the forum is particularly fanciful: as the gold to ransom the city is being weighed out in the presence of the Gallic army, Camillus comes up behind them with his men, orders the weighing stopped and bids the Gauls draw up their forces for battle. The scene is reminiscent of the one between the pirates and policemen at the end of *The Pirates of Penzance*. Yet the effect Livy creates is not one of humour or deflation. Quite the contrary. He writes a fast-paced, compelling narrative, in which he achieves an artful balance between high-principled patriotism and a cheerful disregard for overnice verisimilitude. The result is quite remarkable: a curiously charming blend of gravity and playfulness, of drama and didacticism.

The divergent attitudes of Livy and Dionysius to the reliability of the evidence for this distant period have their analogue in modern reactions to the same evidence. All historians admit that most of the details and some of the episodes must have been invented, but they react in sharply different ways to the rest. Some refuse to treat the period at all. Others credit a limited number of facts, events, and practices as having a basis in fact, but regard the residue as hopelessly mired in falsity, both because of the unlikelihood of much reliable information having survived in oral or written form and because of the universally accepted practice among ancient historians of imaginatively recreating actions and words to flesh out the bare 'facts'—or, in Livy's words, those 'shadowy events that are difficult to make out because they are seen, as it were, from a great distance' (6.1). Still others believe that much more of what we find in Livy and Dionysius is based on authentic data.

In default of written histories, what other sources were there that might have supplied information about the period before 390 BC? Certainly oral transmission is one, both through collective memory, such as the tale of Romulus and Remus, and by way of traditions handed down in noble families, such as the disaster that befell the Fabian clan at the Cremera (2.49–50) or the courageous action of Fabius Dorsuo during the Gallic Sack (5.46: note that Rome's first historian was Fabius Pictor). Yet oral history that goes much beyond three generations in the past is notoriously unreliable. Then again, families were prone to magnify or even to invent the deeds of their ancestors, as Livy well knew (8.40); at one point he catches out one of his authorities, Licinius Macer, in the very act of such fabrication (7.9; cf. 5.20–2). Another source consisted of written texts, few though they were. Certainly one or more lists of the chief magistrates of the early Republic survived, and most scholars are willing to believe that much of it is based on fact, if only because many of the families had long since died out and because the list clashes with later attempts to superimpose an interpretation upon the period that the names fail to support. For example, the struggle between the patricians and plebeians is retrojected into the first years of the Republic, and the chief magistrates are claimed as patricians. Yet many plebeian names appear among them (see e.g. 4.7, 5.12, and the notes to these passages). The list of magistrates preserved in the Linen Books, or *Libri Lintei*, which Livy cites through Licinius Macer (4.7, 20, 23), differed in some important ways from the generally accepted list, although many of these variants are of questionable authenticity. But the most likely source of genuine information were the Pontifical Tablets, or *tabulae pontificum*, known in their published form as the *Annales Maximi*, The Greatest Annals, or possibly The Annals of the Greatest (Pontiff). These records derived from the whitened board that the pontifex maximus, head of the state religion, affixed each year to the outer wall of his official residence in the forum, on which he recorded 'the names of the consuls and other magistrates, followed by notable actions at home and abroad, by land and by sea'.[20] Moreover, the notices were brief

---

[20] Servius on Virgil's *Aeneid* 1.373.

and clipped: 'bare statements of times, persons, places and deeds, without any elaboration', according to Cicero.[21] Scholars presume that these Tablets were used by some of Rome's early historians, from whom later writers such as Livy and Dionysius derived their knowledge of the period. Yet we do not hear of anyone being personally acquainted with them except for Cato the Elder, who died in 149 BC: 'I don't intend to write the sort of thing one finds on the tablet at the pontifex maximus' house: how often there was a famine, how often there was an eclipse of the moon or sun, or what the adverse omens were'.[22] Most scholars believe that much of the history of the third century BC is based on the Pontifical Tablets, less so for the fourth. But there is sharp disagreement about the fifth, the period covered in Books 2–5 of Livy, for almost all written records were destroyed in the Sack by the historian's own admission. Some think that the Tablets were reconstructed soon after the Sack, thereby preserving much of value and that this forms the substratum of the narrative we see in Livy, Dionysius, and others.

The Tablets or Greatest Annals provided Roman writers with a format called annalistic history (a modern term). The narrative proceeds year by year, introduced by the entrance into office of the two consuls, who gave their names to the year, and the other magistrates. Affairs in the city (*domi*) usually come next, including the passing of laws and the reporting of prodigies and their expiation, followed by events abroad, chiefly military (*militiae*), before the narrative returns to Rome for further matters such as trials, deaths, the founding of temples, and new elections. The cycle begins again with the entrance of the new consuls into office. The historian might vary this scheme in conformity with the amount and types of information and with his literary aims. But the regular format produced an orderly and satisfying rhythm because, however elaborated or diffuse certain sections might be, the narrative would return to matters that were associated with the earliest written records, the annals of the pontifex maximus. At such times the style could become terse, even bulletin-like, admitting technical expressions and antique words, all of which were meant to recall the original Tablets, or what the Tablets were imagined to have been like (2.16, 21 and 4.30 are examples). Thus annalistic history was a source of pride

---

[21] *De oratore* 2.52.   [22] Aulus Gellius 1.28.6.

and patriotism, rooted as it was in native tradition and carrying with
it echoes of a distant past.

Unlike Dionysius, who did original research into chronology and
antiquarian matters, Livy was content to draw almost exclusively on
the accounts of earlier historians. It is unclear what criteria he used
in making his selections: for example, despite some severe criticisms
of Licinius Macer and Valerius Antias (of the latter he says at one
point, 'there is no limit to the lies he will tell': 26.49), he continued
to use both writers extensively. One particularly important criterion
was length and fullness, since he intended his history of the Republic to be more comprehensive and richly detailed than those of his
predecessors (on the other hand, his account of the regal period in
Book 1 is abbreviated in comparison to theirs). This means in turn
that while he consulted the shorter works of the earliest historians
such as Fabius Pictor and Calpurnius Piso (e.g. 1.44, 55; 2.32, 40,
58) in writing Books 2–5, he relied largely on the longer histories of
recent writers like Antias and Macer. The passage at 4.23 is illustra-
tive of his methods. Macer and another historian, Aelius Tubero,
gave different consuls for the year 434 BC while citing the same work
as their source, the Linen Books stored in the temple of Juno Moneta
on the Capitol. Livy responds to the dilemma as follows: 'This is
one of many aspects of that distant time that are shrouded in obscurity, which is where I shall leave the matter also.' The thought of
going himself to inspect the Linen Books to find out whether Macer
or Tubero (or neither) was right seems not to have occurred to him
(yet if he *had* discovered who was correct, he probably would not
have been much further along in making a decision, if only because
the oldest historians gave still different names and said that military
tribunes with consular power were the chief magistrates that year).

In adapting his sources Livy's eye was fixed primarily on the
congenial task of composing a well-paced, vivid narrative and of
highlighting the moral lessons, which in his mind constituted the
chief benefit of the study of history. He counted on his sources to
supply the basic facts, such as names, places, and actions, but because of his awareness of their frequent disagreements his habit of
following one as a main source for a particular episode helped to
eliminate many inconsistencies. Occasionally he appended variants
for matters like casualty figures and names. Difficulties—sometimes
grave difficulties—appeared, however, when he switched sources,

for while his account of a given passage might be fairly self-consist-
ent, what followed sometimes fitted badly with what preceded, and
on occasion might contradict it. Livy most often lets these inconsistencies stand unremarked and unacknowledged, and one suspects
that in not a few cases he was unaware of them. A striking instance
comes in chapters 12 and 18 of Book 5. In the first passage he tells
how Publius Licinius Calvus was the first plebeian to be elected
military tribune with consular power and he gives the names of
Calvus' five patrician colleagues. In the second passage, a few pages
and four years later, he states that the same group of men was re-
elected to the same office. But the names are all different, save that
of Calvus, who now has only four colleagues. Occasionally he omits
entire years, doubtless inadvertently (see the notes to 2.15 and 2.39
for examples): 'There are so many chronological uncertainties in the
history of these years, with different authorities giving different lists
of magistrates, that the great antiquity of the events and of the
sources does not permit one to make out which consuls followed
which or what events happened in what year' (2.21).

The Structure and Style of the History

Livy's ability as a writer is shown to excellent advantage in the way
he selected and shaped his material. Dionysius, who wrote some
years later and used many of the same sources, is prolix and slow-
moving, taking over twice as many books to narrate the period 509–
390 BC (Books 5–13 answer to 2–5 of Livy). For example, the first
secession of the plebs to the Sacred Mount takes up three chapters
in Livy, including two brief but memorable speeches (2.31–3);
Dionysius fills some forty-five chapters and inserts numerous orations, some of exceeding length (6.45–90). In fact, Livy's skill is
shown to no greater effect than in what he chose to omit or curtail.
Rome's defeat by the Gauls at the Allia was one of the best known
events of her early history, yet the historian describes it in a few
swift strokes (5.38) because in his narrative it is but one piece in a
complex mosaic of collapse and recovery. Within a given episode
Livy characteristically selects a turning-point or climactic moment
toward which the narrative is moving; extraneous material is stripped
away and the conclusion rapidly rounded off. When faced with a
lengthy sequence of events he usually chooses one or a few episodes

for special elaboration in order to give point and focus to the whole, again sharply curtailing introductory and concluding matter. Such longer units proceed in carefully staggered stages, as in the Gallic Sack, where suspense is created by frequent shifts among the three theatres of operation: Rome, Veii, and Ardea. Thematic unity is given to whole books, as Ogilvie perceptively notes in his *Commentary*: the kings of Rome in the First, liberty and threats to it in the Second, the Decemvirate in the Third, the necessity for restraint and mutual consideration in the Fourth, and respect for religion in the Fifth. Lengthy units are often interpunctuated with speeches in direct and indirect discourse, which articulate the stages in the drama (as in his narrative of the decemvirs and Verginia in Book 3.33–57). Although Livy included many short speeches in the first pentad, he refrained from composing one of any length until the end of Book 3. There are, in fact, only four major orations in 1–5, two of which stand at the ends of their books, summing up and rounding them off (Quinctius at 3.67–8 and Camillus at 5.51–4) and two at the start, introducing new themes (Canuleius at 4.3–5 and Appius Claudius at 5.3–6). Livy's rhetorical abilities were much admired in antiquity. Quintilian praised his 'unrivalled eloquence', emphasizing how splendidly what was said suited both speaker and situation.[23]

In bringing scenes vividly before the readers' eyes Livy eschewed detailed descriptions of externals, choosing instead one or two touches that would stimulate the imagination to supply the rest: the lowering cloud that heralds the destruction of Alba Longa (1.29), the glow of lamplight reflected in the faces of Lucretia and her maids as they bend over their work (1.57), the patrician elders seated like statues on their ivory chairs waiting for death (5.41). Livy is at his best in crowd scenes where emotions run high: agitation and suspense, pity and fear, as in his description of the murder of Servius Tullius (1.46–8) or of the Romans looking down from the Capitol on the Gauls as they move about in the streets below (5.42). He is fond of entering into the thoughts and feelings of his characters, more so for groups, less often for persons: Camillus' musings during his exile at Ardea is an example of the latter (5.43), although speech direct or reported is the normal vehicle for giving expression to an individual's state of mind. No historian, said Quintilian,[24] was better at depicting emotions, especially the gentler emotions (*affectus dulciores*).

Livy's Purpose

In his Preface Livy says that the chief benefit of history 'is to behold evidence of every sort of behaviour set forth as on a splendid memorial; from it you may select for yourself and for your country what to emulate, from it what to avoid, whether basely begun or basely concluded.' This evidence is to be found in 'how men lived, what their moral principles were, under what leaders and by what measures at home and abroad our empire was won and extended', and he draws the reader's attention particularly to the steady erosion of those high principles during the course of the Republic. Yet he seldom steps forward in his own person to articulate the moral lessons: for the most part the stories are left to speak for themselves. Examples played a central role in Roman life and Roman thinking, from models of admired authors that schoolboys copied out and imitated to the examples from Roman history cited by their elders as they argued the best course of action to take in the senate, before the people, or in the courtroom and halls of declamation. When in 2 BC Augustus erected in his new forum a series of statues representing the heroes of Rome's past he declared in an edict that the achievements of these men would serve as models against which both he and future leaders were to be measured.[25] Quintilian in the early empire went so far as to declare that the citing of historical examples in the courtroom was more potent than the testimony of witnesses because the former alone are immune to the suspicion of hatred and favouritism.[26]

Virtue in Livy's eyes was not inborn or spontaneous, but must be acquired and kept in constant repair: virtuous behaviour is the product of environment and education. Similarly, the Roman national character is historically determined in Livy. The first Romans were from the dregs of society: shepherds, displaced persons, and runaway slaves who came seeking asylum. For them to acquire a sense of community and love of country, of lawful behaviour and mutual forbearance, required a long period of nurture and development

---

[24] 10.1.101.   [25] Suetonius, *Augustus* 31.   [26] 10.1.34.

(2.1). This motley and unruly crew had to be taught, and sometimes coerced, into behaving rightly: hence the emphasis on Romulus as lawgiver (1.8), on Numa as the teacher of religion (1.21), on Ancus Marcius as the builder of Rome's first prison, constructed to instil fear into those 'who as yet made little distinction between right and wrong' (1.33). What is particularly remarkable in all this is Livy's emphasis on the people as a whole: they are the real heroes of his narrative. He continually emphasizes their lowly origins because it redounds all the more to their credit that they surmounted their humble beginnings and eventually succeeded as brilliantly as they did. Their courage, resilience in the face of adversity, and high principles produced 'the world's mightiest empire, second only to the power of the gods' (1.4). Many aspects of this conception of early Rome may well be original to Livy, for they stand in marked contrast to what we find in two other historians of his own age, Sallust and Dionysius. The former believed the formation of the state was quick and easy and 'all that Rome achieved was owing to the outstanding virtue of a handful of individuals'.[27] Dionysius, on the other hand, maintained that the early Romans were really cultured and learned Greek émigrés: Rome was a Greek foundation and Latin a dialect of Greek.

In his Preface Livy emphasizes that history when properly written can improve people's lives, both as public officials and in the private sphere (*tibi tuaeque rei publicae*), and at the same time laments the sorry state of contemporary morality, in which 'we can endure neither our vices nor the remedies needed to cure them'. It seems implicit, although he does not make the connection, that recovery through the elimination of vices is possible and that the study of history can be a significant means to that end—that history is, in fact, one of the *remedia*. And in this endeavour Livy struck a sympathetic chord. Men were weary of war, collapse, and decline, and yearned for a return to former glories and to the principles they imagined had guided their ancestors in creating their empire.

The *Ab Urbe Condita* became at once the canonical account of the Republic; no one thereafter seriously attempted to supersede Livy's achievement. Writers as diverse as the two Senecas, Quintilian, and

[27] Sallust, *The War with Catiline* 6, 53.

Tacitus praised him, while Plutarch used the history as a source for the *Lives* and Lucan for his epic poem *Pharsalia*. His fame continued strongly to late antiquity. Although less well known in the Middle Ages, he was embraced in the Renaissance with fervour, notably by Machiavelli in his *Discourses on the First Decade of Titus Livius*.[28] In the seventeenth and eighteenth centuries, when doubt was cast on much that had hitherto gone unquestioned, early Rome was a principal catalyst in the birth of critical history: for example, in L. DeBeaufort's *On the Uncertainty of the First Five Centuries of Roman History*,[29] published in 1738. Once it was admitted that much of what Livy wrote about early Rome must be invention, his reputation took a sharp downturn. The change is illustrated by comparing Dante in the fourteenth century, who spoke of 'Livy who errs not',[30] with Macaulay's pronouncement in the nineteenth: 'No historian with whom we are acquainted has shown so complete an indifference to truth . . . On the other hand, we do not know, in the whole range of literature, an instance of a bad thing so well done.' In the latter half of the twentieth century the historian's reputation has revived somewhat owing to a livelier appreciation of his achievement and of the difficulties any ancient historian faced when narrating the words and deeds of a far-distant past.

But it is as a literary artist that Livy has been judged pre-eminent both in antiquity and in modern times, particularly as a brilliant stylist (Pollio's captious criticism aside). Though a devotee of the Ciceronian period, in which sentences run their leisurely course through complex subordinate clauses before turning for home and arriving at the main verb, Livy, like Cicero himself, is careful to introduce variety of all sorts: in sentence length, word order, rhythm, and vocabulary. Quintilian spoke of history as 'in some sense a poem set free from meter' (*quodam modo carmen solutum*);[31] hence poetic diction was permissible, as was liberal use of figures of thought and speech. In a striking metaphor he also says that history was infused with a sort of nourishing fluid, 'rich and pleasing' (*quodam uberi iucundoque suco*), and he singles out Livy's 'milky richness' for praise (*lactea ubertas*). Hence it is not surprising to find in Livy a wide vocabulary to suit speaker and situation: poetic, sacral, legal, colloquial, and so forth. Yet for all the variety the his-

---

[28] *Discorsi sul primo libro delle deche di Tito Livio.*
[29] *Sur l'incertitude des cinq premiers siècles de l'histoire romaine.*
[30] 'Livio . . . che non erra': *Inferno* 28.12.   [31] 10.1.31–2.

torian has brought to his work this translator has been struck by the elevated tone that pervades and unifies the whole. The touches that Livy employs to characterize, for example, the plain speaker or simple soldier, an archaic religious formula or official bulletin, are just that: touches that suggest these qualities while maintaining the supple elegance that is Livy's trademark. When he reproduces the parable that Agrippa Menenius tells the plebs on the Sacred Mount, he does so in paraphrase, because direct speech would have required 'old-fashioned and homely language' (2.32: *prisco illo dicendi et horrido modo*). Similarly, since the remarks of the soldier Sextus Tempanius were said to have been 'rough-hewn' (4.41: *oratio incompta*), Livy gives them in reported speech using short, vigorous sentences with little subordination to suggest their unpolished nature, without being coarse or ungainly in themselves.

It is doubtful that the young Livy realized the extent of the task that lay before him when he began writing. In Book 10 (31) he interrupts to say that he has taken four books to describe the Samnite Wars and that there are more still to come, which leads him to give a pep talk to his readers: who could begrudge reading about these wars when they did not exhaust the men who fought them? By Book 31 (1) he appears genuinely appalled at the growing dimensions of his task: the first two Punic Wars, which lasted sixty-three years, required as many books to narrate (15) as did the 488 years that preceded them. He compares himself to one who wades into the sea and is carried out over his head 'into depths more vast and, as it were, into the abyss'. At this point 112 books were yet to be written. But he persevered, his fame increasing as the years passed,[32] until in old age he became a living legend: the man who would not stop. In one of his letters the younger Pliny asks (2.3): 'Have you never heard the story of the man of Cadiz, who was so impressed by the name and reputation of Titus Livius that he journeyed from the end of the inhabited world just to see him, looked, turned about and went back home?'

---

[32] Pliny, *Natural History*, praef. 16.

NOTE ON THE TEXT
AND TRANSLATION

The translation follows the 1974 Oxford Classical Text of Livy 1–5, edited by R. M. Ogilvie, and has benefited greatly from the same author's masterful commentary of the same books (Oxford, 1965). The translator owes a great debt of gratitude to Christopher Pelling of University College Oxford for his many suggestions for improvement.

The book divisions are Livy's own; the chapter divisions were made in the Renaissance. The dating system follows Livy's figures for the number of years in the reigns of each of the seven kings (Book 1). The annual dating by consuls begins in 509 BC at the start of Book 2.

Variant spellings of place-names found in the manuscripts, such as Polusca/Pollusca, Bola/Bolae, Ecetra/Ecetrae, have been retained.

SELECT BIBLIOGRAPHY

Text

Titi Livi Ab Urbe Condita Libri I–V, ed. R. M. Ogilvie (Oxford, 1974).

Commentary

Ogilvie, R. M., *A Commentary on Livy: Books 1–5* (Oxford, 1965).

General Works on Historiography

Badian, E., 'The Early Historians', in T. A. Dorey (ed.), *Latin Historians* (London, 1966), 1–38.

Cornell, T. J., 'Aeneas and the Twins: The Development of the Roman Foundation Legend,' *Proceedings of the Cambridge Philological Society*, 201 (NS 21) (1975), 1–32.

—— 'The Formation of the Historical Tradition of Early Rome', in I. S. Moxon, J. D. Smart, A. J. Woodman (eds.), *Past Perspectives: Studies in Greek and Roman Historical Writing* (Cambridge, 1986), 67–86.

—— 'The Value of the Literary Tradition concerning Archaic Rome', in K. Raaflaub (ed.), *Social Struggles in Archaic Rome: New Perspectives on the Conflict of the Orders* (Berkeley, 1986), 52–76.

Fornara, C., *The Nature of History in Ancient Greece and Rome* (Berkeley, 1983).

Laistner, M. L. W., *The Greater Roman Historians* (Berkeley, 1947).

Wiseman, T. P., *Clio's Cosmetics* (Leicester, 1979).

—— 'Monuments and the Roman Annalists', in I. S. Moxon, J. D. Smart, A. J. Woodman (eds.), *Past Perspectives: Studies in Greek and Roman Historical Writing* (Cambridge, 1986), 87–100.

Woodman, A. J., *Rhetoric in Classical Historiography* (London, 1988).

Works on Livy

Konstan, D., 'Narrative and Ideology in Livy: Book I', *Classical Antiquity*, 5 (1986), 199–215.

Luce, T. J., 'The Dating of Livy's First Decade', *Transactions of the American Philological Association*, 96 (1965), 209–40.

—— 'Design and Structure in Livy: 5.32–55,' *Transactions of the American Philological Association*, 102 (1971), 265–302.

—— *Livy: The Composition of his History* (Princeton, 1977).

—— 'Livy, Augustus and the Forum Augustum', in K. A. Raaflaub and M. Toher (eds.), *Between Republic and Empire* (Berkeley, 1990), 123–38.

Luce, T. J., 'Livy and Dionysius,' *Papers of the Leeds International Latin Seminar*, 8 (1995), 225–39.

McDonald, A. H., 'The Style of Livy,' *Journal of Roman Studies*, 47 (1957), 155–72.

Miles, G. B., *Livy: Reconstructing Early Rome* (Ithaca and London, 1995).

Moles, J. L., 'Livy's Preface', *Proceedings of the Cambridge Philological Society*, 39 (1993), 141–68.

Solodow, J. B., 'Livy and the Story of Horatius, 1.24–26', *Transactions of the American Philological Association*, 109 (1979), 251–68.

Syme, R., 'Livy and Augustus', *Harvard Studies in Classical Philology*, 64 (1959), 27–87.

Walsh, P. G., *Livy: His Historical Aims and Methods* (Cambridge, 1961).

Historical Works

Bloch, R., *The Origins of Rome* (New York, 1960).

Cornell, T. J., *The Beginnings of Rome: Italy and Rome from the Bronze Age to the Punic Wars (c.1000–264 BC)* (London, 1995).

Heurgon, J., *The Rise of Rome to 264 BC*, trans. J. Willis (Berkeley, 1973).

Nicolet, C., *The World of the Citizen in Republican Rome*, trans. P. S. Falla (London, 1976, 1980).

Palmer, R. E. A., *The Archaic Community of the Romans* (Cambridge, 1970).

A CHRONOLOGY OF EVENTS

All dates are BC

753　　　　The Founding of Rome

753–716　Romulus
716–673　Numa
673–641　Tullus Hostilius
641–617　Ancus Marcius　　　} The Regal Period
617–578　Tarquinius Priscus
578–535　Servius Tullius
535–510　Tarquinius Superbus

509　　　　Start of the Republic
508–7　　Lars Porsenna's siege of Rome
499　　　　Battle of Lake Regillus
494　　　　First secession of the plebs
488　　　　Coriolanus
479–8　　Disaster at the Cremera
458　　　　Cincinnatus summoned to save the state　　} The Republic
450　　　　Second secession of the plebs
450–49　The Decemvirate
437　　　　Cornelius Cossus wins the spoils of honour
396　　　　The capture of Veii
390　　　　The sack of Rome by the Gauls

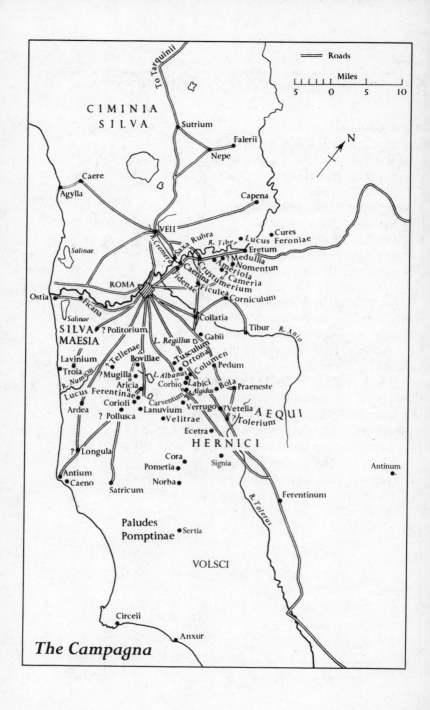

The Campagna

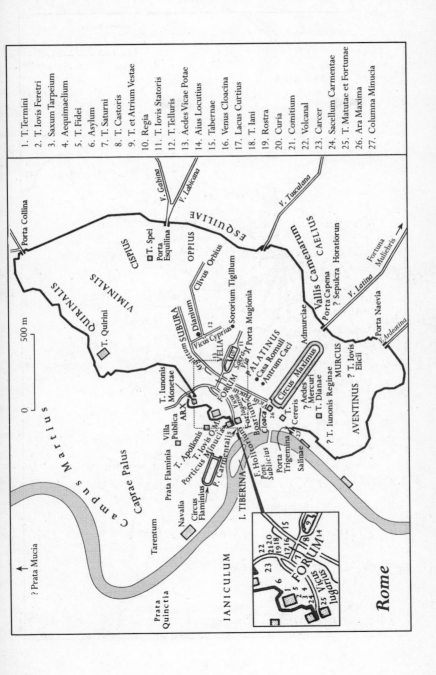

Rome

1. T. Termini
2. T. Iovis Feretri
3. Saxum Tarpeium
4. Aequimaelium
5. T. Fidei
6. Asylum
7. T. Saturni
8. T. Castoris
9. T. et Atrium Vestae
10. Regia
11. T. Iovis Statoris
12. T. Telluris
13. Aedes Vicae Potae
14. Aius Locutius
15. Tabernae
16. Venus Cloacina
17. Lacus Curtius
18. T. Iani
19. Rostra
20. Curia
21. Comitium
22. Volcanal
23. Carcer
24. Sacellum Carmentae
25. T. Matutae et Fortunae
26. Ara Maxima
27. Columna Minucia

THE RISE OF ROME

PREFACE

Whether in writing the history of the Roman people from the foundation of the city the result will be worth the effort invested, I do not really know (nor, if I did, would I presume to say so), for I realize that this is a time-honoured task that many have undertaken, each succeeding writer thinking he will either bring greater accuracy to the facts or surpass his unpolished predecessors in artistry and style. However that may be, it will still be a source of satisfaction to celebrate to the best of my ability the history of the greatest nation on earth; and if in this throng of writers my own fame should be eclipsed, I will console myself with the thought of the nobility and greatness of those who overshadow my own.

What is more, the task is immense, since Rome's history stretches back over seven hundred years and since the state has now grown so large from small beginnings that it struggles under the incubus of its own great size. Moreover, I do not doubt that Rome's foundation and early years will bring less pleasure to the majority of my readers, who will want to press on to recent times, in the course of which the strength of a mighty people has long been bent on its own undoing. I on the other hand shall regard as an additional reward of my labour the opportunity to turn away from the sight of the evils that our age has witnessed for so many years and, for the bit of time my full attention is fixed on those early days, to be wholly free from the anxiety that may assail a writer's mind, although it cannot deflect it from the truth.

Events before the city was founded or planned, which have been handed down more as pleasing poetic fictions than as reliable records of historical events, I intend neither to affirm nor to refute. To antiquity we grant the indulgence of making the origins of cities more impressive by commingling the human with the divine, and if any people should be permitted to sanctify its inception and reckon the gods as its founders, surely the glory of the Roman people in war is such that, when it boasts Mars in particular as its parent and the parent of its founder, the nations of the world would as easily acquiesce in this claim as they do in our rule.

Yet I attach no great importance to how these and similar traditions will be criticized or valued. My wish is that each reader will pay the closest attention to the following: how men lived, what their moral principles were, under what leaders and by what measures at home and abroad our empire was won and extended; then let him follow in his mind how, as discipline broke down bit by bit, morality at first foundered; how it next subsided in ever greater collapse and then began to topple headlong in ruin—until the advent of our own age, in which we can endure neither our vices nor the remedies needed to cure them.

The special and salutary benefit of the study of history is to behold evidence of every sort of behaviour set forth as on a splendid memorial; from it you may select for yourself and for your country what to emulate, from it what to avoid, whether basely begun or basely concluded. Yet either the love of the task I have set myself deceives me or there has never been any state grander, purer, or richer in good examples, or one into which greed and luxury gained entrance so late, or where great respect was accorded for so long to small means and frugality—so much so that the less men possessed, the less they coveted. Recently wealth has brought greed in its train, manifold amusements have led to people's obsession with ruining themselves and with consuming all else through excess and self-indulgence.

But complaints, which will not be pleasing even at a later time when they will perhaps be necessary, should at least be banished from the commencement of such a great undertaking. Rather, if we were to adopt the practice of poets, we would more gladly begin with good omens, and with vows and prayers to the gods and goddesses that they may grant us success as we embark upon this vast enterprise.

BOOK ONE

1. There is general agreement, first of all, that when Troy fell the Greeks punished the other Trojans mercilessly but refrained from exercising any right of conquest in the cases of two men, Aeneas and Antenor, who were connected to them by long-standing ties of guest-friendship and had always advocated the return of Helen.* Thereafter Antenor, having experienced various twists of fortune, penetrated to the furthest reaches of the Adriatic Sea with a large group of Eneti who had been driven by civil strife from Paphlagonia and had been seeking both a place to settle and a new leader after the death of their king Pylaemenes before Troy. The combined Eneti and Trojans expelled the Euganei, who inhabited the district between the Adriatic and the Alps, and occupied their territory. The spot where they first disembarked is now called Troy, the district thereabouts Trojan; the people as a whole were called Veneti.*

Aeneas by a similar misfortune had been driven as a refugee from his homeland, although in his case the fates had destined him for the initiation of far greater things. He first went to Macedonia and then to Sicily in search of a place to settle; from Sicily he steered his ships to Laurentine territory,* which today also bears the name of Troy. There the Trojans disembarked and began to plunder the area, since after nearly limitless wanderings they possessed nothing but their arms and ships. King Latinus and the Aborigines, who inhabited the territory in those days, rushed together in arms from the city and surrounding countryside to repel the attack of the strangers.

There are two versions of what happened next. Some say that Latinus was defeated in an actual battle and made peace with Aeneas, offering him a marriage alliance as well. Others say that, when the battle lines had been drawn up but before the trumpets sounded the attack, Latinus stepped from the front ranks and invited the leader of these strangers to talk matters over. He asked what manner of men they were, where they had come from, by what misfortune they had left their homeland, and what their intentions were in entering Laurentine territory. When he learned that they were Trojans and that their leader was Aeneas, son of Anchises and Venus, and that, since their native land had been put to the torch, they were now exiles seeking a place to found a city, he was much impressed by the fame of both people and leader and by their spirit, prepared as they were for war or peace. He extended his right hand and pledged future friendship. Thereupon the two leaders struck a treaty, while the two armies saluted one another. Aeneas, the story continues, became a guest of Latinus in his home, where the king before his household gods added a personal alliance to the public one by giving Aeneas his daughter in marriage. This act in particular bolstered the Trojans' hope that at long last they had reached a permanent and secure end of their wanderings. They founded a town which Aeneas named Lavinium after Lavinia, his wife. The new union quickly produced a male child, to whom his parents gave the name Ascanius.

2. War was what the Aborigines and Trojans jointly faced next. Because Turnus, king of the Rutuli, to whom Lavinia had been betrothed prior to Aeneas' arrival, was angry that an outsider had been preferred to himself, he took up arms against Aeneas and Latinus together. Neither side emerged from the fight unscathed. The Rutuli were defeated; the Aborigines and Trojans, although victorious, lost their leader Latinus. At this point Turnus and the rest of the Rutuli, no longer trusting to their own resources, appealed to the flourishing Etruscan nation and to Mezentius their king, who ruled the then prosperous city of Caere. From the very beginning Mezentius had been unhappy with the founding of the new city; he was now convinced that the power of the Trojans was growing far too fast for the safety of the neighbouring peoples. He therefore had no hesitation in forming a joint alliance with the Rutuli.

In face of the fear generated by the prospect of such a war, Aeneas wished to win the loyalty of the Aborigines by letting them enjoy the same rights as the Trojans and, what is more, by uniting the two peoples under a common name. So it was that he called them both Latins, thereby making the Aborigines henceforth as dedicated and loyal to Aeneas as were the Trojans. It was on this new spirit of the two peoples, who he could see were becoming more united day by day, that Aeneas was relying when he decided to lead them into the field to do battle, although he could have defended himself from behind the city walls; and he did this despite the fact that Etruria was then so powerful that its fame had filled both land and sea throughout the entire length of Italy, from the Alps to the

Sicilian strait. The battle that ensued went well for the Latins, but for Aeneas it was his last mortal act. He is buried, whether he should be called man or god, on the banks of the Numicus River. Men call him Jupiter Indiges.*

3. Aeneas' son Ascanius was not yet old enough to take over as *interesting if not her son* ruler. Nevertheless the kingdom survived intact for him until he grew to maturity because of Lavinia's guardianship, for she was an able woman; in the interval before he came of age she preserved for her son the Latin community and the throne that his grandfather and father had held. I will not debate—for who could establish the truth of a matter so ancient?—whether the boy in question was this Ascanius or an older brother, born to Creusa before the fall of Troy and a companion of his father in his flight, the same one that the Julian family calls Iulus and claims as its founder.* This Ascanius, wherever born and from whatever mother (certainly it is agreed that Aeneas was his father), handed over to his mother—or stepmother— Lavinium, which now had a surplus population and was prosperous and wealthy, as things were reckoned in that age, while he himself founded a new city at the base of Mount Alba, which, because it stretched out along a ridge, he called Alba Longa.

About thirty years intervened between the founding of Lavinium and of its colony Alba Longa. Even so, their resources had grown so great—especially after the defeat of the Etruscans—that not even the death of Aeneas or the succeeding regency of Lavinia or the apprenticeship of the young king sufficed to provoke Mezentius and the Etruscans or other neighbouring peoples into making any hostile moves. Peace terms had fixed the Albula River, which is now known as the Tiber, as the boundary between Etruscans and Latins. *monarchy*

Silvius, son of Ascanius, was the next ruler,* born by some accident in a silvan setting. He begot Aeneas Silvius, he in turn Latinus Silvius, who was the one who sent out a number of colonies called the Ancient Latins.* Henceforth Silvius was the last name of all kings at Alba. To Latinus Alba was born, to Alba Atys, to Atys Capys, to Capys Capetus, to Capetus Tiberinus, who drowned in crossing the Albula River and gave to the river what was to become a famous name among posterity. Next came Agrippa, son of Tiberinus. After Agrippa, Romulus Silvius succeeded to his father's throne. He was killed by a lightning bolt and left the kingdom to his successor Aventinus, who in turn was buried on that hill which is now part of the city of Rome and bears his name. Proca was the next king. He begot Numitor and Amulius and left the ancient kingdom of the Silvian family to Numitor, the elder son. But violence had greater effect than the wish of the father or respect for seniority. Amulius expelled his brother and seized the throne. He added a second crime to the first: he killed his brother's male issue and, under the pretext of honouring the daughter Rhea Silvia, made her a Vestal,* thus depriving her of hope of children by the constraint of perpetual virginity.

4. But in my view the fates ordained the founding of this great city and the beginning of the world's mightiest empire, second only to the power of the gods. For when the Vestal, having been ravished, became the mother of twin sons, she named Mars as the father of her dubious progeny, either because she thought he really was the father or because naming a god as the one responsible for her transgression made a more respectable story. Yet no divine or human power saved her or her offspring from the king's cruelty. He ordered that the priestess be taken into custody and put in chains, and the twins to be set out on the river where the current flowed strongly. By some providential accident the Tiber had overflowed its banks, forming quiet shallows that made approach to the river's regular channel impossible. Those who were ordered to expose the babies hoped that they would be drowned no matter how weak the current. And so, as if they were carrying out the king's command, they exposed the twins at the edge of the floodland where the Ruminalis fig tree now stands (tradition says it was formerly called the Romularis).

In those days the area was wild and desolate. Legend has it that when the receding water left the basket in which the boys had been placed on a dry patch of ground, a thirsty she-wolf from the surrounding mountains headed toward the sound of their crying; so gently did she lower her teats for them to nurse that the king's chief herdsman came upon her licking the babes with her tongue (Faustulus is said to have been his name). He carried the babies back to the sheepfold for his wife Larentia to rear. There are people who fancy that the shepherds used to call Larentia 'She-wolf' because of her sexual promiscuity and that this was how the miraculous tale originated.*

So were the boys born and so were they brought up. As soon as they had matured, they proved to be energetic young men, who, after finishing their chores around the sheepfold and out in the pastures, used to roam the forests for game. These activities so strengthened them in body and spirit that they would not only confront wild beasts but attack robbers laden with loot, which they would seize and share among the shepherds. With them the lads enjoyed their days together at work and at play, while the number of young men joining them increased day by day.

5. In those days, according to legend, the present festive rite of the Lupercal* was already in existence on the Palatine hill, which received its name from Pallanteum, an Arcadian city, later altered to Palatium. Once upon a time Evander had dwelt there, who was a native Arcadian and had brought from there the custom in which naked young men would cavort about in antic fashion in worship of Lycaean Pan, whom the Romans later called Inuus. The robbers, who knew when the festival was set to occur and who were angry at having lost their loot, ambushed the young men as they were caught up in the festivities. Romulus defended himself by fighting back, but Remus was captured. They took their captive to King Amulius, even going so far as to bring charges against him. The accusation they stressed the most was that the brothers had begun by poaching on Numitor's lands and had ended by plundering them with an organized band of youths like an invading enemy. Remus was therefore bound over to Numitor for punishment.

Now Faustulus from the very beginning had expected that the twins he was raising would prove to be of royal blood, since he knew that infants had been exposed by command of the king and that the date he had found them coincided with that command. But he had not wanted to reveal the situation prematurely unless a favourable opportunity arose or necessity intervened. Necessity came first. Under the stimulus of fear he revealed the situation to Romulus. It chanced that Numitor, too, when he heard from Remus, whom he was holding in custody, that he had a twin brother, and when he compared their ages with the time of exposure and their noble characters with that of the low-born, was set to thinking of his grandsons. By dint of close questioning he in the end was coming quite close to recognizing who Remus really was.

And so on all sides a trap was laid for the king. Romulus ordered the shepherds not to approach the palace in a single group—for he was not equal to such an open display of force—but to split up and come by separate routes at a time agreed upon. This was how he attacked Amulius, while from Numitor's dwelling Remus also helped with another party he had gathered. So it was that Romulus slew the king. *So Numitor rules?*

6. When the uproar was in its early stages Numitor repeatedly insisted that a foreign enemy had invaded the city and had attacked the palace, thereby drawing off the soldiers of Alba to the citadel on the pretext of securing it with an armed guard; but after the murder, when he saw the young men hastening to him to offer their congratulations, he at once called an assembly in which he revealed his brother's crimes against himself, the origin of his grandsons—how they were born, raised, and recognized—and, finally, the murder of the tyrant king, a deed for which he assumed responsibility. The twins with their fighters then marched in through the middle of the assembly and saluted their grandfather as king. The multitude shouted its unanimous assent, thereby confirming Numitor's title and authority.

Now that Alba had passed into Numitor's hands, Romulus and Remus conceived the desire of founding a city in the place where they had been exposed and raised. In fact, the population of Alba and the Latins had greatly increased; in addition, there were the shepherds who had flocked to them, all of whom taken together readily raised the expectation that both Alba and Lavinium would be small in comparison to the city they intended to found. But at this point the family curse—the desire for kingly supremacy—came between them as they were making their plans, and from an innocent beginning developed an ugly fight. Because they were twins no distinction could be made between them on the basis of age. In order that the deities who presided over the area might choose by augury who should give his name to the new city and rule it once it was founded, Romulus occupied the Palatine and Remus the Aventine to mark out the sacred areas where they would look for the signs of heaven's will. 7. To Remus augury came first, legend says: six vultures. After this had been reported to the people, double the number appeared for Romulus. Accordingly, the supporters of each man hailed their candidate as king, one side claiming the sovereignty because of the priority of time, the other because of the number of birds. From a war of words anger turned them to bloodshed. In the

who's using who. Remus' punishment vs Numitor's return

importance of public consent now

heat of the mêlée Remus met his death. The more common story is that in mockery of his brother's claim Remus jumped over the half-built walls, whereupon the enraged Romulus struck him down, crying 'So be it for any other who overleaps my walls!' Romulus thus became sole sovereign and gave his name to the city so founded.

He first fortified the Palatine, where he had spent his boyhood. To the other gods he instituted religious rites in accordance with Alban ritual, but in the Greek manner to Hercules, as Evander had ordained. The tale goes that Hercules, after slaying Geryon,* drove the monster's magnificent cattle to this spot, and after swimming across Tiber's stream, driving the kine before him, he lay down on a grassy bank so that this serene setting with its lush pasturage might refresh his cattle and himself, exhausted as he was from his journey. As slumber stole over him, heavy with food and drink, a native shepherd named Cacus, a creature of ferocious strength, was much taken by the beauty of the beasts: he wanted them for himself. But if he drove off the herd and forced it to enter his cave, the hoofmarks would point their inquiring owner in his direction. What to do? So it was that he selected the handsomest bulls, turned them around and dragged them into the cave by their tails. When the first flush of dawn roused Hercules from sleep and his gaze swept over the herd, he realized that some of them were missing. He headed for the nearest cave to see if perchance their tracks might direct him there. But when he saw that all hoofprints pointed away from the cave and nowhere else, befuddled and uneasy, he began to drive the herd away from the alien spot. At this point certain of the heifers, as they were moving off, mooed because they missed, as is natural, the males left behind. The bulls shut up in the cave lowed in response, and Hercules turned back. When Cacus saw him striding toward his cave he tried to resist by force, but, smitten by the hero's club and calling in vain for help from his fellow shepherds, he expired.

In those days Evander,* a refugee from the Peloponnesus, ruled this area more by personal influence than real power. He was revered for his ability to write, a new and miraculous skill among ignorant men, and revered even more because of his mother Carmenta, whom the natives believed to be divine and whom they held in awe for her prophetic power in the period before the Sibyl* arrived in Italy. At this point in the fracas, then, Evander was summoned by the agitated shepherds as they crowded about the stranger, whom

they had caught in the very act of murder. After listening to what
had happened and the reason for it, and after gazing at the stranger,
Evander realized that he possessed a figure and bearing rather greater
and more august than those of ordinary mortals. He asked what
manner of man he was. When he heard his name, father, and birthplace, he exclaimed, 'Son of Jupiter—Hercules—welcome! My mother,
a true prolocutor of the gods, once foretold to me that you would be
added to the number of the deities in heaven and that on this site an
altar to you would be dedicated which one day the most flourishing
people on earth would call the Greatest Altar and would revere in
the conduct of your cult.' Hercules, extending his right hand, said
he accepted the omen: he would fulfil destiny's decree by building
and dedicating the altar.

There a fine heifer from the herd was for the first time sacrificed
to Hercules, with two of the most prominent families of the area, the
Potitii and Pinarii, being called in to conduct it and to provide a
feast. It chanced that since the Potitii were present at the start, the
entrails were apportioned to them, while the Pinarii who arrived
after the entrails had been eaten received what remained. The custom of not offering the Pinarii the entrails of the sacrifice survived
thereafter as long as the family did. The Potitii, whom Evander had
instructed in the proper ritual, were for many generations the priests
of the sacrifice, but when the family's sacred duties were handed
over to public slaves to perform, the clan of the Potitii perished root
and branch.* This was the only foreign cult that Romulus adopted,
who even then honoured immortality achieved by virtuous deeds,
an honour toward which his own destiny was urging him as well.

8. After duly carrying out religious observances, Romulus summoned the populace to a meeting to promulgate laws that were
essential for the formation of a unified community. He thought that
the rustics would feel bound to observe the laws if he made his own
person more august and imposing by adopting various insignia of
power, both in his dress and particularly by the addition of twelve
lictors* to accompany him in public. Some think he took this number
from the number of augural birds that portended his kingship. I
myself incline to the opinion of those who believe that, just as the
attendants and other paraphernalia of office were borrowed from the
neighbouring Etruscans, who gave us the curule chair and the toga
praetexta,* so also the number twelve was borrowed from the lictors

the Etruscans furnished to the man they elected king of their league, each of the twelve Etruscan peoples contributing one lictor apiece.

Meanwhile the city's protective walls were continually extended as one area after another was annexed, more in the expectation of a large future population than to defend the inhabitants. In order that the enlarged city might not be empty and weak, he resorted to the time-honoured fiction of city founders that the lowly and ignoble folk they attract are children 'sprung from the earth'. He therefore selected a site for an asylum, which is the enclosed area on the left between the two groves as one descends the Capitol. A motley mob from the neighbouring peoples flocked to the spot, with no distinction made as to whether they were free or slave, and all eager for a new start in life. These men were the beginning of the real strength of the city. Satisfied now with the physical power of the citizen body, he next provided it with counsel and guidance. He created one hundred senators, either because this number seemed sufficient or because there were only one hundred suitable to be designated *patres*, or 'Fathers'. At all events, they were styled *patres* because of their rank; their descendants were called patricians.

9. Rome by this time was equal to any of the surrounding cities in her prowess in war, but because of the lack of women her greatness would not last beyond a generation: there was no hope of having children at home, and there existed no right of intermarriage with their neighbours. On the advice of the senators Romulus therefore dispatched ambassadors to the surrounding peoples to seek alliance and marriage rights for the young community. The envoys were instructed to argue that cities, like everything else, had humble beginnings, and those that achieved great prosperity were the ones who enjoyed a great name by their own valour and the help of the gods: Rome's neighbours should realize that the gods had been present to bless Rome's foundation and that the valour of the Romans themselves would never fail in the years ahead. In short, let one group of humans not disdain to unite in blood and kinship with another.

Nowhere did the envoys receive a sympathetic hearing. The neighbouring peoples scorned them, while simultaneously fearing for themselves and their descendants the growing giant in their midst. The envoys were dismissed with the repeated question why they had not also opened up an asylum for women: only this would have provided the sort of brides they deserved! The Roman youth were

seems like major oversight, no women
last resort; steal

stung by the insult: it looked as if the situation could be resolved only by the use of force. With this aim in mind (but disguising his resentment) Romulus purposely instituted games (called the Consualia) in honour of Neptune, patron of horses,* which would provide an opportunity and a site to implement his plan. He ordered that announcement of the spectacle be made to the neighbouring peoples, while the men at Rome prepared to celebrate the games with as much pageantry as they knew or were capable of in those days, their object being to make the festival widely known and anticipated.

Many a man came to see it, with the additional motive of touring the new city. In particular, Rome's closest neighbours came, the people of Caenina, Crustumerium, and Antemnae; the whole nation of the Sabines arrived as well, accompanied by wives and children. They were hospitably lodged in private homes, and when they viewed the site of the city, with its walls and many houses, they were amazed that it had grown so rapidly in so short a time. The day for the spectacle arrived and, while their eyes and minds were intent on it, a prearranged free-for-all began, with the Roman men scattering at an agreed signal to seize the unmarried girls. Most maidens were carried off as each man chanced upon her, but certain beauties, marked out for the leading senators, were hustled off to their homes by hirelings from the plebeian class. They say that as one lass, who excelled all others in bearing and beauty, was being carried off by a gang belonging to a certain Thalassius, many asked to whom they were bringing her. To prevent any interference the gang kept crying out, 'To Thalassius! To Thalassius!' This was the origin of the traditional cry we hear at weddings today.*

As the games broke up in confusion and fear, the grieving parents of the maidens ran off, accusing the Romans of violating their sacred obligations as hosts and invoking the god to whose festival and games they had been deceitfully invited contrary to religion and good faith. The abducted maidens had no better hope for their plight than had their parents, nor was their indignation less. But Romulus repeatedly went about in person to visit them, arguing that what had occurred was due to the arrogance of their parents, who had refused intermarriage with their neighbours. Despite this, he promised that they would enjoy the full rights of a proper marriage, becoming partners in all the fortunes the couple might share, in

Rome's citizenship, and in the begetting of children, the object dearest to every person's heart. So let them now abate their anger, let them give their hearts to those to whom chance had given their bodies. Often, he said, thankfulness replaces a sense of wrong over the course of time. In fact, their husbands would be even more solicitous than they might expect, because each one would do his utmost both to be a good husband and to fill the void created by the loss of parents and country. To Romulus' entreaties the husbands added their own honeyed words, claiming that they had acted out of desire and love, an avowal calculated to appeal most to a woman's nature.

10. The abducted maidens were by now much mollified, but not so their parents who, garbed in mourning attire, were at that moment unsettling their fellow citizens with tears and protestations. They did not restrict their expression of outrage to their own cities, but flocked from all sides to the king of the Sabines, Titus Tatius. Official delegations came as well, since his reputation was the greatest in the region. Now some of the daughters of the peoples of Caenina, Crustumerium, and Antemnae had also been abducted, but to the men of these cities Tatius and his Sabines seemed too slow in retaliating. The three communities therefore prepared to wage a joint war on their own. Yet not even Crustumerium and Antemnae acted fast enough to suit the ardour and anger of the people of Caenina, who invaded Roman territory on their own. Romulus came upon them with his army as they were widely scattered in their plundering and in a quick fight demonstrated that anger without strength goes for nothing. He routed their army, put it to flight, and pursued it as it scattered. He slew their king in battle and stripped the corpse of its armour; when their king had been lost, the city fell to Romulus at the first assault.

Romulus returned in triumph with his army, and, being an extraordinary man in his ability to publicize his achievements no less than in his execution of them, mounted the Capitol bearing the spoils of the slain enemy hung on a frame built for the purpose, and there, after he had propped it against an oak tree sacred to the shepherds, he marked out the boundaries of a temple to Jupiter, invoking him with a new title:* Jupiter Feretrius! I, Romulus, victor and king, bring to you these armaments of a king, and on this site I vow to build a temple that I have just now marked out in my mind, a place for dedicating the spoils of honour, which later leaders, following my example, will offer you after slaying kings and leaders of our enemies.' This was the origin of the first temple that was consecrated at Rome. In the years that followed the gods saw to it that these words of the temple's founder concerning future dedications of the spoils did not go unfulfilled, and at the same time that the honour would not be cheapened by many earning it. Only twice since have the spoils of honour been won, despite so many wars over so many years. The good fortune of attaining such distinction has been rare indeed.*

11. While the Romans were engaged at Caenina, the army of Antemnae took advantage of their absence by invading Roman territory. A legion hastily marched out from Rome against them as well and defeated them as they roamed the countryside. The battle-cry raised at the first charge was enough to put them to flight; subsequently the town itself fell. Romulus' wife Hersilia, yielding to the importunate entreaties of the abducted maidens, begged him as he returned flushed with his double victory to pardon their parents and to grant them citizenship: the state, she argued, could thereby grow in strength and concord. Romulus gave his ready consent.

The people of Crustumerium then began hostilities. When he marched out against them he encountered even less resistance: their own resolution had collapsed in face of the defeat of the others. Colonies were sent to both places, although more volunteers for Crustumerium were found because of the fertile soil. On the other hand many migrated from there to Rome, especially the parents and relatives of the abducted girls.

The war with the Sabines came last in the series, and it proved the greatest by far, for they did not act out of anger or greed, nor even give a hint of their intention before commencing hostilities. They also made subterfuge a part of their strategy. Spurius Tarpeius was in command of the citadel at Rome. Tatius induced Spurius' virgin daughter by a bribe of gold to admit his armed men into the citadel; at that time she used to go beyond the fortifications to seek water for performance of her religious duties.* Once admitted they crushed her under the weight of their weapons either so that the citadel might appear to have been captured by force or to set an example for the future that no one should ever keep faith with a traitor. Another legend has it that because the Sabines regularly wore heavy gold bracelets on their left arms and had splendid jewelled rings, she bargained for what they wore 'on their left arms'; accordingly they heaped upon her not gifts of gold but the very shields they were carrying. A third variant is that according to the agreement of surrender she asked for the actual weapons they had in their left hands and, because she seemed to be trying to disarm them by trickery, was killed by the very reward she had asked for.

12. However it came about, the Sabines had gained control of the citadel. On the next day the Roman army was drawn up, filling the area between the Palatine and Capitoline hills, but before the Sabines descended to level ground, anger and a desire to retake the citadel emboldened the Romans to mount an uphill attack. The commanders of each side led the fray, Mettius Curtius for the Sabines, Hostius Hostilius for the Romans. With *élan* and daring Hostilius placed himself in the front rank and pressed the Roman charge up the steep slope, but when he fell, the Roman line immediately broke and fell back to the ancient gate of the Palatine. Even Romulus was carried along in the crush of those fleeing. Lifting his weapons to the heavens he cried, 'Jupiter, the augural birds you sent commanded me to lay the first foundations of our city here on the Palatine. The Sabines have now bribed their way into control of the citadel; from there in battle array they have won the valley between the two hills and are now upon us. I beg you, father of gods and men, prevent the foe at least from seizing *this* spot. Banish Roman fear, stay their shameful flight! Here I vow a temple to you, Jupiter the Stayer, which shall be a reminder to posterity that the city was saved by your very present help.' And then, as if he had an intimation that his prayer had been heard, he cried, 'On this spot, Romans, Jupiter Optimus Maximus bids us make our stand and renew the fight!' The Romans obeyed as if directed by a voice from heaven. Romulus himself rushed to the front line. ~multiple Jupiters honored?~

Meanwhile Mettius Curtius, the Sabine leader, had plunged down from the citadel, driving the Romans in confusion before him over the entire area of the present forum. Not far from the gate to the Palatine he cried, 'We have vanquished treacherous hosts and a faint-hearted host: they now realize it is one thing to abduct young girls and another to fight with men!' Romulus with a band of the most mettlesome of the Roman youth attacked him in the very act of making this boast. Mettius happened at that moment to be fighting from horseback; it was therefore all the easier to put him to flight. The Romans pursued him as he fled, while the rest of their force, inspired by their intrepid king, routed the Sabines. When his horse took fright from the clamour of those in pursuit Mettius was plunged into a swampy area. The plight of their great leader caused the fleeing Sabines to wheel about and to fight back. The shouts and gestures of his many supporters gave Mettius added heart; he succeeded in extricating himself, but when the two sides renewed the general fight in the valley between the two hills the Roman forces gradually began to get the upper hand.

13. It was at this moment that the Sabine women, whose abduction had caused the war, boldly interposed themselves amid the flying spears. Their misfortunes overcame womanish fear: with hair streaming and garments rent, they made a mad rush from the sidelines, parting the battling armies and checking their angry strife. Appealing to fathers on one side and husbands on the other, they declared that kin by marriage should not defile themselves with impious carnage, nor leave the stain of blood upon descendants of their blood, grandfathers upon grandsons, fathers upon children. 'If you cannot abide the ties between you that our marriage has created, turn your anger against us. We are the cause of this war, we the cause of husbands and fathers lying wounded and slain. Only one side can win this fight. As for us, it is better to die than to live, for we must do so either as widows or as orphans.' Their appeal moved both leaders and the rank and file: silence and a sudden hush fell upon the field.

The commanders then came forward to strike a treaty by which they not only made peace but united the two peoples in a single community. They elected to share the sovereignty, while fixing the seat of government at Rome. As a concession to the Sabines, they styled the doubled population Quirites from the Sabine town of Cures. They called the spot where Curtius' horse had struggled out of the swamp to shallow water the Lacus Curtius,* as memorial to the battle.

The sudden shift from the distress of war to the blessings of peace endeared the Sabine women all the more to husbands and parents, and most especially to Romulus. For in dividing the population into thirty wards or *curiae*, he named them after the women. Tradition does not say—since the women were undoubtedly more than thirty in number—whether the names were chosen by lot, age,

or according to their own or their husbands' rank. At the same time
(three centuries of knights were also created, one called Ramnenses
from Romulus, and a second Titienses from Titus Tatius; the reason for the name of the third century, Luceres, is uncertain.* Henceforth the two kings ruled jointly and in harmony.

14. Some years later relatives of King Tatius did violence to
ambassadors from Laurentian territory. The injured party protested
this violation of international law, but the influence and entreaties of
Tatius' own people had greater weight with him. The consequence
was that what should have been their punishment became his. For
when attending an annual sacrifice at Lavinium, his presence caused
an uproar, and he was killed. They say that Romulus was less upset
by this than he should have been, either because of the untrustworthy nature of shared sovereignty or because he thought Tatius
had been killed for just cause. He did not make a military response,
therefore, but renewed the covenant between Rome and Lavinium
in order to expiate the violence done to the ambassadors and the
king's murder. King killed in a riot (instead of battle)

On this front, then, an unexpected peace prevailed, but on another—much closer to home and, in fact, at Rome's very gates—war
broke out. The men of Fidenae,* believing that the growing strength
of such a close neighbour was dangerous to themselves, decided to
make a pre-emptive strike before Rome should become as powerful
as they believed she soon would be. An armed band of youth was
dispatched and ravaged the land between Fidenae and Rome; then,
because the Tiber barred their way on the right, to the west, they
turned left, where they caused a great panic among the country
dwellers, whose disorderly flight from countryside to Rome was the
first indication that war was upon them. Since a conflict on his
doorstep naturally permitted no delay, Romulus reacted at once by
leading out his army and fixing his camp a mile from Fidenae. After
leaving a small garrison there, he set out with his entire force,
ordering *en route* a contingent to conceal themselves in ambush in a
spot densely overgrown with brushwood; advancing further with
the greater part of his army and the whole cavalry, he executed a
plan to draw out the astonished enemy by riding up virtually to the
city gates in an undisciplined and threatening manœuvre. The enemy was less surprised when the horsemen wheeled and retreated,
although the retreat was feigned. And, while the cavalry appeared to

be hesitating between combat and flight, the foot soldiers too began
to fall back. Suddenly the enemy gates were filled with soldiers, who
poured out pell-mell and, as the Roman line gave way, were drawn
in their eagerness to harry and pursue to the ambuscade. From there
the Romans suddenly rose up and attacked the enemy line on its
flanks. And when the enemy saw standards advancing toward them,
carried by the garrison contingent from the camp, their alarm increased. Terror-stricken by the threat from so many quarters, the
army of Fidenae panicked and ran almost before Romulus and his
men could rein in their horses and wheel about. Those who had
lately been pursuing men pretending flight now found themselves
fleeing back to the town, but in a far more chaotic stampede: their
panic was genuine. Yet they did not escape. The Romans followed
the enemy so closely that both pursuers and pursued burst into the
town in a single thrust before the gates could be shut.

15. War fever then spread from Fidenae to the people of Veii,*
who were provoked because Fidenae was of the same Etruscan stock
as themselves and because their very proximity would, they were
sure, be a stimulus to Roman aggression should Rome begin to view
all neighbours indiscriminately as enemies. They overran Roman
territory as if conducting a raid rather than standard warfare, since
they pitched no camp and did not wait for an enemy response. They
returned to Veii carrying booty taken from the countryside. The
Romans, failing to find the enemy in their territory, crossed the
Tiber prepared and eager for a decisive confrontation. When the
men of Veii heard that the Romans were pitching camp and would
soon be approaching, they sallied forth to decide the issue on the
battlefield rather than defend homes and city from within. By brute
force and without strategy the Roman king prevailed, using the
might of his veteran army alone. He pursued the fleeing enemy to
their walls, but did not attack the city itself, protected as it was by
great fortifications and a naturally defensive site. On his return he
plundered their farmland more to take revenge than for booty. And
so it was that Veii, overcome as much by this misfortune as by their
defeat on the battlefield, sent envoys to Rome to seek peace. Deprived of part of their territory, they were granted a hundred years'
truce.

These were Romulus' chief accomplishments at home and abroad
during his reign, none of which was at variance with belief in his

parallel to Hercules who he honored

divine origin and in the divinity they came to accept after his death—not his valour in recovering his grandfather's kingdom, nor his plan to found the city and to put it on a firm footing in war and peace. He so strengthened the city, in fact, that Rome enjoyed peace and security for the next forty years. Nevertheless, the common people favoured him more than did the senators, while the soldiery showed him by far the greatest affection; from them he selected both in war and in peace three hundred armed bodyguards whom he called Celeres, or 'the Swift'.

16. Such were the earthly deeds of Romulus. One day during a meeting to review his troops on the Campus Martius at the Goat Swamp a sudden storm with mighty thunder claps enveloped the king in such a dense cloud that the crowd lost sight of him. Nor was Romulus seen again on earth. The fear of the young soldiers at last subsided when the turbulence passed and the light of a calm and sunny day returned. Although they readily believed the senators who had been standing closest that he had been snatched up in the air by a whirlwind, still, as they gazed at the empty throne, they were stricken with the fear of having been orphaned, so to speak, and for quite a time stood in mournful silence. Then, after a few proclaimed Romulus' divinity,* the rest joined in, hailing him with one accord as a god born to a god, king and parent of the city of Rome. They asked in prayer for his favour: that willing and propitious he might safeguard his children evermore.

I believe that even then there were some people who maintained privately that the king had been torn apart by the hands of the senators—for this version, though little known, has also been handed down. Still, admiration for the man and the alarm felt at the time gave the other version wider currency, and it was further strengthened by the testimony of a single individual. This man was Proculus Iulius, a highly respected citizen according to tradition. To assuage the distress of his fellow citizens at the loss of their king and to combat their hostility to the senators, he stepped forth in a public meeting to affirm the truth of a most extraordinary event. 'My fellow citizens,' he declared, 'today at dawn's first light Romulus, father of our country, descended from heaven without warning and appeared before me. I was drenched in the sweat of fear and I stood rooted to the spot in veneration, praying that it might be lawful for me to be looking upon him. "Go," he said, "announce to the Ro-

weird

mans that the gods in heaven will my Rome to be the capital of the world. Accordingly, let them cultivate the art of war; let them realize, and let them teach their descendants, that no human power can withstand Roman supremacy." With these words he rose aloft and disappeared.' It is astonishing how absolute was the conviction that Proculus Iulius' words carried and how, once belief in Romulus' immortality had been confirmed, the grief felt by the army and people was mitigated.

17. Meanwhile ambition for royal power took hold of the senators, creating a struggle that did not involve particular persons (for no individuals had as yet emerged as pre-eminent in the new state) but factions from the two constituent groups. Those of Sabine stock wanted one of their own to be named king: since the death of Tatius they had had no share in the kingship, and they now saw power slipping from them, although they were supposed to be partners on equal terms. On the other hand, the old Roman element objected to a foreign king. Nevertheless, despite conflicting choices, they did agree in wanting a king, having as yet no experience of the blessings of liberty. The senators then began to fear that a state without a leader and an army without a commander might fall prey to violence from without, since so many neighbouring states harboured unneighbourly feelings toward Rome. Their dilemma was that though they agreed in needing a head of state, no one could bring himself to yield to another. *funny — later w/ liberty face threats from inside*

It was under these circumstances that the hundred senators divided the government among themselves by creating groups of ten, from each of which individuals were elected to manage affairs of state. Ten held power, but only one of them possessed the insignia of command and the lictors—a command limited to a period of five days and passed round to each in turn. The lapse in kingship lasted for a year. From this fact it was called an interregnum, a term that is still in use today.

The plebs then began to grumble that they were now enslaved to one hundred masters instead of one. It began to look as if they would accept nothing less than that there should be a king and they should be the ones to choose him. Realizing that this was their intention, the senators thought they should offer what they were about to lose in any case: their decision to entrust the people with the final choice created much goodwill, but it was so formulated

#2: Numa

that the senators ended by retaining as much power as they had given up. For they decreed that when the people elect a king, their choice should be valid only if the senators confirm it (today, too, in voting for laws and magistrates the same principle is followed, although the senate's real power has been lost, since before the people vote the senators ratify the outcome in advance).* At that time, the interrex, having summoned a public meeting, declared, 'Fellow citizens, may what you are about to do prove favourable, fortunate, and happy: elect your king, for such is the senate's will. The senators will then ratify your choice, should you elect a man worthy to be Romulus' successor.' This was so pleasing to the plebs that, not to be outdone in goodwill, they merely voted that the senate should choose the next ruler of Rome.

(not real action of Her an thing ease)

18. Numa Pompilius was famed in those days for his justice and piety. He lived in the Sabine town of Cures, and was the most learned man—so far as anyone could be in that age—in all matters of law, both human and divine. People wrongly claim Pythagoras of Samos as his teacher, in default of their discovering any other. Yet it is clear that Pythagoras lived during the reign of Servius Tullius over a hundred years later, and that his school of devoted disciples was located far off in south Italy, in and around Metapontum, Heraclea, and Croton.* Now, even if Numa had been a contemporary, how could Pythagoras' reputation have penetrated to Sabine country from so far away, and in what language could Pythagoras have inspired a neophyte to study with him? And how could a single individual have safely passed through the many intervening peoples, so different from one another in language and customs? I think it more likely that Numa's mind and moral principles were due to his own inborn nature, formed not so much by foreign learning as by the strict and severe manners of the old Sabines, the most incorruptible of ancient peoples.

When Numa's candidacy was broached in the senate, it seemed that power would shift to the Sabines, were one of their number chosen king. Yet because no one could bring himself to oppose the candidacy of this great man in favour of himself or a member of his faction—or, for that matter, any other senator or citizen—the senate decreed unanimously that the kingship should be offered to Numa Pompilius.

After he was summoned he ordered that, as Romulus had received the kingship by augury when founding the city, so the gods should be consulted about himself as well. He was then escorted to the citadel by an augur, who held a sacred office that, as a mark of honour, thereafter became public and permanent. Numa was seated on a stone, facing the south, while the augur sat to the left, his head covered and holding in his right hand a curved staff without knots which they called the *lituus*. Then, looking out over the city and countryside, he prayed to the gods and marked out a field from east to west, designating the areas to the south 'the right', those to the north 'the left'. He fixed in his mind a landmark opposite him far off on the horizon; then, shifting the staff to his left hand and placing his right on Numa's head, he prayed as follows: 'Father Jupiter, if it is heaven's will that Numa Pompilius whose head I am now touching be king at Rome, I ask you to sanction it by sending us incontestable signs within those boundaries I have fixed.' He then enumerated the auspices that he wished to be sent. And sent they were: Numa was declared king and descended from the sacred area of augury.

19. After receiving supreme power in this way Numa determined that Rome, which had originally been established through force of arms, should be re-established through justice, law, and proper observances. But her inhabitants could not be accustomed to such a change, he realized, if they were forever at war, which brutalizes the soul. To soften the bellicose temper of the people by inducing them to give up arms, he made the temple of Janus at the foot of the Argiletum an indicator of peace and war: when open, it signified that the state was in arms; when closed, that all surrounding peoples were at peace. Twice since the reign of Numa it has been closed, once in the consulship of Titus Manlius after the end of the First Punic War, and a second time, which the gods granted our age to see, after the war at Actium when the emperor Caesar Augustus established peace over land and sea.*

After the closing Numa ended fear of attack from Rome's neighbours by winning the goodwill of them all through treaties of alliance. On the other hand, he realized that a people whose aggressiveness had formerly been checked by fear of their enemies and by military discipline might become fractious in their new-found idleness. He therefore first aimed to instil in them fear of the gods, an invaluable constraint in the case of an untutored multitude, which

in those days was rather primitive. Yet because he could not win
them over without some miraculous fiction, he pretended that he   ha
met by night with the goddess Egeria: it was at her prompting, he
claimed, that he was instituting religious rites that would please the
gods most and was assigning a special priest to each of them.

His first measure was to divide the year into twelve months according to the phases of the moon. Yet because a lunar month does
not amount to a full thirty days, the lunar year falls eleven days
short of a full revolution of the sun. He therefore made provision for
inserting intercalary months in such a way that after twenty years
the lunar and solar calendars should again coincide, the days coming
round to the same position of the sun from which they had started.*
He also fixed the days on which one could and could not conduct
public business, since it would be desirable for there to be times
when nothing might be brought before the people.

20. He then turned his attention to instituting various priesthoods,
although he performed very many religious duties himself, particularly those that now pertain to the flamen Dialis, or priest of Jupiter.* But because in a warlike state he judged there would be more
kings like Romulus than himself and that they would take the field
in person, to ensure the proper performance of the king's sacred
duties he created the (flamen Dialis, to be permanent and resident in
Rome, distinguishing him by special dress and the royal curule chair.
To this he added two more priesthoods, one for Mars, the other for
Quirinus; he also appointed virgins to serve Vesta, a priesthood that
had originated in Alba and was therefore closely associated with the
native city of Rome's founder. He paid them from public funds to
ensure that they would be in constant attendance at their temple,
further emphasizing their revered and inviolable status by the rule of
chastity and other marks of sanctity. He likewise enrolled twelve
Salian priests of Mars Gradivus and granted them the distinction of
an embroidered tunic over which they wore a bronze breastplate. He
bade them carry the shields from heaven called *ancilia** and to go
through the city singing hymns and performing their ritual three-
step war dance. From the senators he enrolled as pontiff Numa
Marcius, son of Marcus, and entrusted to his keeping all sacral lore
which, written out and authenticated, specified with what victims,
on what days, and at what temples sacrifices were to be made, and
with what moneys expenses were to be paid. He then subjected all

other public and private religious matters to the decrees of the pontiff; it was to him that the plebs should come for advice, and it was he who was to prevent transgressions of divine ordinances by failure to observe ancestral custom or by the adoption of foreign rites. The same pontiff assumed jurisdiction not only over rituals concerning the gods above but also over proper funerary rites and the placation of the spirits of the dead; in addition, he was to determine what prodigies—whether as thunder or in some other observable form—should be recognized as significant and attended to. To elicit knowledge of these matters from the divine will he dedicated an altar to Jupiter Elicius on the Aventine hill, and consulted the god by augury as to which prodigies it was proper for him to recognize.

21. The entire population, thus diverted from aggression and warfare, concentrated its attention and energy on matters such as these. Because heaven's will was seen to be involved in human affairs, concern for the gods became ever-present and habitual, filling their hearts with such devotion that good faith and regard for their oaths ensured good order rather than fear of punishment under the law. And since men on their own initiative patterned their conduct after the unique example of their king, even Rome's neighbours, who previously had believed that it was not a civilian community but a military camp that had been set down in their midst to menace the peace of all, began to respect them so much that they considered it sacrilege to attack a state wholly devoted to the worship of the gods.

There was a grove watered by a fountain of never-failing water that poured forth from a shaded grotto in its centre. Numa often made solitary visits there to meet, as he said, with the goddess; he consecrated this grove to the Camenae* because it was there that they conferred with his spouse Egeria. He also instituted worship of Fides, or Faith, ordering that the flamens should be borne to her shrine in a covered carriage drawn by two horses and should perform their sacred duties with the hand wrapped to the fingers, thereby indicating that Faith must be safeguarded and that when men join right hands there too Faith has her temple. He ordained many other rites of sacrifice and places for carrying them out, which the pontiffs call Argei.* His greatest achievement, however, was the preservation throughout his reign of peace no less than of his realm.

Thus Rome's first two kings, one by war and the other by peace, fostered Rome's well-being. Romulus reigned thirty-seven years, Numa forty-three. The state had become strong and well-tempered in the ways of war and peace.

22. At Numa's death Rome reverted to an interregnum. The people then elected Tullus Hostilius king, grandson of that Hostilius who had fought the Sabines so brilliantly in the battle at the foot of the citadel, a choice that the senators then ratified. He was not only unlike his predecessor but even more combative than Romulus: his mettlesome nature was the product of youth, strength, and awareness of his grandfather's prowess. And so, believing the state was becoming weak from inaction, he looked about for opportunities to stir up conflict. It so happened that the country people from both Rome and Alba were making cattle raids on each other's territory (Gaius Cluilius was then ruler at Alba). Envoys were sent from each city almost simultaneously to demand restitution. Tullus had told his men to carry out their instructions with dispatch: he well knew the Albans would refuse and that in this way war could in good conscience be declared. The Albans, on the other hand, conducted their business at a leisurely pace: hospitably received by Tullus in ease and good fellowship, they were thoroughly enjoying the king's convivial banquet during the time in which the Roman envoys in quick order demanded satisfaction and, when refused, declared war upon the Albans, to begin at the end of a thirty-day period. After they reported back to Tullus, he gave the Albans' envoys permission to state the purpose of their mission, who, ignorant of what had transpired, hemmed and hawed in apology: they were, they said, reluctant to say anything that might upset such an excellent host, but they were under orders; they had come to seek satisfaction and, if it was not given, they had been commanded to declare war. Tullus replied as follows: 'Tell your king that the king of Rome has the gods on his side: they have witnessed which people first rejected envoys seeking restitution and dismissed them. Utter defeat in this war will befall the guilty party.'

23. When the envoys of Alba reported what Tullus had said, each side began to make an all-out effort for a war that would be much like a civil conflict, virtually between parents and children, since both communities were of Trojan descent, Lavinium having been founded by Trojan stock, Alba by Lavinium, and Rome from the

line of the Alban kings. The war was nevertheless destined to end
with little loss of life, since it was not decided by the opposing
armies in a pitched battle: the peoples would be merged into one,
with the demolition of only the buildings of one of them.

The Albans were the first to attack, invading Roman territory
with a large force. They pitched their camp not more than five miles
from the city and surrounded it with a trench, which was long
known as the Cluilian trench from the name of Alba's general; but
in the course of time both the trench and its name disappeared. It
was in this encampment that Cluilius, the Alban king, died; the
Albans then elected Mettius Fufetius dictator.

In the meantime Tullus, made particularly combative by the king's
death, declared that the power of the gods, which had manifested
itself by first striking down the king himself, would soon exact
punishment from the entire Alban people for this godless war. Slipping past the enemy's camp by night, he invaded Alban territory.
Mettius was thus forced to abandon his position. While taking the
most direct route toward the enemy, he sent an envoy on ahead to
propose to Tullus that they confer before joining battle; if they did
so, he was sure that his proposal would be as much in Rome's
interest as in that of Alba. Tullus accepted and drew up his forces in
preparation for the parley, even though Mettius' proposal was un-
likely to convince. The Albans took up a position facing the Romans.

Accompanied by a few nobles the two leaders met in the area
between the two armies. The Alban spoke thus: 'Our King Cluilius
said, I recollect, that the causes of this war were the wrongs committed and the failure to make restitution according to our treaty, and
I do not doubt, Tullus, that this is your officially stated position.
But if we are to be frank with one another and not indulge in fair-
sounding pretexts, we will concede that the desire to dominate one
another is provoking our kindred and neighbouring cities to go to
war. Whether rightly or wrongly is not the issue. That would be a
concern for the one who began hostilities: as for myself, the people
of Alba have chosen me general simply to prosecute the war. Let me
remind you, Tullus, that the Etruscans surround both of us—and
you in particular, for you know full well which of the two of us is
closer to them, who are even more powerful on the sea than they are
on land. Please remember that the moment you give the signal to

begin hostilities, they will be looking on as our two sides clash, ready to attack simultaneously the victors and vanquished in their exhaustion and affliction. In heaven's name, let us not risk losing the liberty we now possess by a throw of the dice that will bring enslavement to one of us and supremacy to the other; let us rather find a way that will allow one people to rule the other without both of them suffering crippling losses and much bloodshed.' Tullus was not displeased by these words, although he was more combative by nature and confident of victory.

As each side was seeking an answer to this dilemma a solution presented itself for which Fortune herself provided the means of fulfilment. **24.** For it chanced that in each army there were three brothers who were triplets, one set very like the other in age and strength. Tradition agrees on their names, the Horatii and the Curiatii, and there is scarcely a better known episode from antiquity. Still, in an episode so famous there is uncertainty as to which nation the Horatii belonged and to which the Curiatii. There are authorities in support of both beliefs, but I find that the majority identify the Horatii as Roman, and I am inclined to follow them.

Their respective kings encouraged the triplets to take up their swords on behalf of their country: to the victorious side would go dominion. They agreed, and a time and place were fixed. But before the fight, a treaty was struck between the Romans and the Albans upon condition that whosesoever champions should prevail, their country would win sovereignty with full consent of the other.

Now treaties differ, as do their terms, but they are all made in the same way. Tradition has it that this treaty, which is the oldest we know of, was made as follows. The fetial priest* asked King Tullus, 'Do you bid me, O king, to strike a treaty with the *pater patratus* of the Alban people?' When the king so commanded, he said, 'I require of you a piece of sacred turf, O king.' The king replied, 'Take it, free from impurity.' The fetial then took up from Rome's citadel a clump of green grass free from impurity. He then asked the king, 'Do you, O king, grant me, along with my sacred utensils and attendants, royal sanction to represent the Roman people of the Quirites?' The king replied, 'So far as may be done without prejudice to myself and the Roman people of the Quirites, I do.' At that time Marcus Valerius was the fetial priest; he made Spurius Fusius *pater patratus* by touching his head and hair with a ceremonial branch.

The *pater patratus* is appointed to pronounce the oath—that is, to solemnize the treaty; he did this in many words that are not worth repeating, since the formula is a long one. After the provisions had been recited, he said, 'Hear me, Jupiter; hear me, *pater patratus* of the Alban people; hear me, people of Alba. The Roman people shall not be the first to transgress these stipulations which, inscribed on wood or wax, have been read out without malice aforethought from first to last, and whose meaning is clearly apprehended here and now. If by public decision they should be the first to transgress with malice aforethought, then on that day, Jupiter, may you strike the Roman people as I here and now strike this pig; and may you strike with greater force, just as you are greater in potency and power.' When he had said this, he struck the pig with a flint knife. In response the dictator and the *pater patratus* of Alba pronounced a similar formula and oath of their own.

25. On completion of the treaty the triplets, as had been agreed, took up their arms. Each side cheered on its champions, reminding them that ancestral gods, homeland, and parents, together with all their countrymen at home and in the army, were at that moment looking to the weapons they held in their hands for salvation. The fighters, emboldened by the cries of their supporters and by inborn courage, advanced to the open area between the two lines. The armies had settled down before their respective camps and, though exempt from the immediate danger, were filled with apprehension: supremacy was at stake, and it depended on the courage and luck of a handful of men. As they turned their attention upon the discomfiting scene, rapt and keyed up, the signal to begin was sounded.

The three champions from each side fell upon their opponents with swords drawn and filled with the fighting spirit of their mighty armies. They were not concerned about the danger to themselves but by the thought that the future of their countries lay in their hands: supremacy or enslavement. As for the spectators, at the first onslaught they shivered in dread at the clash of arms and flashing swords, and, when neither side appeared to be winning the advantage, voice and breath strangled in their throats. In the hand-to-hand combat that followed they beheld struggling bodies and weapon thrusts that were unable to bring the fight to a decision; then wounds and blood appeared; in the end two of the Romans fell lifeless, one upon the other, but not before they had wounded all three Albans.

At the death of the Romans the army of Alba roared with delight; the Romans, hopes dashed, were now frozen in fear at the plight of the single man whom the three Curiatii had now surrounded. By good luck he was as yet unharmed, and although unequal to the three taken together he knew he was a match for them individually. He therefore took to flight to separate his opponents, expecting that each would give pursuit as his wounds would permit. After spurting ahead some distance from the scene of the fighting, he looked back to see two of them far off and widely separated, and one closing in on him. He wheeled and attacked in a ferocious rush; and even as the Alban army was calling out for the Curiatii to come to their brother's rescue, Horatius was toppling his enemy and looking about for his second victory. A mighty hurrah from his astonished supporters spurred him to finish off the fight. He felled his second foe before the last brother, who was closing in fast, could reach him.

Now only two were left to fight it out on equal terms, but their hopes and strength were not the same. The Roman, as yet unwounded, was eager for the final encounter because of his double victory; confronting him was an opponent weak from wounds and hard running, sick at heart from the slaughter of his brothers. What followed was not a real fight. The exultant Roman cried, 'I have slain two foes to appease the shades of my brothers; I shall slay the third to win dominion of Rome over Alba, the prize of this war.' Looming over his foe who was struggling under the weight of his arms, Horatius buried his sword in his throat. He then stripped the spoils from the corpse as it lay.

The Romans welcomed him to their ranks with rejoicing and congratulations, their joy all the greater because they had been so close to defeat. The two sides then buried their dead, but with very different feelings: one had gained supremacy, the other was now the subject of the victor. The tombs stand today on the spot where each fell, the two Roman ones together toward the site of Alba, the three Alban nearer Rome but at intervals, exactly as the battle had been fought. 26. Before they parted Mettius asked Tullus what orders he had to give in accordance with the treaty; Tullus' command was to keep his soldiers under arms, for he would need them should a war break out with Veii.

The two armies then marched back to their respective cities, with Horatius at the head of the Roman forces and bearing before him the triple spoils. He was met at the Capena gate by his unwed sister, who had been betrothed to one of the Curiatii. When she saw the military cloak over her brother's shoulders that she herself had made for her fiancé, she let down her hair in mourning and tearfully called out his name. His sister's weeping enraged the hot-tempered young man, coming as it did at the moment of his personal victory and of great public rejoicing. Unsheathing his sword, he stabbed her to the heart, crying out in his vehemence, 'Go to your betrothed, along with your ill-timed love—you who have no thought for your dead brothers, for me, or for your country. So may it be for any Roman woman who mourns an enemy.'

The senators and plebeians were shocked at what he had done, but in their minds it was counterbalanced by his splendid action on the battlefield. Nevertheless, they laid hands on him and hurried him off to the king for justice. Tullus, however, did not want to be responsible for convicting and punishing such a man, which would be repugnant in its own right and displeasing to the people. He therefore called the populace together and announced, 'In accordance with the law I hereby appoint a two-man board to convict Horatius of high treason.'* The grim formula of the law was as follows: 'Let a two-man board judge the accused guilty of high treason; if he appeals this verdict, let the appeal be heard; if the verdict stands, let the lictor put a hood over the guilty man's head, let him tie him up and suspend him from a barren tree; let him scourge him to death either within the sacred boundary of the city or without.' These being the terms of their appointment, the two men felt that they were not empowered to acquit even an innocent man. They accordingly condemned him, one of them saying, 'Publius Horatius, I find you guilty of high treason. Lictor, go bind his hands.' When the lictor had approached and was preparing to throw the ropes about him, Horatius, at the prompting of Tullus, whose sympathies were with the defendant, said, 'I appeal.'

The appeal was taken before the people. In this proceeding men were influenced more than anything else by the assertion of the father, Publius Horatius, that his daughter had been killed for cause: if that were not the case, he would have exercised his legal powers as a father against his son.* A short time before, he said, they had looked upon him as the proud father of a splendid family. He now implored them not to take away his only remaining child. With

these words the aged father embraced the young man, while pointing to the spoils of the Curiatii fastened up at that spot now called
the Horatian Spears.* 'Fellow citizens,' he asked, 'can you endure to
look upon this man you have just honoured as he entered the city,
triumphant in victory, tied up spreadeagled on a rack, tortured, and
scourged? The eyes of our Alban enemy could scarcely endure the
sight of such an appalling sight! Lictor, go bind those hands that
with spear and shield have just won for the Roman people dominion
over Alba. Go, put a hood over the head of the liberator of our city,
suspend him from that barren tree. Scourge him to death within the
city's sacred boundary—amid these spears and spoils he has won.
Or do so outside the boundary—amid the very tombs of the Curiatii
he slew! Is there any place you can take him where evidence of the
glory he has won would not exempt him from suffering such a
hideous punishment?'

The people could not bear to see the tears of the father or the
resolute spirit of the son, ready to face every peril. They acquitted
him more out of respect for his noble spirit than for the justness of
his cause. But then, in order to atone for an act of outright murder
by some rite of purification, they bade the father make expiation
and to do so at public expense. Accordingly, after conducting certain sacrifices of atonement that became traditional in the Horatian
clan thereafter, he had a wooden beam built over the roadway, beneath which he required the young man to pass with covered head,
as if passing under a yoke of submission. The beam remains today,
periodically restored with public moneys, and is known as the Sister's Beam. A tomb for Horatia was constructed of hewn stone on
the spot where she fell.

27. Yet peace with Alba did not last long. When the people turned
against him for having placed the fate of the entire city in the hands
of three soldiers, Mettius' unstable nature led him to abandon straight-
forward schemes that had not succeeded in favour of devious ones
that he hoped would reinstate him in his countrymen's eyes: earlier
he had proposed peace in the midst of war, now he looked to war in
peacetime. And because his city's will to fight was greater than its
real strength, he incited other states openly to declare war on Rome,
while reserving for his own people the role of Roman allies bent on
treachery. Fidenae, which enjoyed the privileges of a Roman colony,
was induced to go to war with Rome by the promise of Alba's

defection to her side. The people of Veii were also taken into the
plan as allies.

And so, when the Fidenates broke into open revolt, Tullus summoned Mettius and his army from Alba and marched out against
them. He crossed the Anio River and pitched his camp where it
meets the Tiber. The army of Veii had crossed the Tiber at a point
between the camp and Fidenae, and had now formed up immediately next to the river as the right wing of the battleline. On the left
toward the rising hills the men of Fidenae took up their position.
Tullus stationed his forces opposite the Veientes, and set the Albans
facing Fidenae's legion.

But Mettius proved as cowardly as he was untrustworthy. Daring
neither to stay put nor to desert openly, he withdrew bit by bit
toward the hills, and, when he thought he had put sufficient distance between himself and the others, deployed his whole force on
the high ground, and, still hesitating, spun out the time by marshal-
ling each line of men one after the other. His plan was to go over to
whichever side fortune should give the victory.

At first the Romans closest to Mettius were surprised to find
their flank left undefended by the withdrawal of their allies; then a
cavalry captain swiftly galloped off to inform the king that the Albans
were retiring. At this critical moment Tullus vowed to consecrate
twelve Salian priests, as well as shrines to Pallor and Panic.* Shouting in a voice loud enough for the enemy to hear, he ordered the
captain to return to the fight: there was no reason for alarm—the
Alban army at his command was shifting around to attack the un-
protected rear of Fidenae. He also commanded the cavalry captain
on rejoining his men to order them to raise their spears aloft. This
had the effect of preventing a good many of the Roman infantrymen
from seeing the withdrawal of the Albans. Even those who had seen
what was happening thought it was part of Tullus' plan, and so
fought all the harder.

Now it was the enemy's turn to be alarmed: they had heard what
Tullus had meant them to hear, for many in Fidenae understood
Latin, enjoying as they did the rights of colonists. And so, to avoid
being cut off from their town by a sudden descent of the Albans
from the hills, they turned and fled. Tullus gave pursuit and, after
routing the men of Fidenae, turned even more fiercely upon the
Veientes, who had been panicked by the panic of the others. They

did not withstand his attack, but the river at their back kept them from headlong flight. At the river bank some in cowardice threw down their weapons and plunged pell-mell into the water, while others were overwhelmed as they hesitated between resistance and flight. Never before had Rome fought a bloodier battle.

28. At that point the army of Alba, which had been watching from the sidelines, descended to the plain. When Mettius ventured to congratulate Tullus on his victory, the latter made a courteous response. After praying that heaven would grant its blessing, he ordered the Alban camp to be joined with the Roman and that preparations be made for a sacrifice of purification the next day. When the morrow came and everything needful stood in readiness, he ordered each of the two armies to a meeting. Heralds, beginning on the outskirts of the camp, summoned the Albans first. To them such a gathering was a novelty: curiosity aroused, they crowded round the Roman king to hear what he had to say. By prearranged plan armed Romans stood about them, their centurions having been instructed to execute their orders promptly.

Tullus began as follows: 'Romans, if ever there was a war in which you had reason to be thankful above all to the gods and then to your own courage, it was in the battle we fought yesterday. For we were contending not so much with the enemy, but—what is even more difficult and dangerous—with the treachery and betrayal of our allies. Please do not suppose that I gave the order for the Albans to withdraw toward the hills. That was not my doing: I pretended it was because I did not want your fighting spirit to desert you as your allies were doing; at the same time, by making our foe think they were being attacked from the rear, I hoped they would turn tail and flee. And yet responsibility for this treachery does not fall upon all men of Alba. No, they were following their leader, just as you would have followed me had I decided to pull my troops away from the position we were in at the time. Mettius over there led the retreat, Mettius instigated the war, Mettius broke the treaty between Rome and Alba. I intend to single out this man for an exemplary punishment that will be a lesson to anyone in the future who contemplates such treachery.'

Armed centurions closed in on Mettius. The king continued: 'May what I am about to do prove favourable, fortunate, and happy for the Roman people, for myself, and for the men of Alba. It is my

intention to <u>move all the people of Alba to Rome</u>, to give the plebeians citizenship and to enroll your leaders in the senate: in short, to
create a single city, a single state. Just as Alba once was split into
two peoples, so now let it return to one.' The reaction of the Alban
youth to these words was silence: unarmed, they were surrounded
by those in arms and, though feelings among them differed, they
shared a common fear.

Then Tullus said, 'Mettius Fufetius, if you were able to learn to
keep your word and abide by agreements you have made, I would so
school you and spare your life. But as it is, you are beyond saving.
Your punishment nevertheless will teach mankind to hold sacred
the things you have profaned. Just as yesterday your loyalties were
divided between Fidenae and Rome, so today shall your body be
divided.' At once two four-horse teams were brought forward. Mettius
was tied spreadeagled to the chariots and the teams driven off in
opposite directions. His body was rent, parts of his limbs still tied to
each of the ever-widening chariots. Everyone averted his eyes from
the ghastly spectacle. This was the first and last time the Romans
meted out such uncivilized punishment; in all other cases they are
entitled to boast that no other people have punished wrongdoing in
a more humane way.

29. In the meantime the cavalry had been sent to Alba with orders
to conduct the population to Rome. Soon the legions arrived, whose
job was to level the city. Upon entering the gates they did not
encounter the uproar and panic that are usual when cities are captured: gates breached, walls shivered with battering rams, the citadel stormed, cries of enemy soldiers pounding through the streets
spreading pandemonium everywhere with fire and sword. What met
the Romans were grim silence, wordless grief, fear so paralysing that
the people were heedless as to what they should take or leave behind; in their helplessness they kept asking their neighbours what
they should do, standing now on their doorsteps, now wandering
aimlessly through the houses that were theirs for the last time. But
as the call of the cavalry for them to depart became more insistent,
the crash of the falling buildings at the city's edge reached their
ears; in the distance they could see the dust rising in the air, then
drifting overhead like lowering cloud. At last they took what they
could, abandoning the shrines of their household gods, the homes in
which they had been born and raised. The streets were filled with

an unbroken line of those departing, the sight of the others bringing forth fresh tears and shared anguish, made more intense by the cries of the women, especially as they passed the venerable temples where they had once worshipped and left their gods behind like so many captured prisoners.

When the Albans had gone, the Romans pulled to the ground all public and private buildings. A single hour was enough to reduce to rubble what it had taken four hundred years to build. Yet the temples of the gods were spared, as the king had decreed.

30. The fall of Alba led to Rome's increase. The number of citizens was doubled and the Caelian hill added to the city, which Tullus selected as the site of his palace to encourage others to move there, and which he occupied to the end of his life. He integrated the Alban nobles into the state by enrolling them in the senate: Iulii, Servilii, Quinctii, Geganii, Curiatii, and Cloelii. For this enlarged senate he built and consecrated a building called the Curia Hostilia, or senate-house of Hostilius, a name that endured to the last generation.* To complete the incorporation of all levels of Alban society he created ten squadrons of cavalry; from the same source he added some to the existing legions and used others to form new ones.

Relying on this strength, Tullus declared war on the Sabines, a people in that age second only to the Etruscans in military might. On both sides wrongs had been committed and restitution sought in vain. Tullus charged that during the busy market fair at the shrine of Feronia Roman traders had been seized, the Sabines that some of their people had earlier sought refuge in the grove of asylum at Rome and had been detained there. Such were the causes each side advanced for going to war. Now the Sabines were well aware that their strength had been diminished when Tatius and his followers had moved to Rome and that Rome's power had been further increased by the recent addition of the Albans. They therefore decided they too should seek help from outside. Etruria was near by and, of the Etruscans, Veii was closest. From there came a source of individual volunteers, who were especially prone to defection because of lingering resentment over former defeats; the homeless also flocked to them as mercenaries, attracted by the promise of pay. Yet the Sabines received no public assistance from Veii: their truce with Rome kept the Veian state faithful—behaviour less surprising in the case of the other Etruscan cities.

Since both sides were making an all-out effort to prepare for war and everything seemed to depend on which would strike the first blow, Tullus pre-empted the Sabines by crossing into their territory. A fierce battle took place in the Malitosa forest, where the Roman victory owed much to the effort of the infantry, to be sure, but even more to that of the recently increased cavalry. For it was a sudden charge of the horsemen that threw the ranks of the Sabines into confusion, in which they were not able without great loss either to stand their ground or to extricate themselves for withdrawal.

31. When in consequence of the Sabine defeat both Tullus and Rome were at the zenith of prestige and prosperity, it was reported to king and senators that stones had rained from the sky upon Mount Alba. The Romans were incredulous and dispatched a delegation to look into the prodigy. On arrival they themselves witnessed a great many stones falling from the sky, piling up in drifts on the ground, as if by a wind-driven hailstorm. They even fancied they heard a great voice issuing from the grove on the topmost summit, directing the Albans to resume the religious practices of their ancestors that they had neglected since abandoning their city, behaving as if they had abandoned their gods as well: either they had taken up Roman rites or they had ceased worship of the gods in their understandable anger over what had befallen them. As for the Romans, the same prodigy led them to perform a public sacrifice over a nine-day period, whether bidden to do so by a voice from heaven on Mount Alba—for some sources report this as well—or at the advice of soothsayers. The ceremony survived: whenever the same prodigy was reported, a nine-day religious holiday was celebrated.

Not much later a pestilence struck. The men of military age were in consequence in no condition to take up arms, but their warlike king allowed no respite: he believed they would be more likely to get better through service in the field than at home. But when a lingering sickness struck him as well, it broke his body and proud spirit: he who before had considered that nothing less befits a king than devotion to religion suddenly fell under the spell of all sorts of superstitions both large and small, to the point that the people began to follow his lead as well. Everywhere men now yearned for the days of King Numa, convinced that the only cure for their sickness was to seek the peace and pardon of the gods. Tradition has it that the king consulted Numa's writings privately and, when he found described there certain secret sacrifices to Jupiter Elicius, hid himself away to perform them; but because he did not begin or carry them through correctly, not only did he receive no sign from heaven but, when Jupiter became angered at this perversion of religion, the god blasted him with a thunderbolt. King and palace perished together. Tullus, who had won great fame for his military exploits, reigned for thirty-two years.

32. At Tullus' death the government, as had been the regular practice from the start, reverted to the senate, which named an interrex. He presided over the election at which the people chose Ancus Marcius king, whom the senators confirmed. Ancus Marcius was the grandson of King Numa Pompilius on his mother's side. His grandfather's fame was much in his mind as he began his rule; he was conscious, too, of the reign of the last king, which though excellent in other respects had foundered because of either neglect of religion or the wrongful practice of it. He was convinced that the public performance of sacred rites as instituted by Numa was essential, and accordingly ordered the pontiff to set forth on a whitened board in a public place all matters contained in the royal archive. The citizens, who yearned for a respite from military service, and the neighbouring states were encouraged to hope that the new king would model himself on the behaviour and precepts of his grandfather.

The Latins, who earlier had struck a treaty with Tullus, therefore found their courage reviving. They raided Roman territory and returned a haughty response to the Romans' demand for satisfaction, believing that the Roman king would spend his reign in sedentary fashion amid shrines and altars. But Ancus' character was really a blend of the qualities possessed by Numa and Romulus. Convinced that peace had been imperative in the reign of his grandfather when the nation was young and aggressive, he also believed that at the present time he was not likely to enjoy peace at home without exposing himself to attack from outside; his forbearance, he knew, was being tested and, having been tested, was so far the object of contempt: in short, the times were more suited to a king like Tullus than Numa.

To counterbalance the religious rites Numa had instituted for peacetime, Ancus wished to establish religious ceremonies relating to war—not only for waging it but the rite by which it was declared. He therefore had transcribed from the law of the ancient tribe of the Aequiculi* a ritual which the fetial priests still perform today whereby restitution for wrongs is sought. When the envoy comes to the borders of those from whom restitution is sought, his head is wrapped in a woollen band and he cries, 'Hear me, Jupiter! Hear me, boundaries'—he names the people whose boundaries they are—'Hear me, Righteousness! I am the official spokesman of the Roman people. I come as their envoy just and pious, and may faith attend my words.' He then goes through the demands. Next he makes Jupiter his witness: 'If I demand unjustly and impiously that those responsible and the stolen property be handed over to me, then may you never allow me to see my native land again!' He repeats this when he crosses the boundary, when he meets the first inhabitant, when he walks through the gates and when he enters the market place, with changes of a few words in the formula and oath. If the restitution he seeks is not forthcoming after thirty-three days—for this is the statutory number—he declares war as follows: 'Hear me, Jupiter, and you, Janus Quirinus, and all you gods in heaven, on earth and in the underworld, hear me! I call you to witness that these people'—he names whoever they are—'is unjust and has not made proper restitution, but in reference to these matters we shall consult the senior men back in our homeland as to how we may attain our right.' With these words the envoy returns to Rome for the consultation. The king would consult the senators at once, using some such words as these: 'Concerning the stolen property, disputed items, and the contestation of which the *pater patratus** of the Roman people of the Quirites has given due notice to the *pater patratus* of the Ancient Latins and to the men of the Ancient Latins, and concerning the things they have neither given back nor done nor paid, which ought to have been given back, done, or paid, speak out,' he said, addressing the man whose opinion he requested first, 'How do you vote?' The senator asked would then say, 'I vote that restitution should be sought in a pure and pious war, and so I resolve and so I propose.' Then the others would be called upon in order according to rank, and when the majority of them had spoken to the same effect, war would be agreed on. It was customary for the fetial priest to carry a spear of iron or of fire-hardened cornelwood to the enemy's territory and to say in the presence of no less than three men of military age: 'Whereas the peoples of the Ancient Latins and the men of the Ancient Latins have committed acts and offences against the Roman people of the Quirites, and whereas the Roman people of the Quirites have ordered there be war with the Ancient Latins and the senate of the Roman people of the Quirites has voted, resolved, and proposed it, for this reason I and the Roman people do declare war and do make war on the peoples of the Ancient Latins and the men of the Ancient Latins.' When he had said this, he would throw the spear into their territory. This was the manner in which restitution was demanded from the Latins and war declared at that time, a ceremony that has been passed down from generation to generation.

33. After entrusting religious matters to the flamens and other priests, Ancus set out with a newly conscripted army and took the Latin town of Politorium by storm. Following the custom of earlier kings who had enlarged the city by receiving enemies into citizenship, he moved the entire population to Rome. And because the Palatine (the site of the orginal Roman settlement) was surrounded on both sides by already settled populations—the Sabines on the Capitol and citadel and the Albans on the Caelian hill—he assigned the Aventine to the new arrivals; not much later people from the subsequently captured towns of Tellenae and Ficana joined them. The Ancient Latins then proceeded to occupy the deserted town of Politorium, which the Romans reclaimed after a fight and then demolished so that it would not in the future be a refuge for their enemies. Finally, when the war with the Latins became wholly centred on the town of Medullia, neither side was able to bring the issue to a victorious conclusion, for the city was protected by defence works and manned by a strong garrison, and when the Latins had pitched their camp out in the open, on several occasions they engaged the Romans in hand-to-hand combat. In the end Ancus in an all-out effort won the day on the battlefield, from which he returned to Rome possessed of great plunder. Many thousands of Latins were then received into citizenship, to whom, in order to link the Aventine to the Palatine, the district known as Admurciae was given for settlement. The Janiculum hill too was annexed, not because of a need for room, but lest it should at some time become an enemy stronghold. The decision was taken to join it to the city both by a wall and by a bridge of wooden piles—the first to be constructed over the Tiber—thereby facilitating traffic. The Ditch of

the Quirites was also the work of King Ancus, an important defence
work for those parts of the city approached on level ground.

Yet the huge additions that had been made to the population
brought with them an increase of stealth and crime, since the great
mass of men were conscious of little distinction between right and
wrong. To curb their growing lawlessness a prison was built in the
centre of the city overlooking the forum. In addition to enlarging
the city itself, Ancus also increased Roman territory and pushed out
her boundaries. By depriving Veii of the Maesian forest, he extended Roman control to the seaboard; the city of Ostia was also
founded at the mouth of the Tiber, and salt works established around
it. To mark the many successes in war the temple of Jupiter Feretrius
was enlarged.

34. During Ancus' reign Lucumo, an energetic man whose wealth
gave him great influence, migrated to Rome. He had his heart set on
reaching high public office, an attainment not permitted him in the
Etruscan city of Tarquinii, for he was as much a foreigner there as
at Rome. His father, Demaratus of Corinth, fled his native city
because of civil strife and settled down, as chance would have it, in
Tarquinii, where he married and fathered two sons, Lucumo and
Arruns. Lucumo survived his father and inherited his entire fortune: Arruns died before his father, leaving a pregnant wife, but
because the father survived Arruns only a short time and did not
realize his daughter-in-law was with child, he made no provision for
a grandson in his will. The name Egerius—the Needy One—was
given to the boy after his grandfather's death because of the poverty
resulting from having had no share in the inheritance.

The wealth that Lucumo as sole heir now enjoyed made him
quite ambitious, an ambition further intensified by his marriage to
Tanaquil, a lady of high birth who did not easily brook marrying
into a rank in society beneath the one into which she had been born.
Unable to endure the degrading snub given her husband by the
Etruscans for being the son of an alien exile, and unmoved by any
inborn love of her native city, her one aim was to see her husband
elevated to high position. So she determined to leave Tarquinii and
fixed on Rome as the most promising new home: a brave and energetic man would make his mark in this new city where nobility
could be quickly acquired and came from one's own worth: Tatius
had been king, though a Sabine, Numa had been called to the throne

from Cures, while the nobility of Ancus, born of a Sabine mother, depended on only one distinguished ancestor—Numa himself. She won over her husband easily because of his ambition for high office; nor did attachment to Tarquinii count for much with him, for it was his native city on his mother's side only.

They packed their belongings and headed for Rome. Fortune brought them to the Janiculum. There, as he was seated in his wagon next to his wife, an eagle on motionless wings gently dropped down and seized the cap he was wearing; with a great scream it flew over the wagon and then returned to place the cap deftly back on Tarquin's head, as if it had been divinely sent. Then it rose aloft and flew away. Tanaquil is said to have interpreted this joyfully as an omen, for as an Etruscan she was well versed in the lore of prodigies sent from heaven. Embracing her husband, she told him that he should look forward to something exalted and magnificent: the type of bird was highly significant, as was the place in the sky in which it appeared, to say nothing of the very deity whose messenger the bird was; the omen concerned the crown of his head; the bird had removed the headcovering that had been placed there by a human hand in order that a divine agent might replace it.

Such were the hopes and surmises they brought with them upon entering the city; after acquiring a place of habitation, they told one and all that Lucumo was now Lucius Tarquinius Priscus. The Romans quickly came to know of the new and wealthy *arriviste*. He made strenuous efforts to promote his good fortune further by acquiring as many friends as he could through affable speech, openhanded hospitality, and benefactions. In time his reputation reached even the palace. At first Tarquin and the king were simply acquaintances, but by Tarquin's handsome and unstinting services the acquaintanceship quickly developed into such an intimate friendship that he was admitted to consultations equally on public and private matters, whether pertaining to war or domestic affairs. In the end, having passed every test, he was instituted tutor to the king's children in his will.

35. Ancus reigned for twenty-four years, a king equal to any of his predecessors in the fame of his achievements in war and peace. Since his sons by this time were almost grown, Tarquin began to press ever more insistently that the assembly for electing a king be held as soon as possible. As the time approached he got the boys out

#S: Tarquinius Priscus
Etruscan

of the city by sending them on a hunting foray. He is said to have
been the first to canvass for the throne and to have delivered a
speech aimed at winning the votes of the plebs: he was not, he said,
seeking anything unusual, since he would not be the first but the
third foreigner at Rome to aspire to sovereignty, an achievement at
which no one could take offence or be surprised: Tatius began not
just as a foreigner but as an enemy, yet was made king, while Numa,
who knew nothing of the city and did not seek the throne, was even
solicited to accept it; as for himself, he had immigrated to Rome
with his wife and all his wealth the moment he was no longer under
his father's power; the greater part of adult life that men devote to
service of the state he had spent in Rome and not in his native city;
at home and in the field he had learned the ways of the Romans in
law and religion under the best of teachers, King Ancus himself; he
had vied with everyone in the obedience and attendance he paid the
king, while vying with the king in his benefactions to others.

The Roman people elected him king overwhelmingly, for what he
said was perfectly true. Tarquin, outstanding in other respects, continued during his reign to be driven by the self-seeking he had
shown when he was aiming at the throne. Since he was as anxious to
consolidate his own power as to promote the welfare of the state, he
enrolled a hundred men in the senate who were thereafter known as
senators 'of the lesser families'—future supporters of the man who
had elevated them to senatorial rank.

He waged his first war with the Latins and took by storm the
town of Apiolae. When greater booty was brought back than might
have been expected, he celebrated games on a more lavish and elaborate
scale than had the earlier kings. Then for the first time a site was
selected for a circus, now known as the Circus Maximus. Areas were
assigned to senators and knights* where each order might raise viewing
stands for its use; these were called *fori*, or seating sections, which
stood on pilings twelve feet high from which the spectators could
view the contests of horses and boxers, most coming from Etruria.
Thereafter the games were held at regular annual intervals, variously called the Roman or Great Games. In addition, Tarquin assigned sites around the forum for private individuals to build on;
colonnades and shops were also added.

36. While he was preparing to encircle the city with a stone wall,
war with the Sabines interrupted his plans. The crisis was so sudden

that the enemy crossed the Anio River before the Roman army could confront and drive them off. Rome was filled with alarm. At first no one could gain the upper hand and there were grievous losses on each side. The enemy's withdrawal to their encampment gave the Romans time to regroup and rearm; Tarquin, believing that his cavalry in particular was not up to needed strength, decided to add new centuries to the Ramnes,* Titienses, and Luceres that Romulus had once created and to distinguish them by naming them after himself. But because Romulus' action had come only after the taking of the auspices, Attus Navius, a famous augur of that time, said that a change should not be made nor a new action taken unless the birds gave their consent. This made Tarquin angry; the story goes that he mocked his skill by saying, 'Well now, gifted seer that you are, determine by augury whether what I am now thinking of is capable of accomplishment.' Attus then took the auspices and said that what the king contemplated could certainly be done. Tarquin responded, 'Ah, but what I have in mind is for you to slice this sharpening stone in two with this razor. Here, take them and do what your birds say can be done.' According to the legend Attus sliced the sharpening stone in two without hesitation. His statue, with head covered, stood on the spot where this took place, on the steps of the Comitium, or place of assembly, to the left of the Curia. Tradition says that the sharpening stone too was deposited in this location as a memorial of the miracle for later generations. What is certain is that such honour accrued to augury and its practitioners that thereafter nothing was done at home or abroad without taking the auspices and that meetings of the people, the mustering of the army, and other proceedings of the greatest importance were postponed whenever the birds refused their assent. Nor did Tarquin venture to make any changes at that time concerning the centuries of cavalry; he simply doubled the number of men, with the result that the total came to 1,200 horsemen enrolled in the three centuries. The names of the centuries stayed the same, but the word *Posteriores* or 'Supplementary Ones' was used to denote those who had been added. Nowadays they are known as the six centuries because of the doubling of the number.

37. A second battle was fought with the Sabines, but now with the enlarged cavalry. A stratagem gave further help to the increased strength of the Roman army: men were secretly sent to gather a

large quantity of wood lying along the banks of the Anio, set it on fire, and push it out into the current: the wind fanned the flames, while a good part of it, packed on rafts, jammed into the wooden piles of the bridge spanning the river and set it afire. This, in addition to the new cavalry, caused the Sabines to panic during the fighting; the loss of the bridge hindered their flight from the enemy, and many a man drowned in the current. The distinctively Sabine armaments that floated down the Tiber to the city apprised the Romans of the great victory almost before the official news arrived from the battlefield. The cavalry performed outstanding service in the fight: the story is that when the centre line of the infantry was being pushed back, they, stationed on the wings, made such a furious charge on the enemy's flanks that the Sabines, who were aggressively hounding the retreating Romans, were not only stopped in their tracks but put to flight in a trice. The Sabines scattered and headed pell-mell for the hills, which a few succeeded in reaching; most of them, as was said before, were driven into the river by the cavalry. Tarquin sent the booty and captives to Rome and burned a great pile of the spoils, fulfilling a vow he had made to Vulcan. Then, thinking he ought to pursue the thoroughly frightened enemy, he hastened to lead his army forthwith into Sabine territory. Although things had gone badly for them and they could not hope they would get any better, still, because the situation gave no time for deliberation, the Sabines went out to meet Tarquin with a hastily levied force; routed for a second time and in desperate straits, they sued for peace.

38. Collatia, together with territory of the Sabines between the town and Rome, was taken from them. Egerius, son of the king's brother, was put in charge of the garrison at Collatia. I find that the people of Collatia capitulated according to the following formula of unconditional surrender. The king asked, 'Are you the envoys and spokesmen sent by the people of Collatia to surrender yourselves and the people of Collatia?'—'We are.'—'Are the people of Collatia free to make decisions for themselves?'—'They are.'—'Do you surrender yourselves, the people of Collatia, city, territory, water, boundary stones, shrines, moveables and all things divine and human into my control and that of the Roman people?'—'We do.'—'Then I so receive you.'

At the conclusion of the Sabine war Tarquin returned to Rome in triumph. He then made war on the Ancient Latins, but when no single battle could decide the whole issue, he fought the war town by town. In the end he subdued the entire Latin nation: Corniculum, Old Ficulea, Cameria, Crustumerium, Ameriola, Medullia, and Nomentum—these were the towns of the Ancient Latins or those who had defected to them that were captured. Peace was then made.

Thereafter Tarquin put a greater effort into his building projects in the city than he had expended in the field, so much so that the people had as little leisure at home as they had had on campaign. For he resumed the enclosure of those parts of the city as yet undefended with a stone wall, the start of which had been interrupted by the Sabine war; and, because the low-lying parts of the city, including the forum and the other flat areas between the hills, did not allow for easy run-off of water, he drained these level areas by constructing sewers on a grade leading to the Tiber. He also built substructures over an area on the Capitol that would support a temple of Jupiter. He had vowed the temple in the Sabine war, and in his mind he already foresaw the future greatness of the place.

39. A prodigy occurred in the palace about this time, miraculous to those who saw it and in its outcome. The story is that the head of a boy named Servius Tullius burst into flame as he lay sleeping and that many people saw it. This extraordinary event naturally caused an uproar that brought the royal pair hurrying to the scene, and when one of the servants brought water to put it out, the queen held him back; she called for quiet and forbade the boy to be disturbed until he woke of his own accord; soon, as sleep left him, the flames died out.

Tanaquil then took her husband aside. 'Do you realize who this child is who is being raised in our household in such humble circumstances? It is evident that one day he will turn out to be the beacon and bulwark of our royal house in its hour of need. Let us in all sufficiency nurture this youth who will prove a great blessing to us and to the state.' Thereafter, the story continues, they looked upon the boy as their son and gave him the sort of education that would inspire him to reach the loftiest of stations in life. The queen's presentiment came to pass, for such was heaven's will: the young man turned out to be of a truly royal nature, and when the king found that none of the Roman youth could be compared with Servius as a prospective son-in-law, he betrothed his daughter to him.

Whatever the reason for it, the honour accorded to Servius was so great that it is difficult to believe he was the son of a slave and as a youth was himself a slave.* I am more inclined to follow those who give this account: that at the capture of Corniculum the pregnant wife of Servius Tullius, the leading man of the city who was killed in the sack, was recognized among the mass of women captives and that because of her singular dignity the Roman queen saved her from enslavement and took her to Rome, where she gave birth to her child in the home of Tarquinius Priscus; that this great generosity then brought the women together in close friendship, while the boy was raised in the palace in love and high regard; and that the reason why Servius was believed to have been born of a slave woman was the fate that befell his mother when she fell into the enemy's hands upon the capture of her native city.

40. It was now about the thirty-eighth year of Tarquin's reign, and Servius held a position of pre-eminent honour not only in the eyes of the king but of senators and plebeians as well. The resentment of the two sons of Ancus had all along been at a dangerous simmer, for they had been smarting under the indignity of having been kept from their father's throne by the deceit of their tutor, to say nothing of the fact that a foreigner was king at Rome—a man not even from Italy, much less from one of the neighbouring peoples. But now their sense of outrage had reached the boil: it looked as if they were not even in line to succeed Tarquin, but that the throne was about to be sullied by one of servile origin: in short, that their city, which some hundred years before had been ruled by Romulus as long as he was on earth, born of a god and himself a god, was about to pass into the hands of this Servius person, a slave born of a slave. It would be a disgrace to the entire city and particularly to their house if, while the sons of King Ancus were alive, the throne should be occupied not just by foreigners but by slaves. They therefore decided to forestall insult by murder.

Their sense of wrong was keener against Tarquin than Servius; besides, should the king somehow survive, he would be a more formidable avenger of an attempted assassination than would a person in private life; what is more, if they killed Servius, who knew whom the king might choose as his next son-in-law, who would then be heir to the throne? For these reasons the plot was directed against Tarquin himself. They suborned two shepherds to do the deed, both utter ruffians. These fellows, armed with the tools that shepherds use, staged as unruly an altercation as they could in the forecourt of the palace. As all the king's attendants crowded round, they appealed to Tarquin at the top of their lungs; the outcry penetrated to the palace, and soon the king summoned them in for a hearing. At first each tried to drown the other out in a shouting match, but when checked by a lictor and ordered to speak in turn, they at last ceased abusing one another. By prearrangement one of them began to argue his case and, while the king's attention was wholly fixed on him, the other brought down an axe upon Tarquin's head. Leaving the weapon fixed in the wound, both bolted for the doors.

41. The bystanders had scarcely caught the dying Tarquin as he fell when the lictors seized the fleeing assassins. There followed an uproar as the people thronged together, wondering what the matter was. In the midst of the commotion Tanaquil ordered the palace to be shut and any witnesses sent home. She made elaborate preparations for tending to the wound, as if there still was hope, while at the same time, should hope fail, she made provision for a different sort of protection. Servius was hastily summoned, and after showing him that her husband was near death, she grasped his right hand and begged him not to allow himself as the son-in-law to let the murder go unavenged, nor herself as his mother-in-law to be mocked by her enemies. 'The throne is yours, if you are man enough to take it, not theirs who suborned others to do this terrible deed. Take heart! Obey the will of the gods, who long ago encircled this head of yours with fire to portend its future greatness. May that heavenly flame truly waken you now! We too were foreigners, yet we ruled. Think not of your birth but what kind of man you have grown to be. And should your mind be too clouded to make plans to meet this crisis, then follow mine.'

When the outcry and the crush of people could no longer be ignored, Tanaquil addressed the crowd from the window of the palace's upper storey that faces New Street (the king lived near the temple of Jupiter Stator). She bade them be of good hope; the king had been stunned by a sudden blow; it was a surface wound; he was now coming to his senses; the blood had been wiped away and the wound examined; the situation was quite all right, and she was sure they would see him very soon. In the meantime she bade the people

#6: Servius
unelected
unclear parentage

to obey Servius Tullius: he would dispense justice and undertake the other duties of the king.

Servius stepped forth wearing the royal robe, surrounded by lictors. Taking his seat on the throne he made certain decisions, but about others pretended he would consult the king. And so for some days after Tarquin had died his death remained concealed, while Servius strengthened his position by appearing to be standing in for him. Then at last the truth was revealed when the ritual lament for the dead was heard coming from the palace. Servius used bodyguards to protect his person, and was the first to rule without having been elected by the people, albeit with the blessing of the senate. The sons of Ancus, at the point when they learned that their hired assassins had been caught, that the king was still supposedly alive, and that Servius' support was so strong, had gone into exile in Suessa Pometia.

42. Servius was as concerned to buttress his position within his household as in the state at large, for he feared that the sort of hostility that had been directed against Tarquin by the sons of Ancus might also be directed against himself by the sons of Tarquin. He therefore decided to marry his two daughters to the young princes, Lucius and Arruns Tarquinius. But he could not alter the course of destiny by this human contrivance, for even within his own house certain members wanted the throne for themselves, creating a situation of poisonous perfidy and malevolence.

By great good fortune a war with Veii—the truce had run out—and with other Etruscan states contributed to the peaceful stability of the nation. For in it the courage and good fortune of Tullius showed forth, and on his return to Rome after defeating the vast army of the enemy his position as king was unquestioned in the minds of both senators and plebeians.

He then embarked on a great project relating to the nation in peacetime: just as Numa had been the author of the religious system, so Servius' aim was that posterity should remember him as the one who established all the distinctions and ranks in society whereby groups are differentiated from one another by station and wealth. What he created was the census, an invaluable institution for a nation destined to be so great: a man's duties to the state in war and peace would no longer be determined randomly one by one but in proportion to the amount of money he possessed.

more money, had to serve?-

It was then that he fixed the classes and centuries, which proved adaptable to the needs of the state, whether in peace or in war. They were arranged in the following way.* 43. For those who possessed 100,000 asses or more he created eighty centuries, forty for seniors and forty for juniors; taken together they were called the First Class. The seniors were to stand ready to guard the city, the juniors to wage war in the field. The arms they were to provide were helmet, round shield, greaves, and breastplate, all of bronze. This was their defensive armour; for offence they were to supply a long spear and a sword. Added to this class were two centuries of carpenters and metalworkers who were to serve without arms; their job was to carry the siege equipment in war. The rating of the Second Class ranged from 100,000 to 75,000 asses, and to them, juniors and seniors, twenty centuries were assigned. The armour they were to provide was the same as for the First Class except that they had no breast-plate and carried an oblong rather than a round shield. For the Third Class he fixed 50,000 as the rating; they had the same number of centuries as the Second Class, and were also divided between juniors and seniors; their arms were the same as well, save that they wore no greaves. For the Fourth Class the rating was 25,000; the number of centuries was the same, but not their arms: they were expected to provide nothing but a long and a short spear. The Fifth Class was larger: 30 centuries. They carried with them slings and stones as missiles. To this class were added supernumeraries, bu-glers, and trumpeters distributed over three centuries. The census rating for the Fifth Class was 11,000. The rest of the population that was rated below 11,000 was assigned a single century and was ex-empt from military service. Such was the equipment and distribu-tion of the infantry.

He next formed twelve centuries of knights or equestrians from among the leading men of the state. He likewise included six addi-tional centuries, three of which had been instituted by Romulus, although all six still used the same names they had received when inaugurated.* Ten thousand asses were allotted from public funds for purchasing the horses, and for their upkeep unmarried women were assessed two thousand asses annually.

All these expenses were shouldered by the rich rather than by the poor. The former were then compensated by a special privilege. Under Romulus and the other kings each citizen, no matter who he was, had by right a <u>vote</u> that possessed the same weight as that of anyone else; now the <u>weighting was calibrated</u> so that all real power rested with the nation's leading men, although no one was ostensibly deprived of his right to vote.* For the knights were called to vote first, then the eighty centuries of the First Class. If they did not agree—which rarely happened—the procedure was then to call on the centuries of the Second Class. It virtually never happened that the voting descended to the lower classes on the scale.

One should not be surprised that the system that exists today, in which there are a full complement of thirty-five tribes and their number has been doubled in the centuries of juniors and seniors, does not agree with the total of centuries instituted by Servius Tullius.* For when the city was divided into four parts according to the regions and hills that were inhabited, he called those parts tribes, I think, from the word 'tribute.'* In fact, Servius established the same method of collecting tribute: that is, proportionally according to the amount of one's census rating. But these original four tribes did not have anything to do with the distribution and number of centuries.

44. Servius completed the census quickly by passing a law threatening imprisonment and death for those who failed to register. He then issued an edict commanding all Roman citizens, cavalry and infantry, to present themselves in the Campus Martius* at dawn, each man in his assigned century. When the army had assembled in battle array, he purified the whole of it by sacrificing a pig, sheep, and bull; the name for the purification was *lustrum*, and on completion of the census the ceremony was called 'closing the *lustrum*'. Eighty thousand citizens are said to have been registered in this *lustrum*; our oldest authority, Fabius Pictor,* maintains that this figure represents the men able to bear arms.

The city seemed to need enlarging in order to accommodate this multitude. Hence Servius added two hills, the Quirinal and Viminal; he then extended the area of Esquiline, which he selected for his palace in order to enhance the prestige of the site. When he surrounded the city with an embankment, ditch, and wall, he was obliged to extend the sacred boundary of the city, called the *pomerium*. Those who look solely to the literal meaning of the word *pomerium* understand it as *postmoerium*, 'beyond the wall'. But it should rather be *circamoerium*, 'on both sides of the wall', because in founding cities the Etruscans, whenever they selected a site for a wall, used to consecrate the area by taking the auspices at specific points along the boundary lines. The result was that within the wall buildings could not touch it (whereas today they are commonly built into it) and on the outside a strip of land was left fallow, uncontaminated by human cultivation. This space, which religion forbade be built upon or farmed, the Romans called the *pomerium*, as much because the wall lay beyond it as it lay beyond the wall. Accordingly, as the walls were advanced to accommodate the constant enlargement of the city, the consecrated boundary stones were moved forward as well.

45. The city had now been enlarged and each rank in society assigned its duties in war and peace. But Servius, dissatisfied that hitherto Rome's prosperity had depended on warfare, decided to promote her ascendancy through diplomacy, while simultaneously adding distinction to the city. The temple of Diana at Ephesus was already famous in that age, and it was well known that it had been built as a joint effort by the cities of Asia. Servius was lavish in his praise of their co-operation in uniting for religious purposes when speaking to the Latin nobles, with whom he had purposely culti-vated ties of hospitality and friendship, both official and personal. His constant talk on the subject finally led to the agreement that the Latin peoples would unite with the Romans in building a temple of Diana at Rome.

This was tantamount to conceding primacy to Rome, the very issue over which they had fought for so long. In fact, after their long string of defeats, none of the Latins seemed to care any longer about the matter; but chance seemed to offer one man from Sabine coun-try the opportunity to win supremacy by a stratagem of his own devising. On this Sabine's homestead a heifer of astonishing size and beauty is said to have been born, whose horns for many years were displayed in the portico of the temple of Diana as proof of its extraordinary nature. Its birth was regarded as a prodigy, which indeed it was, and seers predicted that the state whose citizen sacri-ficed it to Diana would achieve supremacy. Now the priest of the temple of Diana had heard of this prophecy, and when on the first day suitable for sacrifice the Sabine brought the heifer to Rome for sacrifice and placed it at the altar of Diana's temple, the priest was much impressed with the great size of the victim that so many had talked about. With the prophecy uppermost in mind, he accosted the Sabine. 'Stranger, what is this? Surely you cannot be getting ready to sacrifice to Diana in an unclean state! Please have the decency to wash yourself first in running water. If you look, you will see the Tiber flowing by in the valley below.' The stranger was sensitive to such religious scruples, for he wanted everything to be done properly so as to ensure the outcome that the prophecy had foretold. So he immediately walked down to the Tiber. While he was gone, the Roman sacrificed the heifer to Diana. King and country welcomed the news with delight.

46. Servius was no doubt *de facto* king, but from time to time the young Tarquin ventilated in public his contention that Servius ruled without the people's consent. In response the king first won the goodwill of the plebeians by dividing up land captured from the enemy and giving it to them in individual allotments; he then ventured to ask the people for their formal consent to his rule, which they gave with more unanimity than for any of the earlier kings.

But this did not stop Tarquin. Quite the contrary: he wanted the throne for himself and, when he perceived that the senators were displeased in the matter of the land distribution to the plebs, he saw his opportunity to worm his way into their good graces by censuring the king on the senate floor. He was a restive and ambitious young man, to be sure, but at home he had a wife—Tullia—who inflamed that ambition still further. From this the Roman royal house produced a tragic spectacle to rival those of Greece, in order that disgust with kings might all the sooner usher in an era of liberty and that the last king would be one who seized the throne through crime.

This Lucius Tarquinius—whether he was the son or grandson of King Tarquinius Priscus is not at all clear, but I follow the majority of writers in saying he was the son*—had a brother, Arruns Tarquinius, a youth of mild disposition. These two had married the two Tullias, daughters of the king, as I said before, who were likewise very different in character. It happened by chance that the two of violent temperament were not married to one another—or rather, I think, it was owing to the Fortune of the Roman people, whose purpose it was that the reign of Tullius endure long enough to lay a firm foundation for the building of Rome's national character.

Tullia—the one who was so headstrong—was greatly aggrieved because her husband did not have the stuff of manhood, neither hungry for power nor two-fisted; turning from him, she set her sights on the other Tarquin, confessing her admiration for someone who was a real man, a true son of a king, while ridiculing her sister for having married such a fine specimen, while lacking the backbone a woman should have. Their similar natures swiftly drew them together, as so often happens: evil attracts evil. Yet it was the woman who began the débâcle. Conversing secretly with another woman's husband became normal for her: she had no scruples in damning her husband to his brother, her sister to her sister's husband; she maintained it would have been better if she had remained a spinster and he a bachelor than to be married to such unsuitable spouses: as it was, their enterprising nature was being stifled by the spinelessness of others; if the gods had given her a husband who was worthy of her, she would soon see in her own house the royal power she now saw in her father's. It did not take long for her to fill the young man with her own recklessness. Lucius Tarquinius and the younger Tullia emptied their houses with virtual back-to-back funerals. They married, with Servius not forbidding it more than with his approval.

47. From then on Tullius' old age proved an increasing source of danger and his hold on the throne became more precarious with each passing day: the woman, having committed one crime, was now looking to commit another. Night and day she pressured her husband not to let the previous murders go for nothing. What she had previously, she said, was a man to whom she could be said to be married and with whom she wordlessly served those in power; what she had not had was a man who thought himself worthy of the throne, who remembered he was the son of Tarquinius Priscus, who preferred to take the throne than to hope for it. 'If you are the man whom I think I married, I salute you as husband and king. If not, my situation is worse than before, for what I have now is a criminal as well as a coward. Why not arm yourself for action? You are not from Corinth or Tarquinii. You do not, like your father, have to win a kingdom in a foreign land. The gods of your house and of your ancestors, the image of your father, the palace that was your home, the royal throne in that home, the very name of Tarquin—they all declare and make you king. If you lack the nerve, then why disappoint everyone's expectations? Stop parading around as a prince of the blood royal. Clear out of Rome, slink back to Tarquinii or Corinth. Revert to what your family once was, more like your brother

than your father!' With taunts such as these she goaded the youth to act. Yet she was equally hard on herself: if a spirited woman like Tanaquil—and a foreigner as well—could act as a kingmaker twice in a row, first for her husband and then for her son-in-law, then why was she, who was of royal blood, unable to make headway in making and unmaking a king?

Tarquin, goaded by the frenzied ambition of his wife, went the rounds, seeking in particular the support of the senators from the lesser families: he reminded them of the favour his father had done them, and now sought their support in return. He won over the younger men with gifts, and increased his influence everywhere by making extravagant promises and denouncing the king. Finally, the moment to strike was at hand. Escorted by a cadre of armed men he burst into the forum. When everyone was stricken with fear, he took his seat on the king's throne in the entrance to the senate-house and ordered a herald to summon the senators into the presence of King Tarquin.

They gathered at once, some acting on cue, others fearful that non-appearance might get them in trouble; people were dumbfounded by this brazen step: Servius, they thought, was doomed. Tarquin began by attacking the king, going back to his base origin: a slave born of a slave, he seized the throne after the shameful murder of Tarquin's father, without the customary interregnum, without calling the assembly, without a vote of the people, without the sanction of the senate: the throne was the gift of a woman! Such was his birth, such was how he became king, a champion of the dregs of society from which he himself came; in his hatred of others' nobility he took land from the high-born and gave it to riff-raff; all the burdens that once had been shared in common were now piled on the backs of the nation's leaders; he had instituted the census so that the rich might be singled out as objects of jealousy, while providing a perpetual source, whenever he wanted, of lavishing gifts upon the needy.

48. In the midst of this harangue Servius burst upon the scene, alerted to the alarming news. In a great voice he called out from the antechamber of the senate-house, 'Tarquin, what is the meaning of this? How dare you presume to call the senate or take my seat while I am alive?' Tarquin snarled in reply that he was sitting in his father's seat; the son of a king had a far better claim to the throne

than a slave; Servius had flouted his masters long enough with an insulting licence that knew no limits. An uproar arose from the supporters of each man; a crush of people pushed into the senate chamber; it was clear that the victor would be king. Tarquin was forced to stake everything on his next move. Much younger and stronger, he seized Servius about the waist, carried him out of the room and flung him down the steps of the senate-house to the ground below. He returned to the chamber and ordered the senators to resume their places. Servius' attendants and companions took to their heels, while Servius himself, faint from the loss of blood and close to death, headed back to the palace, assisted by some of the royal bodyguards. But Tarquin had sent men after him, who caught him as he fled and cut him down. Some believe that this was done at Tullia's prompting: it certainly fits in with the other terrible things she did. For all agree that she rode into the forum in a wagon and, unabashed by the presence of the males gathered there, called her husband forth from the senate-house and was the first to salute him king. He told her to clear out and fast, for the situation was dangerous. When she was heading back home and had reached the top of Cyprius Street (where the chapel to Diana was until recently), and as she made a left turn on Urbius Street *en route* to the Esquiline hill, her driver started in horror and, reining in, pointed out to his mistress the body of the slain king. She is said to have committed an appalling and barbaric crime there—and the place is a reminder of it, for they call it the Street of Crime: maddened by the avenging spirits of her sister and former husband, Tullia, so the story goes, drove the wagon over Servius' body. Spattered and defiled by the blood of her murdered father, she brought back part of it to her own household gods and those of her husband, who in their anger saw to it that the evil beginning of the reign would soon have a suitably bad ending.

Servius Tullius reigned for forty-four years, and even a good and temperate successor would have found it difficult to come up to Servius' standard. Servius' renown was further enhanced by the fact that his death marked the end of just and legitimate rule by kings at Rome. And, mild and restrained though his was, certain authorities affirm that he intended to abdicate precisely because it was rule by one man, but that—alas—villainy within his own family prevented him from carrying out his plan to give freedom to his country.

sympathetic to king on the side of the poor

49. Such was the commencement of Lucius Tarquinius' reign.
He was given the name of Superbus, or the Proud,* because of his
actions: first, he forbade the burial of his own father-in-law (which
he justified by saying that Romulus had not received burial after
death either!); second, he killed off prominent senators who he believed had favoured Servius' interests. But then, realizing that seizing the throne in the terrible way he did might set a precedent to be
used against himself, he surrounded his person with an armed guard,
for violent usurpation constituted his only claim to the throne, since
he had received neither the vote of the people nor the consent of the
senate. Worse still, because he could not count on the affection of
the citizens, he was forced to cow them into submission. He spread
fear still further by trying people on capital charges* in a court
where no one save himself was the judge; under this charade he was
able to execute, exile, and fine not just those he suspected or disliked, but those from whom he wanted nothing but their money.
This more than any other measure shrank the number of men in the
senate, nor did he replenish the losses, for small numbers would
diminish the prestige of that body, which in turn would leave that
many fewer people disgruntled with the senate's lack of participation in Rome's governance. Indeed, Tarquin was the first king to
allow the custom to lapse of asking advice of the senate on all
matters, a custom that all his predecessors had followed. He administered affairs of state by consulting only his personal friends. On his
own initiative he made and unmade war, peace, treaties, and alliances as he pleased, and did so with those whom he liked without
the consent of the people and senate. He won in particular the
support of the Latin peoples, conciliating them through ties of hospitality and marriage alliances, in order that through foreign support
he might be more secure at home. He gave his daughter in marriage
to Octavius Mamilius of Tusculum, who was far and away the most
important man among the Latins—descended, if we can believe
legend, from Ulysses and the goddess Circe. Through this union he
secured Mamilius' many relatives and friends as adherents.

50. When Tarquin's influence among the Latins had grown great,
he fixed a day for a meeting at the grove of Ferentina: there were
matters, he said, that he wanted to discuss. Early on the appointed
day a great crowd gathered. Though Tarquin kept the appointment,
he arrived only a little before sunset. Those who had assembled

talked over the situation variously throughout the day, and Turnus Herdonius from Aricia sharply attacked the absent Tarquin. No wonder the name Superbus or the Proud had been given him at Rome—for that is what people there called him behind his back. What was more arrogant than to insult the entire Latin nation in this fashion? Heads of state had been bidden to come here from homes far away, while he who had called the meeting failed to appear. His aim, no doubt, was to find out how much abuse they would take: if they allowed their necks to be put in the yoke, he would force them to do his bidding. And wasn't it obvious that control over the Latins was his goal? If his own citizens had done well in bestowing power on him—and if it really was a matter of bestowal rather than usurpation through a father-in-law's murder!—then the Latins would do well to do the same. But no—not even in this case, for it ought not to be given to a foreigner. But if this was something his own people regretted—whom, in fact, he was killing, exiling, and stripping of property one after another—how could the Latins hope for anything better? If they listened to him, each man would go back to his own home and have no more concern for the meeting than the man who had called it.

Now Turnus, a rebel and troublemaker at home in Africa, had become powerful there by tactics such as these; and just as he was making these remarks and others to the same effect, Tarquin arrived. This ended the speech. Everyone turned away to greet Tarquin, who called for silence and, when advised by those near by to explain why he had come so late, said that he had been acting as a mediator between a father and son; his concern to oblige them and to effect a reconciliation had caused the delay; but because the day was now over, he would bring before them on the morrow the subject he wished to raise. Turnus is said not to have let even this pass without comment: no inquiry took less time than that between father and son, he said, for it could be dealt with in a word or two: if the son did not obey the father, he would be mighty sorry for it.

51. The man from Aricia finished his attack on the king of Rome and left the meeting. Tarquin was considerably more affronted by it than he showed, and at once began to plot Turnus' murder: he wanted to intimidate the Latins in the same way he had broken the spirit of the citizens at home. But because his power at Rome did not allow him openly to kill Turnus in this place, he trumped up a

false charge that proved the undoing of an innocent man. Using certain men from Aricia who were political enemies of Turnus as his agents, Tarquin bribed with gold one of Turnus' slaves to look the other way as a great quantity of swords were secretly introduced into the quarters where Turnus was staying. A single night was enough to set the scene. A little before dawn Tarquin summoned the leaders of the Latins, pretending to be upset at some new discovery. Divine providence, he said, must have been at work the day before, for his delay proved to be his salvation as well as theirs. He had been told that Turnus was plotting to murder him and the other nobles so that he might assume leadership of the Latins. He had planned to mount his attack at the previous day's meeting, but had to put off his scheme because the man who had called it and who was his principal target was absent. That explained his belligerent remarks against himself! The delay had frustrated his plans. If what was reported was true, he did not doubt that at dawn Turnus would come to the meeting he had called armed and accompanied by a gang of conspirators. Moreover, it was said that he had collected a great number of swords. Whether this was true or not could quickly be determined, and he asked them to accompany him to Turnus' quarters. That man's pugnacious nature, his speech the day before, and Tarquin's delay made it plausible that there was indeed a plot and that it had been called off for this reason. They therefore went with Tarquin, inclined to believe the worst, but had the swords not been found they would undoubtedly have discounted the other charges. On arrival they roused Turnus from sleep and stationed guards around him. Turnus' slaves then tried to resist in their determination to protect their master and were seized, and when the swords were pulled from their hiding places in every nook and corner, Turnus seemed truly to have been caught red-handed. He was put in chains and brought to a meeting of the Latins that was hastily called amid great commotion. There the sight of the swords displayed for all to see roused such hostility that they refused to let Turnus defend himself, but voted to carry out a new kind of execution: Turnus was plunged into the headwaters of Ferentina and sunk beneath a wicker frame piled with rocks.

52. When the Latins were summoned back into session, Tarquin heaped praises upon those who had caught Turnus in the act of plotting murder and revolution and who had punished him as he

deserved. He continued by saying that he was perfectly within his rights to act on the basis of the ancient treaty made under King Tullus in which the entire Alban community along with its colonies had passed into Roman control: since all Latins originated from Alba, all were bound by the treaty. But everyone's advantage would be better served, he believed, if the treaty were now renewed. In doing so, the Latins would share in the good fortune of the Roman people rather than be continually expecting or suffering destruction of cities and devastation of territories, which they had experienced twice, once under Ancus and again under his own father.

It was not difficult to persuade the Latins, even though Rome's superiority was acknowledged in the treaty: besides, it was clear that the Latin ruling élite sided with Tarquin, and after what had just happened to Turnus, no one needed a reminder of what would happen to a man who ventured to oppose him. So the treaty was renewed and, in accordance with it, Latin youth of military age were ordered to gather at the grove of Ferentina on a fixed day, armed and in full force. Recruits from all the Latin peoples assembled in response to Tarquin's command. But because he did not want them to have their own leaders or be under an independent command or follow their old standards, he created new tactical units from both peoples by halving the pre-existing Roman and Latin maniples and forming new ones from each half. The maniples under Roman command were thus recombined, and Roman centurions put over them.

53. Unjust though his behaviour was in peacetime, he was not an ineffective leader in war; in the military sphere he would have been deemed equal to the earlier kings had not even this distinction been spoiled by his degeneracy in other respects. He was the first to fight the Volsci, a conflict that was to last more than two hundred years. In taking Suessa Pometia from them by force, he realized forty talents of silver from the sale of the booty. He then conceived a plan for a temple of Jupiter whose magnificence would be worthy of the king of gods and men, of Rome's empire, and of the majesty of the site itself. He set aside the money realized from the capture for the building of the temple.

He then undertook a war against the neighbouring city of Gabii that dragged on longer than he expected. When he failed to take the city by storm and could not carry on a successful siege after being repulsed from the walls, he fell back on a wholly un-Roman stratagem, deceit and treachery. For, while pretending to be intent on laying the foundation of the temple and on other urban projects—having seemingly abandoned the war—he arranged for Sextus, the youngest of his three sons, to flee to Gabii as a deserter. This Sextus did, and on arriving he complained of Tarquin's insupportable cruelty toward himself: the situation had reached the point where he had turned the arrogance he had shown others upon his own family; even the number of his children had become an irritant; he was bent on killing off his household as he had the senate so that he might die childless and without an heir. In fact, he said, now that he had dodged his father's weapons and swords and made good his escape, he considered that there was no safe haven for him anywhere except among Tarquin's enemies. Let them make no mistake: abandoning the war was only a pretence; they were not safe, and he would attack them unawares the moment an opportunity offered. But if there was no place for suppliants among them, he would wander the length and breadth of Latium, and from there he would go to the Volsci, Aequi, and Hernici until he found someone who knew how to protect a child from a father's cruel and unnatural punishment. Possibly he could muster some fighting spirit that would enable him to take up arms against the most arrogant king and most bellicose people in the world.

When it seemed that turning him away would prompt him to make an angry and immediate departure, the people of Gabii opened their hearts and took him in. They told him he should not be surprised if his father in the end had turned against his children as he had against citizens and allies; he would no doubt end by turning his savagery upon himself when there was no one left upon whom he could vent it. They truly welcomed his coming, and believed that soon, with his help, the war would be shifted from the gates of Gabii to the walls of Rome.

54. He was then invited to take part in the councils of state, in which he said he deferred to the long-time residents in regard to matters with which they were better acquainted than he. But he never ceased to be a staunch advocate of war, in which he was thought to possess special expertise because of his knowledge of the strength of each people and his familiarity with the hatred the Romans had for their king's arrogance, which not even his children had been able to abide. Thus he prodded the leaders of the city bit

by bit to reopen the war, while he would select the most intrepid of the young soldiers to accompany him on sallies to secure plunder and to reconnoitre. Everything he did and said was designed to deceive them, and in this he succeeded so well that their misplaced trust led them in the end to choose him commander-in-chief.

The civilians were ignorant of what was afoot, but when minor clashes between the forces of Rome and Gabii frequently resulted in Gabii getting the best of it, everyone in the city, from highest to lowest, were quick to believe that Sextus Tarquinius had been sent to them as a gift from the gods. As for the soldiers, by risking his life and sharing in their hardships, and by doling out booty with a free hand, they came to hold him in such affection that he became as powerful in Gabii as his father was in Rome. And then, when he judged his strength was up to any eventuality, he sent a confidant to Rome to ask his father what he wanted him to do: by the will of the gods everything at Gabii now was in his hands. No doubt it was difficult for the father to believe this message and that is why he said nothing in reply. Instead, the king took a walk in the garden around his house as if to mull things over, with his son's messenger following, and as he strolled about in silence he is said to have struck off the heads of the tallest poppies with his staff. The messenger finally grew tired of asking for a response and receiving none; so he returned to Gabii, thinking his job only half done. He reported what he had said and seen: the man hadn't uttered a word, whether out of anger or hatred or the arrogance that was part of his nature.

But Sextus knew what his father meant and what he was hinting at by this wordless charade. He proceeded to kill off the city's leaders, some by convicting them on various charges before the people and others who were vulnerable because of their own unpopularity. Many were thus dispatched quite openly, but others against whom he could not plausibly bring charges he murdered in secret. Exile was open to those who chose it, but if not, they were forced into it. He then would divide up and distribute the property of those in exile and of his victims. And so the people at large, privately enriched by such largess and by booty won in the field, felt this public wrongdoing much less keenly. In the end, unable to help themselves or to seek help from others, they and their city passed into the hands of Rome's king without a fight.

55. Upon taking over Gabii, Tarquin made peace with the Aequi and renewed the treaty with the Etruscans. He then turned his attention to the city itself, his prime object being to make the temple of Jupiter on the Tarpeian summit of the Capitol a memorial to himself and to his family: both Tarquin kings had had a hand in it, the father who made the vow to build it and the son who fulfilled that vow. But because he wanted the site to be devoted solely to Jupiter and his temple, he decided to remove in a ceremony of deconsecration the shrines and chapels already there, several of which had been vowed by King Tatius at the critical moment of the battle he fought with Romulus and which had been consecrated and inaugurated later. During the laying of the foundation it is said the will of the gods was revealed concerning the magnitude of Rome's future empire; for when the augural birds permitted all the chapels to be deconsecrated with the exception of the shrine to Terminus,* this was interpreted as an omen in the following way: the fact that Terminus' dwelling was not to be moved and that of all the deities he alone was to remain within the boundaries sacred to him meant that all things in Rome's future would be stable and secure. This guarantee of permanence was followed by another prodigy that portended the greatness of empire: a human head with features intact is said to have been unearthed by those digging the foundations of the temple. The sight of this made it unequivocally clear that this spot would be the seat of empire and the head of the world, an interpretation confirmed by the prophecies of the seers in the city and of those summoned from Etruria for consultation on the matter.

The king was thereby encouraged to make lavish outlays of money on the project; but the spoils realized from Pometia, which he had thought would cover the expenses of the temple from start to finish, were scarcely enough to pay for the cost of the foundation. Hence I am more inclined to follow Fabius here—apart from the fact that he is the older authority—that the spoils amounted to only forty talents, than Piso,* who writes that forty thousand pounds of silver were reserved for the project; one could scarcely expect the spoils of a single city in that age to produce such an amount; in fact, it would more than suffice for the grandiose structures we build nowadays.

56. Tarquin was intent on completing the temple. He brought in workmen from every part of Etruria, using not only public moneys to pay for it but conscript labour of the plebeians. Though the work involved was scarcely negligible in itself, the plebs were obliged for military service as well. Building temples of the gods with their own hands bothered them less than other construction projects to which they were later transferred, which, though less impressive in outward appearance, involved considerably greater labour: these were the seating sections of the Circus and the Cloaca Maxima, or Great Sewer, the underground drain for the whole city. The renovations made recently to these two works, magnificent though they are, do not begin to match the magnitude of the original constructions.*

After the plebs had finished these labours, he felt their large numbers to be a burden on the city, where there was no regular employment for them. He therefore extended the bounds of Roman control by establishing two colonies that would in the future serve as defensive outposts for the city, Signia in the interior and Circeii on the coast.

A terrifying portent was seen in the midst of these activities: a snake* darted out from a wooden column. People ran into the palace in fright, but when the king heard of it, he was not so much immediately fearful as anxious as to what it meant for the future. Etruscan seers were summoned when it was a question of public prodigies, but Tarquin took this one as affecting his household, and in his apprehension he decided to consult Delphi, the most famous oracle in the world. He did not think it safe to entrust the oracle's response to any but his two sons, whom he dispatched to Greece through lands unfamiliar in that age and over seas more unfamiliar still.

Titus and Arruns set out, accompanied by Lucius Iunius Brutus, son of Tarquinia, the king's sister, a young man very different in intelligence from the dullard he pretended to be. For since his uncle had killed the leading men of the state, including his own brother, he decided to leave nothing in his person for the king to fear or in his possessions for him to covet: safety lay in being an object of scorn, now that justice was no more. He therefore deliberately began to act the part of a dull-witted fellow, allowing the king to control himself and his property. Nor did he object to the name Brutus,* but rather used it as a shield, waiting for the moment to show himself as the great-hearted liberator of the Roman people he proved to be. In this role he accompanied the two Tarquins to Delphi, more a figure of fun than a companion. He is said to have brought as a gift to Apollo a golden staff hidden inside a larger one made of cornelwood and hollowed out to receive it, a riddling symbol of his own character. When they arrived and had carried out their father's instructions, the two Tarquins conceived the desire to ask which of them would succeed their father as king of Rome. From the inmost recess of the sanctuary this response is said to have issued: 'Whoever of you, my lads, first brings a kiss to his mother shall hold supreme power at Rome.' The Tarquins gave orders that no one say anything about this: they intended to keep their brother Sextus back in Rome in the dark and to eliminate him as a possible successor. Between them they agreed to draw lots to determine which, on reaching Rome, would be the first to kiss his mother. But Brutus thought the Pythia's words meant something quite different. Pretending to slip, he fell to the ground and pressed his lips to the earth, the mother of us all.

Upon returning to Rome they found that preparations for war against the Rutuli were in full swing. 57. These people inhabited the city of Ardea and were very wealthy for that time and place. Their wealth was the cause of the war: Tarquin wanted to enrich himself, now that his resources were exhausted from his many public works, and to mollify the plebeians with Ardea's plunder, for they disliked his rule both because of his general arrogance and because of their resentment at having been kept so long at work fit for ordinary workmen and slaves. Tarquin tried to take Ardea in an initial assault, but when this did not succeed, he fell back on blockading the city from behind siegeworks.

A permanent camp grew up and, as happens in a war that is long but not hard-fought, furloughs were freely granted, but more for the officers than for the rank and file. Now the young princes of the royal house were in the habit of spending their free time feasting and carousing among themselves. It so happened that when they were drinking in the quarters of Sextus Tarquinius, where Tarquinius Collatinus, the son of Egerius, was one of the guests, they fell to discussing their wives. Each man praised his own extravagantly. When the dispute heated up, Collatinus said there was no need of talk. Why, in a few hours they could see for themselves that his Lucretia was the best of the lot. 'We're young and red-blooded. Why don't we ride off and see with our own eyes just what sort of wives we've got? The surest proof will be what each man finds when he shows up unexpectedly.' By this time they were quite drunk.

'Well then, let's go!' Spurring their horses they flew off to Rome.

The evening shadows were lengthening when they came upon the royal princesses feasting and frolicking with their friends. Then they sped off to Collatia: though the evening was late, they found Lucretia still in the main hall of her home, bent over her spinning and surrounded by her maids as they worked by lamplight. Lucretia was the clear winner of the contest. She graciously welcomed her husband and the Tarquins as they approached; Collatinus, happy in his victory, issued a comradely invitation for the royal young men to come in. When Sextus Tarquin set eyes upon her he was seized by the evil desire to debauch her, spurred on as he was by her beauty and redoubtable chastity. In the meantime, with the youthful lark now at an end, they returned to camp.

58. After a few days Sextus Tarquin, without Collatinus' knowledge, came to Collatia with a single companion. He was graciously welcomed, for no one suspected what he was up to, and after dinner was shown to a guest room. When the household was safely asleep, in the heat of passion he came to the sleeping Lucretia sword in hand and, pressing his left hand on her breast, whispered, 'Say no word, Lucretia. I am Sextus Tarquin. There is a sword in my hand. You die if you make a sound.' She awoke in fright, and when she realized she could not call for help with the threat of death hanging over her, Tarquin confessed his passion, pleaded with her, intermingling threats with entreaties and working in every way upon her feelings as a woman. When he saw she was resolute and would not yield even out of fear for her life, he threatened to disgrace her even in death by placing the naked body of a murdered slave next to her corpse, evidence that she had been killed in the act of committing adultery of the basest sort. When by this threat his lust vanquished her resolute chastity, he left the house exulting in his seeming conquest of the woman's honour.

Lucretia, stricken to the heart at the disgrace, sent the same messenger to her father in Rome and husband in Ardea: each was to come with one trustworthy friend; it must be done this way and done quickly: a terrible thing had happened. Spurius Lucretius arrived with Publius Valerius son of Volesus, Collatinus with Lucius Iunius Brutus, in whose company he was travelling *en route* to Rome when his wife's messenger chanced to meet him. They found Lucretia seated downcast in her bedchamber. At the arrival of her father and husband tears welled up, and when her husband asked, 'Are you all right?', she replied, 'Indeed, no. What can be right when a woman's virtue has been taken from her? The impress of another man is in your bed, Collatinus; yet only my body was defiled; my soul is not guilty. Death will be my witness to this. But pledge with your right hands and swear that the adulterer will not go unpunished. Sextus Tarquin did this, a guest who betrayed his host, an enemy in arms who last night took his pleasure, fatal, alas, to me—and, if you act as you should, to him.' Each pledged his word in turn and tried to comfort the heartsick woman by fixing the guilt not upon the victim but the transgressor: the mind sins, they said, not the body, and there is no guilt when intent is absent. 'It is up to you', she said, 'to punish the man as he deserves. As for me, I absolve myself of wrong, but not from punishment. Let no unchaste woman hereafter continue to live because of the precedent of Lucretia.' She took a knife she was hiding in her garments and drove it into her breast. Doubling over, she collapsed in death.

Husband and father raised a ritual cry of mourning for the dead. 59. While they were taken up with lamentation, Brutus pulled the knife dripping with blood from Lucretia's body. Holding it before him he cried, 'By this blood, so pure before defilement by prince Tarquin, I hereby swear—and you, O deities, I make my witnesses—that I will drive out Lucius Tarquinius Superbus together with his criminal wife and all his progeny with sword, fire, and whatever force I can muster, nor will I allow them or anyone else to be king at Rome.' He then handed the dagger to Collatinus, and next to Lucretius and Valerius, who stood amazed at the miraculous change that had come over him. They repeated the oath after him; from that moment on, anger overmastering grief, they followed Brutus' lead in bringing the monarchy to an end.

They bore Lucretia's body from the house to the forum, where they drew a large crowd that was scandalized by the extraordinary turn of events, as anyone would be. Each man expressed his personal sense of outrage at the rape the prince had committed. And not just the father's grief moved them, but Brutus also, when he rebuked them for tears and useless complaints when what they should be doing as men and Romans was to take up arms against those who had dared such violence. The most spirited young men were quick to seize weapons and join the cause; the rest followed their lead. Then, leaving a garrison at Collatia's gates to prevent anyone from getting out and reporting the uprising to the royal family, Brutus led the rest of the warriors to Rome.

The arrival of a large group of armed men caused fear and commotion wherever it went; on the other hand, the sight of the nation's leaders at the forefront made people think that whatever was afoot there must be a good reason for it. Moreover, men were as appalled by Sextus' heinous deed at Rome as they had been at Collatia. From all quarters of the city people crowded into the forum, where a herald summoned them to assemble before the tribune of the Celeres, or king's bodyguard, a post that Brutus chanced to be holding at that moment. He then delivered a speech that was wholly at odds with the spirit and character he had pretended to have up to that day. He spoke of the violence and lust of Sextus Tarquin, of the unspeakable rape of Lucretia and her wretched death, of the bereavement of Lucretius Tricipitinus and the cause of his daughter's death, which for him was more unworthy and more pitiable than the death itself. He mentioned also the arrogance of the king himself and how the plebs had been forced underground to dig out trenches and sewers: the men of Rome, victorious over all their neighbours, had been turned into drudges and quarry slaves, warriors no longer. He recalled the appalling murder of King Servius Tullius and how his daughter had driven over her father's body in that accursed wagon, and he invoked her ancestral gods as avengers. After saying these things and, I am sure, even more shocking ones prompted by his outrage of the moment, which are not easy for writers to capture on paper, he brought his listeners to such a pitch of fury that they revoked the king's power and ordered the exile of Lucius Tarquinius, together with wife and children.

Brutus armed a group of select young volunteers and with them set out for Ardea to rouse the army against the king. He left Lucretius in control of Rome, whom Tarquin had appointed prefect of the city some time before. In the midst of the tumult Tullia fled from her home. Wherever she went men and women reviled her, calling down on her head the vengeance that the spirits of kindred inflict upon those who have wronged them.

60. When the news of these events reached the camp, the king in fear at the sudden crisis hastened to Rome to suppress the distur-

bance. Brutus anticipated that he would be on his way and, not wanting to meet up with him, took a different route: at almost the same moment Brutus arrived at Ardea and Tarquin in Rome. The gates were closed to Tarquin and his exile proclaimed. The liberator of the city received a delighted welcome in the camp, and the king's sons were expelled from it. Two of them accompanied their father into exile at Caere among the Etruscans. Sextus Tarquin went to Gabii, apparently regarding it as his personal fiefdom; but there he was killed by those who had witnessed his murders and depredations and were bent on settling old scores.

Lucius Tarquinius Superbus reigned for twenty-five years. The monarchy at Rome from her foundation to her liberation lasted two hundred and forty-four years. Two consuls were then elected, in accordance with the precepts laid down by Servius Tullius, by the Comitia Centuriata under the presidency of the prefect of the city. They were Lucius Iunius Brutus and Lucius Tarquinius Collatinus.

BOOK TWO

1. The history of a free nation in peace and war will be my theme from this point on, the election of annual magistrates and greater obedience to the commands of law than to those of men. The arrogance of the last king caused the advent of liberty to be all the more welcome, whereas the rule of the earlier monarchs was such that they are deservedly reckoned successive founders of at least those parts of the city that they annexed to accommodate the new peoples each had added to the state. Nor is there any doubt that the same Brutus, who won so much glory in expelling Superbus, would have done a grievous wrong to the state if out of a premature desire for liberty he had wrested rule from one of the earlier kings. The plebs were a mixture of shepherds and adventurers who had fled their own lands. What would have happened to them when they won immunity if not liberty under the sacred protection of asylum? Uncowed by the absolute power of a king, they would have been stirred up by tribunician agitation and would have begun battling with the senators in a city not their own, before they had become united in spirit by commitment to wives and children and by love for the soil—a love that takes a long time to develop. The nation, not yet grown up, would have been torn apart by dissension. But as it was, a calm and moderate exercise of governmental authority fostered and nourished it so that when it matured and grew strong it was able to enjoy the excellent fruits of liberty.

One might more correctly say that the birth of liberty was owing to the annual nature of the consuls' tenure than to any lessening of the power the kings had possessed. The first consuls enjoyed all the rights and insignia of the highest office: they were only forbidden to hold the fasces* at the same time, lest double intimidation of the people should appear to be their aim. By agreement with his colleague Brutus was the first to hold the fasces, and he proved thereafter to be as keen a guardian of liberty as he had been its initial champion. First of all, while the people were in the first flush of enthusiasm for liberty, and to obviate their possibly succumbing to the entreaties or bribes of princes in the future, he had them swear an oath that they would allow no man to be king at Rome. Next, he

brought back the senate to its former strength of three hundred
members, for its numbers had been much reduced by the murders
committed by Tarquin; the new members were drawn from the
leaders of the equestrian class. The tradition is also said to have
grown up that when the senators are summoned into session they
are styled Fathers and those Conscripted; for those he enrolled were
called *conscripti*. This action contributed wonderfully to harmony
within the state by emphasizing the joint interests of plebeians and
senators.*

2. They then turned their attention to religious matters: those
public rites that the kings had performed in person they now assigned (since no one wanted the return of a king) to an official called
the King of Sacrifices. The priesthood was made subordinate to the
pontiff, lest the title and office should in any way infringe their
freedom, which was then a concern uppermost in people's minds.
And in fact this concern, which extended to all areas and the most
minute matters, may well have caused them to go beyond a reasonable limit. The mere name of one of the consuls, for example, who
had never given offence in anything he had done, was detested.
People said that the Tarquins had become all too used to monarchical rule; Priscus began it; then came Servius Tullius; but not even
this interruption, when the throne belonged to someone outside the
clan, had caused Tarquinius Superbus to forget it; through violence
and crime he had claimed it as his birthright; and now, after Superbus'
expulsion, Tarquinius Collatinus was in power! The Tarquins did
not know how to live as private citizens; the name was an anathema
because it was a threat to liberty.

Such talk had at first a gradual effect on men's feelings, but when
it became widespread and had upset the people greatly, Brutus called
them to a meeting. He first read out their oath that they would not
allow anyone to be king and that no one at Rome should be a threat
to liberty: this, he said, must be cause for the greatest vigilance, and
nothing that might affect it should be misprized. He was reluctant
to speak out of regard for the man in question, nor would he have
said anything had not the love he bore his country compelled him.
The Roman people were not convinced that their freedom had been
fully realized: not only were members of the royal family who bore
the name Tarquin present in the state, they were even heads
of state. This compromised liberty, this prejudiced it. 'Lucius

Tarquinius,' he said, 'remove this apprehension of your own accord. We remember and we admit that you helped in expelling the king: complete now the good work you began by removing the royal name from Rome. Your fellow citizens here—and I strongly support them— will not only grant you all your property but, should it in any way be deficient, will add to it handsomely. Depart in an amicable spirit; relieve your country of what is possibly a groundless fear. People are convinced that monarchy will depart only when those bearing the name Tarquin depart as well.'

At first Collatinus could not speak from amazement at this strange and unexpected turn of events; and as he collected his thoughts to make a response, the leading men crowded about and begged him to follow the course Brutus had urged. He was less influenced by these others, but after Spurius Lucretius, his father-in-law and an older man for whom he had greater respect, began to ply him with entreaties and persuasive arguments to yield to the consensus of the nation, the consul feared that when he left office he would hear the same sentiments and would suffer the loss of his property and other humiliation besides. So he resigned the consulship and with all his property left Rome for Lavinium. Brutus, in accordance with a decree of the senate, proposed to the people that the entire Tarquin family should go into exile; in the Comitia Centuriata he declared Publius Valerius elected as his colleague, with whose help he had expelled the kings.

3. No one doubted that the Tarquins would try to regain the throne by force, but the war was slower in coming than people expected. What nearly destroyed liberty was something they had not feared: deceit and treachery from within. Among the Roman youth there were several of high birth who had lived under the monarchy a more irresponsible and pleasure-seeking life than they could at present, for as peers and companions of the young Tarquins they had grown accustomed to living in a royal manner. They missed the licence that had once been theirs; and with everyone now enjoying equal rights they began to complain among themselves that the freedom of others had brought subjection to themselves: the king was a fellow who could accede to one's requests, whether just or not; there were opportunities for receiving and doing favours; he could be both angry and forgiving, for he made a distinction between a friend and an enemy; the laws, on the other hand, were deaf

and unapproachable, more a prop and defence for weaklings than for men of standing; there was no complaisance, no indulgence in them if one stepped over the line; mankind can go wrong in so many ways that living a life of perfect rectitude was fraught with pitfalls.

They were thus already in a disgruntled mood when envoys from the royal family arrived on the scene to ask for the restitution of their property, although making no mention of their return to Rome. The senate gave the envoys a hearing and took some days to debate the proposal: if the property were not returned it would be a cause for war, and if returned it might provide the means and opportunity for prosecuting one. In the meantime the envoys got to work on other matters. While their stated mission was recovery of the property, they were secretly laying plans to restore the monarchy. They went their rounds as if doing what they were sent to do, but they were really testing the temper of the young nobles. And to those who gave their proposals a favourable hearing they gave a letter from Tarquin and proposed that the royal family be secretly introduced into the city under cover of darkness.

4. The job of carrying this out was in the first instance given to the Vitellii and Aquilii brothers. The sister of the Vitellii was married to the consul Brutus, from which union there were now grown sons, Titus and Tiberius, whom their uncles brought into the plot (certain other young nobles were also members of the conspiracy, but over the course of time their names have been lost). In the meantime the senate voted that the property be returned. The envoys now had an excuse for staying longer in the city because the consuls had granted them a period in which to procure transport for conveying the king's property. All this time they devoted to making plans with the conspirators; in the end they prevailed on them to write a letter for delivery to the Tarquins: otherwise how would the king believe that the report brought by the envoys on such a momentous matter was really true?

The letter that the young nobles wrote as proof of their good faith was to provide proof of their crime. For on the day before the envoys were to return to the Tarquins the Vitellii gave a banquet at their home during which none but those who were part of the conspiracy were present. The impending plot naturally required detailed discussion, in the course of which one of the slaves overheard them. This fellow had guessed even before what was afoot but was waiting for the moment when the envoys would be given the letter, which when seized would be proof of what was going on. When he saw that it had indeed been handed over, he reported the matter to the consuls. They left their houses and took the envoys and conspirators into custody, crushing the whole business without disturbance: their chief concern was to put their hands on the letter. The traitors were put in chains at once, but for a while there was doubt about what to do with the envoys; and although they seemed to have committed hostile acts, the dictates of international law concerning the neutral status of ambassadors prevailed.

5. The senators earlier had voted that the royal property be returned, but now, overcome by anger, they took up the question anew and forbade that either it be returned or the proceeds assigned to the public treasury. Instead, the plebs were permitted to loot it, in order that plundering the royal possessions would forever forestall the possibility of peace with the Tarquins. Their land, which lay between the city and the Tiber, was consecrated to Mars, becoming the Campus Martius. On this property a crop of wheat is said to have been ready by chance for harvesting, and because religion now forbade the consumption of the produce of the Campus, the crop was cut down, stalks and all, by a great number of men, who carried it in baskets to the Tiber and dumped it into the slow-moving current, it being midsummer. The heaps of grain got caught in the shallows and settled in the mud. In this way an island took form, gradually growing as other detritus chanced to pile up against it. I believe that the embankments were added later and the area so improved that it became high enough and strong enough to support safely temples and porticoes.*

Following the looting of the royal property the traitors were condemned and punished, a spectacle made all the more conspicuous because the consulship imposed on the father the duty of carrying out the penalty on his sons: the man who should not even have witnessed the scene was the one fortune had chosen as executioner. Youths of the highest birth stood bound at the stake; yet people scarcely regarded them, for all eyes were fixed on the consul's sons. Men felt as much sorrow for the crime for which they were being deservedly punished as for the punishment itself: to think that in this year of all years, when their country had won its freedom, when their father was its liberator, and when the consulship had origi-

nated in their own family, they had taken it into their heads to
betray everything—senators, plebeians, the gods and men of Rome—
all in favour of that arrogant ex-king who was now threatening their
country. The consuls proceeded to take their seats, and the lictors
were ordered to carry out the sentence. They stripped, flogged, and
beheaded the young men. During the whole time all were painfully
aware of Brutus' eyes and expression, for as he fulfilled his duty as
a public official the natural feelings of a father could be read in his
face. After the offenders had been punished and as a conspicuous
measure to prevent further crime, the slave was rewarded with a
grant of money from the treasury, with freedom and with citizenship. He is said to have been the first slave to have been freed
uindicta.* Some think the word *vindicta* derived from his name,
which they say was Vindicius. Thereafter those who were freed in
this manner were regarded as having been received into Roman
citizenship.

6. Tarquin was enraged at the news of what had happened. The
disappointment of his great hopes produced feelings of pain, hatred,
and anger and, seeing that deceit had not furthered his designs,
decided to issue an open call for war. So he went around as a
suppliant to the cities of Etruria, entreating Veii and Tarquinii in
particular not to let him, an Etruscan blood brother, perish with his
grown sons before their eyes—he who had once been a powerful
monarch but now was reduced to an impoverished exile. Rome's
other kings, he said, had been called from outside to take the throne;
he, who had been born to it and had extended Rome's dominion,
had been expelled by his own kinsmen in a criminal conspiracy. The
Romans, he maintained, had then carved up the state among themselves because not one of them seemed good enough to be king; and
they had given the people his own property to loot, so that everyone
would share in the guilt. He aimed to recover throne and country,
and to make those ungrateful citizens smart for what they had done.
He needed their help and assistance. What is more, they should
avenge the wrongs they had long suffered: armies repeatedly slaughtered, their land confiscated.

These last arguments won over the Veientes, each man asserting
belligerently that at least under a Roman general their humiliations
would be cancelled and their losses in war made good. His very
name and relationship prevailed with the people of Tarquinii: it

seemed a fine thing for one of their own to be king at Rome. So the armies of two states followed Tarquin's lead: they aimed to restore the monarchy and to punish the Romans in war. When they entered Roman territory the consuls confronted them. Valerius led the infantry, formed into a hollow square; Brutus went ahead with the cavalry to reconnoitre. The enemy horsemen had been similarly sent on in advance, commanded by Arruns Tarquinius, son of the king. Tarquin himself was following with the legions. When Arruns perceived from the lictors that the consul was in the distance and was coming his way, and when he recognized Brutus' features close up, he was incensed. 'There is the man', he cried, 'who drove us from our country into exile. Just look! He parades about in pomp, flaunting our royal emblems. Help us now, O gods, avengers of kings!' He spurred his horse and charged directly at the consul. Brutus realized that he was coming against him. Since it was an honourable thing in those days for the commanders themselves to engage in the fighting, he eagerly threw himself into the fray. They charged one another with such vehemence that neither thought of safeguarding his own person if only he could wound his opponent. Each man was struck through the shield by his adversary's blow and, impaled on the spear, tumbled from his horse in death. At the same time the rest of the cavalry began to fight, and not long after the infantry also joined the conflict. There the fight wavered back and forth almost as if there could be no clear winner, the right wing of each side prevailing, the left going down to defeat. The Veientes, accustomed to being beaten by the Roman soldiery, were routed and put to flight. The men of Tarquinii, a new enemy, not only held their ground but even drove back the Romans on their end.

7. Although the battle ended in this fashion, such fear overcame Tarquin and the Etruscans that the armies of both Veii and Tarquinii abandoned their efforts and left by night for home. Tradition connects the following miraculous event with the battle: a great voice issued from the Arsian forest, believed to be that of the god Silvanus, saying that since one more Etruscan than Roman had fallen in the fight, Rome had prevailed. However this may be, the Romans returned from the battlefield as victors, the Etruscans as the losers. For after it grew light and none of the enemy was in sight, the consul Valerius gathered the spoils and returned to Rome in triumph.* He conducted a funeral for his colleague with as much

pomp as he could. Yet Brutus' death was honoured far more by the grief of the people, marked above all by the matrons who for a year mourned for him as for a parent because he had been such a stout champion of a woman's honour.

As for the surviving consul, the fickleness of public opinion brought a shift from popularity to hostility, and even to a suspicion that culminated in a nasty accusation. Gossip said he was aiming at the throne because he had not replaced his colleague and was building a house on the Velian hill: there on a lofty and protected site an impregnable bastion was under construction. The consul was distressed at the groundless nature of the accusation, which was widely repeated and believed. He therefore summoned the people to a meeting and himself entered the assembly with *fasces* lowered. The crowd was pleased at the sight of the symbols of office being made subordinate to themselves, for it was an admission that the people's power was superior to that of the consuls. When Valerius had called them to order, he praised the good fortune of his colleague, who had died after seeing his country freed, while yet holding the highest office and fighting for his country, and with his reputation still at its height and not yet the target of ill will; as the survivor he found that he had been reduced to the likes of the Aquilii and Vitellii. 'Will there ever exist', he asked, 'a man whose integrity is great enough to withstand the taint of suspicion? What grounds were there to fear that I, the implacable foe of monarchy, would ever be subject to the charge of seeking the throne? Even had I lived on the citadel and Capitol, how could I have believed I would be the object of fear on the part of my fellow citizens? Does my reputation in your eyes depend on so trivial a circumstance? Is your confidence in me so shaky that it matters more where I am than who I am? Fellow citizens, Publius Valerius will never be an obstacle to your freedom. The Velia will not threaten your safety. Nor will I move my house to just any piece of level ground, but shall place it at the foot of the hill so that you may dwell above the one you suspect. Let those men build on the Velia whose love of liberty you believe to be greater than that of Publius Valerius.' All the building material was brought down at once to the base of the hill and a house built at the bottom of the slope where the temple of Vica Pota now stands.

8. A series of laws was then passed whose effect was not only to relieve the consul of suspicion of aiming at the throne but to make

him widely popular; hence came his cognomen of Publicola, or People's Friend. Those laws were above all pleasing to the masses that sanctioned appeal to the popular assembly from decisions of the magistrates* and that made a man who tried to seek the throne a sacrificial victim to the gods.* Valerius as sole consul presided over the passing of these laws so that he alone would receive the credit for them. Only then did he hold an assembly to elect a colleague. Spurius Lucretius was chosen consul, but his advanced age did not give him the strength to carry out his consular duties, and within a few days he died. Marcus Horatius Pulvillus was elected in Lucretius' place. I do not find Lucretius listed as consul in certain old sources, for they put Horatius immediately after Brutus. I believe that because he did nothing of note in his consulship men forgot about it.

The temple of Jupiter on the Capitol had not yet been dedicated, and it fell by lot to Horatius to perform the ceremony. Publicola set out for war against Veii. Valerius' relatives were more disgruntled than was seemly that the dedication of such a great temple had been given to Horatius. They tried to block it in every way and, when their other efforts ended in failure, at the very moment when the consul was in the middle of his prayer as he held on to the doorpost, they struck at him with the ill-omened message that his son had just died and that he could not dedicate the temple with his house in the shadow of death. Whether he refused to believe this or possessed great strength of spirit tradition does not say, nor is interpretation easy. He permitted himself to be deflected from his task only long enough to order the body carried out for burial; then, keeping his grip on the doorpost, he completed the ritual prayer and dedicated the temple. Such were the events at home and abroad in the first year after the expulsion of the kings.

9. Publius Valerius for the second time and Titus Lucretius were the next consuls. The Tarquins had by this time fled to Lars Porsenna, king of Clusium. There they mingled pleas with advice, now begging him not to suffer them, Etruscans by origin and of the same blood and nationality, to be penniless exiles, now warning him not to allow the growing habit of expelling kings to go unpunished; unless kings defend their thrones with as much vehemence as nations seek liberty—which itself is sufficient attraction—the highborn will find themselves on the same level as the lowest; there will be nothing left in nations that is exalted, that rises above the ordi-

nary; monarchy would soon be a thing of the past, although it is the finest form of government among gods and men.

Porsenna, thinking it a good thing for there to be a king at Rome and one of Etruscan stock, advanced on the city in hostile array. Never before had such fear gripped the senate: the state of Clusium was at that time very strong and Porsenna's reputation formidable. Yet their fear concerned not just the enemy but their own citizens as well: the plebs might in their terror accept monarchical rule, willing to settle for peace at the price of liberty. The senate therefore took a number of steps to win the people's goodwill during this period. Special care was given to the grain supply, some being sent to the Volsci to secure it, others to Cumae.* Oversight of the salt supply, which was being sold at exorbitant prices, was taken out of the hands of individual entrepreneurs and wholly taken over by the state. The plebs were also exempted from custom duties and tribute, which were to be paid by the rich, who could afford them. The poor, they argued, made a sufficient contribution by rearing their children. This beneficence on the part of the senators proved in the hard times of famine and siege that were to come such a unifying force in the state that the thought of monarchy was as much an anathema to the lowest elements of society as to the highest. No single individual thereafter ever attained as much popularity by demagoguery as the senate did then by wise governance.

10. At the enemy approach all the country folk came into the city on their own initiative. The city itself was surrounded by a garrison force. Some parts seemed adequately protected by walls, others by the barrier of the Tiber. The wooden pile bridge, however, almost gave the enemy entrance into the city, but a single man, Horatius Cocles, stopped them; it was Rome's good fortune to have had him as her sole bulwark on that day. He happened to be stationed at the bridge when the Janiculum hill was captured by a sudden assault. As the enemy hurtled down the slope on the double and a swarm of his fearful fellow soldiers began to drop their weapons and withdraw from their place in the ranks, he grabbed one man after another and blocked his way; he swore by all that was sacred to gods and men that abandoning their posts was utter folly: if they left the bridge in their rear for the enemy to cross there would soon be more Etruscans on the Palatine and Capitol than on the Janiculum. He urged and pleaded with them to break down the bridge, using steel, fire, or

whatever means was to hand; he would take the brunt of the enemy onslaught with as much strength as a single man could muster. He then strode to the bridge's entrance; conspicuous amid the visibly retreating backs of those abandoning the fight and brandishing his arms in the enemy's face as he entered the fray, he stunned his opponents by his astonishing bravado. Yet shame kept two of his companions by his side, Spurius Larcius and Titus Herminius, both distinguished for high birth and achievement. With their help he withstood for a time the first burst of the battle's tumultuous storm; when only a small part of the bridge was still intact and those who were cutting it down screamed for them to get back, he forced them to retire to safety as well. Then his defiant gaze swept menacingly over the assembled Etruscan leadership; he challenged them by name and taunted them as a group: pawns of arrogant kings and careless of their own liberty, they had come to attack that of others. They held back for a time, each man looking to another to begin the fight. Shame then prompted them to move forward; raising a shout from every side, they hurled their weapons at their sole opponent. All those spears stuck fast in his out-thrust shield, nor did they cause him to bestride the bridge any less stubbornly, his feet firmly planted wide apart. They kept trying to drive him off by one assault after another; but the crash of the broken bridge and the shout of the Romans, exuberant at finishing the job, stopped them in their tracks in sudden panic. Then Cocles cried, 'Father Tiber, may you, I humbly pray, receive these arms and this soldier into your favouring stream.' Thereupon he leaped into the Tiber in full armour and, with many spears raining down upon him, swam in safety to his comrades on the shore, a bit of daring that posterity was to find more praiseworthy than credible.

His country showed its gratefulness for such courage: his statue was placed in the Comitium and as much land as could be traced around by a plough in a single day was given him. The enthusiasm of individuals was also conspicuous in the midst of such public honours, for each man, despite the great personal privation that followed, gave him something from his meagre private store.

11. Porsenna, repulsed at his first attempt, abandoned his plan to take the city by storm. He turned to besieging it by placing a garrison on the Janiculum, while he himself pitched camp on level ground along the Tiber's bank. Ships were brought in from many quarters

to prevent grain being brought into Rome and to provide transport to the other bank for raiding parties to fan out in various directions as opportunity offered. In a short time all Roman territory was so full of marauders that not only did everything portable have to be brought into the city from the countryside but all the livestock as well, nor did anyone thereafter dare to drive them to pasture outside the gates. The Etruscans were allowed to do this as much by design as from fear, for Valerius was awaiting an opportunity to attack a large number of them unexpectedly as they roamed the countryside, whereas retaliation for small injuries did not concern him, inflicting punishment for more serious offences did. And so in order to set a trap for the marauders he ordered a great many men on the next day to drive the livestock from the Esquiline gate, which was furthest away from the enemy. He was sure they would learn of it through the faithless slaves who were deserting a city besieged and suffering from privation. And they did in fact come to know of it from a defector, in consequence of which many more of the enemy than usual crossed the river in expectation of securing a great deal of booty in a single sweep. Publius Valerius then ordered Titus Herminius with a few troops to lie in ambush at the second milestone along the road to Gabii and Spurius Larcius with a light-armed contingent to stand in readiness at the Colline gate until the enemy passed by; they were then to go out and block the way, should the Etruscans seek to return to the river. Titus Lucretius, the other consul, deployed selected cohorts from the Caelian hill; these last were the first the enemy caught sight of. When Herminius perceived that the skirmish was under way he rose up from his place of ambush and cut down the Etruscans from the rear as they were confronting Lucretius. On the right and on the left, from the Colline and Naevian gates, the war cry was raised. In this way the plunderers were hemmed in and cut down, not having the strength to fight a battle and with all escape routes cut off. This proved the end of indiscriminate raiding on the part of the Etruscans.

12. The siege continued none the less, as did scarcity of grain and the high prices people had to pay for it. Porsenna's hope of capturing the city by entrenching himself in one position was interrupted by the scheme of Gaius Mucius, a noble youth. To Mucius it was intolerable that the Roman people, when subject to a monarch, had never been besieged in any war or by any enemy, but now, having

gained their freedom, were hemmed in by the same Etruscans whom they had so often defeated. This outrage, he thought, should be avenged by some great and daring deed. A plan to sneak into the enemy camp was at first formed on his own initiative, but second thoughts supervened: if he slipped away without consular permission or without telling anyone and by chance were caught by the Roman sentries, he would be dragged back and charged with desertion, which the present plight of the city would make quite plausible. He therefore approached the senate. 'I wish, senators, to cross the Tiber and enter, if I can, the enemy camp; my aim is not to plunder or avenge their raids, but, with the gods' help, to accomplish something far greater.' The senate gave its approval, and he set out with a sword concealed in his clothing.

When he had penetrated to the very heart of the camp, he found a dense crowd milling around the king's tribunal where the soldiers happened to be receiving their pay. Much of the business was being done by the king's secretary, who was seated next to Porsenna and was dressed much like him. Since it was he whom most of the soldiers were approaching Mucius was in doubt as to which of the two Porsenna was. Fearing to ask—for that would give his game away—fortune led him to make a random choice: alas, he cut down the secretary instead of the king. As he strode away, clearing a path through the panicked throng with his bloodstained sword, the uproar attracted an even greater crowd. The king's bodyguard seized him. Dragging him back, they placed the solitary prisoner before the royal tribunal where, even in this well-nigh hopeless situation, he was more an object of fear than afraid himself. He addressed Porsenna: 'I am Gaius Mucius, a citizen of Rome. I came here as an enemy to kill my enemy, and I am as ready to die as I am to kill. We Romans act bravely and, when adversity strikes, we suffer bravely. Nor am I the only one who feels this way; behind me stands a line of those who seek the same honour. If this is the sort of fight you want, go ahead; but it is one in which your life is at risk from hour to hour, one in which an assassin lurks at the very entrance to your palace, sword in hand. Such is the war the youth of Rome have declared against you. Pitched battles and the clash of arms are not what you should fear. Our business is with you alone, one on one.'

The king reacted in both anger and fear. He decided on a course of intimidation by ordering Mucius to be cast into the flames unless he told him at once exactly what lay behind these dark threats of assassination. 'Look upon me,' Mucius replied, 'and realize what a paltry thing the body is for those who seek great glory.' So saying he thrust his hand into the fire that had been lit for sacrifice, and as it burned he gave no sign of feeling the terrible pain. The king was dumbstruck by this extraordinary act. He leaped from his seat and ordered the young man pulled from the altar. 'Leave this place. You have proved a stouter foe against yourself than against me. If you were a member of my own country I would congratulate you with bravos. But you are not, and I now release you untouched and unharmed, exempt from the laws that apply to prisoners of war.' As if to repay his generosity Mucius replied, 'Because you value bravery so highly, I will tell you as a favour what you could not wrest from me by threats: three hundred of the finest Roman youth have sworn to ambush you as I have done. The lot fell to me first. The others, as each man's lot comes up, will attack you in turn and in their own time, until fortune grants one of us to strike you down.'

13. Mucius was dismissed, and thereafter bore the cognomen Scaeuola from the maiming of his right hand.* Envoys from Porsenna followed him to Rome, for the king was greatly upset by the thought that he had escaped this first attempt on his life because of the assassin's mistake and that in the future he would have to undergo as many attempts as there were those who had sworn to kill him. He therefore took the initiative in offering peace terms to the Romans.

The proviso that the Tarquins be restored was rejected (Porsenna brought the issue up more in deference to the wishes of the Tarquins than out of ignorance that the Romans would refuse). He did prevail in his demand that territory taken from Veii be returned and that, if the Romans wanted him to remove his garrison from the Janiculum, they would have to give hostages. Peace was made on these terms; Porsenna led his army down from the Janiculum and withdrew from Roman territory. To honour his courage, the senate gave Gaius Mucius land across the Tiber that was thereafter known as the Mucian Fields.

Courage so rewarded filled the female sex with similar patriotic ardour. The maid Cloelia was one of the hostages and, when Porsenna chanced to pitch camp not far from the Tiber's bank, she led a group of young girls in escaping the guards, swimming the river as the enemy's weapons rained down, and safely restoring them all to their relatives in Rome. When the king learned of this, he was at first incensed; he sent spokesmen to Rome to demand the return of the hostage Cloelia: he was, he said, not much concerned about the others. Admiration followed upon anger; what she did, he realized, surpassed the deeds of men like Cocles and Mucius; he then took the position that if the hostage were not returned, he would consider the treaty broken, but if she were given back, he would restore her to her people untouched and unharmed. Both sides kept their word. The Romans gave back Cloelia in accordance with the treaty, while the Etruscan king not only safeguarded and honoured her, but allowed the brave girl to choose some of the remaining hostages to take back to Rome. When all were brought before her, maidenly modesty is said to have led her to select boys of tender years, a choice that the remaining hostages approved, for the young were the most vulnerable to mistreatment by the enemy. With peace re-established, the Romans marked the woman's unprecedented courage with an unprecedented honour, an equestrian statue; a maiden seated on a horse was placed on the highest point along the Sacred Way.

14. The Etruscan king's peaceful departure from the city is not consonant with the custom of auctioning off 'the property of King Porsenna' that has, among other formalities, been handed down from antiquity and is still in use today. The origin of this custom must either have begun in the midst of war and continued on in peacetime or have developed from a more peaceable beginning than the notice of a sale of enemy property would indicate. From the available evidence the most likely solution is that the property in question was what Porsenna left in his camp on the Janiculum, where he had conveyed the finest goods and choicest produce of nearby Etruria, and that he left it as a gift to the Romans, who were then in dire straits from the long siege; this property was then sold—rather than leaving it for the people to plunder as if it were that of an enemy—and that the phrase 'the property of Porsenna' signified more gratitude for his beneficence than auction of his royal fortune, which, after all, the Roman people did not possess.

Now that he had abandoned his war against Rome, Porsenna did not want his foray into the area to appear to be without result. He therefore gave his son Arruns part of his forces and ordered him to attack Aricia. The people of the city were at first stricken by this unexpected development, but when the reinforcements they had summoned from the Latins and from Cumae arrived, they were so emboldened as to decide the issue in a pitched battle. At the start of the fight the Etruscans' onslaught was so furious that they routed the Aricians by sheer momentum. The cohorts of Cumae countered force with stratagem, steadily retreating to one side and then, when the enemy rushed past pell-mell, wheeling about and attacking them from the rear. Thus the Etruscans, nearly the victors, were cut down between the two forces. A very small group, now leaderless, ended up in Rome in default of a nearer refuge, without weapons and behaving like the suppliants that their plight had made them. They were welcomed in kindly fashion and quartered among various hosts. After their wounds had been attended to, some set out for home, bringing news of the warm hospitality they had received; affection for their hosts and for the city caused many to remain in Rome. The area assigned to them for habitation was thereafter called the Tuscan Quarter.

15. Publius Lucretius and Publius Valerius Publicola were elected the next consuls.* In this year envoys came from Porsenna for the last time concerning the restoration of Tarquin to the throne. When the senators determined to deal with the king directly they dispatched at once a delegation consisting of their most distinguished members. Admittedly, they said, this determination not to allow restoration of the monarchy could simply have been conveyed to his envoys at Rome; but they had decided to send this special delegation to emphasize that on this issue discussion was not possible. Should Porsenna continue to seek what was inimical to Rome's freedom and should the Romans—unless they consented to the ruination of their most cherished ideal—be obliged to refuse the request of one to whom they wished to refuse nothing, the resulting friction would be a constant irritant to the good relations that now obtained between them. The Roman people were living not under a monarchy but in freedom. They would sooner open their gates to an enemy than to an autocrat, and it was their resolve that the end of freedom would be the end of the city. Accordingly, if he wished Rome to prosper, he should suffer her to be free. The king was deeply impressed by this impassioned plea. 'Since your resolve', he said, 'is fixed and unshakeable, I shall not dun you by fruitlessly raising the issue in the future nor shall I disappoint the Tarquins in their expectation of

help that is not mine to give. To avoid any compromise of the peace I have made with you, they must find another place, whether by war or diplomatic means, in which to find a home in exile.' His subsequent actions gave even greater proof of his friendship, for he returned the remaining hostages and restored the Veian land that had been taken away by the treaty struck on the Janiculum. Tarquin, with all hope of return cut off, went into exile in Tusculum with his son-in-law Octavius Mamilius. Thus was the peace between Rome and Porsenna scrupulously maintained.

16. The next consuls were Marcus Valerius and Publius Postumius. In this year a successful war was fought against the Sabines; the consuls celebrated a triumph. The Sabines then prepared to wage war on a greater scale. To meet this threat, and to be in readiness against a sudden incursion of Tusculum, from which quarter war was anticipated but not yet under way, experienced leaders were elected as the next consuls: Publius Valerius for the fourth time and Titus Lucretius for the second. The Sabines then became sharply divided between those advocating war and those advocating peace. Rome was the beneficiary of this dispute; for Attius Clausus, whose Roman name was to become Appius Claudius, fled to Rome from Inregillum with a great number of clients* when he found himself as an advocate of peace no match for harassment at the hands of his political opponents. Citizenship and land across the Anio were given them: collectively they were styled the Old Claudian Tribe, although later new members who settled in the area were added as well. Appius was chosen to sit in the senate; he soon rose to be reckoned among the most prominent leaders of the state. The consuls made an offensive strike into Sabine territory; devastation of their land was followed by defeat in battle, such that for a long time afterward there was no fear of the Sabines renewing the war. The consuls returned to Rome in triumph.

In the following year, when Menenius Agrippa and Publius Postumius were consuls, Publius Valerius died, the foremost man in war and peace by universal consent. Although he enjoyed a great reputation, his private fortune was so slender that there was not enough to pay for the funeral; so he was buried at public expense. The married women went into mourning for him as they had for Brutus. In the same year two Latin colonies, Pometia and Cora,* defected to the Aurunci. War was begun with the Aurunci; as the consuls entered their territory a huge army put up a fierce resistance but was routed. The war was then centred on Pometia. The slaughter was as great after the battle as during it; more were killed than captured, but even the latter were subject to general massacre. Anger over the war prompted even the killing of three hundred hostages that had been given.

17. The following consuls, Opiter Verginius and Spurius Cassius, first attacked Pometia in force and then besieged the city with moveable towers and other siege works. The Aurunci counter-attacked more out of an unappeasable hatred than because they had some particular expectation of success or to take advantage of a favourable opportunity. They rushed out, more of them carrying firebrands than weapons, and filled the entire field with slaughter and fire. They set the towers ablaze, wounded and killed many of the enemy, and came close to killing one of the consuls (which, the sources do not specify) when he fell from his horse, gravely wounded. The Romans went back to the city after this unsuccessful effort, bringing among the many wounded the consul, who hovered between life and death. After a short interval, but sufficient to attend to the wounded and resupply the army, they returned to Pometia, their anger much fiercer and in even greater force. The towers were rebuilt and the siege intensified to the point that the soldiers were about to scale the walls when the city surrendered unconditionally. Yet the fate of the Aurunci in surrender was no less terrible than if their city had been captured. Its leaders were beheaded, surviving colonists sold into slavery, the city demolished, its territory sold. The consuls triumphed more because Rome's anger had been savagely satisfied than from the magnitude of the war they had brought to a finish.

18. In the following year Postumus Cominius and Titus Larcius were consuls. In that year during the licence of games held in Rome Sabine youths abducted some whores. A brawl broke out in the crowd and almost turned into a full-scale battle; from this trifling incident a renewal of hostilities loomed. What is more, there was fear of war with the Latins, for few doubted that the thirty Latin peoples were conspiring against Rome at the instigation of Octavius Mamilius. At this critical juncture, when men feared the worst, the idea of appointing a dictator* was first mooted. But authorities do not agree in what year this happened or which consuls were mis-

trusted because they belonged to the faction of the Tarquins—for this too is part of the tradition—or who the first dictator in fact was. Still, among the oldest authorities I find Titus Larcius was named the first dictator and Spurius Cassius his master of the horse.* The choice was made from among ex-consuls, for this was a provision of the law that was passed concerning the dictatorship. I am therefore more inclined to think that Larcius, who was an ex-consul, rather than Manius Valerius, son of Marcus and grandson of Volesus, who had not yet been consul, was put in a position superior to the consuls; if they had been looking to choose a dictator from this particular family they would rather have selected his father Marcus Valerius, a consular of proven merit. Thus a dictator was named for the first time at Rome, and when the people beheld the axes carried before him,* they were greatly afraid and were all the readier to obey his orders, for there was no help from a second person as there was with the consuls nor did the right of appeal exist: nothing mattered save concern for obedience. The naming of the dictator at Rome filled the Sabines with fear as well, especially since they believed it had come about because of them. So they sent envoys to sue for peace, who begged the dictator and senate to pardon the young men for their error. They were told that forgiveness was possible in the case of the young men, but not their elders, who from the seeds of one war sowed another. Nevertheless, peace was in the process of negotiation and would have succeeded could the Sabines have brought themselves to pay the costs Rome had incurred in the war—for this was one of the demands. War was declared; a tacit suspension of hostilities then followed in this otherwise quiet year.

19. The next consuls were Servius Sulpicius and Manius Tullius. Nothing noteworthy occurred. Then came Titus Aebutius and Gaius Vetusius. In their consulship Fidenae was besieged, Crustumeria captured; Praeneste defected from the Latins to Rome, nor was war with the Latins, which had been smouldering for some years, longer delayed. Aulus Postumius as dictator and Titus Aebutius as master of the horse set out with a great force of infantry and cavalry and met the enemy at Lake Regillus in the territory of Tusculum; when it was learned that the Tarquins were present in the enemy army, anger prompted the Romans to join battle at once. The ensuing fight was consequently a good deal fiercer and harder fought than

earlier encounters, for the leaders were not content to stay behind
the lines as strategists but entered the fray and fought in person; in
fact, scarcely any of the nobles on either side left the battlefield
unwounded save for the Roman dictator. Tarquinius Superbus, somewhat slowed by age and in failing strength, let his horse go full tilt
at Postumius as he was exhorting and deploying his men in the front
line. A missile pierced Superbus' side; his men rushed to his aid and
dragged him to safety. And on the other wing Aebutius, master of
the horse, made a rush at Octavius Mamilius, who saw him coming
and drove straight at him to meet the attack. The clash was as
horrific, as the two men, lances lowered, bore down on one another.
Aebutius' arm was pierced through, Mamilius struck in the chest.
The Latins opened their ranks and pulled him to the rear, while
Aebutius, no longer able to hold a spear because of his crippled arm,
retired from the field. Mamilius continued to stir up the fight in
spite of his wound and, when he saw his men in retreat, called up
the cohort of Roman exiles led by the son of Lucius Tarquinius.
Anger at the loss of his patrimony and homeland caused Tarquin to
battle all the harder, and for a while he succeeded in renewing the
struggle.

20. While the Romans were in retreat in this part of the field,
Marcus Valerius, brother of Publicola, caught sight of the young
Tarquin aggressively parading about in the front line of the exiles;
this spectacle fired his own aggression, for he hoped that, just as it
had been the glory of the Valerian house to expell the Tarquins, so
it would be theirs to finish them off. So he spurred on his horse and,
levelling his spear, attacked. Tarquin avoided the charge by withdrawing into his own ranks, but as Valerius recklessly stampeded
into the exiles' battleline someone blind-sided him with a spear
thrust; his horse continued hurtling forward with its wounded rider,
who tumbled to the ground in the throes of death, his arms piling
upon his body as he fell. When the dictator Postumius beheld the
death of this great fighter and the retreat of his stricken forces
before the swift and ferocious charge of the exiles, he signalled the
select cohort that was his own bodyguard to treat any soldiers who
took flight as an enemy. Threatened from two sides at once, the
Romans stayed their flight and turned against the enemy. The battle
was renewed. It was then that the dictator's cohort entered the fray
for the first time; fresh in body and spirit, it assaulted the tiring

exiles and cut them down. This triggered a second fight among the nobles. When Mamilius, the Latin general, saw the exile cohort nearly surrounded by the Roman dictator, he quickly brought forward a few maniples from the rear to the front line. But a captain, Titus Herminius, caught sight of these men as they were forming up and he recognized Mamilius among them by his distinctive uniform and armour. Herminius attacked the Latin general, but with so much greater fury than the master of the horse had exhibited a little before that a single thrust into his side was enough to dispatch Mamilius; yet Herminius was himself struck by a spear as he despoiled his enemy's body. Carried back to camp as the victor, he expired as the first efforts were being made to save his life. The dictator then rushed to where the cavalry was stationed, bidding it to dismount and take up the fight in the place of the exhausted infantry. Obeying his command, they leaped from their horses, rushed to the fore and threw up their shields to protect the soldiers on the front line. The infantry instantly recovered its spirit when it saw these noble youths sharing in their danger and ready to fight as the rank and file did. This assault was what finally broke the Latin battleline and made it give way. The horses were then brought forward so that the cavalry could remount and pursue the enemy; the infantry followed. At this point the dictator, calling on both divine and human aid, is said to have vowed a temple to Castor and to have announced a reward for the first and second soldiers to enter the enemy camp. So great was the enthusiasm that they defeated the enemy and captured his camp in the same forward thrust. Thus was fought the battle at Lake Regillus. Dictator and master of the horse returned in triumph to the city.

21. For three years there was neither an assured peace nor open war. The consuls were Quintus Cloelius and Titus Larcius, then Aulus Sempronius and Marcus Minucius. Under the latter the temple to Saturn was dedicated and the Saturnalia instituted as a holiday.* Then Aulus Postumius and Titus Verginius were elected consuls. I find that certain sources do not date the battle of Lake Regillus until this year, when Aulus Postumius, because his colleague's loyalty was suspect, abdicated the consulship, at which point a dictator was named. There are so many chronological uncertainties in the history of these years, with different authorities giving different lists of magistrates, that the great antiquity of the events and of the

sources does not permit one to make out which consuls followed which or what events happened in what year.

Appius Claudius and Publius Servilius were elected the next consuls. This year was noteworthy for the news of Tarquin's death. He died at Cumae, where he had taken refuge with the tyrant Aristodemus after the defeat of the Latin coalition. The senators were cheered by this news, as were the plebs. But the senators' joy proved excessive, for the leading men began to mistreat the plebs, whose interests up to that time they had wholeheartedly served. In that same year the colony of Signia that King Tarquin had founded was refounded by the addition of new colonists. At Rome twenty-one tribes were created. The temple of Mercury was dedicated on 15 May.

22. There had been neither peace nor war with the Volscian people during the Latin war, for the Volsci had levied support troops which they were intending to send to the Latins had not the Roman dictator moved quickly. But move quickly he did, so as not to have to confront both Latin and Volscians in a single fight. Hence anger prompted the consuls to lead the legions into Volscian territory. This unexpected move took them by surprise, for they had not expected retaliation for what they had planned to do; without thinking of resistance they gave as hostages three hundred children of the leading men from Cora and Pometia. Thus the legions were led back without a fight.

And yet not much later, when the Volsci no longer feared retaliation, their old inclination returned. Again they clandestinely prepared to go to war after taking the Hernici as their allies in arms. They also sent envoys everywhere to rouse the Latins to action; yet the thought of the recent defeat they had suffered at Lake Regillus filled the Latins with such anger and hatred for anyone who would urge them to take up arms that they actually laid hands on the envoys, whom they arrested and brought to Rome. There they were handed over to the consuls: evidence that the Volsci and Hernici were preparing for war against the Romans. When the matter was brought before the senate, its members were so grateful that they sent back to the Latins six thousand captives; as for a treaty (which the senate had hitherto refused to negotiate as a virtually permanent policy) they instructed the incoming magistrates to take up the matter. The Latins were then indeed overjoyed at this turn of events, and the advocates of peace were much honoured. They sent a gold

crown to Jupiter on the Capitol. Along with the envoys and the gift
came a great throng of the captives who had been sent back to their
own cities. Each man hastened to the home of the family in which
he once had been in a position of a slave and gave thanks for having
been treated as a free man and attended to in his misfortune; all
entered into formal ties of hospitality with their Roman hosts. Never
before was the Latin nation more closely joined to the Roman state
by public and private ties.

23. Yet war with the Volsci was threatening, while on the home
front the state was at odds with itself, rent by hostility between
senators and plebeians, the chief cause of which were those who had
fallen into debt.* They complained that while fighting in the field
for liberty and empire they were taken prisoner and maltreated at
home by their fellow citizens: the liberty of the plebs was better
served in war than in peace and among the enemy than among
citizens.

While this animosity was increasing of its own accord the conspicuous misfortune of a single individual fanned it into open flame.
An elderly man burst into the forum displaying the marks of all his
misfortunes. His clothing was filthy, his person more repellent—
wasted, pale, and haggard; in addition, his bushy beard and hair
gave him the appearance of a wild man. Still, he was recognized
even in this appalling state by some of the bystanders, who said he
had been a company commander and, in the general pity for him,
credited him with other military honours. The man himself repeatedly pointed to the scars on his chest as proof of honourable service
in many a battle. The crowd pressed round him as if attending a
public meeting and asked how he had fallen into such a terrible
state. He answered that while he was serving in the war against the
Sabines his crops had been ravaged, his farmhouse burned down, all
possessions looted, his flocks driven off. Then, at this worst of
moments, a war tax was levied. So he borrowed money, and as the
interest piled up he first lost the land that had belonged to his father
and grandfather and then all his moveable goods, until the debt
spread like a cancer to his very person: his creditor led him not into
slavery but into a torture chamber and prison. He then showed
them his back, hideously scarified from recent whippings. A great
outcry arose when the people heard and saw these things. Nor was
the uproar confined to the forum, but spread through the city in all

directions. Debtors, both those in chains and those released from them, rushed out in public and implored their fellow citizens for protection. Everywhere men joined the disturbance, filling the streets as they shouted and streamed toward the forum. Those senators who chanced to be there found themselves in great danger as the crowd pressed around them, and it would even have laid hands on them had not the consuls, Publius Servilius and Appius Claudius, quickly intervened to quell the strife. But the mob turned upon them and pointed to its chains and other marks of degradation. These, they said, were the rewards they had earned, each man making a bitter reproach of his military service on different campaigns. Their demand that the senate be summoned was couched more as a threat than an entreaty. They ranged themselves round the senate-house in order to oversee and regulate the deliberations of state.

The few senators who chanced to be present were convened by the consuls. Fear kept the rest not just from the senate-house but from the forum; yet no business could be conducted because of the lack of a quorum. This completely convinced the mob that it was being mocked and strung along: the missing senators were absent not out of chance or fear but to frustrate their demands, while the consuls themselves were playing a double game; no doubt they all were out to make a joke of their misery. The situation had nearly reached the point where not even the consuls' power and position could check the hostility, when the senators, uncertain whether they would incur more danger by delaying or coming, finally convened. But even with a full house no agreement could be reached among its members or between the consuls. Appius, a man of vehement character, thought the situation should be handled by consular authority: when one or two had been arrested, the rest would lie low. Servilius, more inclined to a conciliatory solution, thought it safer and easier to assuage such angry feelings than to crush them.

24. In the midst of these concerns another and greater fear arose. Latin horsemen came on the double with the alarming news that the Volsci were advancing in hostile array to attack the city. The reactions of the senators and plebeians to this report were very different: the hostility between them was such that there were now two communities instead of one. The plebs were exultant: the gods, they said, were at hand to avenge senatorial arrogance. They exhorted one another not to enlist: better that all should perish than they alone; let the senators don their armour and fight the fight so that the same group would face the peril and reap the rewards! The senate, on the other hand, was dispirited, fearful of both citizen and enemy; it entreated the consul Servilius, whose temperament was more in tune with popular feeling, to extricate the republic from the great fears that beset it. The consul accordingly adjourned the senate and called a public meeting. In it he argued that the senators had the welfare of the plebs at heart, but that anxiety about the republic as a whole took precedence over concern for them—admittedly the largest part of the state, but still only a part; with the enemy virtually at the gates nothing was more important than going to war, and, even if the danger abated, it was not honourable for the plebs to refuse to serve under arms unless they first received some recompense, just as it was unseemly for the senate to consult about the distressed circumstances of their fellow citizens out of fear rather than at a later time of their own free will. He convinced the assembly of his sincerity by the edict he issued: no one might keep a Roman citizen in chains or confine him so that he could not join the military levy held by the consuls; nor might anyone take possession of or sell the property of a soldier while he was on active duty, nor interfere with his children or grandchildren. When this edict had been issued, the debtors present enlisted on the spot, while those whom their creditors no longer had the right to confine burst forth from their places of detention and rushed to the forum to take the oath. Their numbers were very great, and no others surpassed them in courage and service during the Volscian war.

The consul led out his forces against the enemy and pitched camp a short distance away. 25. On the next night the Volsci, counting on the likelihood of desertion or betrayal under the cover of darkness on the part of the disaffected Romans, attacked the camp. The sentries perceived this and the army was alerted; on command men rushed to arms; the Volscian attempt was thus frustrated. For the rest of the night both sides were quiet. At dawn on the next day the Volsci filled in the trenches and attacked the rampart. They tore up the palisades everywhere while the consul, despite the unanimous clamour (especially from the debtors) that he give the signal to attack, delayed for a bit to test the mettle of the soldiers; when he was satisfied that their ardour was at its pitch, he at last gave the signal to break out; the soldiery was let loose, clamouring to get at the enemy. The first clash was enough to rout the enemy on the spot. Those fleeing were cut down from the rear to the extent that the infantry could pursue them; the cavalry then drove them in their panic all the way to their camp. Soon the camp itself was surrounded by the legions and, when fear drove the Volsci out, it was captured and plundered. On the next day the legions were led to Suessa Pometia, where the enemy had fled; the town was captured within a few days, and on its capture was given over to plunder, from which the poorer soldiers realized a bit of money. The consul led his victorious army back to Rome to his own great glory. As he was departing for Rome envoys of the Volsci of Ecetra approached him, fearful for their own situation after the capture of Pometia. Peace was granted them by a decree of the senate and territory taken away.

26. Immediately thereafter the Sabines too gave the Romans a scare, although it was really more of a fracas than a war. At nightfall the city learned that a Sabine army had gone on a plundering raid as far as the Anio River, and that there had been widespread looting and burning of the farmsteads. Aulus Postumius, who had been dictator in the Latin war, was sent at once with the entire cavalry; the consul Servilius followed with a select detachment of foot soldiers. The cavalry cut off a great many as they were dispersed in pillaging, nor did the Sabine troops put up resistance when the infantry approached: tired from their march and from looting throughout the night—and stuffed with food and wine they had found in the farmhouses—most scarcely had the strength to run away.

The Sabine war was finished in the same night the Romans heard of it, but on the next day, just when there was hope that peace had been secured on all fronts, envoys of the Aurunci came to the senate saying that there would be war unless the Romans evacuated Volscian territory. An army of the Aurunci had set out from home together with the envoys, and when it was reported that it had been sighted not far from Aricia, the Romans were thrown into such disarray that it was impossible to consult the senate in regular fashion or to give a peaceful response to those bearing arms while they themselves were taking up arms. The Romans headed for Aricia to make an offensive strike; not far from the city they clashed with the Aurunci. A single engagement ended the war.

27. After the defeat of the Aurunci, the soldiers in the rank and

file, victors in many a battle within a few days, looked to the consul to fulfil his promises and the senate to keep its word. But Appius, from inborn arrogance and aiming to frustrate his colleague's pledge, began to render the harshest possible decisions in trials concerning debt. The result was that those who had been bondsmen before were handed over to their creditors and others were bound over for the first time. All soldiers to whom this happened sought the help of his colleague. There were a great many of them, and they vociferously rehearsed Servilius' promises, making their service in the war and the wounds they had received matters of reproach. They demanded that he either bring the matter before the senate or as consul come to the aid of his fellow citizens, as general to the aid of the soldiers who had served under him. The consul felt the force of these appeals, but the situation forced him to equivocate; not only did his colleague vehemently support the other side, but the faction of nobles did as well. And so by steering a middle course he neither escaped the hatred of the plebs nor won the senators' goodwill. The latter thought the consul weak and aiming to win popularity; the plebs, untrustworthy; in a short time the hatred they felt for him was as great as they felt for Appius.

Rivalry arose between the consuls as to which would dedicate the temple of Mercury. The senate referred the choice to the people, stipulating that the man to whom the people voted the dedication should also oversee the grain supply, establish a guild of merchants, and perform the dedication in the presence of the pontiff.* The people then voted the dedication to Marcus Laetorius, a centurion of the first rank; this was plainly meant not so much as an honour for a man whose position in the state was not commensurate with so exalted a duty as to show contempt for the consuls. This infuriated Appius and the senators, whatever their feelings had been before. The self-confidence of the plebs, on the other hand, increased, and they ventured on a course of action far different from the one they had first essayed. For, despairing of help from the consuls and senate, whenever they beheld a debtor being hailed into court, they would rush to his aid from every quarter. The consul's decision could not be heard above the clamorous din, nor when he did issue it would any obey. The situation was becoming violent: instead of the debtors, the creditors were now the ones fearful and their persons in danger, since in the presence of the consul each was roughed

up by the assembled mob. On top of all this there was growing fear
of war with the Sabines. No one reported when the recruitment levy
was announced. Appius was enraged. He accused his colleague of
self-promotion: by saying nothing he was courting popular favour
and betraying the interests of his country; and in addition to refusing to hear cases involving debt he was not even conducting the levy
that the senate had decreed. Still, he said, the state had not been
completely left in the lurch and consular authority wholly flouted:
single-handed he would himself step forth as the champion of the
majesty that was his and the senate's by right. While the mob that
assembled daily crowded about him, fired up and unruly, he ordered
the arrest of one of the most conspicuous ringleaders. As the culprit
was being dragged off by the lictors, the man appealed;* Appius
would have refused to yield to the appeal (for he had no doubt what
the verdict of the people would be) had not his obstinacy been
overcome—but with difficulty—more by advice and the influence of
the leading men than the clamour of the crowd; Appius' proud
spirit was more than prepared to endure the abuse from the people.
From this point on the crisis deepened day by day not only through
open protests but, what was far more ominous, by secret and seditious plotting. At last the term of the consuls whom the plebs hated
expired, Servilius leaving office with the approval of neither side,
Appius with that of the senators.

28. Aulus Verginius and Titus Vetusius next entered the consulship. At this juncture, the plebs, uncertain what sort of consuls they
would turn out to be, began to gather nightly, some on the Esquiline,
others on the Aventine, because they did not wish to be stampeded
in the open forum into making hasty decisions and conduct all their
business in impetuous and haphazard fashion. The consuls, regarding this behaviour as pernicious (as it was), referred the matter to
the senate. But when they did so, usual protocol was thrown to the
winds: the senators erupted into shouts of outrage that the consuls
would shift upon them the odium for dealing with a matter that they
were obliged to handle by virtue of their consular power; real magistrates would assuredly countenance no assembly at Rome save
one—and that out in the open; as things were, the state had been
broken up into myriad senates and assemblies; a real man, by god—
someone a lot better than a consul—Appius Claudius, for instance—
would have broken up those meetings in a trice!

The chastened consuls then asked what the senate wished them to do, for they would not act with any less decisiveness or energy than the senate wanted. The senators decreed that the consuls conduct as stringent a levy as possible: the plebs had become a shiftless and unruly lot. When the senate broke up the consuls mounted the tribunal and summoned the young men by name. When none responded to his name, the multitude came crowding around as if at a meeting and declared that the plebs could be duped no longer; not a single soldier would step forth unless the state made good on a solemn pledge: it must guarantee every single individual his freedom before issuing him his weapons, for men would fight for country and countrymen, not for people who owned them. The consuls were aware of the senate's instructions, but of those who had spoken so vehemently within the walls of the senate-house, not one was present to shoulder a part of the odium; and there was good reason, for a terrible fight with the plebs was in the offing. Therefore, before resorting to desperate measures, they decided to consult the senate a second time. When it met the youngest members virtually milled about the consuls' seats, bidding them resign their office and lay down their power, for the exercise of which they had no stomach.

29. Now that they had made a genuine effort both to recruit the plebs and to satisfy the demands of the senate, the consuls in the end made this statement: 'Because we do not want you to complain that you were not given advance warning, conscript fathers, we tell you this: a massive revolt is upon us. We ask that those persons among you who have been quick to rebuke us for inaction stand by to support us as we conduct the levy, the performance of which we guarantee will satisfy the severest critic present.' They returned to the tribunal, where they intentionally called up one of the men standing before them by name. When the man stood silent and a small group clustered about to prevent him from possibly being manhandled, the consuls sent a lictor to him. The lictor was shouldered aside, and the senators who were standing by the consuls exclaimed that this was the last straw. Leaping down from the tribunal, they rushed to the lictor's defence. But when the crowd turned from the lictor (who had only been prevented from seizing the man) and vented its fury upon the senators, the consul intervened to quiet the fracas—one, however, in which no stone or weapon had been used and in which angry shouts were more in evidence than physical contact.

The senate was frantically called into session; the meeting itself proved more frantic. Those senators who had been jostled about demanded that a special judicial inquiry be instituted, the most excitable ones not waiting to make a formal motion but breaking into clamorous outcries. Passions cooled after the consuls rebuked them by saying there was no more sanity in the senate-house than in the forum. Normal deliberations then began. There were three proposals. Publius Verginius was against extending debt relief; he proposed that it be restricted to those who, in accordance with the pledge given them by the consul Publius Servilius, had served in the Volscian, Auruncan, and Sabine wars. Titus Larcius countered by saying that this was not the time to recompense only those who had seen service; the plebeians as a whole were mired in debt, and no stable solution was possible unless it applied to everyone; if there were different rules for different people, the discord would be fanned into greater flame, not quenched. Appius Claudius, hard-hearted by nature and goaded by the hatred of the plebs on the one side and the praises of the senators on the other, said that these mob scenes were sparked not by miserable living conditions but by unruliness, and that the plebs were revelling in hooliganism rather than smarting from maltreatment. The root of this evil was to be found in the right of appeal, as one would expect; in fact, the consuls could only threaten, not enforce, when a miscreant had the right of appeal to his fellow miscreants. 'Come now,' he said, 'let us appoint a dictator, from whose decisions there is no appeal; then this madness that has fanned everything into flames will die down. I very much doubt that a man will interfere with a lictor when he knows that the right to flog and kill him rests with that very individual whose power he has flouted.'

30. Many thought Appius' motion outrageous and cruel, as indeed it was, but those of Verginius and Larcius unhealthy precedents for the future. Larcius' proposal was viewed as leading to the complete undermining of credit; Verginius' motion seemed to strike a reasonable balance between extremes, but because there existed a private interest group concerned for its own aggrandizement—which always has and always will eclipse concern for the general good—Appius won the day. The man even came close to being appointed

dictator himself, which absolutely would have alienated the plebs at a most critical moment, when the Volsci, Aequi, and Sabines all happened to be in arms at the same time. But the consuls and older senators wanted the office with its formidable power to go to someone of humane temperament: so they named Manius Valerius, son of Volesus, as dictator. The plebs knew perfectly well that the appointment of the dictator was meant to thwart them; but because the dictator's brother had been the one who had carried the law on appeal, they were not afraid of harsh or untoward treatment from a member of that family. An edict of the dictator gave them further encouragement, since it was nearly identical to the one issued by the consul Servilius. Believing they would do better to put their trust in the man and his power, they gave up their resistance and enlisted. This was Rome's largest army to date, a total of ten legions, the consuls each commanding three, the dictator four.

War could no longer be put off. The Aequi invaded Latin territory. Spokesmen of the Latins asked the senate either to send help or to allow the Latins themselves to take up arms in defence of their borders. It seemed safer to have unarmed Latins defended by Romans than to permit them to rearm. The consul Vetusius was dispatched. He put an end to the plundering raids, whereupon the Aequi retired from the plains and, relying more on situation than weapons, protected themselves by settling high in the mountains. The other consul, setting out against the Volsci, wanted to come to a quick decision also. Ravaging their fields was what helped most to induce the enemy to bring its camp nearer and to fight it out in a pitched battle. In the area between the camps each side lined up before its rampart, ready to do battle. The Volscian force was somewhat larger, which caused it to enter the fray in an uncoordinated and careless manner. The Roman consul did not move his battleline forward and forbade the battle-cry to be raised in response; instead, he ordered his men to stand with their pikes grounded until the enemy were at close quarters, and then with all their might to attack in a body, swords in hand. The energy of the Volsci had been sapped from their running and shouting as they bore down upon the Romans, who they fancied were standing still because they were paralysed with fear; but when they ran into resistance and saw the swords flashing in their faces, they were thrown into confusion and turned tail, just as if they had fallen into an ambush. Nor could they even summon the energy to flee, having gone into battle on the run. The Romans, on the other hand, were still fresh, for they had been standing quietly until the fighting should commence. They easily caught up with the exhausted Volsci, took their camp by assault, and, after driving the enemy from it, pursued them to Velitrae, where victors and vanquished burst into the city in a single column. There more blood was spilled through the indiscriminate slaughter of its many inhabitants than on the battlefield itself. Pardon was granted to those few who threw down their weapons in unconditional surrender.

31. While these things were going on in Volscian territory the dictator routed and put to flight the Sabines, the most formidable of Rome's opponents. He then stripped them of their camp. By sending in the cavalry he had thrown the centre line into confusion, where, as they extended their wings, efforts to strengthen the battleline by deepening it had proved ineffective.* The infantry then penetrated their disordered ranks. In the same assault their camp was captured, the war finished. No other battle was more famous in those days after the battle at Lake Regillus. The dictator entered the city in triumph. In addition to the customary honours a permanent seat in the circus was assigned to him and his descendants from which to watch the games; a curule chair was set up on the spot. After the defeat of the Volsci the territory of Velitrae was taken from them; colonists were sent to Velitrae from Rome and a colony established.

A battle was fought with the Aequi a bit later, but against the will of the consul, since he was forced to move over unfavourable terrain to engage the enemy. His soldiers charged that the campaign was being drawn out so that the dictator could resign his office before they themselves returned to the city and his promises might thereby go unfulfilled, just as had happened before in the case of the consul. So they compelled him to move his forces in haphazard fashion up the mountains before them. The unenterprising enemy allowed this unwise manœuvre to succeed: stunned by the audacity of the Romans, they abandoned their camp, which was situated on a most defensible site, and, without even discharging their javelins, plunged down the slopes to the valleys on the other side. The Romans enjoyed much booty and a bloodless victory.

War had been thus successfully waged on three fronts, but at home senators and plebs were still anxious about the outcome of the internal crisis because the creditors had, in the meantime, used considerable private pressure and manœuvrings to frustrate the wishes of not only the plebs but even of the dictator himself. For after the return of the consul Vetusius, Valerius first placed the question before the senate that most concerned the victorious Roman populace: what the senate's pleasure was concerning the debtors. When the senate would not debate the issue, he said: 'When I champion the cause of harmony, you do not like it. Soon, by heaven, you will wish the Roman plebs had men such as myself as their advocates. As for me, I shall no longer frustrate the will of my fellow citizens nor the obligations of my office. Internal discord and external wars created a need for a dictator: peace has been won abroad but is crippled at home. I shall confront the impending sedition as a private citizen rather than as dictator.' He then left the senate-house and resigned the dictatorship. The reason was clear to the plebs: he had quit his magistracy out of indignation at their plight. And so, just as if he had fulfilled his promise—since its non-fulfilment was not his fault— they escorted him home with enthusiasm and praises.

32. The senators were then filled with apprehension lest disbandment of the army should lead to the renewal of secret gatherings and conspiracies. Hence they took the position that the soldiers were still bound by the oath they had taken to obey the consuls, although the levy itself had been conducted by the dictator. On the pretext that war had been renewed by the Aequi they ordered the legions to be marched out of the city. This proved the catalyst for secession. It is said that at first there was debate about releasing themselves from the oath by murdering the consuls; but on being told that they could not be absolved from their oath by the commission of a crime, under the prompting of a certain Sicinius, but without the consuls' permission, they seceded to the Sacred Mount. The Mount is situated on the far side of the Anio, three miles from the city (this account is more common than the version of Piso that they seceded to the Aventine). They fortified their camp with a rampart and ditch without the need of a leader and remained quiet, having taken nothing with them except subsistence items. For some days they kept to themselves, neither suffering nor provoking hostilities. The city was in great apprehension; all business came to a halt from mutual dread: the plebs left behind feared violence from the senators, while the

senators, wary of the plebs who remained, could not decide whether they preferred them to have stayed or to have departed. Besides, how long would the multitude that had seceded remain quiet? And what would happen if some outside military emergency arose in the meantime? They became convinced that no solution existed except in concord among all citizens: the plebs must be reconciled to their country at all costs.

So they decided to send to the plebs Menenius Agrippa as their spokesman, a forceful speaker whom the plebs liked, for he had come from their ranks. On being admitted to the camp his speech is said to have consisted simply of the following parable, couched in old-fashioned and homely language. Once upon a time man's bodily parts did not work as one as they do now, but each limb went his own way and had his own voice. The other parts unhappily complained that the belly received the benefit of their care, help, and hard work and that it stayed contentedly in the middle doing nothing but enjoying the good things they gave it. They then concocted a plan: the hands would not carry food to the mouth, the mouth would not accept it if given, the teeth would not chew it. They aimed to starve the belly into submission, but their anger brought the limbs and the whole body close to wasting away completely. Then it dawned on them that the belly's job was important: it received as much nourishment as it gave back, carrying everywhere that by which we live and breathe—our blood, which, enriched by the food we digest, spreads through the blood vessels to all parts of the body. By comparing the internal revolt of the body with the anger of the plebs against the senators, Agrippa brought the plebs round to his way of thinking.

33. Negotiations then began about restoring concord, and agreement was reached on the following terms: the plebs should have their own sacrosanct magistrates,* who would have the right to help plebeians against actions by the consuls, and no senator would be allowed to hold this magistracy. Two tribunes of the plebs were accordingly elected, Gaius Licinius and Lucius Albinius; they in turn elected three colleagues, among whom was Sicinius, who had urged the secession. There is less agreement as to who the other two were. Some say only two tribunes of the plebs were elected on the Sacred Mount, and that it was there the law on sacrosanctity was passed.

During the secession of the plebs Spurius Cassius and Postumus Cominius entered the consulship. Under these consuls a treaty was struck with the Latin peoples. One consul stayed to preside over the formalities, the other was sent to fight the Volscian war, in which he routed and put to flight the Volsci of Antium. After driving them into the town of Longula he captured it. From there he straightway took Polusca, also a town of the Volsci. He then attacked Corioli in great force.

There was at that time in the camp a prominent young noble named Gnaeus Marcius, an intrepid and articulate young man, whose later cognomen was Coriolanus. During the siege of Corioli, when the Romans were intent on keeping the townspeople penned within and had no fear of an attack from outside, Volscian legions from Antium suddenly descended upon them; at the same time the enemy burst forth from the town. Marcius happened to be on guard duty at that moment. With a band of picked men he not only beat back the assault of the inhabitants but boldly burst through the open gate into the town; cutting down those in the surrounding area who opposed him, he grabbed a firebrand that chanced to hand and threw it into the buildings that overtopped the walls. The townspeople began to shout, the women and children to scream, who were naturally terrified; this lifted the Romans' spirit and confounded the Volsci, since the city they had come to help was now in enemy hands. So the Volsci of Antium were routed and the town of Corioli captured. Marcius' own glory so eclipsed that of the consul that, had there not been an engraved bronze column stating that Spurius Cassius struck the treaty with the Latins by himself because his colleague was absent, the fact that Postumus Cominius was the one who fought the Volsci would not have been remembered at all.

In this same year Menenius Agrippa died, who throughout his life had been pleasing to senators and plebeians alike, and even more pleasing to the plebs after their secession. This man, who had been the advocate and mediator of concord among the citizens, who had been the envoy whom the senators chose to be their spokesman before the plebeians, and who had restored the plebs to the community, did not leave enough money to pay for his funeral. The plebeians buried him, each contributing a copper coin apiece.

34. The consuls elected next were Titus Geganius and Publius Minucius. In this year of respite from wars and alleviation of dis-

cord at home, another much more serious calamity struck the community: scarcity of grain caused by the fields having been left fallow during the secession of the plebs led to famine of the kind that those under siege are accustomed to suffer. It doubtless would have ended in starvation for the slaves and plebeians had not the consuls seen to it that emissaries were sent to all quarters, not only to buy grain from communities along the Etruscan shore north of Ostia and from the coastal areas beyond Volscian territory to the south all the way to Cumae, but to ask for contributions in Sicily as well. From so far away had the enmity of Rome's neighbours forced her to seek help. But after buying grain at Cumae, the tyrant who ruled the place, Aristodemus, appropriated the ships in payment for the property of the Tarquins, to which he was the heir. The Volsci and people of the Pomptine district refused even to sell; in fact, those sent to buy the grain were in danger of their lives. From the Etruscans grain was floated down the Tiber; it was this that fed the plebs. In these straitened circumstances Rome would have been faced with an inopportune war had not a great plague struck the Volsci as they were in the midst of arming themselves. Their spirits were so stricken by the disaster that even after it abated they continued in the grip of fear; this enabled the Romans to increase the number of colonists at Velitrae and to plant a new colony at Norba, a stronghold in the mountains of the Pomptine district.

In the consulship of Marcus Minucius and Aulus Sempronius a large amount of grain arrived from Sicily, and there was debate in the senate at what price it should be given to the plebs. Many thought the time was right for cowing them and recovering the rights that had been extorted from the senate by secession and violence. Prominent among them was Marcius Coriolanus, an enemy of the tribunes' power, who addressed his colleagues as follows: 'If they want the grain supply they used to enjoy, then let them restore to us senators the rights we used to enjoy. Why do I see plebeian magistrates and Sicinius strutting about, when I have bent my neck beneath the yoke of submission, like a man ransomed from brigands? Should I submit to these outrages any longer than I have to? If I would not put up with Tarquin as king, why put up with Sicinius? I would like to see him secede now, and summon the plebs along as well. Let them try to seize the grain from our fields as they did three years ago. Let them know first-hand the high cost of food which their own madness has brought about. I venture to say that, overmastered by the calamity, they will sooner till the fields themselves than prevent their cultivation by armed secession.' (I believe the senators were in a position to annul the tribunes' power and all the rights that had been unwillingly extorted from them by setting harsh terms for selling grain at a reasonable cost; whether they ought to have done this is hard to say.)

35. This proposal seemed to the senate unduly severe. The plebs were so angry that they came close to taking up arms: they were, they said, already being starved out like a foreign enemy, deprived of food and the necessities of life; grain that had been imported, that fortune had unexpectedly given them as their sole sustenance, would be snatched from their mouths unless the tribunes were tied up and handed over to Gnaeus Marcius and he were allowed to vent his savagery on the hides of the plebeians, a sadist newly fledged, who bade them die or be slaves. He would have been attacked as he left the senate-house had not the tribunes at the last moment brought an indictment against him. Thereupon plebeian anger subsided, for they realized that *they* would be the judges, *they* would decide whether their enemy would live or die.* At first Marcius listened to the threats of the tribunes with contempt: they were empowered to help the oppressed, he said, not to punish people; what is more, they were tribunes of the plebs, not of the senators. But the plebs' hostility was such that the senators were forced to make one of their number the scapegoat. Yet they did not do so without putting up a fight both individually and as a body, despite the unpopularity it engendered. They first attempted to quash proceedings by having their clients* use scare tactics on individual plebeians to deter them from gathering together or holding meetings. They then stepped forth in public in a body (you would have thought they were all on trial) and with prayerful entreaties begged the plebs, if they were unwilling to acquit an innocent man, to concede to them as a gift this single citizen, this single senator, even though they might think him guilty. But when the defendant himself did not appear for trial, the anger of the plebs hardened further. Found guilty *in absentia*, Coriolanus went into exile among the Volsci, threatening his homeland and even then beginning to regard it as his enemy.

The Volsci welcomed him kindly when he arrived and, as they noticed his anger against his countrymen growing and his grievances and threats mounting, their kindnesses increased proportionately. He was lodged in the home of Attius Tullius, who was the undisputed leader of the Volscian people and an inveterate enemy of Rome. And as both old and fresh hatreds exacerbated one another, the two began to make plans to wage war against Rome. Yet they knew it would not be easy to bring the Volscian people around to their way of thinking, who had so often been worsted when they had gone to war: their spirits had been crushed by the loss of so many young men in these frequent wars and in the recent pestilence. The two men would have to proceed in a roundabout way to revive by some fresh provocation feelings of hostility to which men had become largely insensible.

36. A repetition of the Great Games happened to be in preparation at Rome.* The cause of the repetition was as follows. On the morning of the games a certain householder tied a slave's hands to a wooden fork placed about his neck, whipped him, and before the games got under way paraded him about in the middle of the circus. When the games began, this incident seemed to have no connection with the religious nature of the occasion. Not much later Titus Latinius, a plebeian, had a dream: Jupiter appeared to him and said 'the lead dancer'* at the games displeased him; unless the games were repeated on a lavish scale, the city would be in danger; he should go and report this to the consuls. Although Latinius was a man of religious scruples, shyness in approaching such lofty personages proved greater than his religious fear, for he did not want to become a laughing-stock in men's eyes. His hesitation cost him dearly, for within a few days he lost his son. Lest there be any doubt as to the cause of this sudden disaster, the same figure appeared to the anguished man as he slept, asking whether he had paid a sufficiently high price for disregarding the will of the gods; a greater disaster was imminent unless he went quickly and told the consuls. He now came closer to realizing what was at issue. Yet still he hesitated and procrastinated and, as he did so, collapsed from a terrible malady. This punishment from the gods finally brought him to his senses. Enfeebled by past and present misfortunes, he called a family council and told them of what he had seen and heard—of Jupiter appearing so often to him in a dream and of the god's angry threats being translated into his own calamities. Everyone present was in instant agreement. Carried in a litter to the forum where the

consuls were, he was conveyed on their orders into the senate-house; when to everyone's astonishment he told those assembled what had happened, lo and behold, another miracle occurred, for tradition has it that he who had been brought into the building a complete cripple walked home on his own power, having discharged the duty he owed the god.

37. The senate decreed that the games be celebrated as splendidly as possible. A great many Volsci under the leadership of Attius Tullius came to attend them. Before they began, Tullius, following the plan he had hatched with Marcius at home, approached the consuls, saying there were matters of state he wished to discuss with them in private. When all but the consuls had been ushered out, he spoke as follows: 'I am loath to say anything discreditable about my countrymen. I have come here not because they have as yet done any wrong but rather to prevent them from possibly doing so in the future. The nature of my countrymen is more mercurial than I would wish. We know this from our many defeats; we have escaped harm so far not because we deserve it but because of your forbearance. A great many Volsci are now here in Rome; the games are about to begin; the city will be intent on the spectacle. I remember what the Sabine youth did in your city on the same occasion; I shudder at the thought of some rash or impetuous act occurring now. I believed, consuls, that I should tell you my thoughts before-hand, both for our sakes and for yours. As for myself, I intend to go home at once to avoid being implicated in anything that might be said or done were I to remain.' With these words he left them. The consuls reported the conversation to the senators, the content of which was vague enough but the source known to them all. As is usual in such matters, the status of the speaker had greater influence than what he said in prompting them to take precautions, needed or not. The senate decreed that the Volsci should leave the city.

Heralds were sent to order them to depart before nightfall. At first they were filled with fear as they scattered to fetch their belongings from their lodgings. Later, *en route* home, indignation supervened: like godless outlaws they were being expelled from the games on a day that was sacred, a day on which men and gods meet in assembly, so to speak. 38. Since they were travelling almost in a body, Tullius went ahead to the headwaters of Ferentina to greet them severally as they arrived; he plied their leaders with protests

and expressions of outrage, who gave a ready ear to words that
answered to their own angry feelings. Tullius then conducted these
men—and they in turn their followers—to a level area below the
road, where he delivered a speech as if to an assembly, in which he
rehearsed the old injuries done by the Romans and the disasters
suffered by the Volsci. 'But forget past history. How did you feel
about the insulting treatment you received yesterday, when they
inaugurated the games by mocking us? Or didn't you realize that
they were actually celebrating a triumph over us? That as you left,
every citizen, every foreigner, every one of Rome's neighbours was
looking down upon you? That your wives and children were made
to parade in front of everyone's eyes? What do you think the people
thought when they heard the herald's announcement? or those who
saw us as we shuffled out? or those who encountered our humiliated
group as it travelled here? What else but that our presence at the
games was an unholy abomination, an obscene pollution deserving
of heaven's wrath! *That* is why we were driven from the assembly of
the pious, the throng of the pure in heart! What else can we conclude except that we owe our lives to the fact that we departed
quickly?—if you can call eviction departure! After all that has happened, do you not regard Rome as your enemy, where, had you
delayed a single day, every one of us would now be dead? They have
declared war against you—but, if you are real men, they will live to
regret it!'

The crowd had come to the gathering already in an angry mood,
and Tullius' words further provoked them. When they arrived home,
each so inflamed his own townsmen that the entire Volscian nation
rose up in revolt. 39. They all agreed that the generals for the war
should be Attius Tullius and Gnaeus Marcius, the Roman exile, in
whom they reposed somewhat greater hope than their own man.
Marcius more than fulfilled their hopes, making it clear that Rome's
leaders were superior to the armies they led. Advancing first upon
Circeii, he expelled the Roman colonists and handed over the liber-
ated city to the Volsci; then, crossing over to the Via Latina by a
side-road, he captured from the Romans the towns of Satricum,
Longula, Polusca, Corioli, and Mugilla. He next seized Lavinium,
then Corbio, Vetelia, Tolerium, Labici, and Pedum. Finally, he led
his forces from Pedum to Rome and, striking camp at the Cluilian
trench five miles from the city, he ravaged Roman territory, sending

overseers with the pillagers who were to see to it that the land of the patricians was spared, either because his anger was greater against the plebeians or to provoke conflict between senators and plebeians. And this indeed would have been the result, for by their accusations against the leading men the tribunes were goading the plebeians, who were already spoiling for a fight, still further; but fear of an outside enemy, the greatest stimulus to internal harmony, united them, however much they were at odds with one another. Their only point of disagreement was this: the senate and consuls put their hope in a military solution, the plebeians in any course save a military solution.

Spurius Nautius and Sextus Furius were now the consuls,* and as they were reviewing the troops and assigning guards to man the walls and other places where they had decided to station sentries and watchmen, a great multitude of those calling for peace at first caused them alarm by their mutinous clamour. In the end they were compelled to call the senate into session and to raise the question of sending envoys to Gnaeus Marcius. The senators accepted the proposal when they realized that the plebs' resolve was wavering. Spokesmen sent to Marcius to treat for peace brought back his harsh response: if their land was returned to the Volsci, negotiations about peace could begin; but if it was the Romans' intention to sit back and hold on to the land they had seized, he—mindful of the wrongs the Romans had done him and of the kindness shown him by the Volsci—would prove that exile had not broken his spirit but had toughened it. When the same men were sent a second time they were turned away from the camp's entrance. Priests, too, tradition says, went to the camp in the dress and role of suppliants, but had no more influence on him than had the envoys.

40. The married women then gathered in large numbers at the home of Veturia, mother of Coriolanus, and of Volumnia, his wife. I am uncertain whether this was public strategy or the result of the women's fear, but, whatever the motive, they prevailed on both Veturia, who was advanced in years, and Volumnia to take with them Marcius' two small sons and to go to the enemy camp in order that the women might with prayers and tears defend the city that the men were unable to defend by force of arms.

They arrived in the camp and Coriolanus was informed that a large group of women were present. At first female lamentations impressed him less than had the solemn embassy of state and the august religious dignitaries who had come before. But when one of his friends recognized Veturia standing with her daughter-in-law and grandsons in the crowd, marked out by her great distress, he said, 'Unless my eyes deceive me, your mother, wife, and children are present.' Coriolanus leaped from his seat, beside himself with shock. As his mother saw him hurrying to embrace her, anger won out over tears: 'Permit me, before I receive your embrace, to know whether I am greeting an enemy or a son, whether I am your mother or a prisoner of war in this place. Have a long life and hapless old age brought me to this: to see you in exile and an enemy of your country as well? How could you bring yourself to lay waste the land in which you were born and brought up? However bitter and disaffected you felt on your way here, why did your anger not fall away as you crossed your country's boundaries? When the city itself stood before your eyes why did you not think to yourself "Within these walls are hearth and home, my mother, wife and children"? As for myself, had I not given birth, Rome would not now be under siege; if I had not had a son, I would die a free woman in a free country. I cannot suffer anything more disgraceful to you or more grievous for me than what I am suffering now; but, wretched as I am, my wretchedness will soon be over. These young people here must look forward to an early death or a long life of slavery if you continue on as you have begun.'

Hugs from his wife and children and the wailing of the crowd of women as they lamented the fate of their country and themselves finally broke the man. Embracing his loved ones, he let them go and himself went back to the camp. The legions were then led out of Roman territory. One story is that the disgrace of what he had done killed him; others give different reasons. I find that Fabius, our oldest authority by far, says he lived until quite old; he affirms that in his declining years he used to say that for an old man exile becomes worse the longer he lives.

Back in Rome the men did not stint in their praise of the women, for people in those days were not jealous of another's glory. In addition, the temple of Fortuna Muliebris, or Women's Fortune, was built and dedicated as a memorial to what they had accomplished.

The Volsci then returned with the Aequi to Roman territory; but there came a time when the Aequi would no longer brook Attius Tullius as leader. A struggle ensued as to whether the Volsci or Aequi would supply the general for the united army; a falling out was followed by a terrible battle. It was the good fortune of the Roman people that two enemy armies perished in a fight that was as murderous as it was stubborn.

Titus Sicinius and Gaius Aquillius were the consuls. To Sicinius fell the Volscian war, to Aquillius the Hernican—for these people too were in arms. In this year the Hernici were defeated; the fight with the Volsci ended in a draw.

41. Spurius Cassius and Proculus Verginius were elected the next consuls. A treaty was struck with the Hernici; two-thirds of their territory was taken from them, which Cassius proposed to split evenly between the Latins and the plebs. To this grant he tried to add some of the state-owned land that, he charged, private individuals had appropriated. Many senators, who had occupied the land, were alarmed at the possibility of losing this property; but the general welfare concerned them as well, since the consul by his largess was building a source of personal power inimical to liberty. A land law was then proposed, the first in Rome's history, a form of legislation that has invariably been the cause of agitation and upheaval down to the present day. Cassius' colleague resisted the largess with the support of the senators, and even some of the plebs were sympathetic with Verginius' stance, since from the first they had been averse to the citizens sharing such a boon with the allies. Frequently thereafter the consul Verginius used to warn them in public meetings, in mantic fashion, of the pernicious result his colleague's largess was likely to have: that land would enslave those who received it; a road to kingship was being built. For what was the point of siding with the Latin allies or of returning to the Hernici, Rome's recent enemy, a third of the land taken from them, if it was not to put Cassius as their head in lieu of Coriolanus? Verginius' arguments against the law and his attempts to block it began to win him popular support. Each consul became a rival, as it were, of the plebs' affections. Verginius said he would allow the land to be distributed if it were given to none save Roman citizens; Cassius, whose efforts to ingratiate himself with the allies had brought a corresponding drop in his popularity among the plebeians, tried to win the citizens' goodwill by a second largess: he ordered that moneys

realized from the Sicilian grain be distributed among the people. The plebs rejected this outright as nothing but a blatant bribe to win absolute power; the deep-seated suspicion of kingship was such that they spurned his proposed generosity as if they had no money worries whatever.

Tradition is firm on the fact that as soon as he left office he was convicted and executed. Some say his father carried out the punishment: he tried the case at home, and then had him whipped and executed; he consecrated his son's savings to Ceres; a statue of the goddess was then made, the inscription reading, GIVEN FROM THE PROCEEDS OF CASSIUS' PROPERTY.* I find in certain authorities—which is easier to believe—that he was charged with treason by the *quaestores*, or investigators, Caeso Fabius and Lucius Valerius, was convicted in a court of the people, and his house pulled down in a public ceremony. The date of his conviction was the consulship of Servius Cornelius and Quintus Fabius, whether the trial be reckoned private or public.

42. The people's hostility against Cassius was short-lived. The land law in its own right, even with its author gone, held them in thrall, their desire for it becoming greater when mean-spiritedness prompted the senators, after the defeat of the Volsci and Aequi in this year, to deprive the soldiers of the booty. Fabius the consul sold whatever was captured from the enemy and placed the proceeds in the treasury.

The Fabian name was hateful to the plebs because of what this last consul had done; still, the senators retained their grip with the election of Caeso Fabius as consul along with Lucius Aemilius. This estranged the plebs still further, and their seditious behaviour at home led to war abroad. Civil struggles were put on hold for the war; senators and plebeians united to fight a successful battle under the leadership of Aemilius against the Volsci and Aequi, who had renewed hostilities. But more of the enemy perished as they fled than in combat, so dogged was the cavalry pursuit after they were routed. The temple of Castor was dedicated in the same year on 15 July; it had been vowed in the Latin war by Postumius the dictator; his son was one of the two men elected for the ceremony, and he performed the actual dedication. In this year also eagerness for the land law continued to agitate the plebs. The tribunes kept popular power in the spotlight by their advocacy of a popular law; the senators, thinking the multitude was unruly enough without rewarding it, were horrified by such give-away programmes and incitements to misconduct. The consuls led the senatorial resistance. Their faction therefore prevailed not only in the present crisis but also in electing as consuls for the coming year Marcus Fabius, Caeso's brother, and Lucius Valerius, who was even more hateful to the plebs because of his accusation of Spurius Cassius.

This year also saw conflict with the tribunes. The proposed law was brought into contempt, along with its sponsors, because they had made a great fuss about something they could not accomplish. The reputation of the Fabii was at its height after three successive consulships, all of them having been tested in the conflict with the tribunes, which comprised a single, ongoing movement in these years. So the office, like money well invested, remained in the family for some time. War with Veii then broke out, and the Volsci renewed hostilities; but while Rome's strength was more than sufficient for waging wars in the field, it was dissipated by infighting among themselves. Added to this unhealthy atmosphere were threatening prodigies from heaven that occurred almost daily in the city and countryside. Seers, on looking both publicly and privately into the cause of divine displeasure by inspecting entrails and observing the birds, affirmed that no other cause existed save the improper performance of religious rites. The upshot of these fears was the conviction of the Vestal Virgin Oppia for unchastity and her punishment.*

43. Quintus Fabius and Gaius Iulius were the next consuls. In this year the discord at home did not slacken, while war abroad proved more trying. The Aequi took up arms; the Veientes even entered Roman territory on a plundering raid; as anxiety about these wars was increasing, Caeso Fabius and Spurius Furius became consuls. The Aequi attacked Ortona, a Latin city; the Veientes, having now had their fill of plunder, threatened to attack Rome itself. These reverses ought to have dampened rather than raised the spirits of the plebs; and although they refused enlistment as they had in the past, it was not of their own accord but at the instigation of Spurius Licinius, tribune of the plebs, who thought the time was right to force the land law upon the senate by the extreme measure of thwarting the military effort. However, the invidiousness of holding tribunician power fell wholly upon him when the other tribunes

joined the consuls in blocking him; with their help the consuls held the levy.

Soldiers were recruited for two wars at once, one army being assigned to Fabius to lead against the Veientes, the other to Furius against the Aequi. Little worthy of record was accomplished against the Aequi.* Fabius had considerably more trouble with his own citizens than with the enemy. He alone, by virtue of his office, saved the day for Rome, which the army out of hatred of the consul tried its best to betray. For the consul, in addition to the good generalship he consistently displayed in preparing for the war and in conducting it, drew up his forces in such a way that the cavalry alone was sufficient to rout the enemy's army; but the infantry refused to pursue them as they fled. It is perhaps understandable that the orders of a hated commander had no effect on them, but even their own disgrace and their country's present dishonour—to say nothing of the later peril should the enemy's spirits revive—could not make them pick up their speed or, if nothing else, keep to their places in the ranks. Without orders they retreated and returned to camp grim-faced (you would have thought they were the vanquished), now cursing their commander, now the energetic effort of the cavalry. Nor did the commander discover any correctives to this pernicious behaviour; defeating an enemy is more easily accomplished by men of talent than governance of citizens. The consul returned to Rome with his military glory not so much enhanced as his soldiers' hatred of him was quickened and aggravated. Still, the senators prevailed in having the consulship stay in the Fabian clan: they elected Marcus Fabius consul, with Gnaeus Manlius as his colleague.

44. This year also saw a tribune sponsoring a land law, Titus Pontificius. Behaving as if the attempt of his predecessor, Spurius Licinius, had been successful, he impeded the levy for a short time. The senators were again alarmed; Appius Claudius suggested that the tribune's power had been worsted in the previous year because, it had been discovered, the power of the office could be the source of its own undoing: this was proving true at the present moment and would serve as a blueprint for the future. There would always be some tribune, he argued, who would want to get the best of a colleague and win the goodwill of true patriots for the public good; and more tribunes (if more were needed) would be ready to come to the consuls' aid, even though one was quite enough to thwart the

rest.* The consuls and leading senators should now make an effort
to reconcile, if not all, then at least some of the tribunes with their
country and with the senate.

The senators followed Appius' advice, all of them treating the
tribunes in a courteous and friendly manner, while any consulars
who had private claims upon individual tribunes used their personal
influence and standing in the community to convince them to em-
ploy their power as tribunes to promote the health of the state; thus,
four tribunes enabled the consuls to hold the levy by blocking the
one colleague who was thwarting the public good.

They then set out for war against Veii, where from all parts of
Etruria auxiliary contingents had gathered, prompted not so much
by the desire to do Veii a favour as by the prospect of Rome being
broken up by internal discord. Whenever all the Etruscan peoples
would meet, their leaders would set them abuzz with the following
reflections: Rome's strength would be everlasting unless they turned
their savagery upon themselves in civil strife: this was the one poison, the one cancer of wealthy states that led to the demise of great
empires. Rome had long been able to survive, sick though it was, by
the leadership of the senators and the long-suffering of the plebeians, but now it had reached the crisis stage. Where there had been
one state, there were now two; each side had its own magistrates, its
own laws. At first they had confined their violence to times when
the levy was held, but obeyed their leaders in the field; however bad
conditions might be in the city, they could survive because of military discipline. But now the Roman soldiery had extended its habit
of not obeying the magistrates to the camp. In the latest war, in the
battleline itself, in the very midst of fighting, the army conspired
actually to hand the victory to the defeated Aequi—abandoning the
standards, leaving their commander on the front line, returning to
camp without orders. If her enemies would keep the pressure up,
Rome's own forces could defeat her. All one had to do was declare
war and make a show of it; fate and the gods would take care of the
rest as a matter of course. Such were the hopes that caused the
Etruscans to arm, the victors and losers in the shifting hazards of
many a war.

45. The Roman consuls were also apprehensive of nothing other
than their own strength and military might: recollection of the terrible incident during the last war made them hesitant to risk having

to face two armies at once. And so they kept to the camp in order to avoid this insidious double peril: time and circumstance, they thought, might possibly mitigate the soldiers' anger and restore them to sanity. The Veientes and other Etruscans therefore tried to stampede the Romans into fighting, attempting to provoke hostilities at first by riding up to the camp and issuing a challenge; but when this had no effect, they fell back on hurling insults at both consuls and army: they were afraid to fight and were using internal discord as an excuse; it wasn't so much that the consuls mistrusted their soldiers as that they had no confidence in their fighting ability. Here was a new kind of mutiny: saying nothing and doing nothing while armed to the teeth! They also jeered at the newness of Rome and her people, some of which was true, some false.

The consuls listened to this noisy ridicule going on before ramparts and gates quite calmly; but rage and shame filled the breasts of the ignorant multitude and kept them from dwelling on their domestic grievances. They did not want the enemy to get away with this, but equally did not want the senate and consuls to win out. Their minds were a battlefield of conflicting hatred for the enemy within and the enemy without. In the end those without prevailed, so haughtily and arrogantly did the enemy taunt them. The soldiers gathered in large numbers at camp headquarters and demanded that the trumpet be sounded to start the battle. The consuls put their heads together as if deliberating and spent a long time talking. They wanted to fight, but they reined in this desire, concealing it in order to sharpen further the soldiers' will to fight by balking and stalling. So the reply came back: it was too soon to act; this was not the time for battle; they should keep to the camp. An edict was accordingly issued forbidding battle; if anyone fought without orders, he would be subject to the death penalty as if he were one of the enemy.

They were thus dismissed, but the more they believed the consuls did not want battle, the greater was their ardour for it. The enemy fired them up to fever pitch when it became known that the consuls had decided not to fight: obviously they could jeer at the Romans with impunity; soldiers could not be trusted with weapons; mutiny had reached the point of no return; Rome's rule was at an end! Buoyed by these hopes, they made sallies against the gates, heaped up the insults, and with difficulty refrained from attacking the camp head-on.

The Romans could endure the abuse no longer. From all parts of the camp they converged on the consuls and made their demands not indirectly as before, through the leading centurions, but all shouting furiously together. The situation was reaching a head, but still the consuls held back. Fabius, in face of the growing uproar and seeing his colleague giving way in fear of an outright mutiny, called for silence through a trumpet blast, and said, 'I know, Gnaeus Manlius, that these men *can* win, but I do not know from their previous actions that they really *want* to. No signal for attack will be given unless they swear to leave the battlefield as the winners. Once the Roman soldier broke his oath to the consuls on the battlefield, but he will never break his oath to the gods.' Marcus Flavoleius, a centurion who was one of those who had called most loudly for battle, declared, 'Marcus Fabius, I shall return from battle as victor.' If he broke his oath, he declared, he called down upon himself the wrath of Father Jupiter, Mars Gradivus, and the other gods. Each soldier then swore the same oath for himself. Once the oath was taken the signal was given; seizing their weapons, they went to the fight filled with anger and hope, challenging the Etruscans to hurl their insults now, to show off their braggadocio now that they were holding their weapons in their hands.

The courage displayed by everyone that day was extraordinary, both plebeians and senators. Members of the Fabian clan fought with special distinction; they had decided to win back in that battle the goodwill of the plebs, who had become estranged by so much civil conflict. 46. As the Romans drew up their battleline, the Veientes and the Etruscans did not hang back, for they were almost certain that the Romans would no more fight with them than they had with the Aequi: besides, it was not too much to hope that their behaviour might be even worse, given their present exasperation and the unpredictable situation.

The outcome proved far different, for the Romans entered the battle more eager for a fight than in any war before, so greatly had they been goaded by the enemy's insults and the consuls' delay. The Etruscans scarcely had time to deploy their forces when the Romans, hurling their pikes helter-skelter in their initial excitement rather than in a regular volley, began to engage at once in the most brutal type of fighting: face to face, swords in hand. The Fabian clan was in the forefront, and they set a most conspicuous example

to their fellow citizens. Quintus Fabius, who had been consul three
years before, led the charge into the closely packed line of the Veientes;
and as he heedlessly plunged into their crowded ranks an Etruscan
of formidable strength and fighting skill drove his sword into the
Roman's breast. When the weapon was pulled out, Fabius doubled
over and toppled headlong. Though it was the fall of a single man,
both sides perceived it, and as the Romans began to retire from their
position, the consul Marcus Fabius leaped over the body of the
fallen man and, thrusting his shield forward, cried, 'Is this what you
swore, men—to return to camp in flight? Are you more fearful of
this craven enemy than of Jupiter and Mars by whom you swore? I
did not take the oath, but I shall either return in victory or shall fall
fighting here beside you, Quintus Fabius.' Then Caeso Fabius, consul the previous year, said to the consul, 'Do you think, my brother,
that what you have said will make them fight? The gods will make
them, by whom they swore. Let us, as befits noblemen and as is
worthy of the Fabian name, kindle the soldiers' fighting spirit by
action rather than talk.' So did the two Fabii fly to the fore with
spears poised to strike, and they carried with them the entire battleline.

47. While the fighting was being renewed on this wing, the consul
Gnaeus Manlius hurled himself into the fray with equal vigour on
the other. The outcome was similar also, for Manlius' soldiers followed their commander's lead in virtually routing the enemy with as
much valour as had Fabius' men; and when Manlius, gravely
wounded, was retiring from the field, his soldiers began to retreat
likewise, thinking he had been killed. And they would have given
ground had not the other consul with some cavalry galloped to the
spot on the double, shouting that his colleague was alive and that he
was here to help them, having routed the enemy on the other wing.
Fabius thus restored the line as it wavered, assisted by Manlius'
reappearance as he too endeavoured to stem the tide. The sight of
their commanders fired the soldiers' courage.

At the same time the enemy, relying on their superior numbers,
depleted their ranks by sending their reserves to attack the Roman
camp. After a brief skirmish they forced their way in, but wasted
more time in plundering than in fighting. The Roman reserves from
the third line, who had been unable to withstand the initial irrup-
tion, sent to the consuls news of their present plight and, after
reforming, returned to camp headquarters. They renewed the fight-

ing on their own initiative as the consul Manlius was returning to the camp; when he arrived, he posted guards at all the gates, thereby blocking the enemy's escape. The Etruscans, in desperate straits, resorted to actions more mad than daring. For as they were running in any direction that promised a way out and were making ineffectual attacks here and there, a squad of young men set upon the consul himself, conspicuous in his armour. Their first volley struck those surrounding him; yet their onslaught could not be withstood: the consul fell mortally wounded; all those around him fled. Etruscan boldness increased; fear drove the Romans in panic throughout the camp, and the worst would have happened had not some officers caught up the consul's body and opened one gate through which the enemy might escape. From there they broke out, but rushing off pell-mell, they fell in with the other consul who had been victorious; once again they were cut down and put to flight in all directions.

A great victory had been won, made sombre by the deaths of two such distinguished men. And so the consul, when the senate endeavoured to vote him a triumph, replied that if an army could triumph without its commander, he would readily consent to it in view of the army's outstanding effort in the fight; as for himself, because his family was in mourning for the death of his brother, Quintus Fabius, and the state had been orphaned by the loss of his colleague, he would not accept something so out of place as a laurel crown when family and country were plunged in grief. His refusal of a triumph became more famous than any triumph ever celebrated: seasonable avoidance of glory can sometimes bring more renown than pursuit of it. He then conducted the two funerals, one for his colleague, the other for his brother, the same eulogist for each in turn, wherein he earned greater praise by ceding to them praises that were rightfully his.

Nor did he forget the policy he had adopted at the start of his consulship of winning the goodwill of the plebs, for he divided the wounded soldiers among the senators to convalesce. The majority were given to the Fabii, who lavished as much care upon them as did anyone. Thereafter the Fabii enjoyed popular favour—a favour won by no other means than those which promoted the health of the state as a whole.

48. The result was that Caeso Fabius, elected consul along with

Titus Verginius, won with equal support of plebs and senators. No concern, not even preparing for war or holding the levy, took precedence in his mind over strengthening at the earliest possible moment the unity between plebs and senate, now that a start had been made toward realizing this goal. Consequently, at the start of the year he thought that before anyone—any tribune—should step forward to sponsor an agrarian law, the senators themselves should pre-empt such a move by assigning the captured land to the plebs in as even-handed a manner as possible: it was right that those whose blood and sweat had won the land should possess it. The senators scouted the scheme; certain of them even groused that Caeso's once vigorous nature had grown rank from excessive glory and was now in its decline.

Yet no party strife ensued. The Latins were being harassed by raids of the Aequi. Caeso therefore set forth with an army, crossing into the territory of the Aequi themselves to lay waste their land; in response the Aequi retired to their towns and kept within the walls, thus forestalling any noteworthy military engagement. But a defeat was received at the hands of the Veientes because of the rashness of the other consul, and it would have been the end of the army had not Caeso Fabius opportunely come to the rescue. From that moment there was neither peace nor war with the Veientes; the situation resembled banditry more than anything else. The enemy would retire to their city as the Roman legions approached, and when they perceived the legions had been withdrawn, they would raid the countryside, parrying in turn war by quiescence, quiescence by war. Thus the situation as a whole resulted in a contretemps that could not be ignored or brought to a resolution. Moreover, fighting on other fronts was pressing the Romans, whether actually imminent, as from the Aequi and Volsci, who were quiescent only as long as the pain of their latest defeat lasted, or soon to be realized, when the ever hostile Sabines and the whole of Etruria should bestir themselves.

Yet the Veientes affronted Roman feelings more often by causing annoyance than by doing actual harm, since the Romans could never forget them nor turn their attention to other fronts. The Fabian clan then approached the senate, the consul acting as spokesman: 'As you know, conscript fathers, the Veian war requires a continuous rather than a sizeable defence. We urge you to concern yourselves with the other wars and leave Veii to the Fabii. We pledge that we will not tarnish Rome's great name. We propose to carry on hostilities from our own home, as it were, and at our expense; the state will need to provide neither men nor money on this front.' They were heartily thanked. The consul left the senate-house and went home, accompanied by the Fabii in marching order, who had stood in the vestibule awaiting the senate's decision. He bade them present themselves the next day in arms at his house. They then retired to their several homes.

49. The news spread throughout the city. People praised the Fabii to the heavens: a single family had assumed the responsibility of the state; the war against Veii had become a private enterprise, a private vendetta; if there were two more clans of the same strength in the city, one would claim the Volsci for its own, the other the Aequi; all the neighbouring peoples could be subdued while the Roman people enjoyed a peaceful holiday!

The Fabii took up their weapons the following day and gathered at the appointed place. When the consul, garbed in a general's cloak, walked into the forecourt, he beheld his entire clan drawn up in marching order; entering their ranks, he ordered the standards raised and carried forward. No army had even marched through the city smaller in size or greater in distinction and in men's regard: three hundred and six soldiers, all patrician, all of the same clan, were passing by, of whom none would have been deemed an unworthy commander of a great army at any point in Rome's history: the might of a single family was threatening to destroy the people of Veii. A crowd followed; some were relatives and friends, who were beset not by the ordinary emotions of hope and concern, but of the limitless possibilities of the outcome; others, held in the grip of fervour and wonderment, were anxious for the community at large. They bade them march out bravely and with high hope, to crown this splendid show with splendid success; in return they would heap upon them consulships and triumphs, every honour and office. As they passed by the Capitol, citadel, and other temples, the crowd prayed to the divinities as they beheld or thought of them to send forth the army with favour and good fortune, to bring it back swiftly and in safety to kin and country.

Their prayers went for naught. Setting out on that ill-fated journey through the right portal of the Carmental Gate, they came to the Cremera River, which seemed ideal for establishing a fortified outpost.*

Lucius Aemilius and Gaius Servilius were elected the next consuls. The Fabii, as long as they were engaged simply in raiding, were not only enough to protect the outpost but, by controlling the entire region where Etruscan and Roman territories met, to render their own land safe for themselves, the enemy's unsafe for him. Then came a brief respite from the raiding; the Veientes summoned an army from Etruria and attacked the garrison at the Cremera. In response the consul Lucius Aemilius brought up the Roman legions and engaged in a hand-to-hand fight with the Etruscans; or rather, the Veientes scarcely had enough room to deploy their battleline: thus, while in their initial disorientation they were filling up the ranks behind the standards and stationing their reserves, a squadron of Roman cavalry attacked suddenly on their flank, depriving them of room not only to begin the fight but even to hold their ground. Thus they were driven back to the Red Rocks where they had pitched their camp; they sought peace in suppliant fashion, which was granted. But true to their character, they had a change of heart even before the Romans were to withdraw the garrison from the Cremera.

50. So the Fabii and the people of Veii were once again pitted against one another. There was no intent to escalate the conflict to a higher level: raids were made in the countryside or sudden reprisals upon the raiders, although from time to time they confronted one another in regular battle array; when this happened a single clan of the Roman people frequently prevailed over the most powerful of Etruscan states, as power and wealth were reckoned in those days. At first the situation seemed humiliating and unworthy to the Veientes, but from it a plan was devised to entrap the arrogant enemy in an ambush. They were happy to see how success was making the Fabii reckless; accordingly, cattle would often be placed in the path of the freebooting Romans, as if they had come there by chance; fleeing peasants would desert the countryside, while detachments of armed men, sent to drive off the pillagers, would retreat from fear more feigned than real. Soon the Fabii developed so much contempt for the enemy that they viewed their unbeaten record as a guarantee of success at any time and any place.

On one occasion they espied cattle ranging far from the Cremera over a wide expanse of plain and with little evidence of the enemy's presence: they swooped down. Careless and in a disorganized rush they passed beyond an enemy ambush placed on either side of their path* and dispersed in order to seize the cattle that were widely scattered, as happens when they are frightened. At this juncture the enemy rose from his ambuscade and appeared before them and on every side. At first they were frightened by the shout the enemy raised all about them; then missiles began raining down from every quarter; and as the Etruscans began to draw their forces together, the Fabii were hemmed in by a continuous line of armed men: the more the enemy squeezed them, the smaller the space into which they were forced to contract their circle. This manœuvre made evident their few numbers and the great size of the Etruscan army, as its ever deepening ranks tightened their grip. They gave up having to fight the enemy in all directions at once and pressed forward as a unit to one place, forcing their way in wedge formation with bodies and weapons. The way led up to a slightly elevated slope on the side of a hill. There they made a stand; soon their superior position gave them a chance to catch their breath and recover from the great fear they had felt; they then endeavoured to drive back their attackers, and their small numbers would have prevailed because of the opportune elevation had not a Veian detachment, sent round behind them over a ridge, occupied the crest of the hill, thereby giving them the advantage. The Fabii were slaughtered to a man and their fortified position stormed. Three hundred and six perished, as is generally agreed; one survived because of his tender years, who would carry on the Fabian line and prove possibly the greatest bulwark to the Roman people at home and on campaign in the many crises that lay ahead.

51. When news of the disaster arrived Gaius Horatius and Titus Menenius had already entered the consulship. Menenius was dispatched at once to confront the Etruscans, elated by their victory. Another defeat followed, and the enemy occupied the Janiculum. In addition to the fighting a scarcity of food had resulted from the Etruscans crossing the Tiber: the city would have been besieged had not the consul Horatius been summoned back from the Volscian front. Fighting was carried on so close to the city walls that a battle at the temple of Hope* was fought to a stand-off, while another took place at the Colline Gate. There, although the Roman side proved

only slightly superior, the soldiers' old spirit revived, which made them readier to face future battles.

Aulus Verginius and Spurius Servilius became the next consuls. The Veientes were shy of engaging the Romans in battle after their last defeat; they went on plundering raids and attacked Roman territory everywhere from the Janiculum, using it like a fortified sanctuary; there was no place where cattle or the country people were safe. They were then trapped by the same stratagem they had used against the Fabii. In pursuit of cattle that had been deliberately placed in their way as a lure, they fell into an ambuscade; since their number was greater than that of the Fabii, the slaughter was correspondingly larger.

Yet their intense anger engendered by this disaster led to a greater one. For, after crossing the Tiber by night, they attacked the camp of the consul Servilius. Repulsed with great losses they found their way back to the Janiculum with difficulty. The consul in turn hastily crossed the Tiber and fortified a camp at the base of the Janiculum. On the next day at dawn, no doubt rather intoxicated by his day-old success, but more because a lack of provisions was pressing him into measures that, however impetuous, might lead to a speedy solution, Servilius recklessly led his troops up the slope of the Janiculum to the camp of the enemy, where he received a more disgraceful repulse than he had dealt the enemy the day before. He and his army were saved by the intervention of his colleague. The Etruscans now had their backs to two armies in turn, and were wiped out. Thus the Veientine war was ended by a rash act that had a lucky outcome.

52. Peace brought considerable relief from the food shortage both because of the importation of grain from Campania and because individuals, no longer fearful of personal privation, brought out what they had been hoarding. Yet abundance and idleness caused the people to grow fractious yet again and to return to their old destructive ways, now that destruction no longer threatened from without. Tribunes began to stir up the plebs with their customary poisonous brew: an agrarian law. When the senators resisted, they incited the plebs against them both as a body and individually. Quintus Considius and Titus Genucius, sponsors of the agrarian law, indicted Titus Menenius. The garrison lost at the Cremera was a source of his unpopularity, since as consul he had been encamped not far off; this unpopularity proved his undoing, though the sena-

tors supported him no less than they had Coriolanus and though the high regard men had felt for his father, Agrippa, had not faded away. The tribunes followed a lenient course and assessed him a fine: even though they had indicted him on a capital charge, the fine on conviction amounted to two thousand asses.* But the penalty crushed him; they say he could not bear the disgrace and consequent ill health, and that he was carried off by sickness.

On the expiration of his consulship Servilius, too, was indicted. This occurred at the very start of the new year when Gaius Nautius and Publius Valerius entered office; the accusers were the tribunes Lucius Caedicius and Titus Statius. Servilius did not, as had Menenius, defend himself against the tribunes with pleas for mercy made by himself or by the senators; instead, he had full confidence in his innocence and popularity. In his case the charge concerned his conduct of the battle with the Etruscans at the Janiculum. But he was a man of strong will, which was as much in evidence when defending himself as it had been when defending the state. In a trenchant speech he upbraided both tribunes and plebs, rebuking them for the conviction and death of Titus Menenius; it was by the good offices of this man's father, he reminded them, that the plebs had been restored to the state and enjoyed the magistracies and laws that they were now using to vent their savagery. His doughty speech saved the day. His colleague Verginius also helped by appearing as a witness and sharing his own credit with Servilius; but Menenius' trial helped even more—such was the revulsion of feeling that had come over the people.

53. The conflict on the home front was over. War broke out with Veii, and the Sabines joined them. The consul Publius Valerius, after summoning help from the Latins and Hernici, was sent to Veii with his army and at once attacked the Sabine camp, which had been placed next to the walls of their allies; this caused such consternation that, as different contingents ran out helter-skelter to repulse the enemy attack, the camp gate against which Valerius first directed his assault was captured. Inside the rampart more of a massacre than a fight ensued. The uproar spread from the camp into the city. The Veientes fearfully rushed to arms as if it was their city that had been taken. Some went to aid the Sabines, others attacked the Romans, who were wholly occupied with their assault on the camp. Bit by bit the Romans were dislodged and confounded; now

they were the ones who were fighting on two sides at once. The consul then sent in the cavalry, which routed the Etruscans and put them to flight. In one and the same hour two armies belonging to two of Rome's most powerful neighbours were defeated.

While these events were taking place at Veii, the Volsci and Aequi had struck camp on Latin soil and had ravaged the territory. The Latins on their own, with help from the Hernici, drove them from the camp without Roman leadership or help; besides the recovery of their own property, much booty came into their hands. Nevertheless, the consul Gaius Nautius was sent from Rome against the Volsci; the Romans, I believe, did not like their allies waging war with their own strategy and resources without a Roman as commander and without a Roman army. Despite visiting upon the Volsci every sort of injury and humiliation, they could not force them to engage in a pitched battle.

54. Lucius Furius and Gaius Manlius were the next consuls. Command against Veii fell to Manlius, but no war ensued; instead, they asked for a truce of forty years, which was granted; a contribution of grain and money was imposed. Discord at home immediately followed upon peace abroad. The plebs were in an uproar because of tribunician agitation for an agrarian law. The consuls, undeterred by the conviction of Menenius or the trial of Servilius, resisted with the strongest of strong-arm tactics. On their leaving office Gnaeus Genucius, tribune of the plebs, brought an indictment against them.

Lucius Aemilius and Opiter Verginius entered the consulship. I find Vopiscus Iulius listed as consul in place of Verginius in certain historical accounts. Whoever the consuls were, it was in this year that Furius and Manlius, upon being indicted before the people, donned mourning attire and went about soliciting the sympathetic support of both plebs and younger senators. They cautioned the latter not to seek office or engage in running the country; in fact, they should view the consular fasces, toga praetexta, and curule chair as nothing other than the trappings of a funeral; decked out in honorific regalia, like those headbands worn by sacrificial victims, they were marked for death. But if they found the consulship so appealing, they should realize at the start that the office had been taken over and stifled by the power of the tribunes; all things must be done with the tribune's approval and at his behest, with the consul following in his train like some lackey; if a consul should take the initiative, if he should have regard for the senate, if he should think that any element other than the plebs existed in the state, then these young senators should have before their eyes the exile of Gnaeus Marcius and the conviction and death of Menenius.

Fired up by these words, the senators no longer held public deliberations but met in private so that people would not come to know of them. They all agreed on this: whether it was done by fair means or foul, the defendants must be saved. The most extreme proposals were greeted enthusiastically; there was someone to champion any deed, however terrible.

And so, on the day of the trial, as the plebs were standing in the forum in eager anticipation, their first reaction was surprise when the tribune failed to appear; they then became increasingly suspicious as the delay continued, coming to believe that he had been frightened off by the higher-ups and had abandoned and betrayed his public trust; finally those who had been waiting in his vestibule announced that he had been found dead in his home. When the report spread throughout the assembly, the plebs ran off in every direction like an army that scatters at the death of its commander. The rest of the tribunes took the death of their colleague as a fearful warning: the laws that had made them sacrosanct offered no protection whatever.* Nor did the senators moderate their joy. So little regret did any of them have for this unjust act that even those who had had no part in it wanted to be thought guilty. It was openly bruited about that the tribune's power required outright chastisement to bring it under control.

55. This victory, won by setting a grim precedent, led to the announcement of a military conscription, which the consuls carried out because the tribunes were afraid and would not use their veto. The silence of the tribunes fired the plebs' ire even more than had the consular order. They affirmed that their freedom was over and done for; the conditions of old had returned; the power of the tribunate had died and been buried along with Genucius. They would have to devise some other means to counter the senate. One course was open to them: the plebs would have to defend themselves on their own, since no one else would. Twenty-four lictors attended the consuls, plebeians at that. No force is more contemptible or infirm than when people contemn it; it is great and terrifying because people think it is.

After they had egged on one another by such arguments, the
consul sent a lictor to Volero Publilius, a plebeian, because he claimed
that as a former company commander he ought not to be conscripted now as an ordinary soldier. Volero appealed to the tribunes.
When none of them came to his aid, the consuls ordered him to be
stripped and the rods taken from the fasces. 'I appeal,' cried Volero,
'since the tribunes prefer a Roman citizen to be flogged with rods in
their sight than themselves be murdered in their beds by you!' The
louder he shouted, the more roughly the lictor tore at his clothing
and stripped him. Then Volero, who was a strong man in his own
right, was helped by those who rushed to his side as he called upon
them; they pushed the lictor away. Volero withdrew into the close-
packed crowd where the shouting of his outraged supporters was
the loudest, shouting, 'Stand by me, citizens! Stand by me, comrades in arms! You can look to the tribunes for nothing, for it is they
who are in need of your help!' The bystanders were galvanized and
readied themselves as if for battle. It was clear that the situation had
reached a point of no return; the dictates of religion, public law, and
personal rights would count for nothing. The consuls, who were
exposed to this mighty storm, quickly learned how unsafe high
station is without power. After their lictors had been manhandled
and the fasces broken, they were driven from the forum into the
senate-house, uncertain as to what lengths Volero might go in his
victory. Then, when the tumult died down, they ordered the senate
into session, at which they complained of the injury they had suffered, the violence of the plebs, and Volero's shameless behaviour.
After many harsh proposals had been made, the older senators prevailed, who would not brook a fight between an angry senate on the
one side and plebeians run amok on the other.

56. The plebs became enthusiastic supporters of Volero and, in
the following year when Lucius Pinarius and Publius Furius were
consuls, elected him tribune of the plebs. Despite everyone's expectation that he would use the office to wage a vendetta against the
consuls of the year before, he placed the public good before personal
resentment and refused to assail the consuls by so much as a word.
Instead, he proposed to the people that plebeian magistrates should
thereafter be elected in the tribal assembly. At first sight his proposal did not seem particularly revolutionary, although it aimed at
completely eliminating the ability of the patricians to elect the trib-

unes they wanted through the votes of their clients.* The plebs
supported the proposal strongly; the senators resisted it with all
their might. Yet the authority of neither the consuls nor the other
leading men was sufficient to induce one of the current tribunes to
veto the bill, which was the only effective counter-measure the senators had. Nevertheless, the gravity and importance of the matter
provoked such a battle that it was still unresolved at the year's end.

The plebs re-elected Volero tribune; the senators, believing the
struggle would reach crisis stage, elected as consul Appius Claudius,
son of Appius, who, after his father's clashes with the plebs, detested them and was detested by them.* His colleague was Titus
Quinctius.

From the moment the year began nothing but the proposed law
was discussed. Although Volero was the one who originated the bill,
his colleague Gaius Laetorius proved a fresher and more passionate
advocate. His great reputation as a soldier filled him with bravado,
the most intrepid man of his day. While Volero spoke of nothing
except the law and refused to inveigh against the consuls, he launched
into an attack on Appius and his family as insufferably arrogant and
utterly ruthless toward the plebeians; but when he began to assert
that the senators did not elect Appius as consul but as a cut-throat
to harry and savage the plebeians, his unpractised soldier's tongue
could not do justice to his meaning or his free-spokenness. And so,
as words began to fail him, he cried, 'I am not a ready speaker, but
I do make good on what I say. Come here tomorrow and give me
your support. I shall either push this law through or perish in your
sight!'

The tribunes took over the speaker's platform before anyone else
could on the following day; the consuls and nobles stood together in
the assembly with the intention of blocking the law.* Save for those
who were going to vote, Laetorius ordered the rest to be removed.
The young nobles stood their ground and would not yield to the
tribune's attendant. Laetorius thereupon ordered some of them to
be apprehended. The consul Appius declared that a tribune had the
right to do this only in the case of a plebeian; he was not a magistrate of the people but of the plebs; by ancestral custom even a
magistrate of the people did not have the power to exclude, since the
law said, 'Go, Quirites, if it seems best to you.'* He was able to
confound Laetorius easily by speaking derisively about his rights.

The result was that the tribune, hot with anger, sent his attendant to the consul, the consul his lictor to the tribune, thundering that he possessed no official standing, had no power, and occupied no magistracy. The tribune would have been assaulted had not the entire assembly furiously united to defend him against the consul and had not an excited mob of men streamed into the forum from all parts of the city. Still, the obdurate Appius stood his ground in face of the raging storm, which doubtless would have ended in bloodshed, had not Quinctius, the other consul, instructed the ex-consuls to extricate his colleague from the forum. He himself calmed the enraged plebeians with entreaties and begged the tribunes to dissolve the assembly. They should, he said, give breathing-space to their anger; time would not diminish their strength but would add wisdom to it; the senators would be subject to the people, the consul to the senators.

57. Quinctius calmed down the plebs with difficulty; with even greater difficulty the senators calmed his colleague. When the assembly at last broke up, the consuls convened the senate, where fear and anger produced conflicting opinions. Yet the more emotion gave way to reason as the debate went on, the more they shrank from a fight. They ended by thanking Quinctius because by his effort the conflict had abated. They requested Appius that he consent to the enjoyment of consular prerogatives only as great as could exist in a harmonious commonwealth: when each consul and tribune tried to wrest control for himself, the centre was left powerless; the republic had been rent and wounded; it was more a question of who would control it than that it be unharmed. Appius in reply called upon gods and men as witnesses of how the republic was being betrayed through fear and abandoned; the consul was not failing the senate but the senate the consul; this law was harsher than those that were imposed on them from the Sacred Mount.

Nevertheless, the united feeling of his senatorial colleagues caused him to quiet down. The law was carried without incident. 58. Then for the first time tribunes were elected in the tribal assembly. Piso says that three were added to the original two. He gives their names as Gnaeus Siccius, Lucius Numitorius, Marcus Duilius, Spurius Icilius, and Lucius Maecilius.

During Rome's internal troubles war with the Volsci and Aequi broke out. They invaded Roman land on a plundering raid, hoping that, should the plebs secede, they would find a refuge among themselves; but when the strife abated, they withdrew their encampment. Appius Claudius was sent against the Volsci, while to Quinctius fell the Aequi. Appius behaved in the field with the same harshness as he had in the city, but with fewer constraints, since there were no tribunes to keep him in check. His hatred of the plebs was greater than that of his father: they had worsted him, he admitted to himself; although he had been elected with the sole purpose of opposing the tribunes' power, the law had been passed, which earlier consuls had blocked with less effort but not with the senators' same expectation of success. The anger and indignation these thoughts roused goaded his tyrannical nature to rule the army with an iron fist. But no power could control it, so great had the breach become between him and his men. They balked at all tasks, doing them in an off-hand, careless, and insubordinate manner. Neither shaming them nor intimidation had any effect. If he ordered them to speed up the march, they would deliberately slow the pace; if he appeared in person to urge them to greater effort, all would spontaneously slacken whatever they were doing; they refused to look him in the eye when he stood before them; when he passed by they cursed him under their breath, so that even he who had been unaffected by their hatred before was now shaken from time to time. After every sort of harsh measure had failed, he ignored the soldiers completely; the army, he alleged, had been corrupted by the centurions, whom he would mockingly address now and then as his 'tribunes of the plebs' and even 'Voleros'.

59. The Volsci, well aware of all that was going on, stepped up the pressure, expecting that the will of the Roman army would clash with that of Appius, as it had previously with Fabius; in fact, it proved far more extreme against Appius than in the earlier instance, for the army not only did not want to win, as was true of Fabius' army, but actually wanted to be beaten. When led out to the battleline it turned tail and ran for the camp in a disgraceful rout, not stopping until the Volscian army had penetrated the defence works and wreaked a terrible slaughter of those bringing up the rear. They were now forced to fight back, with the result that the enemy, on the point of victory, was expelled from the rampart; but it was all too clear that the Roman soldier's only wish was that the camp not be captured: in all else he revelled in his defeat and disgrace. Appius' combative spirit remained unbroken, and when he wanted to call an assembly to vent his rage upon them, his lieutenants and military tribunes hastened to warn him not to put his authority to the test, for it depended wholly upon the willingness of those under his command to obey. Soldiers everywhere, they reported, said they would not attend the assembly, and from every side there was a demand that the camp be moved from Volscian territory: the victorious enemy a little while before had been virtually at the gates and rampart, and a great disaster was not merely possible, but was staring them in the face. Appius gave way finally and cancelled the assembly, since they were only putting off their punishment to a later time. He announced that they would be moving the next day, and at early dawn the trumpet signalled departure. The moment the line of march had cleared the camp, the Volsci, as if answering the same trumpet call, attacked the rear. Turmoil spread to those in front, where the standards and ranks were thrown into such confused panic that orders could not be heard nor a battleline formed. No one thought of anything save flight. They dodged around the heaps of bodies and arms in such disorder that the enemy gave up pursuit before the Romans gave up running. The consul had no effect in getting them to stop, and when the soldiers finally regrouped after this wild stampede, he pitched camp in friendly territory. They were ordered to assemble, where with much truth he inveighed against the army as a traitor to military discipline and for its desertion of the standards, singling them out individually and asking them where their standards and weapons were. The bearers who had lost their standards, as well as the centurions and previously decorated soldiers* who had deserted the ranks, he ordered scourged and beheaded; from the rest every tenth man was selected by lot for execution.

60. On the other hand, the consuls and soldiers who were facing the Aequi vied with one another in goodwill and mutual support. Quinctius had a more easygoing nature, and the untoward harshness of his colleague made him all the more pleased with his own disposition. The Aequi, not daring to face this harmonious union of commander and troops, allowed the enemy to range over their land seeking plunder; never before had booty been taken from them over so wide an area. All of it was given to the soldiers, to which Quinctius added his praises, which soldiers take as much pleasure in as they do

in tangible rewards. The army returned more obedient to its commander and, because of him, to the senate, saying that the senators had given a father to them, a tyrant to the other army.

This was a year of varying fortune in war and of frightful discord at home and in the field, but the inception of the tribal assembly made it especially noteworthy—more important, however, in marking a victory of the plebeians than in its practical advantage. For in forbidding the senators to participate in it, more prestige was lost than power was added to the plebs or taken from the senators.

61. A more turbulent year followed under the consuls Lucius Valerius and Titus Aemilius both because of the struggle of the orders* over an agrarian law and because of the trial of Appius Claudius, whom Marcus Duilius and Gnaeus Siccius indicted, for he was a bitter opponent of the law and defended the claims of those occupying public land as if he were a third consul.* No man ever stood trial so hateful to the plebs, who were angry at how he and his father had treated them. The senators for their part supported him as they had no other, and not without reason: this champion of the senate, this defender of their dignity—who may have stepped over the line a bit in his fervent opposition to all the trouble-making of the tribunes and plebeians—was now being sacrificed to the anger of the plebs. Alone of the senators Appius himself paid no heed to tribunes, plebs, or the impending trial. The plebs threatened, the senators entreated, but he could not be moved. He refused to don the squalid raiment of a defendant or go the rounds seeking support in suppliant fashion. When it came time to plead his case he would not deviate a jot from his customary acerbity of speech nor humble himself. They saw the same expression in his features, the same defiant look, the same vehement speech—so much so that most of the plebs feared Appius as much as a defendant as they had as a consul. He pleaded his case on only one occasion, and did so in that accusatorial spirit he used on all occasions; the upshot was that his fearlessness so overawed the tribunes and plebs that on their own initiative they adjourned the trial to a later time and then let the matter be postponed still further. The interval was not long; but before the day arrived, he fell sick and died. The tribunes of the plebs tried to prevent the funeral eulogy from being pronounced, but the plebs did not, on the day of burial, want such a man cheated of this traditional tribute. They heard the eulogy of the dead man

with the same receptiveness they had heard his accusers when he was alive, and attended his funeral in great numbers.

62. In the same year the consul Valerius set out against the Aequi with his army; when he could not induce them to fight, he attacked their camp. A great storm from heaven, accompanied by hail and thunder, stopped him. Wonderment increased when, upon sounding the signal for retreat, such a peaceful hush fell over the scene that it seemed some divine force was protecting the place and that it would be a violation of divine will to attack the camp a second time. And so they vented their anger by devastating the countryside. The other consul Aemilius waged war with the Sabines, where too, because the enemy kept within his walls, his territory was ravaged. But when not just their farmhouses but the villages in which the Sabines concentrated some of the country dwellings were put to the torch, they went out to confront the marauders; after an indecisive battle they withdrew the next day and fixed their camp on a more protected site. The consul viewed this as sufficient reason to consider the enemy defeated; he left with the war scarcely begun.

63. While these wars were in progress and discord continued at home, Titus Numicius Priscus and Aulus Verginius were elected consuls. When it seemed that the plebs would not brook further delay of the agrarian law and were gathering all their strength for a final push, smoke from burning farmsteads and flight of the country people brought the news that the Volsci were upon them. This was enough to abort the political discord, which was far advanced and had nearly broken out. When the senate instantly ordered the consuls to conscript the younger plebeians and lead the army out to war, the plebs who remained behind quieted down. The enemy in fact beat a hasty retreat, although they had done nothing but cause the Romans baseless panic. Numicius went to face the Volsci at Antium, Verginius the Aequi. On the latter front the Aequi ambushed the army and nearly won a great victory, but the courage of the Roman soldiers restored a situation that had been all but lost because of the consul's negligence. Numicius did better against the Volsci. The enemy was routed at the first encounter and driven in flight to Antium, a very strong and wealthy city for those days. The consul did not venture to attack, but took from Antium the town of Caeno, which was by no means as strong and wealthy. While Rome's armies were occupied with the Aequi

and Volsci, the Sabines reached the gates of the city on a plundering raid. But when anger drove both consuls to invade their territory a few days later, they ended by suffering more casualties than they had inflicted.

64. By the end of the year some measure of peace had been achieved but, as was always the case in the past, it was a peace disturbed by the struggle between the senate and plebeians. Anger caused the plebs not to participate in the consular elections. Through the senators and their clients Titus Quinctius and Quintus Servilius were elected. These consuls experienced a year like the last: political discord at the start, which abated when war threatened. The Sabines in a quick march crossed into the district of Crustumerium, burning and slaughtering around the Anio River; they nearly reached the Colline Gate and the walls of Rome, taking much booty in the form of captives and cattle. The consul Servilius and his army went on the offensive, and although they did not succeed in catching the Sabines on level ground where they might engage them, they ravaged their land so widely that no place was untouched by their depredations and they returned with many times more booty than had been taken from them earlier.

Against the Volsci the state was also excellently served by the efforts of commander and soldiers. A pitched battle was first fought in a hand-to-hand encounter, with many dead and many wounded on both sides. Because of their small numbers the Romans were quicker to perceive their losses, and they would have begun to retreat had not the consul shouted to them that the enemy had fled on the other wing. They had not, in fact, but the opportune fiction fired the Romans up. They went on the offensive and won because they thought they were winning. The consul, fearing to renew the fight by pressing the enemy too hard, gave the signal for retreat. For a few days both sides rested as if an undeclared truce obtained. During this time many reinforcements from all peoples of the Volsci and Aequi came to the camp. They were sure that if the Romans perceived this, they would withdraw under cover of darkness. And so at about the third watch* they approached the camp, making ready to attack. This sudden manœuvre threw the Romans into great confusion and fear, which Quinctius brought under control: he ordered the soldiers to stay quietly in their tents, while stationing a cohort of Hernici at an outpost before the rampart. He

mounted the buglers and trumpeters on horses and ordered them
to sound their instruments, thereby keeping the enemy on tenter-
hooks till dawn. For the rest of the night the Romans were secure
in the camp and even had time for sleep. The Volsci in the meantime were looking at armed soldiers whom they took to be numerous and Roman; the horses stamped and neighed, made fractious
because of the unfamiliar riders and the din grating on their ears.
So the Volsci were kept on the alert, as if the enemy were going to
attack at any moment.

65. When it grew light the Romans were led into battle fresh and
rested, where they repulsed the Volsci on contact, who were tired
from standing guard and loss of sleep. Yet the enemy withdrew
rather than fled because at his rear were hills that offered a safe
refuge while the front line gave protection as he retreated, thereby
keeping the formation intact. When the consul came to the steep
slope, he called a halt. It was difficult to restrain the foot soldiers as
they loudly demanded permission to go after those they had repulsed. The cavalry was the more vociferous; they milled about the
commander, vowing to enter the fray in advance of the standards.
The consul, who was confident of his soldiers' courage but wary of
the terrain, hesitated. But as he did so, they shouted that they
would get under way in the very act of doing so. Fixing their pikes
in the ground so that they would not be encumbered in scaling the
heights, they went up on the run. The Volsci discharged their missiles at the first charge, then rained down rocks they found lying at
their feet. From their superior position they began to press the
Romans hard, throwing them into confusion by the incessant volley.
The Roman left wing was near to being overwhelmed and was beginning to retreat when the consul shook the fear out of them by
berating their earlier bravado and present lack of grit. They responded by first holding their ground obstinately, which enabled
them to recover their strength. They then had the pluck to go on
the offensive and, renewing the battle-cry, to move the line forward;
and as they regained their momentum, they overcame the difficulty
of the terrain. They had almost reached the summit when the
enemy turned tail. Rushing pell-mell, pursuers and pursued burst
into the enemy camp almost in a single line. During the ensuing pandemonium the camp was taken. Those of the Volsci who managed
to escape headed for Antium, the Romans following. The city was

given up after a siege of a few days, not because of some fresh effort on the part of the Romans but because the loss of the battle and the capture of their camp had left the Volsci without the will to continue the fight.

BOOK THREE

1. After Antium had been captured, Titus Aemilius and Quintus Fabius became consuls. This was the Fabius who was the only survivor of the massacre of his clan at the Cremera. In his earlier consulship Aemilius had advocated giving land to the plebs; accordingly, in this, his second, consulship those advocating land distribution had reason to hope for passage of such a law, and the tribunes, thinking that a proposal often attempted in opposition to the consuls could certainly be carried through with the consul's assistance, undertook to sponsor it; the consul, moreover, continued to champion it. Those who had occupied the public land, most of whom were senators, complained that a chief of state was ostentatiously behaving like a tribune in order to court popularity by giving away what belonged to others. Hence they shifted the invidiousness of the proposal from the tribunes to the consul.

A terrible struggle was looming, but Fabius helped settle the crisis by a proposal offensive to neither side: in the previous year under the leadership and auspices of Titus Quinctius a certain amount of land had been captured from the Volsci; a colony, he suggested, could be established at Antium, a city on the sea that was near by and accessible; thus, without disturbing the occupiers of public land, the plebs could move to this place and harmony could be preserved in the state. His proposal was accepted. They elected a three-man board for assigning the land, consisting of Titus Quinctius, Aulus Verginius, and Publius Furius; those who wanted to receive allotments were told to make application. The great amount of land that became available produced the not unnatural reaction of misprizing it. Volscian colonists were added to fill out the requisite number; the rest of the multitude preferred to demand land at Rome than to accept it elsewhere.

The Aequi sought peace from Quintus Fabius after he had marched against them with an army, but they broke it themselves by a sudden raid into Latin territory.

2. In the following year the consul Quintus Servilius—his colleague was Spurius Postumius—was sent against the Aequi and fixed a permanent camp in Latin territory;* sickness forced the army into inactivity. The war was prolonged into the third year when Quintus Fabius and Titus Quinctius were consuls. Command was assigned to Fabius by exceptional appointment* because he had defeated the Aequi and had dictated peace terms to them. He set out, confident that his reputation would bring the Aequi to terms. He ordered envoys to say to an assembly of the Aequan peoples that, whereas earlier the consul Quintus Fabius had brought peace from the Aequi to Rome, he says he now brings war in the reverse direction, and holds weapons of destruction in the same right hand he had extended to them in peace; the gods know who broke faith and forswore their oaths and they will soon exact punishment; however that may be, he personally prefers the Aequi to repent even at this late date of their own accord than to suffer hostilities; should they repent, they would find refuge in the clemency they had experienced in the past; if forswearing their oath were their pleasure, they would be waging war more with the angry gods than with a human foe. These words so failed to persuade anyone that the envoys came close to being assaulted and an army was sent to occupy the pass at Mount Algidus against the Romans.

When these events became known at Rome the other consul hurried to the front, prompted more by outrage than a sense of real danger. Two consular armies thus bore down upon the enemy in battle array in order to come to an immediate decision. But since it chanced that the day was nearly over, someone shouted from an enemy outpost, 'This is only pretend warfare, Romans, not the real thing. Here you are, drawing up your forces as night is coming on! We will need more light for the battle to come. Tomorrow as the sun rises return to the battleline: you'll have your fill of fighting, never fear!' The soldiers were angered by this taunt and returned to camp to await the dawn, thinking that the night which delayed the fight would be a long one. They used the time to eat and rest; when dawn came, the Romans drew up in battle order some time before the enemy did; eventually the Aequi took up their position as well. It was a tough fight for both sides: the Romans were battling in anger and hate, whereas the Aequi, conscious that their present predicament was their own fault, had no hope of being trusted in the future; so they were driven to stake everything on this one battle. Yet they did not withstand the Roman line; driven back, they withdrew into their own territory, where the rank and file, uncowed and not at all inclined to peace, criticized their commanders for choosing to decide the issue in a pitched battle, a type of warfare in which the Romans excelled; the Aequi, they said, were better at hit-and-run tactics in which numerous contingents fanned out to raid the countryside rather than at fighting in massed array on a single spot.

3. And so, having left a guard in their camp, they set out and invaded Roman territory, causing such confusion that panic penetrated even to the city. This unexpected move was even more alarming because the last thing anyone feared was that an enemy who had been defeated and nearly besieged in his camp would be bent on plundering. The terrified country people poured in through the gates shouting that this was no raid by a few bands of marauders (their fears were unfounded and they exaggerated everything) but that legions and armies of the enemy were bearing down on the city for an attack. Those who heard these exaggerations relayed the news to others, which became even more exaggerated in the retelling. The rushing about and the shouting of those calling the people to arms much resembled the terror of a city upon capture. Quinctius the consul had returned by chance from Algidus to Rome, which allayed the fear; after quieting the tumult and rebuking them for fearing an enemy that had been defeated, he stationed guards at the gates. The senate was then called into session and a cessation of public business voted.* He next set out to secure Rome's borders, leaving Quintus Servilius as prefect of the city; but he did not come upon the enemy in the field.

Fabius, the other consul, turned in an excellent performance, for he attacked the enemy at the spot he knew they would be passing by, laden with booty and therefore moving along sluggishly. Successful pillaging led to disastrous defeat. Few of the enemy escaped the trap; all the booty was recovered. The return of his colleague Quinctius to the city thus ended the cessation of business, which had lasted four days.

A census was next conducted and the *lustrum* was closed by Quinctius.* 104,714 citizens are said to have been enrolled, not counting widows and orphans. Thereafter nothing memorable was done against the Aequi; they retired to their towns and allowed their property to be burned and ravaged. Several times the consul roamed through the whole of their territory on plundering raids, prepared for battle. He returned to Rome with great praise and much booty.

4. Aulus Postumius Albus and Spurius Furius Fusus were the next consuls. Some spell Furius as Fusius; I say this lest anyone should fancy that the variant in spelling signifies different men. There was no doubt that one of the consuls would wage war with the Aequi. And so the Aequi asked for a military force from the Volsci of Ecetra. This was promptly given, so great was the rivalry of these peoples in their undying hatred of Rome: they were preparing for all-out war. When the Hernici came to know of this, they informed the Romans that Ecetra had espoused the cause of the Aequi. The colony at Antium also fell under suspicion because, when the town was captured, a great number had fled from there to the Aequi, and they proved throughout the Aequan war to be the fiercest fighters. But when the Aequi were subsequently penned up in their towns, this large group got away, and on their return to Antium won over the colonists to their side, who were already disaffected on their own account. Before the revolt actually broke out, the senate was informed that defection was imminent; the consuls were instructed to summon the leading men of the colony to Rome and ask what was going on there. They answered the summons promptly but, after being ushered into the senate by the consuls, gave such unsatisfactory replies to the questions posed that they were dismissed under a greater cloud of suspicion than they had been under when they arrived. War was then considered certain.

One of the consuls, Spurius Furius, was chosen by lot for the campaign against the Aequi; he set out and came upon the enemy plundering the territory of the Hernici; but, unaware of their great numbers because they had nowhere been sighted all in one group, he rashly committed to battle an army much smaller than that of the enemy. Repulsed at the first clash, he withdrew to his camp. Nor did this end the danger; for on the next night and following day the camp was besieged on all sides by such a great force that not even a messenger could get through to Rome. The Hernici were the ones who brought the news that the battle had been lost and that the army was under siege. This so alarmed the senate that it issued a resolution which has always been passed in the direst emergencies: the other consul Postumius was instructed that he 'should see to it that the state suffer no harm'.* It was decided that the consul should stay in Rome to enrol personally all those capable of bearing arms and that in place of the consul Titus Quinctius be dispatched with allied contingents to come to the aid of the camp. Latins, Hernici, and the colony at Antium were ordered to supply 'emergency soldiers' to Quinctius for this contingent—for so were irregular supporting troops styled in those days.

5. During this period many isolated skirmishes and attacks took place because the enemy with his superior numbers was bent on eroding Rome's strength on many fronts at once, thinking she could not adequately respond on all of them. The camp was under assault at the same time that another division was dispatched to devastate Roman territory and, should an opportunity arise, even to make an attempt on the city. Lucius Valerius was assigned to guard the capital, the consul Postumius to drive off those pillaging along the borders. Both maintained vigilance and energy. A night watch was stationed in the city, outposts before the gates and a defensive force on the walls; a cessation of public business, which was necessary in such an emergency, was observed for some days.

At the same time the consul Furius, who had at first endured the siege of the camp without making a countermove, burst from the gate next to the tenth cohort's station and surprised the enemy; though able to give pursuit, he held back from fear that the camp might be open to attack from some other direction. But the foray carried the military legate Furius—he was the commander's brother— too far afield; in his eager pursuit he did not see his own men turning back nor the enemy bearing down on him from behind. And so he was cut off and, after making many unsuccessful attempts to battle his way back to the camp, fell fighting bravely. When he heard his brother was surrounded by the enemy, the consul turned back to make a fight of it, hurling himself into the thick of the fray with more recklessness than good sense. He was wounded, his companions whisking him off the field in the nick of time. This reverse disheartened his men and increased the enemy's aggressiveness. The Aequi, fired up by the death of the legate and the wounding of the consul, could not now be stopped. The Romans were driven back to the camp and would again have been put under siege, no match for the enemy either in morale or strength, and the entire operation would have ended in disaster, had not Titus Quinctius come to the rescue with a contingent of foreign troops composed of Latins and Hernici. He attacked the Aequi from the rear as they were parading the legate's severed head about menacingly and their attention was concentrated on the Roman camp. A sally was made simultaneously from the camp at a signal he gave from a distance. A great number of the enemy were thus surrounded. As for the Aequi who were ranging about in Roman territory seeking plunder, fewer were killed, while most took to their heels. These Postumius attacked from fortified positions he had taken up for such an eventuality. As they scattered haphazardly in flight they fell in with the victorious Quinctius as he was returning with the wounded consul. It was then that the consular army in a splendid fight avenged the wounding of the consul and the killing of the legate and his cohorts.

Those days were marked by much slaughter suffered and committed on both sides. In a matter so ancient it is difficult to believe one can fix the exact number of those who fought or died. Valerius Antias nevertheless presumes to work up the totals: 5,800 Romans, he affirms, fell in Hernican territory; of those Aequi who were ranging along Rome's borders seeking plunder, 2,400 were killed by the consul Aulus Postumius; the rest of this large group (the one that fell in with Quinctius as it was carrying off booty) did not get off so lightly: the dead, he says, amounted to four thousand two hundred and—keeping the count running down to the last corpse—thirty.*

On the return to Rome the cessation of business was lifted. The heavens were seen to blaze with fire, while other portents were either observed or falsely interpreted by the frightened people. A three-day religious holiday was decreed to allay these fears, during which all the shrines were thronged by men and women seeking to appease the gods. The cohorts of Latins and Hernici were then thanked by the senate for their energetic service and sent back home. A thousand soldiers from Antium who had arrived after the battle was over and hence too late to be of use were dismissed in virtual disgrace.

6. Elections came next, with Lucius Aebutius and Publius Servilius winning the consulship. They entered office on 1 August, which in those days marked the start of the year.* An oppressive time of year to begin with, a plague chanced to fall upon the city and countryside, striking humans and animals alike; and when in fear of enemy pillaging they allowed cattle and farmers to crowd into the city, the disease grew more virulent. In the consequent intermingling of all these creatures, the city dwellers suffered from the stench, the countryfolk from heat and sleeplessness caused by being packed into

makeshift shelters. The disease spread further, as the healthy ministered to the sick, and then themselves became infected. At a time when they were barely able to bear up under the misfortunes afflicting them, envoys of the Hernici suddenly appeared with the news that the Aequi and Volsci had joined forces and had pitched camp in their territory, from which they were devastating the borders with a huge army. The small attendance at the senatorial session in which they made this announcement showed the Hernici how greatly the pestilence had afflicted the state. In addition, they received the disheartening response that they along with the Latins must safeguard themselves by their own devices: the city of Rome was being devastated by sickness because of the sudden anger of the gods; if respite to this evil should come, Rome would bring help to her allies as she had the year before and as she always had done in times past. The allies departed, bringing home in response to their grim report a grimmer one, for they would have to face the conflict alone, which they would have been hard-pressed to face even with Roman support.

No longer did the enemy confine themselves to Hernican territory; from there they invaded Roman land, which had already been depopulated, quite apart from the ravages of war. No one challenged them, not even a civilian; all the places they passed through lay undefended and untenanted until they came to the third milestone on the road to Gabii. The consul Aebutius had died; his colleague Servilius was barely breathing and there was little hope for him; a large number of the leading men, the greater part of the senate, and almost all men of military age had been stricken to the point that they lacked the strength not only to counter-attack, which the emergency situation required, but scarcely to stand guard. The senators who were young and healthy enough volunteered for sentry duty; inspection and supervision of the guards fell to the plebeian aediles, for upon them had devolved the governance of the country and the majesty of consular power.*

7. In the helpless state of the city, which was without a head and without strength, Rome's patron deities and good fortune saved her, for it was they who caused the Volsci and Aequi to consider themselves on a looting raid instead of as invading enemies. It did not occur to them even to approach, much less seize, the walls: the buildings seen from afar and the towering hills overawed them.

Everywhere in their camp they began to fret as to why they were wasting time sitting idle and getting no booty in this desolate and forsaken land surrounded by the rotting carcasses of men and animals, when they could be attacking places like Tusculum, as yet untouched and full of riches. So they abruptly pulled up their standards and marched by side roads through the territory of Labici to the hills of Tusculum, where the storm of war with all its violence was now centred.

In the meantime the Hernici and Latins, prompted by shame as much as by pity should they fail to confront their common enemy in his assault upon Rome and to aid their beleaguered ally, joined forces and hastened to Rome. When they failed to encounter the enemy there, they followed the route they were reported to have taken and came upon them as they were descending from the valley of Tusculum into the valley of Alba. There they engaged on terms by no means equal, and the faithful response of Rome's allies failed for the present to meet with success.

The disaster suffered at Rome from the plague was no less than that which the allies suffered by the sword. The surviving consul died, as did other distinguished men: the augurs Marcus Valerius and Titus Verginius Rutulus, as well as the curio maximus, Servius Sulpicius.* The virulence of the plague had also spread throughout the lower classes; it was then that the senate, despairing of human help, turned the people and their prayers to heaven: they were bidden to go with wives and children to supplicate the gods and to seek their appeasement. The shrines were thronged with those constrained by personal misfortune and now called forth by public decree. Everywhere the matrons prostrated themselves, their hair sweeping the temple floors as they beseeched the deities to abate their anger and the disease.

8. The plague then gradually began to wane and the survivors to recover, either because the gods had been appeased or the oppressive season of the year had passed. They now attended to public business and, after more than one interregnum had gone by, Publius Valerius Publicola on the third day after beginning his interregnum appointed as consuls* Lucius Lucretius Tricipitinus and Titus Veturius Geminus (Vetusius is an alternate spelling). They entered the consulship on 11 August, the state being now strong enough not only to protect itself but even to go on the offensive.

Therefore, when the Hernici announced that the enemy had crossed into their territory, help was promptly forthcoming. Two consular armies were enrolled. Veturius was sent to invade Volscian land. Tricipitinus, who was to protect the allies from depredation, went no further than the Hernici. Veturius in his initial battle routed the enemy and put them to flight. But an army of pillagers slipped by Lucretius' position among the Hernici, passing over the mountains of Praeneste and then descending to the plain. They devastated the territory of Praeneste and Gabii; from Gabii they headed for the hills of Tusculum. This caused great fear even in the city of Rome more because of the unexpectedness of the situation than because of inability to defend themselves. Quintus Fabius was in charge of the city; he ensured safety and calm by arming the young men and stationing them as guards here and there. And so the enemy, after seizing booty from the places nearest to hand, did not venture to approach the city, but started back by a roundabout route, their confidence growing greater the further the distance they put between themselves and Rome. They came upon Lucretius, who had previously reconnoitred their line of march and now, reinforced by auxiliary troops, was ready for a fight. And so in high spirits they attacked, the suddenness of it terrifying the enemy. Though rather fewer in number, they routed and put to flight a great multitude, herding them into deep valleys from which escape was not easy. There the Volscian nation was nearly wiped out. I find one historian claiming that 13,470 fell in battle, 1,750 were captured, and twenty-seven military standards taken; even though these figures are somewhat exaggerated, the slaughter was undoubtedly great. The victorious consul took possession of much booty and returned to his standing camp by the route by which he had come. Then the consuls joined camps, while the Volsci and Aequi brought together their shattered forces. The third battle of the year followed. Good fortune continued; the Romans won and, after routing the enemy, even captured their camp.

9. Rome thus went back to what she had been before, and success against her enemies immediately triggered upheaval in the city. Gaius Terentilius Harsa was tribune of the plebs that year. Thinking that the absence of the consuls from the city had created an opportunity for the tribunes to take action, he inveighed for some days against the arrogant behaviour of the senators before the plebs, criticizing

particularly the power of the consuls as excessive and intolerable in a free state: their power, he said, was ostensibly less objectionable but actually more oppressive than that of the kings; two masters had in fact been placed over them instead of one, enjoying unbounded and unlimited power; with free rein they turned all the terrors of the law and all its punishments upon the plebs. This licence ought not to go on indefinitely. He would, he said, propose a law that five men be elected to prepare legislation concerning the consuls' power;* the people would decide what sanctions might be invoked against themselves, and it was these the consul would follow; these, not their own whim and passion, would determine what the consuls would interpret as law.

After the law was proposed, the senators feared that they would be forced to submit in the absence of the consuls. But Quintus Fabius, the prefect of the city, called them into session, in which he denounced the bill and its proposer with such vehemence that even if the consuls had been present to menace the tribune, they could not have been more intimidating. Terentilius, he said, had set a trap and, capitalizing on the situation, was making an attack on his country. Had the gods in their anger seen to it that someone of his ilk had been tribune the year before when plague and war beset the state there would have been no resisting him. When the two consuls had died, when the state lay sick and prostrate, when everything was utterly confounded, he would have proposed laws doing away with consular power in the state: in short, he would have been the commander the Volsci and Aequi needed in order to attack the city. What then was his motive? Did he not have the power, if the consuls behaved arrogantly or cruelly to some citizen, to bring an indictment and to accuse them before a jury composed of the very peers of the victim? He was not making the consuls' power hateful and intolerable but that of the tribunes—a power which the senators had been brought to countenance and to live with, but which now was reverting to its pernicious character of old. But he was not begging Terentilius not to continue as he had begun. 'We ask you, the other tribunes,' said Fabius, 'to remember that your power was designed above all to help individuals, not to destroy us all. You were elected tribunes of the plebs, not foes of the senators. It brings unhappiness to us and odium upon you when our defenceless country is attacked. We ask not that you diminish your rights but your unpopularity. Convince your colleague to bring up the matter anew when the consuls return. After all, when the consuls perished from the plague in the previous year not even the Aequi and Volsci continued their war against us, cruel and arrogant though it was.' The tribunes talked with Terentilius and, with the proposal ostensibly postponed but in reality thwarted, the consuls were immediately recalled.

10. Lucretius returned with considerable booty and far greater renown; on arrival he increased that renown by setting out all the booty in the Campus Martius so that over a three-day period individuals could identify their property and take it away. The belongings of those owners who were not forthcoming was sold off. Everyone agreed that the consul had earned a triumph; but discussion of it was put off while the tribune argued for his law, for this took precedence in the consul's eyes. The bill was discussed for some days both in the senate and before the people; in the end the tribune yielded out of respect for the consul's office and desisted. Then the honour due commander and army was realized. He celebrated his triumph over the Volsci and Aequi, his legions following him in the triumphal procession. An *ouatio** was given the other consul, who entered the city without his soldiers.

Then in the following year the new consuls, Publius Volumnius and Servius Sulpicius, were confronted by the threat of the Terentilian law, which was sponsored by the entire college of tribunes. In this year the sky was seen to glow with fire, and a great earthquake occurred. That a cow spoke was given credence, something that in the previous year had not been admitted as a prodigy. Among other portents there was a rain of flesh, which as it showered down a great number of birds are said to have caught in mid-air; the part that reached the ground lay for some days without decay. The Sibylline books* were consulted by a two-man board in charge of sacred rites: danger was predicted from 'a concourse of strangers, lest the highest places in the city suffer attack and killing ensue'. Among other items there was a warning to abstain from political strife. The tribunes charged that the prediction was designed to block the law, and a great struggle loomed.

In order that the same cycle might repeat yet again this year, lo and behold, the Hernici announced that the Volsci and Aequi were fitting out their armies again, despite their crippling losses: that

Antium was the centre of it all; that at Ecetra the colonists from Antium were holding public meetings and that from Antium the impending war had its origin and drew its strength. When the senate heard the news, a levy was announced; the consuls were ordered to divide the conduct of the war between themselves, one to hold command against the Volsci, the other the Aequi. The tribunes proclaimed quite openly in the forum that the scenario of a Volscian war was a fiction and that the Hernici had been rehearsed in their role. The liberty of the Roman people was not now under attack by blunt and manly means but was being subverted by artifice. Because, the tribunes continued, no one believed that the Volsci and Aequi, virtually wiped out in the massacre, could be preparing for war of their own accord, a new enemy had been trumped up: a faithful colony near by was being falsely traduced. War was being declared upon the innocent people of Antium but waged against the plebeians of Rome, whom the authorities were going to load with weapons and march precipitously out of the city, thereby striking back at the tribunes with the exile and banishment of the citizens. They should therefore not think that there was any other purpose in all this than to defeat the law. But before it was too late—while they were still in the city and in civilian dress—they should see to it that they were not driven from the city and forced to knuckle under. If their determination was strong, help was at hand: all the tribunes were in agreement; there was no threat, nothing to fear, from abroad; the gods the previous year had seen to it that liberty could be defended in safety. Such were the arguments of the tribunes.

11. But on the other side of the forum the consuls placed their seats where the tribunes could see them and began to hold the levy. The tribunes hurried over and drew the crowd with them. A few people were called up as a test, and at once violence erupted. Whenever at the consul's order the lictor laid hands on anyone, the tribunes would order his release; no one moderated his behaviour according to the rights that were his due, but felt he had to resort to physical force to get what he wanted.

The conduct of the tribunes in prohibiting the levy corresponded to that of the senators in blocking the law, which was brought forward every day on which a voting assembly could be held. The uproar was triggered when the tribunes ordered the people to separate into their voting units but the senators refused to budge. The older ones were seldom involved, for this was a situation that was not amenable to reason but was at the mercy of reckless defiance. For the most part the consuls kept aloof, lest in the general mêlée their own high office be at risk to affront.

But Caeso Quinctius was there, a youth fiercely proud of his noble birth and of his size and physical strength. In addition to these god-given attributes he had by his own talents won many military awards and a reputation for eloquence in the forum; there was no man at Rome who was considered a readier speaker or a more energetic soldier than he. When he took his stand in the midst of the senators, he towered above the others and, as if embodying all the dictatorships and consulates in his voice and physique, he alone withstood the tribunes' attacks and the popular agitation. He took the lead in frequently driving the tribunes from the forum, in routing and putting the plebs to flight. Those who opposed him were stripped and beaten before being let go: it became clear that if he were allowed to go on in this way, the law was as good as defeated.

Then, after the other tribunes had been pretty thoroughly cowed, Aulus Verginius, one of their number, indicted Caeso on a capital charge. This action, far from frightening him, exacerbated his passionate nature; he opposed the measure even more fiercely, harassing the plebs and harrying the tribunes as if he were on the battlefield. The accuser allowed the defendant to rush about unchecked, as he added fuel to the hostility he had already aroused and exposed himself to additional charges; in the meantime Verginius introduced the measure not so much in hopes of seeing it passed as to provoke Caeso's rash nature even further. Many things said and done by the young nobles were often attributed solely to the already suspect behaviour of Caeso. Still, he continued to oppose the law. And Aulus Verginius repeatedly harangued the plebs: 'Don't you now see, fellow citizens, that you cannot at the same time have Caeso as a member of this community and the law that you desire? Yet the law is not the issue. It is your liberty that he opposes: in arrogance he surpasses all the Tarquins together. You see that as a private citizen he behaves with the power and wilfulness of a despot. Just wait until he becomes consul or dictator!' Many agreed, complaining that they had been manhandled and even urging the tribune to carry the matter through to the end.

12. When the day set for the trial drew near, it was clear that men

believed their liberty depended on Caeso's conviction. He was at last forced, with much loss of face, to solicit the support of individuals, accompanied by relatives, all prominent statesmen as they were. Titus Quinctius Capitolinus, who had three times been consul, in emphasizing the many honours of his family and himself, affirmed that no man in the Quinctian family or in the state had ever attained to such perfection of character and manliness; Caeso had been his most prized soldier; he had personally seen him battling the enemy on many occasions. Spurius Furius asserted that, when sent by Quinctius Capitolinus, Caeso had come to his rescue at a critical moment; there was no one who he thought had done more to save the day. Lucius Lucretius, consul the preceding year, took advantage of his recent glory by giving Caeso a share of it; he described the fighting and rehearsed Caeso's superlative service in forays and pitched battle. He urged them not to prefer this outstanding young man to be a member of any state save their own, blessed as he was by every gift of nature and fortune, an invaluable asset to any state that might claim him as a member. Hotheadedness and audacity, which they found objectionable in him, was decreasing daily as he grew older; what they missed in him—steady good sense—was growing from day to day. Since his faults were fading and his virtues coming into flower, they should permit him to live out his life in Rome. Among Caeso's advocates was his father, Lucius Quinctius, whose cognomen was Cincinnatus; he forbore repeating Caeso's praises for fear of adding to the resentment felt for his son, but sought forgiveness for his youthful waywardness by begging them to pardon Caeso as a favour to himself, who had never offended anyone by word or deed. Yet some silently rejected these entreaties out of diffidence or fear, while others, complaining that they and their friends had been roughly handled, made no secret of their impending verdict by returning a harsh response.

13. One of the charges against Caeso proved especially damaging, in addition to the widespread resentment felt for him. Marcus Volscius Fictor, who had been tribune of the plebs some years before, testified that not long after the plague had struck the city he fell in among a gang of young men who were roaming the Subura district of the city. A brawl developed, and his older brother, who had not fully recovered from the effects of the plague, collapsed when Caeso struck him with his fist; half-dead he was carried home, and Marcus

believed his brother's subsequent death was the result of the attack. Moreover, the consuls of the last few years had refused him access to legal recourse, despite the aggravated nature of the assault.

The vehemence of Volscius' speech so upset the people that they came near to attacking and killing Caeso. Verginius ordered him to be arrested and put in chains. The patricians countered force with force. Titus Quinctius cried that a man who had been indicted on a capital charge and was shortly to be tried ought not to be subject to physical restraint, unconvicted and unheard. The tribune said his intention was not to punish a man as yet unconvicted, but to keep him in chains until the day of the trial so that the Roman people would not be deprived of the opportunity to punish one who had murdered another. The other tribunes were appealed to and in a compromise decree came to Caeso's rescue.* They forbade him to be put in chains, but they announced that it was their will that the accused should appear for trial and that a sum of money be pledged to the people in case he should fail to do so. There was doubt as to how much money might equitably be required and the question was referred to the senate. While the senators deliberated, the accused was kept in public detention. They decided that bail should be required, which was to be calculated in units of three thousand asses, leaving it to the tribunes to determine the number of units. They proceeded to fix the number at ten. The prosecutor therefore required the accused to pledge this amount; this was the first case of a man giving public bail.

After he was allowed to leave the forum, Caeso went into exile the following night among the Etruscans. On the day of the trial, when it was stated that he had changed his residence and was now in exile, even though Verginius was presiding, his colleagues, when appealed to, stopped the trial from proceeding *in absentia* and dismissed the assembly. The bail money was mercilessly exacted from Caeso's father to the extent that, after selling off all his property, he lived for a time in a remote hut on the other side of the Tiber, as if in banishment.

14. The city's attention was fixed on the trial and the promulgation of the law that Terentilius had proposed earlier; peace prevailed abroad. The tribunes, now that the senators had suffered a defeat in Caeso's exile, considered themselves the winners and the law as good as passed. And while the older senators had let their control of

the government slip from their grasp, their younger counterparts, especially those who had been Caeso's close associates, felt increasingly angry with the plebs and did not abate their resolve. Yet the situation improved to the extent that they now tempered their passions with a certain restraint. When first after Caeso's exile the law came up for passage, they organized a great army of their clients and, when the tribunes provided an excuse by trying to remove them from the assembly, they staged an attack in which no individual stood out for bravado or unpopularity, with the result that the plebs complained that they were now facing a thousand Caesos in place of one. In the intervening days when the tribunes were not trying to pass the law, these same men were invariably mild and peaceable. They greeted the plebs kindly, conversed with them, entertained them in their homes, appeared in the forum to give them their support and allowed the tribunes to hold all other meetings without interference, never behaving harshly to anyone in public or private save when the law was coming up for a vote; in all else the young nobles were like members of the popular party. The tribunes thus carried through other measures in peace, and, more than this, their re-election for the following year brought no objection, much less a physical response. The young nobles, by soothing the plebs and handling them gently, tamed their high spirits bit by bit. By such devices the passing of the law was frustrated for the entire year.

15. The next consuls, Gaius Claudius, son of Appius, and Publius Valerius Publicola, took over a less troubled state. The new year had brought no new concern: men continued to be preoccupied with either passing the law or having to accept it. The more the younger senators tried to win the plebs' goodwill, the fiercer the tribunes resisted. Aiming to make them suspect in the plebeians' eyes, they accused them of mounting a conspiracy: Caeso was in Rome; plans were being laid to kill the tribunes and slaughter the plebs; the older senators were behind this, having suborned their juniors to eliminate the tribunes' power so that the state might go back to what it had been before the plebs had seceded to the Sacred Mount. There was also fear of a war with the Volsci and Aequi, which had become a regular occurrence, if not quite an annual ritual.

Moreover, a new menace closer to home unexpectedly threatened. Up to 4,500 exiles and slaves under the leadership of Appius

Herdonius occupied the Capitol and citadel by night. Those on the citadel who had refused to join the conspiracy and to take up arms on its behalf were immediately killed; some escaped in the tumult and ran down in fear to the forum crying, 'To arms!' and 'The enemy is in the city!' The consuls were as much afraid of arming the plebs as of leaving them defenceless, not knowing what sort of disaster had suddenly befallen the state, whether from within or without, whether prompted by plebeian hatreds or treachery of the slaves. Yet in attempting to calm the uproar they sometimes added to it, for the multitude could not be controlled in their shocked and fearful state. Nevertheless, they issued weapons, yet not to all, but only enough to ensure that there would be a dependable defence force prepared for any eventuality, given their ignorance of who the enemy really was. They passed the rest of the night in anxious state, uncertain as to the identity and number of the foe, but setting up guard posts at all strategic spots throughout the city.

Dawn revealed the nature of the crisis and its instigator. From his position on the Citadel Appius Herdonius was calling the slaves to assert their freedom: he had, he proclaimed, espoused the cause of all Rome's downtrodden so that he might bring back to their country those who had been wrongfully driven into exile and might lift the heavy yoke of slavery from those who bore it; he hoped that the Roman people would support him; but if they did not, he would summon the Volsci and Aequi and would not hesitate to resort to the most extreme measures to achieve his aims.

16. The senators and consuls could now see the crisis more clearly. In addition to Herdonius' threats they feared that the Veientes and Sabines were behind him and that with so many enemies already in the city Sabine and Etruscan troops would soon be on the scene by prearrangement, while those perpetual foes, the Volsci and Aequi, would be coming not to devastate their territory as before, but to the city itself, now that part of it had been captured. Many and various were the fears that beset them; yet the slaves alarmed them particularly. Each man had a potential enemy within his house whom he could not safely trust nor, lest disaffection grow, mistrust: living in harmony scarcely seemed possible.

Confronted by so many overwhelming fears, they scarcely thought of the tribunes and plebs: *that* problem was mild by comparison, one that arose when others were in abeyance and now seemed lulled to rest in face of this foreign threat. But in fact it nearly proved the most crushing weight of all upon their sinking fortunes. For madness held the tribunes in its grip; it was not a war, they said, but a sham war that was now being waged on the Capitol; the aim was to divert the plebs' attention from the law; once it had been passed these foreign friends and clients of the patricians would realize their mock war had been in vain and would tiptoe away in even greater silence than they had come. They then proceeded to call an assembly to pass the law, summoning those in arms to abandon their posts. The consuls simultaneously convened the senate, the tribunes posing a far greater threat than the enemy's night attack had ever done.

17. On hearing the report that his men had laid down their weapons and were abandoning their posts, Publius Valerius left his colleague to preside over the senate while he rushed from the building and hurried to the place in the forum where the tribunes were holding their meeting. 'What do you think you are doing, tribunes? Are you bent on destroying the state under the leadership and auspices of Appius Herdonius? Have you succumbed to his corrupting influence while the slaves have not? Do you really intend to put aside your weapons to enter the voting booths while the enemy is upon you?' He then turned to the gathering crowd: 'Citizens, you may care nothing for the city or yourselves, but surely on seeing your gods in enemy hands you must feel fear. Jupiter Optimus Maximus, Queen Juno and Minerva, the other gods and goddesses— all are under siege. A camp of slaves possesses the tutelary deities of our country.* Is this what you call a healthy state of affairs? A huge enemy force is not only within the walls but on the citadel that overlooks this forum and senate-house; in the meantime you are down here passing laws as the senate debates: as if we hadn't a concern in the world, the senator speaks his piece while the rest of the citizens enter the polling place! Should not every senator and plebeian—consuls, tribunes, gods, and men—have rushed in arms to the Capitol to bring help, to free and bring peace to the august dwelling of Jupiter Optimus Maximus? Father Romulus, I call on you to instil in your descendants that spirit you once showed when recapturing the citadel from those same Sabines. Command them to follow the same path you and your army took. Look upon me as I, the consul, follow where you once trod, as much as mortal man can

emulate a god.' He ended his speech by saying that he was taking up arms and was calling on all citizens to do the same; if there was any resistance, he would disregard consular protocol and the tribunes' sacrosanct power, he would treat anyone he met as an enemy, whoever he was, wherever he was, on the Capitol, in the forum. Should the tribunes order their followers to take up arms against Publius Valerius, the consul (since they had forbidden it against Appius Herdonius), he threatened to do to the tribunes what the founder of his family had done to the kings.

It looked as if only force could resolve the impasse, a spectacle to delight the onlooking enemy. But the law could not be passed nor the consul proceed to the Capitol: darkness put an end to the struggle. The tribunes gave way as night came on, fearful of the military force at the consuls' disposal. Now that the leaders of the sedition were out of the way, the senators circulated among the plebs, joining their groups and planting words of advice apposite to the situation. They advised them to reflect on the crisis that they had brought on the state: the fight was not between senators and plebeians; rather, the senators and plebs, together with the citadel of the city, the temples of the gods and the tutelary gods of Rome and of each household, were being handed over to the enemy. While these attempts were being made in the forum to quell the discord, the consuls had made separate rounds of the gates and walls, lest the Sabines or Veientes should be on the move.

18. On the same night news reached as far as Tusculum that the citadel had been captured, the Capitol occupied and that dissension was rife in the city. Lucius Mamilius was then the dictator of Tusculum.* After the senate had been convened and the messengers given a hearing, he recommended in a forceful speech that they should not wait until ambassadors come from Rome seeking help. The very danger, the crisis itself, to say nothing of the gods invoked in their treaty and the obligation to uphold it, demanded this course: the gods would present them with no better opportunity of winning the goodwill of such a powerful state, and one so close by. They decreed that help be given; youths of military age were enrolled, arms distributed. When at dawn they arrived in Rome, they appeared from afar to be enemies, like the Aequi or Volsci on the move.

When fear subsided, they were admitted into the city, entering the forum in marching column. There they found Publius Valerius drawing up his men in battle order, his colleague having been left to guard the gates. Valerius had a powerful effect on his men when he made the following promise: after the Capitol was retaken and peace had returned to the city, if they would allow him to explain what hidden mischief lay in the law the tribunes were trying to pass, he would be mindful of his ancestors who had handed down to him the cognomen Publicola, People's Friend, which carried with it an inherited responsibility, and would do nothing to impede the plebs as they assembled to vote. And so they followed him, as the tribunes tried in vain to call them back. Up the slope of the Capitol they mounted the battleline. The legion from Tusculum formed part of the force. Tusculans and Romans vied as to which would win the glory of having recovered the city; each commander spurred his men forward. The enemy had confidence in nothing save their superior position; they were stricken with fear as Rome and her ally advanced the standards against them. At the moment the Romans burst into the vestibule of the temple, Publius Valerius was slain as he urged on the fight in the forefront. Publius Volumnius, an ex-consul, saw him as he fell and, after instructing his men to protect the body, himself flew to the fore to take the consul's place. As they hurtled forward in the heat of the fight, the soldiers were unaware of their grievous loss; they won the battle before they realized they had done so without their commander. Many of the exiles were slaughtered in the sacred precinct, many were captured, while Herdonius was killed. Thus the Capitol was retaken. As for the captives, each was punished according to his status, whether free or slave.* Thanks were given to the Tusculans, the Capitol cleansed and purified. The plebs are said to have tossed quarter-coins into the consul's house so that his burial might be conducted on a more impressive scale.

19. When peace had been restored the tribunes began to press the senators to honour the promise made by Publius Valerius and to press Gaius Claudius to permit the law to be discussed, which would free the departed spirit of his colleague from the dishonour of its non-fulfilment. The consul replied that he would allow no such discussion until a replacement for Valerius had been chosen, thereby initiating a dispute that continued until the day of the election, which took place in December. Lucius Quinctius Cincinnatus,

father of Caeso, was elected with the enthusiastic support of the senators and at once entered office. The plebs were dismayed at facing a hostile consul whose power stemmed from the high regard the senators had for him, from his own courageous nature, and from his three sons, each of whom was Caeso's equal in greatness of spirit but, when the situation required, his superior in good sense and restraint.

On entering office Cincinnatus held a series of meetings in which he proved from the tribunal to be more vehement in castigating the senate than in restraining the plebs: that body, he charged, had proven so permissive that one set of tribunes after another had by their abusive language acted not as in a commonwealth but like petty tyrants in an ill-run household. Courage, steadfastness, and all the glory young men could win in war and at home had been driven from Rome along with his son Caeso, and sent into exile. Glib-tongued and seditious, sowing the seeds of discord, tribunes were now re-elected two and three times over, stooping to the vilest practices and acting with the licence the kings had once enjoyed. 'Just because he was not on the Capitol does not make Aulus Verginius any less deserving of punishment than Appius Herdonius, does it? By god, any man of sense would say he deserved it more. At least Herdonius, in declaring himself your enemy, gave notice that you should take up arms. This man, by denying there was a war, took away your weapons and exposed you to your slaves and to the exiles with no means of defending yourselves. I mean no disrespect to Gaius Claudius or to the late Publius Valerius—but did you actually advance the standards up the Capitol without first ridding yourselves of these enemies here in the forum?

'What happened then was an outrage in the eyes of gods and men. The enemy was in the citadel and on our Capitol; their leader commanded a bunch of exiles and slaves; they profaned all the sacred places there, actually occupying the shrine of Jupiter Optimus Maximus himself. And what was the response? Arms were taken up at Tusculum before they were at Rome! There was a real question whether the Tusculan commander Lucius Mamilius or our own consuls, Publius Valerius and Gaius Claudius, would liberate Rome's citadel. In time past we would not allow the Latins to arm themselves even in self-defence against an enemy that had invaded their territory; yet now, had they not taken up arms of their own accord, we would have been captured and wiped out! Do you tribunes claim to be "aiding the plebeians" when you expose them unarmed to enemy slaughter? I have no doubt that if the lowliest plebeian, a member of that cadre you have split off from the rest of the populace and formed into a second country which you have made your personal fiefdom—if any one of these fellows claimed that his slaves had weapons and had taken over his house, you would think that "aid should be given". Was Jupiter Optimus Maximus, when he was besieged by armed exiles and slaves, deserving of no human help? Do these tribunes really demand to be held sacred and inviolate who hold the gods themselves to be neither? And yet, though steeped in wickedness against gods and men, you tribunes keep saying you will pass the law this year. By god, the day I was elected consul will mark a catastrophe far worse for Rome than when Publius Valerius perished: it will—but only if you succeed in passing it.

'Fellow citizens, the first thing my colleague and I intend to do is to march the legions against the Volsci and Aequi. By some mysterious fate our gods favour us more in war than in peace. How great the danger would have been had these peoples known exiles were besieging the Capitol is better left for you to imagine from their past conduct than to experience in actual fact.'

20. The consul's speech impressed the plebs; the senators were convinced that the republic had been restored to its old self. The other consul, more spirited as a supporter than a leader, although he had been willing to cede to his colleague the initiative in devising so bold a course of action, now claimed for himself a consul's share in carrying it out. The tribunes scoffed at Quinctius' declaration as empty show, persistently asking how the consuls intended to lead out an army that they would not be permitted to recruit. 'Recruitment is not necessary,' Quinctius replied, 'because, at the time when Publius Valerius gave the plebs arms for retaking the Capitol, all swore an oath to assemble at the consul's bidding and not to disband without his permission. Accordingly, we order all of you who swore this oath to present yourselves in arms at Lake Regillus tomorrow.' The tribunes then began to quibble, aiming to relieve the soldiers of their religious obligation: Quinctius, they said, was a private citizen at the time when the soldiers bound themselves by the oath.

But the disregard of religious scruple that so pervades the present age had not yet arrived; no one then interpreted oaths and laws to suit personal convenience, but behaved according to their dictates. And so the tribunes gave up hope of blocking the levy and now moved to delay the army's departure, especially when they heard the rumour that the augurs had been ordered to be present at Lake Regillus and to inaugurate a site where the popular assembly might be held after the auspices had been duly taken: any measure passed at Rome by tribunician violence could be rescinded in this assembly. In this event, the tribunes believed, everyone would vote as the consuls wanted, since the right of appeal did not extend more than a mile from the city, and the tribunes, if they came to Regillus, would be subject to consular power along with everyone else. These facts were upsetting enough, but what frightened them most was Quinctius' repeated avowal not to hold consular elections. The sickness of the state, he said, was too grave to be cured by conventional remedies; a dictator was needed so that he who tried to disturb the status quo would discover that there was no right of appeal when a dictator was in power.

21. The senate was in session on the Capitol. The tribunes went there accompanied by the thoroughly agitated plebeians. With a great outcry the crowd implored the consuls and the senate to support them, but the consul did not change his mind until the tribunes pledged to follow the will of the senate. Thereupon the consul raised the question of the demands made by the tribunes and plebs. Two decrees followed: first, the tribunes should not attempt to pass the law that year; second, the consuls should not march the troops out of the city. As for the future, the senate judged it contrary to the national interest for magistrates to succeed themselves or for tribunes to be re-elected. The consuls said they acceded to the will of the senate, but the tribunes were returned to office despite the consuls' loud protest. The senators retaliated by working to re-elect Lucius Quinctius as consul. The consul's speech proved his most uncompromising of the whole year. 'Should I be surprised, conscript fathers, if your authority has no weight with the plebs? You yourselves cheapen it: in response to the plebs annulling the senate's decree in re-electing their officials, you show that you too wish it annulled, as if superior power in the state were equivalent to superior irresponsibility and excess. For surely it is more irresponsible and senseless to subvert one's own decrees and decisions than for others to do so. Go, conscript fathers, ape the witless crowd; do

wrong by following the example of those to whom you should be setting an example of right conduct. As for me, I will not ape the tribunes; I will not allow myself to be declared consul contrary to the senate's decree. I urge you most earnestly, Gaius Claudius, not to permit the Roman people to attempt such folly and to believe me when I say that you will not be preventing my re-election; rather, greater glory will come to me by refusing it and I will escape the odium that would befall me should I continue in office.' Together they issued an edict to the effect that no one should vote for Lucius Quinctius as consul; if anyone did, they would disregard his vote.*

22. The consuls elected were Quintus Fabius Vibulanus for the third time and Lucius Cornelius Maluginensis. A census was conducted in this year; religious law forbade that the *lustrum* be closed because of the capture of the Capitol and the death of the consul.*

From the very start the consulship of Quintus Fabius and Lucius Cornelius proved turbulent. The tribunes egged on the plebs. The Latins and Hernici reported that the Volsci and Aequi were mounting a great war and that the Volscian legions were already at Antium. And it was much feared that the colony itself would defect. The tribunes with great reluctance allowed the war to take precedence.

The consuls were then allotted their provinces.* Fabius was given command of the legions to be led against Antium, Cornelius command of troops in Rome in order to counter any plundering raid of part of the enemy, which the Aequi were particularly prone to do. The Hernici and Latins were ordered to provide soldiers in accordance with their treaty; the army consisted of two-thirds allies and one-third citizens. When the allies arrived on the appointed day, the consul pitched camp outside the Capena Gate. From there, after the army had been ritually purified, he set out for Antium and settled down not far from the town and the enemy encampment. The Volsci did not venture to fight because the troops of the Aequi had not yet arrived; so they prepared to remain quiet, protected by their camp's palisade. On the following day Fabius did not form a single army composed of allies and citizens together, but assigned each of the peoples to its own part of the battleline around the enemy rampart, himself commanding the Roman legions in the centre. He then ordered Romans and allies to obey together the signal to begin the fight and to retreat, should the trumpet sound a recall. At the same time he stationed the cavalry of each people behind its own detach-

ment on the front line. In this fashion he attacked the encircled
camp on three fronts and drove the Volsci from the palisade, who
were unable to withstand the assault that pressed them on all sides.
He breached their defence works, drove the frightened throng forward in a single direction, and expelled it from the camp. The
cavalry, which could not easily cross the palisade, had up to this
point been spectators of the battle; but now it had a share of the
victory by catching up with the terrified enemy as they fled in
disorder over open ground and by cutting them down. The slaughter inside and outside the camp of those fleeing was great, but the
booty was greater still because the enemy had been scarcely able to
take even their weapons with them as they fled. Their army would
have been wiped out had they not found concealment in the forests
thereabout.

23. While these things were going on at Antium, the Aequi sent
a crack division ahead of their main army and in a surprise move
seized by night the citadel of Tusculum. The rest of the force took
up a position not far from the city's walls in order to stretch thin the
enemy's forces. News of what happened, which was quickly brought
to Rome and from Rome to the camp at Antium, caused the Romans
to react no differently than if the Capitol had been reported captured; besides, Tusculum's service to Rome had been so recent and
the similar plight of the two cities seemed to demand a similar
response. Fabius, dropping all else, quickly hustled the booty from
the camp to Antium and, after leaving a small garrison there, marched
swiftly to Tusculum. The soldiers were allowed to take nothing save
their weapons and what ready-to-eat food was on hand. The consul
Cornelius sent regular supplies from Rome.

The war at Tusculum went on for some months. With part of
the army the consul attacked the camp of the Aequi; part had been
assigned to the Tusculans to recapture the citadel, but there sheer
force had no effect. In the end hunger forced the enemy to give
up. When they had been reduced to these straits, the Tusculans
sent them under the yoke of submission, stripped and without
weapons. The consul caught up with them as they were hurrying
homeward in ignominious flight at Mount Algidus and slaughtered
them to a man. The victorious consul then marched back and fixed
his camp at a place called Columen. The other consul, now that
the enemy defeat had removed any threat to the city itself, set out

from Rome. And so together they entered enemy territory on two fronts at once, devastating in a mighty sweep the land of now the Volsci, now the Aequi. Most authorities, I find, say that the people of Antium defected in this same year and that the consul Lucius Cornelius fought them and retook the town. I would not venture to affirm the truth of this because I find no mention of it in older writers.*

24. Although this war was over, the war with the tribunes at home alarmed the senators. The tribunes cried that keeping the army in the field was a trick designed to frustrate the passing of the law but that they were determined to finish what they had begun. Nevertheless Lucius Lucretius, prefect of the city, succeeded in having the tribunes postpone any further move until the consuls returned.

And a new cause of unrest had also arisen. The quaestors Aulus Cornelius and Quintus Servilius indicted Marcus Volscius for having committed outright perjury against Caeso. For there was a good deal of evidence about Volscius' brother: once he had fallen ill, not only had he never appeared in public again but in fact had not recovered at all, but had died from a wasting disease of many months; what is more, during the time that Volscius had charged Caeso with having committed the crime, Caeso had not been seen at Rome; in fact, those who had served with him affirmed that he had been regularly on duty in the field and had taken no furloughs. Many proposed that a private arbitrator determine the truth of the matter. But Volscius did not dare to subject himself to such a proceeding. In fact, with all this new information pointing to his guilt, his conviction seemed as likely as Caeso's had been when Volscius testified against him. But the tribunes impeded the proceedings; they said they would not allow the quaestors to convene the people to try the defendant unless the people were first convened to decide on the law. And so both issues remained undecided until the consuls returned. When they entered the city in triumph with their victorious army and found no one speaking of the law, many assumed the tribunes had been worsted. But they—for it was already the end of the year—now put their energies into being returned for a fourth term, thereby shifting the struggle from the law to a dispute over their re-election. The consuls fought against their continuation in office as vigorously as they would have opposed the passing of the

law that aimed to curtail their power; but victory in the struggle
went to the tribunes.

In the same year peace was granted the Aequi at their request.
The census, which had been begun the previous year, was completed, and is said to have been the tenth *lustrum* since the beginning
of the city. Enrolled were 117,319 citizens. Great was the glory of
the consuls of that year for what they had accomplished at home and
in the field: peace was achieved abroad, while at home, although
harmony eluded them, the state had been less troubled than in
earlier years.

25. Lucius Minucius and Gaius Nautius, who were elected the
next consuls, faced the two disputes of the previous year that had
been left unresolved. As before, the consuls tried to block the law,
the tribunes to block Volscius' trial; but the new quaestors proved
stronger and more influential. Titus Quinctius Capitolinus, who had
been three times consul, was quaestor along with Marcus Valerius,
the son of Manius and grandson of Volesus. Since it was not possible to restore Caeso to the Quinctian family or this finest of the
Roman youth to his country, Capitolinus elected to wage a just and
pious war against the perjurer who had kept an innocent man from
defending himself. Verginius was the most energetic advocate of the
law among the tribunes. A period of two months was granted the
consuls to analyse the law and instruct the people about the hidden
traps it contained; at its expiration a vote could be taken.

During these two months the city enjoyed a welcome respite. But
the Aequi did not remain quiet; breaking the treaty they had struck
the year before with Rome, they chose as their commander Gracchus
Cloelius, who was easily the most prominent leader among them.
With Gracchus as their captain they first raided Lanuvian territory
and then that of Tusculum; laden with booty, they pitched camp on
Mount Algidus. Quintus Fabius, Publius Volumnius, and Aulus
Postumius came there as envoys from Rome to complain of the
wrongs and to demand satisfaction in accordance with the treaty.
The commander of the Aequi told them to deliver their message
from the Roman senate to an oak tree near by: he had, he said, other
business to attend to. This mighty oak towered over the general's
tent and cast a deep shadow over the ground beneath. Thereupon
one of the envoys said as he was leaving, 'Let this sacred oak and
whatever divinities may be in this place know that you have broken

the treaty; let them stand by us now as we give voice to our grievances and later when we shall take up arms to punish this outrage that has violated the laws of gods and men alike.'

When the envoys returned to Rome, the senate ordered one consul to lead the army against Gracchus at Algidus; to the other it assigned the task of devastating the lands of the Aequi. The tribunes, as was their custom, moved to block the levy and possibly would have blocked it to the bitter end, but a new disaster suddenly struck: (26) a huge Sabine force on a plundering raid nearly reached the city walls. The countryside lay devastated, the city was in the grip of fear. The plebs then readily took up arms; and though the tribunes protested loudly two great armies were raised. Nautius led one against the Sabines; he pitched camp at Eretum, and by making small forays, chiefly night raids, he devastated the Sabine countryside so thoroughly that in comparison Roman territory appeared virtually unscathed. As for Minucius, he had neither the same good fortune nor the same pluck in carrying out his assignment, for when he pitched camp not far from the enemy and received a minor defeat, he took fright and shut himself up inside the camp. When the enemy saw his reaction, the fear of one side increased the boldness of the other, as is often the case; so they attacked the camp by night, but when sheer force proved ineffective, they encircled it the next day with siegeworks. But before they had completed the rampart and could shut off all escape, five cavalrymen slipped past the enemy outposts and brought the news to Rome that the consul and his army were under siege. The city was caught completely off guard; the ensuing fear and panic were such that one would have thought the enemy were besieging the city rather than the camp. The consul Nautius was recalled, but when he seemed unequal to the task the decision was taken to name a dictator to solve the crisis. Lucius Quinctius Cincinnatus was the unanimous choice.

Let those hearken to the following tale who prize money above all worldly things and think that great honour and merit fall to none save the extravagantly rich. Lucius Quinctius, the sole hope of his country, was at that moment toiling on his three-acre farm across the Tiber, which was opposite the present-day dockyards and is now known as the Quinctian meadows. The delegation from the senate found him there—possibly spading out a ditch or ploughing (whatever it was, all agree it was some simple farming chore). After an exchange of greetings they requested he don a toga to hear the senate's decree, which they prayed might prove auspicious for himself and for his country. 'Is everything all right?' he asked in wonderment, as he bade his wife Racilia fetch his toga quickly from the farmhouse. After he had wiped off the dust and sweat from his person and stepped forth clad in the toga, the delegation saluted him as dictator and gave their congratulations. They explained the dire straits into which the army had been plunged and summoned him to the city. The state had provided a boat to bring him across and, when he landed, his three sons greeted him, followed by other friends, and then by most of the senators. Surrounded by the throng and with the lictors leading the way, he was conducted to his city residence. There they found a great gathering of plebeians, who, however, were not so happy to see him, since they considered the power of the dictator to be excessive and that this man would prove an overzealous holder of it. No further steps were taken that evening except to post a night watch in the city.

27. When on the next day the dictator entered the forum before daybreak, he named Lucius Tarquinius master of the horse,* a patrician by birth who, though constrained by poverty to do his military service as an infantryman, was considered the foremost soldier in Rome. In an assembly conducted with the master of the horse he decreed a cessation of public business, ordered the shops throughout the city be closed, and forbade private business to be conducted as well; he decreed further that all of military age should present themselves in arms on the Campus Martius before sunset, bringing rations for five days and twelve stakes with which to build a palisade.* He ordered those too old for military service to prepare the rations for soldiers who were their neighbours, while the latter got their gear ready and looked for the stakes. These the recruits scattered to find, taking whatever came nearest to hand. No one tried to stop them, and everyone appeared promptly as the dictator had ordered. Then, with his troops so arranged that they were as ready for battle, should the situation require, as for marching, the dictator led out his men, the master of the horse his cavalry. Each commander gave the sort of speech to his troops that the present emergency demanded: to pick up speed, to reach the enemy while it was still dark; the consul and his army were surrounded; they had been under siege for three days now; no one knew what the coming night

or day might bring; great events often turned on a single moment. In response the soldiers shouted encouragement to one another, which much pleased the commanders: 'Forward, standard-bearer! Soldiers, follow his lead!'

They arrived at Mount Algidus in the dead of night and, upon realizing the enemy was hard by, halted their march. **28.** There the dictator went round on horseback to find out as best he could in the darkness the size and layout of the camp; he told the military tribunes to issue orders for all backpacks to be piled up in one spot and for the soldiers to return to their place in the ranks with their weapons and stakes. After this had been done, he stationed the whole army in a long line surrounding the enemy camp in the order they had taken on the march, and he commanded them to shout in unison when the signal was given, after which each man was to dig a trench in the area in front of him and throw up the dirt to form a rampart for the palisade. The signal quickly followed the order, and the soldiers acted upon it. Their combined shout rang about the enemy and, rising above his camp, penetrated to the consul's position. Fear descended on one side, great joy on the other. The Romans took heart and told one another that these were the voices of their fellow citizens and that help was at hand; they even struck fear into the enemy by attacking beyond their outposts and guard stations. The consul said they must act at once, for that shout meant not only that help had arrived but that battle had been joined, adding that he would be surprised if the enemy's outposts were not at that moment under attack. And so he ordered his men to seize their weapons and follow him. They began the battle in darkness; the shout they raised told the dictator's troops that they too were attacking the enemy. And so, just as the Aequi were preparing to prevent being encircled, the enemy they were surrounding began its assault; to stop them from breaking through into their camp, they concentrated their fighting on this front, which lasted until dawn and gave their encirclers time to complete their investiture.

First light revealed that they were now surrounded by the dictator's forces and were scarcely a match for one army. The dictator's men, shifting quickly from work with the spade to that of the sword, stormed the rampart. Now the enemy faced a new assault while the earlier continued unabated. Threatened with disaster on two fronts at once, they turned from battle to prayer, entreating the dictator on

one side and the consul on the other not to let their victory end in
a bloodbath but to take their weapons from them and let them go.
The consul told them to go to the dictator: the decision was his to
make. Quinctius in his anger added certain humiliating conditions:
their commander Gracchus Cloelius and other officers were to be
brought to him in chains and they were to evacuate the town of
Corbio. He had no need, he said, of spilling Aequan blood; but, to
exact a complete confession of their defeat and subjugation, they
were to pass under the yoke. One was made from three spears, two
fixed in the ground and the third tied across. It was under this that
the dictator caused the Aequi to pass.

29. The captured enemy camp was found full of their possessions, for the dictator had sent them away with nothing save their
lives. But he assigned all the plunder to his soldiers alone, while
rebuking the army of the consul and the consul himself. 'You soldiers will not share in the booty of an enemy to whom you so nearly
became the booty. As for you, Lucius Minucius, until you show you
know how a consul should behave, you will command these legions
as my subordinate.' So Minucius abdicated his consulship and, as
ordered, stayed with the army. But this army proved so ready to
submit to a man of superior power that, remembering what good
Quinctius had done rather than his rebuke, it voted him a crown of
gold, a pound in weight, and saluted him on his departure as their
protector.

At Rome the senate, when called into session by Quintus Fabius
the city prefect, ordered that Quinctius should enter the city in
triumph with his army following in the order it had taken on the
march. The enemy leaders were paraded before the chariot; military
standards headed up the procession; the army followed, laden with
booty. Tables of food are said to have been set before each house,
from which the soldiers ate as they followed the chariot, singing a
song of triumph and shouting traditional jibes in the manner of
revellers. On that day with everyone's approval citizenship was given
to Lucius Mamilius. The dictator would have immediately resigned
from office had not the trial of Marcus Volscius, who had perjured
himself, made him postpone doing so. The tribunes feared his power
and so did not try to block the trial. Volscius was found guilty and
went into exile at Lanuvium. Quinctius abdicated the dictatorship
within sixteen days, although his term was for six months.* During

those days the consul Nautius fought successfully against the Sabines at Eretum; this defeat followed upon the devastation of their territory. Fabius was sent to Algidus to succeed Minucius. At the end of the year there was agitation by the tribunes about the law; but because two armies were out of the city, the senate prevailed in not having any bill brought before the people; the plebs showed their power by re-electing the same tribunes for the fifth time. Dogs are said to have been seen chasing wolves on the Capitol. In response to this prodigy the Capitol was ritually purified. Such were the events of this year.

30. The next consuls were Quintus Minucius and Marcus Horatius Pulvillus. The year began with peace abroad and the same tribunes at home causing dissension over the same law. The situation would have worsened—so high were feelings running—had not the report come that, as if by design, the Aequi in a night raid had wiped out the garrison at Corbio. The consuls convened the senate; they were to enroll emergency soldiers and lead them to Algidus. Then, with the struggle over the law in abeyance, a new fight arose over the levy; the tribunes were getting the better of the consuls when a new crisis loomed: a Sabine army had invaded Roman territory on a plundering raid and was now heading for the city. People reacted in such fear that the tribunes allowed the soldiers to be enrolled, but not before an agreement was struck that, since their plans had been frustrated for five years and the interests of the plebs had been poorly served during this time, the number of tribunes of the plebs should hereafter be ten. The senators felt they had no choice but to agree: they accepted on the condition that they not see the same tribunes returned to office. And so, lest this concession come to nothing after the war as others had, tribunician elections were held at once. Thirty-six years had passed since the first tribunes; now ten were elected, two from each class,* and it was stipulated that they be elected in this manner hereafter.

After the levy had been held, Minucius set out against the Sabines but failed to encounter them. Horatius, since the Aequi after the massacre of the garrison at Corbio had gone on to seize Ortona also, fought them at Algidus; many a man was killed among the enemy; he drove the enemy not just from Algidus but from Corbio and Ortona as well. He razed Corbio to the ground because of the betrayal of the garrison.

31. Marcus Valerius and Spurius Verginius were elected the next consuls. There was peace at home and abroad; excessive rain led to a shortage of grain. A law was passed allowing the Aventine hill to be settled. The same tribunes of the plebs were re-elected. In the following year when Titus Romilius and Gaius Veturius were consuls, they constantly brought up in every public meeting they held the law Terentilius had once proposed: they would be ashamed, they said, at the pointless increase in their number if this law should hang fire during their two years of office as it had in the previous five. When this agitation was at its height, the worrisome report came from the Tusculans that the Aequi were in their territory. The recent service of Tusculum made the Romans ashamed to hold back in giving help. Both consuls were sent out at the head of an army, and found the enemy in its usual haunt in Algidus. There a battle was fought. Over seven thousand of the enemy were killed, others put to flight. The booty was enormous, which the consuls proceeded to auction off in order to refill a depleted treasury. This the army resented, and it became the basis of charges the tribunes brought against the consuls, which were to come before the people for decision. And so, on handing over their office to the new consuls, Spurius Tarpeius and Aulus Aternius, Romilius was indicted by Gaius Calvius Cicero, tribune of the plebs, Veturius by Lucius Alienus, plebeian aedile. Each was found guilty, to the great indignation of the senators; Romilius was fined ten thousand asses, Veturius fifteen. But the condemnation of their predecessors did not deter the new consuls. They said that it was possible for them, too, to be condemned, but it was not possible for the tribunes to pass the law.

The law that Terentilius had proposed long ago was abandoned, having outlived its time; the tribunes now began to treat with the senators in a more conciliatory spirit, proposing to end their contentiousness at last: if they disliked laws proposed by plebeians, they should at least permit the election of lawmakers selected jointly from plebeians and senators, whose task would be to propose measures to benefit both sides and aimed at ensuring equality before the law. The senators did not reject the general idea, but they maintained that none save the senators could be lawgivers. And so, with agreement over the legislation but not the legislators, Spurius Postumius Albus, Aulus Manlius, and Publius Sulpicius Camerinus were sent on an embassy to Athens with instructions to record the famous laws of Solon and to acquaint themselves with the institutions, customs, and laws of other Greek states.

32. The year was free from foreign wars. The one that followed, when Publius Curiatius and Sextus Quinctilius were consuls, was even more peaceful because of the complete inactivity of the tribunes. They were waiting for the envoys to return from Athens with copies of Greek laws; in addition, two terrible misfortunes struck simultaneously, famine and pestilence, devastating to man and beast alike. The countryside was a wasteland, the city prostrate from the long series of deaths. Many distinguished families were in mourning: the flamen of Quirinus, Servius Cornelius, died, as did the augur Gaius Horatius Pulvillus, in whose place the augurs chose Gaius Veturius, all the more eagerly because of his recent conviction by the plebs. The consul Quinctilius also died, as well as four tribunes of the plebs. And while the year was dreadful because of these multiple disasters, Rome's enemies were inactive.

The next consuls were Gaius Menenius and Publius Sestius Capitolinus. No foreign conflict occurred this year, although disturbances arose in the city. The envoys had now returned with the laws of Athens. With even greater urgency the tribunes pressed that there should finally be a start in writing down the laws. The decision was taken to appoint a board of ten men, the decemvirs, from whose decisions there would be no right of appeal, and that there be no other magistrates in their year of office. For a while there was a dispute as to whether plebeians would participate; in the end the senators had their way, with the proviso that the Icilian law about opening the Aventine to settlement and other sacred laws should not be abrogated.*

33. Three hundred and two years after Rome's founding the form of her government changed for the second time: power shifted from the consuls to the decemvirs, as it had before from the kings to the consuls. The change made less of an impression because it did not last long, for from an auspicious beginning the office grew rank like an overgrown plant, dying back rather quickly; thus, from ten men the state would soon go back to two vested with the title and power of consuls.

Those decemvirs chosen were Appius Claudius, Titus Genucius, Publius Sestius, Titus Veturius, Gaius Iulius, Aulus Manlius, Publius Sulpicius, Publius Curiatius, Titus Romilius, and Spurius Postumius.

Claudius and Genucius had been elected consuls designate for the coming year and now were named to the new office by way of compensation; Sestius, one of the consuls the year before, was also picked because he had brought the proposal for constitutional change before the senate despite his colleague's opposition. Those holding the next places of honour were the three envoys who had gone to Athens; the office was a reward for their having travelled so far afield; besides, people thought their knowledge of foreign legislation would prove useful for establishing the law at Rome. The other four, who were voted in last to make up the requisite number, were chosen, tradition says, because of their advanced age: they were thought less likely to offer spirited opposition to the others.

Appius assumed the leadership of the board because of plebeian support. He had changed his behaviour to such a degree that instead of being considered a savage and cruel persecutor of the plebs, he suddenly turned into their champion, seeking every opportunity to ingratiate himself with them. Each decemvir dispensed justice in rotation, one day in ten. On that day the twelve fasces belonged to the one administering the law; a single attendant each was assigned to the other nine. And while enjoying unparalleled harmony among themselves (although in the past such consensus had at times not proved beneficial to the governed), on this occasion they treated others with absolute fairness.* The following example will suffice to illustrate their even-handedness. The decemvirs were elected without the right of appeal. Even so, when a dead body was unearthed at the home of Lucius Sestius, a patrician by birth, and the corpse displayed in a public assembly, Gaius Iulius, one of the decemvirs, indicted Sestius and acted as the prosecuting attorney in a trial before the people. Sestius was clearly guilty of murder, and Iulius had the legal right to act as the judge; but he gave up this right so that he might add to the people's liberty by refusing to make use of his power as a magistrate.

34. While the decemvirs were dispensing justice that was accessible to high and low alike and was as scrupulous as if it came from an oracle, the board of ten was also concentrating on setting down the laws. People looked forward with keen expectation to what they would produce, and when ten tables were set up for all to see, the decemvirs prefaced their edict with a prayer that what was to happen would prove favourable, fortunate, and happy for them, their

children, and their country: they were to assemble and read the laws; they themselves, as much as the talents of ten men would allow, had made the laws applicable to high and low equally; yet when many people contribute talent and suggestions, the better the results; hence, they should consider carefully each particular, discuss it privately, and then let everyone know what they found that was negative or positive in it; the legislation would then seem to be what the Roman people as a whole had decided for itself rather than accepted from others. After the laws were amended in response to comments the people made on each provision, the Laws of the Ten Tables were passed in the Centuriate assembly; even now, despite the plethora of legislation that has followed, they stand as the fount of all law, public and private.

The people began to say that if two more tables were added, the body, so to speak, of the whole of Roman law would be complete. In expectation of this, there was a feeling as election day approached that the decemvirs should be re-elected. The plebs, apart from the fact that they hated the name of consuls as much as they had that of the kings, did not even seek to have the tribunes back as their protectors, since the decemvirs recognized the right of appeal from one to another.

35. But after the election of the new decemvirs was fixed in twenty-four days' time, the political climate became so heated that even the leading men of the state—no doubt dismayed at the prospect of less worthy men holding this powerful office if they chose not to run—began to buttonhole prospective voters and to beg support from plebeians with whom they had been at odds for an office they had vehemently opposed. Appius Claudius believed that now, in the prime of life and with the high offices he had held, his political eminence was now threatened, and he reacted accordingly. You would not have known whether he was a decemvir or seeking to become one: at times he acted more like a candidate than an incumbent. He began to assail the conservative establishment and to praise the meanest and shallowest among the candidates, while flying around the forum accompanied by the likes of Duilius and Icilius, former tribunes, and using their influence to sell himself to the plebeians. Finally his colleagues, who up to then had been his wholehearted supporters, looked askance at him and began to wonder what it all meant: clearly he was up to no good; when a proud aristocrat

behaves so chummily he must have an ulterior motive; to go to the extreme of acting like one of the rank and file and to hobnob with ordinary people is not so much the mark of a man hastening to lay down his office as of one looking for a way to continue in it.

Not daring openly to block his desire, they proceeded to disguise a blocking manœuvre by playing up to his vanity. They all agreed to do him the honour of putting him in charge of presiding over the electoral assembly, as the youngest among them. He could not elect himself—this was their thinking—for this was something that no one had ever done, save for some tribunes of the plebs, who had set an utterly repugnant precedent in doing so. He promptly agreed to act as the presiding officer, adding a prayer that it might turn out for the best; in doing so he changed an obstacle into an opportunity. For he joined a cabal to defeat the two Quinctii, Capitolinus and Cincinnatus, as well as his own uncle, Gaius Claudius, the most stalwart of the conservatives, and other candidates of the same eminence: he then proceeded to announce the election of much less distinguished decemvirs, himself chief among them; the strength of good men's disapproval was as great as their belief had been that he would not dare to do it. Elected with him were Marcus Cornelius Maluginensis, Marcus Sergius, Lucius Minucius, Quintus Fabius Vibulanus, Quintus Poetelius, Titus Antonius Merenda, Caeso Duilius, Spurius Oppius Cornicen, and Manius Rabuleius.

36. This was the end of Appius' pretending to be what he was not. From then on he started to follow the dictates of his own nature and to impose his way of doing things on his new colleagues even before they entered office. They began to meet daily with no witnesses present, where they secretly cooked up despotic plans; no longer bothering to conceal their arrogance, they made themselves largely unapproachable and would speak to few—behaviour that persisted until the fifteenth, or Ides, of May (in those days the Ides of May was the regular date for magistrates to enter office). The announcement they made on their first day caused every one to shiver in apprehension, for, while the previous decemvirs had observed the rule that only one of them should hold the fasces and that this symbol of royalty should pass to each of them in turn, every one of them appeared in the forum with twelves fasces of his own. One hundred and twenty lictors filled the forum carrying before them the axes bound up with the rods; there was no point in removing the

axes, they explained, since they had been elected without the right of appeal.*

They paraded about like ten kings, increasing the fear felt not just by the lower orders but by the leading senators as well, who suspected that an opportunity was being sought to begin a bloodbath: if any of them should utter a cry for liberty in the senate or before the people, the rods and axes would be readied for use, which would serve to intimidate the rest of the population as well. For apart from the fact that there was no protection in the people, with the right of appeal having been taken away, the new decemvirs had also agreed that none of them would recognize intercession, whereas the earlier ones had permitted their decisions to be amended by appeal to one of their colleagues and certain matters that might be thought within their power to be referred to the people.

For a time fear affected all alike; but bit by bit the plebeians began to bear the brunt of it. Senators were not the targets. The lower orders were treated in an arbitrary and cruel fashion: who you were, not the merit of your case, was all that mattered; justice was determined by favouritism. They held counterfeit trials in the privacy of their homes and announced the verdicts in the forum. If anyone appealed to a colleague, he left wishing he had been satisfied with the first decision. There was also the belief, though no one would personally vouch for it, that they had conspired to commit such outrages not just for the present but had sworn a secret oath among themselves not to hold elections but to continue to exercise the power of the Decemvirate now that they had secured it.

37. The plebeians then looked to the reaction of the patricians and began to catch at some hope of liberty from them, on whose account, in their fear of subjection, they had brought the state to the present pass. The leading senators hated the decemvirs and hated the plebs. They did not approve of what had transpired, yet thought the plebs had got what they deserved; they were pleased that the plebs in their headlong rush to liberty had fallen into subjection; yet they did not want their suffering multiplied: their aim was that the plebeians in their revulsion from the present conditions would want the two consuls and the former constitution back. Most of the year had gone by and two tables of laws had been added to the ten tables of the previous year; when the new laws were also passed by the Centuriate assembly, there would be no reason for the Decemvirate

to continue to exist. People expected that the consular elections would soon be announced. The plebeians were concerned only with the re-establishment of the tribunes' power, the safeguard of their liberty that was no longer theirs.

In the meantime no mention was made of any elections. The decemvirs, who had earlier courted popularity by being seen in the company of former tribunes, now kept a cadre of young patricians as a bodyguard. They planted themselves in squads around the tribunals, manhandling the plebeians and robbing them of possessions and property, as if the stronger had the right to take whatever they wanted. Physical abuse occurred. Some were beaten with the rods, others beheaded with the axe. And so that such cruelty might not go unrewarded, the property owner's punishment was followed by the awarding of his property to his persecutor. Such rewards corrupted the young nobles: not only did they not oppose such outrages, but openly showed they preferred the licence to act as they pleased to the liberty of everyone else.

38. The Ides of May arrived. No magistrates had been elected, and although they appeared in public not as decemvirs but private citizens, they had every intention of holding on to their power and insignia of office. This was tyranny undisguised: liberty was given up as forever lost; no one attempted to reclaim it, nor was anyone likely to make the attempt in the future. The Romans had not only lost their spirit themselves, but began to be looked on with contempt by neighbouring peoples, who thought those who had lost their liberty were unworthy holders of imperial power. A large detachment of Sabines raided Roman territory and plundered widely, taking with impunity humans and animals as booty; after recalling their wide-ranging raiding parties, they pitched camp at Eretum, putting their hopes in Rome's discord, which would, they thought, prevent the mobilization of an army. Reports of what had happened and the throng of peasants that filled the city created panic. The decemvirs debated what to do: hated by senators and plebeians alike, they felt themselves quite alone. Fortune brought a second source of fear. The Aequi on another front fixed camp at Algidus, from which they laid waste Tusculan territory in a series of raids; envoys from Tusculum arrived, reporting what had happened and asking for help.

The decemvirs became so frightened that they determined to

consult the senate in face of this simultaneous double threat to the
city. They ordered that the senators be summoned into session, not
unaware how great a storm of hostility they were likely to face:
everyone would blame them for the devastation of the land and the
dangers that threatened; and there would be an attempt to abolish
their office unless they united to resist and, by using their power
ruthlessly to crush their most outspoken critics, bring the rest to
heel. The cry of the herald was heard in the forum summoning the
senators into session before the decemvirs. This novel occurrence
(the custom of consulting the senate had long been in abeyance)
made the plebs wonder what had happened to cause the decemvirs
to revive the practice: Rome should be thankful for the enemy attacks because they had led to the revival of at least one aspect of her
days of freedom. They looked everywhere in the forum to find a
senator but saw scarcely any, and beheld the decemvirs sitting alone
in an empty senate-house. The latter took the failure of the senators
to assemble as proof of the hatred felt for their rule, the plebs as
evidence that those who held no office did not have the right to call
the senate. A start had been made toward the recovery of liberty, the
plebeians believed, provided they allied with the senate and refused
recruitment, following the lead of the senators who had not convened when summoned. Such was the talk among themselves. There
was scarcely a senator in the forum and few in the city. Out of
disgust with present conditions they had retired to their country
farms, where they busied themselves with their personal affairs rather
than those of the state, in the belief that the greater the distance
they put between themselves and their despotic overlords the safer
they would be.

    After they had failed to assemble when summoned, officers were
sent around to their homes to exact fines for non-attendance and to
ascertain whether their absence was deliberate. When the report
came back that the senators were on their country estates, the
decemvirs' spirits lifted: this was better than if the order to convene
had been refused outright. They commanded that all be sent for and
fixed the senate meeting for the next day. Attendance proved somewhat greater than they had hoped. At this juncture the plebs thought
the senators had betrayed the cause of freedom: they were obeying
those whose magistracy had expired and who were no different from
private persons, save in their use of force, and were behaving as if

these persons had the right to give them orders. **39.** But we are told that their obedience in coming to the senate chamber was greater than the submissiveness of the speeches they delivered. Tradition says that Lucius Valerius Potitus, after Appius Claudius had put the question to the house but before opinions were asked for in order of precedence, demanded that he first be permitted to speak on the state of the nation; when the decemvirs forbade this and threatened him, he created an uproar by declaring he would go before the people.

With equal vehemence Marcus Horatius Barbatus went on the offensive, calling them ten Tarquins and reminding them that the kings had been expelled under the leadership of the Valerii and Horatii. This happened, he continued, not because men rejected the idea of a king—after all, Jupiter rightly had the title, as had Romulus, the city's founder, and the kings who succeeded him, and it was even retained as the traditional title of those performing sacrifices*— no, what was hated was the last king's arrogance and violence. Who would put up with behaviour in so many private persons that had then been intolerable in a single king,* or the king's son? They should see to it that they did not provoke speech outside the senate-house by forbidding free speech within it; as for himself, he did not see that it was any less permissible for a man in private life to summon the people to an assembly than it was for the decemvirs to convene the senate. Let them find out, if they wished, how much stronger is a man's resentment in defending his rights than is the determination to exercise an unjust despotism. They put the question to the house about war with the Sabines, as if the Roman people had no less of a war with those who were elected to write up the laws but had left no law in the state! Men who had done away with assemblies, annual magistracies, and the passing of power from one set of officials to another, which was the sole safeguard of freedom; men who were merely private citizens yet held the fasces and kingly power. After the kings had been expelled there had been patrician magistrates; plebeian magistrates came into being after the secession of the plebs. To what party did they belong? The people's? What had they done through the people? The conservative cause? For nearly a year they had refused to hold a meeting of the senate, but now, when they have, they forbid speaking about the state of the nation! Let them not put much hope in the fear of others; what they feared seemed by now less oppressive than what they were already putting up with.

40. As Horatius gave this fiery speech, the decemvirs did not know how much anger or forbearance to show, nor did they see how the situation would resolve itself. Gaius Claudius, the uncle of Appius, the decemvir, then took the floor; his speech was more like an entreaty than a rebuke, for he invoked the departed soul of his brother, Appius' father, and begged his nephew to remember the citizen society into which he had been born rather than the unsavoury compact he had struck with his colleagues. He begged this much more for Appius' sake than for that of the state: the latter would seek redress from the decemvirs whether they consented or not; on the other hand, from great struggles great passions almost always arise: he shuddered, he said, to think what such passions would lead to in this case. While the decemvirs wished to forbid discussion of anything except the question they had put before the house, they hesitated to cut Claudius off. He therefore completed his speech, saying that in his opinion no decree of the senate should be issued whatever. Everyone interpreted this to mean that Claudius judged the decemvirs to be private citizens; so many of the consulars rose thereafter simply to express agreement with him. Another proposal was that the patricians should assemble to name an interrex,* which at first sight seemed harsher but was in reality something of a compromise, for if they issued any sort of decree, it would show that they judged those who convened the senate to be magistrates, while by advocating the issuance of no decree they were judging them to be persons in private life.

As the position of the decemvirs became ever more doubtful, Lucius Cornelius Maluginensis, the brother of the decemvir, Marcus Cornelius, rose to respond, having been deliberately reserved as last to speak among the consulars. He defended his brother and his brother's colleagues by feigning concern over the war: by what coincidence of fate, he wanted to know, had it happened that the people attacking the decemvirs were the very ones—or at least most of them were—who had been the unsuccessful candidates for the Decemvirate; and why was it that for months on end, when the state was at peace, no one had questioned whether the heads of state were proper magistrates, but that now, when Rome's enemies were practically at her gates, was the time they chose to create civil discord—

unless they thought that dissension would help to conceal what they
were really up to. What is more, at a time in which Rome was more
worried about war with her enemies, it was not right for such an
important matter as the legitimacy of the decemvirs to be prejudged.*
As for the claim of Valerius and Horatius that by the Ides of May
the decemvirs had ceased to be magistrates, he proposed that this
question be decided by the senate after the wars that faced them
were over and the state was once more at peace, and, further, that
Appius Claudius should realize he must be prepared at that time to
explain how he viewed the election of decemvirs over which he as
decemvir had presided: whether they were elected for one year or
until the laws that were still missing had been written up and passed.
In his view, everything except the war should be disregarded for the
present; if they thought the rumours about the war were false and
that the messengers and the Tusculan envoys were not to be believed, he proposed that scouts be sent who should report on what
they discovered; but if they trusted the messengers and envoys, that
a levy be held at the first opportunity and the decemvirs lead the
armies where it seemed best to the several commanders and that no
other matter take precedence.

41. The younger senators pressed to have the house divide on this
proposal and seemed to be winning their point.* In response Valerius
and Horatius became even more insistent than before, demanding
loudly that they be permitted to speak on the state of the nation: if
they were prevented from doing so by a cabal, they would address
the people; those having no official standing could not stop them
either in the senate or in an assembly, nor would they defer to the
bogus fasces of those present. Appius thought that his authority
would collapse unless he countered their attack with equal boldness.
'You will be well advised', he said, 'to say nothing except what
pertains to the question before the house.' When Valerius retorted
that only an officer of state had the right to prevent him from
speaking, Appius ordered the lictor to arrest him. From the threshold of the chamber Valerius implored his fellow citizens outside to
protect him, but Lucius Cornelius clutched Appius in suppliant
fashion (he was acting in Appius' interest, not Valerius'), thereby
putting an end to the struggle. As a favour to Cornelius, Valerius
was allowed to say what he wanted; but liberty went no further than
speech: the decemvirs had their way. In addition, the consulars

and senior senators continued to be hostile to the power of the tribunes, which they thought the plebs missed much more than that of the consuls; and so they almost preferred that the decemvirs should voluntarily resign their magistracy at some later date than that hatred for them should prompt another uprising of the plebs: if the situation were handled gingerly, they thought, and popular outcry avoided, the consulship might be revived and, either because of intervening wars or the moderate behaviour of the consuls in exercising their power, the plebs could be induced to forget the tribunes.

Amid the silence of the patricians the levy was announced. Those of military age answered when their names were called, since there was no right of appeal. When the legions had been enrolled, the decemvirs decided among themselves which ones ought to serve in the war and which should command the armies. The chief decemvirs were Quintus Fabius and Appius Claudius. Since a greater war undoubtedly loomed at home than abroad, they thought Appius' militant nature was better suited to suppress civil unrest, while Fabius' character was not so much actively bad as unsteady. Indeed, the Decemvirate and his colleagues had so changed Fabius that he no longer was the great soldier and statesman he once had been, but preferred to model his conduct after Appius than after his former self. The Sabine war was assigned to him, with Manius Rabuleius and Quintus Poetelius acting as his lieutenants. Marcus Cornelius was sent to Algidus with Lucius Minucius, Titus Antonius, Caeso Duilius, and Marcus Sergius. They decreed also that Spurius Oppius should help Appius Claudius in protecting the city, holding power equal to all other decemvirs.

42. The interests of the nation were no better served in the field than at home. The only fault of the commanders was that their conduct had made them hateful to the citizens: the soldiers were responsible for the disaster in every other respect, for they were determined that nothing should succeed under the leadership and auspices of the decemvirs; so they allowed themselves to be beaten, to the disgrace of themselves and their commanders. Armies were defeated both by the Sabines at Eretum and on Algidus by the Aequi. In the dead of night refugees from Eretum pitched camp on an elevation nearer to the city between Fidenae and Crustumeria; they had refused a direct fight at any point during the enemy's

pursuit, and found protection in the nature of the terrain and the palisade they built, not in their weapons or courage. At Algidus both the disgrace and the slaughter were even greater. They, too, lost their camp and all the supplies in it; they went to Tusculum, counting on the loyalty and pity of their hosts to ensure their survival, which, despite what had happened, was readily given. The reports brought to Rome were so frightening that, putting aside their hatred for the decemvirs, the senators voted that sentries be posted in the city, ordering everyone who was of an age to bear arms to guard the walls and to man outposts beyond the gates; they also decreed that arms and reinforcements be sent to Tusculum, that the decemvirs remove the soldiers from the citadel at Tusculum and put them in a military camp, that the other camp be moved from Fidenae to Sabine territory and that they make an offensive strike to deter the enemy from attacking the city.

43. In addition to these defeats inflicted by the enemy, the decemvirs did two terrible things, one at home and the other in the field. Lucius Siccius was part of the force sent against the Sabines. In his hatred of the decemvirs he began to talk with the common soldiers over a period of days about electing tribunes and seceding. So the decemvirs sent him out, along with some other soldiers, as a scout to select a site for the camp. They ordered his companions to attack and kill him during their foray. Kill him they did, but he was not unavenged, for some of the assassins fell around him as he fought back: though surrounded, he defended himself, a strong man with courage to match his strength. The survivors returned to camp and reported that Siccius had fallen in an ambush: he had put up a stout fight and some of his companions had been lost with him. The report was believed at first; but when a cohort was sent out by permission of the decemvirs it found that no spoils had been taken from the fallen and that Siccius lay in the middle fully armed, with the other bodies facing against him, and that there were no enemy casualties or even a sign of the enemy having been there. So they brought back the body, saying that he had been undoubtedly killed by his own men. The camp seethed with outrage, and they would have decided to take Siccius' body straightway to Rome had not the decemvirs been quick to give him a military funeral at public expense. He was buried to the great distress of the soldiers, while the reputation of the decemvirs among the rank and file sank to its lowest point.

44. A second outrage took place in the city, originating in sexual passion and ending as ignobly as that which drove the Tarquins from the city and their throne, when Lucretia was raped and died: the same fate befell the decemvirs as the kings and the same cause precipitated their fall from power.

Appius Claudius lusted for a plebeian girl and was intent on possessing her. Her father, Lucius Verginius, was a centurion of high rank in the camp at Algidus, a man of exemplary character at home and in the field. His wife had been imbued with his high principles and his children were being trained in them. He had betrothed his daughter to Lucius Icilius, a former tribune who had demonstrated energy and devotion to the plebeian cause. Appius, crazed by passion, began to ply this grown and beautiful girl with presents and promises; but when he realized her decency was proof against all advances, he turned to cruel and overbearing force. He suborned his client, Marcus Claudius, to claim the girl as his slave and told him not to give in to those who would demand interim possession of her until the question of her free status was decided; Appius thought the father's failure to appear in the girl's defence would enable him to flout the law.*

As the girl was entering the forum (she went to school in make-shift quarters near by), this minister to the decemvir's lust laid hands on her, saying she was a slave born from one of his slave women; he ordered her to come with him; if she resisted, he would take her by force. As the girl stood there paralysed with fear, her nurse cried out and begged the citizens to protect her. People gathered round. They reminded one another that her father Verginius and her fiancé Icilius were supporters of the people's cause; their friends took the girl's side out of regard for them, while the crowd at large did so because of outrage at what was happening. But now that she had been saved from force, the claimant said there was no need for the crowd to be upset; he was proceeding legally, not by force. He summoned the girl to court; her supporters advised her to follow.

And so they came before Appius' tribunal. The prosecutor told the story he had rehearsed with the judge, the author of the scen-ario: the girl had been born in his house but had been stolen and whisked off to Verginius' house, where she had been fobbed off on him as his child. He had been given evidence of this and was now coming forward: he would prove his case even to Verginius, were he the judge, who was more in the injured party than he: in the mean-time it was only right that the slave go with her owner. The girl's supporters pointed out that Verginius was absent in the service of his country and that he would appear on his daughter's behalf in two days' time if he were apprised of the situation: it was unfair to fight over his child in his absence. They requested Appius to decide nothing until the father arrived, since the law he himself had passed gave interim possession to those who argued for freedom; he should not permit a grown girl to suffer her good name to be called into question even before her free status had been decided.

45. Before issuing his decree Appius said that the very law which Verginius' friends adduced in support of their case showed how strongly he himself favoured the presumption of liberty, but that the law would be a reliable stronghold of liberty only if it were applied to cases and persons without variation. As for those who were claimed to be free, anyone had the legal right to make the claim, but in the case of things that fell under a father's jurisdiction, the father and no one else controlled their disposition. It was accordingly his deci-sion that the father be summoned; in the meantime the claimant should not lose his right of taking the girl and guaranteeing her appearance at such a time as the man said to be her father should present himself.

This unjust pronouncement elicited grumbling on the part of many, but outright protest by no one. Publius Numitorius, Verginia's grandfather, and Icilius, her betrothed, then intervened. As they made their way through the crowd, people thought that Icilius' intervention in particular would open the way to resisting Appius. But a lictor declared that the decree had been issued, and pushed the protesting Icilius out of the way. Such blatant manhandling would have outraged even a man of peaceable temperament. 'You will have to kill me, Appius, if you want no outcry as you carry out your secret design. As her intended husband, I will preserve the purity of my wife to be. Go ahead, summon all the lictors of your colleagues also. Order the rods and axes to be readied. Icilius' be-trothed will stay nowhere but in her father's house. You have done away with the protection afforded by the tribunes and the right of appeal to the Roman people, the two bulwarks in freedom's defence. But this does not mean you have absolute power and can force wives and children to satisfy your unholy appetites. Take out your savagery by beating and killing us, but at least let the virtuous be untouched. If violence should threaten this maiden, I will beseech the citizens present to protect my betrothed, Verginius will beseech his fellow soldiers to protect his only daughter, and we all will beseech the protection of gods and men. You will never carry out that decree of yours without my dying first. Again and again I ask you, Appius, to consider where you are heading. Let Verginius decide when he comes what he should do about his daughter. Let him only know that he will have to find another son-in-law if he capitulates to the claim of this man there. As for me, I will sooner die than fail in my duty to defend the free status of my betrothed.'

46. The crowd was in an ugly mood and a fight seemed imminent. Lictors surrounded Icilius but had not gone beyond threatening him, when Appius spoke up: Icilius, he said, was not defending Verginius, but was looking for a chance to create dissension by stirring up trouble and behaving like the tribune he once had been. He would not give him an excuse to act at present, but would reserve his final decision and not enforce his decree: Icilius should realize that he was doing this not in response to Icilius' effrontery but in deference to the absent Verginius, to the rights of fatherhood and to the claim of liberty. He therefore would request Marcus Claudius to forgo his right and to allow his claim on the girl to be decided the following day; but if the father was not present then, he wanted Icilius and his sympathizers to know that he would enforce the law he had passed and would act with the fearlessness befitting a decemvir; he would not, in any event, summon the lictors of his colleagues to force compliance on the fomentors of sedition; his own lictors would be quite sufficient for this.

Now that Appius had put off enforcing his iniquitous decree, the girl's defenders withdrew and decided first that Icilius' brother and Numitor's son, venturesome young men, should head straight for the city gate and summon Verginius from the camp as speedily as possible: the girl's safety depended on his appearing the next day to defend her claim to be free. Acting on these instructions, they brought the message to the father after a hard ride. Back in the forum, the claimant of the girl pressed Icilius to provide money that would guarantee the girl's appearance, and Icilius replied this was just what he was doing (his aim was to spin out the time while the messengers hurried to the camp). Hands were raised everywhere in the crowd signifying willingness to Icilius to guarantee the money. 'Thank you,' he said with tears in his eyes. 'Tomorrow I will need your help. For the present I have enough guarantors.' And so Verginia was taken by her relatives, who had put up the necessary sum. Appius continued on the tribunal for a time so he would not seem to have been there for this matter alone, but when no one approached him because everyone's thoughts were of this case alone, he went home and wrote to his colleagues in camp not to give Verginius permission to leave, and even to hold him in custody. His wicked design came too late, as it deserved; Verginius secured his leave and set out at the first watch. It was not until the next morning that Appius' letter asking for his detention arrived.

47. The entire population in the city assembled at dawn in keen anticipation. Verginius, in rags of mourning, ushered in his daughter, who was clad in a shabby garment and accompanied by a number of married women.* Many supporters followed. He began to move through the crowd and buttonhole individuals, appealing not just to their sense of fair play but saying that they owed him their support: he took his place in the battleline every day in defence of their wives and children; no other fighter was reckoned as brave and daring as he. Yet what was the use of safeguarding a city in which one's children must suffer the horrors they would face had the enemy captured it? So he moved about, speaking as if he were making a public address, while Icilius echoed his sentiments. But the silent weeping of the women moved the crowd more than anything they said.

Appius defiantly mounted the tribunal, determined to brook no opposition: it was madness, if one is to be truthful, rather than lust that held him in its grip. Marcus Claudius began by complaining that the day before partiality had prevented a decision being rendered in his favour, but before he could finish or Verginius could even make a response, Appius interrupted. Just what he uttered in defence of his decision is unclear. Possibly something of what he actually said has been preserved in our oldest authorities, but I myself find nothing plausible, given the appalling nature of the decree. It seems best simply to record what all agree on: namely, that he ruled in favour of the complainant: the girl was his slave. At first everyone stood rooted in shock and amazement at this monstrous decision. The silence continued until Marcus Claudius pushed his way through the throng of matrons to seize the girl. The women raised great cries of distress; Verginius shook his fist at Appius and said, 'I betrothed my daughter to Icilius, not to you, and I raised her to be married, not defiled. Animals and wild beasts fornicate indiscriminately. Is that your aim? Possibly those who support you will allow this. But I feel sure that those who have weapons will not.'

After Marcus Claudius had been pushed back by the women and the other supporters standing by, a herald called for silence. **48.** Passion made the decemvir lose self-control. He declared that Icilius' noisy disturbance the day before as well as Verginius' outrageous behaviour—which the Roman people had witnessed—had hinted at trouble, but he had now learned from reliable informants that meetings had been held in the city throughout the night aimed at stirring up revolution. Accordingly, aware of the impending danger, he had come to the forum accompanied by men in arms, not to intimidate law-abiding citizens but to curb those disturbing the peace by virtue of his superior authority. 'These person would be well advised to behave peaceably,' he said. 'Lictor, go disperse the crowd and open up a path for the owner of the girl to take possession of his property.' His thunderous rancour caused the crowd to shrink back of its own accord. The girl was left standing alone, a defenceless victim of this outrage.

Verginius, seeing that all support had melted away, turned to the tribunal. 'Appius,' he cried, 'if I have offended you in any way, I ask you to forgive a father's distress. Allow me to question the nurse here, in the girl's presence, about this business. If I find I have been falsely claimed as the girl's father, I will depart in a calmer state of mind.' When permission was granted, he took the girl and her nurse aside next to the shops near the temple of Venus Cloacina, now known as the New Shops, and, snatching a knife from a butcher's stall and saying, 'I am asserting your freedom in the only way I know how, my daughter,' stabbed her to the heart. As he did so he looked back at the tribunal and cried, 'With this blood, Appius, I curse you and your life.' This shocking act ignited an uproar. Appius jumped up and ordered Verginius arrested, but the latter, brandishing his weapon, made his way to the city gate; by now a throng of supporters was accompanying him. Icilius and Numitorius lifted up the corpse and displayed it to the people; they bewailed Appius' wickedness, the girl's fatal beauty, and the necessity that had driven

her father to commit such an act. The women followed with loud
laments—was this what it meant to have children, was this the
reward of a woman's purity?—along with other things which distress suggested to them in the situation, the more pitiable, given
women's more emotional nature. The men's talk, and particularly
that of Icilius, centred wholly on the loss of the tribunes' power and
of the right of appeal to the people, as well as on the indignity
suffered by the nation at large.

49. The crowd was thrown into turmoil, partly because of the
shocking nature of what Verginius had done and partly because it
seemed to offer an opportunity of regaining liberty. Appius first
ordered Icilius to be summoned back, and then, when he kept going,
to be arrested; but the decemvir's attendants could not get near him.
In the end Appius himself waded into the crowd accompanied by a
cadre of young patricians and ordered him to be put in chains. But
by this time not only had the crowd surrounded Icilius, but the
crowd's leaders as well, Lucius Valerius and Marcus Horatius, who
repulsed the lictor and declared that, if Appius were acting in a legal
manner, he was a private citizen and they had the right to protect
Icilius; if he tried to use force, they would answer in kind. This
triggered a terrible riot. A lictor of the decemvir went after Valerius
and Horatius: the crowd smashed his fasces. Appius mounted his
tribunal to address the people. Horatius and Valerius followed. The
crowd listened to them but shouted down the decemvir. Then, acting as if he were a magistrate, Valerius ordered the lictors to cease
serving someone who was a private citizen.

Appius, broken in spirit and fearing for his life, hid his face and
slunk away to his house near the forum unnoticed by his adversaries. Spurius Oppius hurried to help his colleague, bursting into the
forum from the other end. He realized that force had won out over
his power as a magistrate. He wavered, as suggestions were made on
all sides and he inclined now to one, now to another. In the end he
ordered the senate into session. This step calmed the crowd because
most of the senators were believed to be opposed to the actions of
the decemvirs; the hope was that the senate would put an end to
their power. The senate decided that the plebs must not be provoked further and that, more importantly, steps should be taken to
prevent disturbance among the soldiers when Verginius arrived among
them. **50**. And so junior senators were dispatched to the camp,

which then was on Mount Vecilius; they instructed the decemvirs to take every precaution against mutiny in the ranks.

There Verginius created even greater ferment than he had in the city. For as he approached, he was seen to be accompanied by nearly four hundred men from the city, who had joined him because of the outrage they felt for the shocking way he had been treated. The entire camp was even more stirred by the sight of his drawn sword and bloodstained clothing. Moreover, the sight of men in civilian dress everywhere in the camp made their number seem somewhat greater than it really was. When those he encountered asked what was the matter, he stood weeping silently for a time, but after a crowd had gathered round and was waiting in anxious silence, he told them everything as it had happened. Then with palms upraised to heaven and appealing to them as fellow soldiers, he begged them not to find him responsible for Appius Claudius' crime and not to spurn him as the murderer of his child. His daughter's life had been dearer to him than his own, but she could not live that life as a free and chaste woman. When he saw her being hurried off like a slave to be debauched, he thought it better to lose her to death than to defilement. The pity he had felt for her made what he did seem cruel, and he would have killed himself as well, had he not hoped to avenge her death with the help of his fellow soldiers before him. They, too, had daughters, sisters, and wives: Appius Claudius' lust had not died with his daughter: the longer he went unpunished, the more bestial his behaviour would become. Another's tragedy was a warning to protect themselves from suffering a like fate. As for himself, his wife was deceased and his daughter, because she could no longer live with honour, had met an unhappy but honourable end. There was no one left in his house to fall victim to Appius' lust: he would defend himself from any other sort of indignity that Appius might inflict in the same spirit he had defended his daughter. Others should look to what was best for themselves and their children.

In response to Verginius' declaration, the crowd shouted that it would not fail to avenge his loss or assert its own liberty. The civilians intermingled with the troops bewailed Verginia's fate also, and said that the soldiers' shock would have been far greater had they witnessed what had happened rather than hearing of it, and that the decemvirs' power was near collapse in Rome: then others added still more, saying that Appius had nearly lost his life and had gone into exile: in response to all this the soldiers gave the call to arms, seized the standards, and were ready to set out for Rome.

At the same time the decemvirs, dismayed by what was going on before their eyes and by the news from Rome, split up and hurried off in different directions throughout the camp to calm the disturbance. Conciliatory moves brought no response, while displays of force were met with the assertion that they were men and were armed. So the soldiers marched to the city and settled down on the Aventine, urging the plebeians they met to reclaim their liberty and elect tribunes of the plebs. No extreme actions beyond these were proposed.

Spurius Oppius convened the senate, which advised against harsh measures: responsibility for the mutiny lay with themselves, after all. Three consular envoys were sent, Spurius Tarpeius, Gaius Iulius, and Publius Sulpicius, who were instructed to ask in the name of the senate by whose order they had left their camp and what their aim was in settling on the Aventine in arms and in occupying their own country, while abandoning the fight against the enemy. The crowd knew what its response should be but not who was the right person to give it, since they had no recognized leader and no one was willing to expose himself to such an invidious role. The crowd only shouted that Lucius Valerius and Marcus Horatius should be sent for: to them it would give its response.

51. When the envoys had left, Verginius pointed out to the soldiers that they had been somewhat at a loss just now because they lacked a leader and that their response, while perfectly adequate, had resulted more from a chance consensus than concerted strategy. He proposed that they elect ten men as their leaders to be styled tribunes of the soldiers by way of honour to the military. When they moved to bestow the office first on him, he said, 'Reserve your judgement of me to a better time for myself and for you. I cannot hold office as long as my daughter's death remains unavenged, nor should you have leaders in the present crisis who labour under the notoriety I do at present. I can serve you equally well if I remain in private life.' And so they proceeded to elect military tribunes, ten in number.

Nor was the army quiet on the Sabine front. There, too, with Icilius and Numitorius taking the lead, the soldiers mutinied against the decemvirs, their feelings roused no less by the memory of the murdered Siccius than by the news of Appius' shocking attempt to abduct and rape Verginia. When Icilius heard that military tribunes had been chosen on the Aventine, he did not want the citizen assembly in the city to follow the lead of the soldiers by electing the same men tribunes of the plebs. So, as an experienced popular leader and ambitious for the office himself, he took care before going to the city that his men elect an equal number of their own. They entered the city through the Colline Gate under the standards, and marched to the Aventine through the middle of the city. There they joined up with the other army and entrusted the twenty tribunes of the soldiers with selecting two from their number as heads of state. They picked Marcus Oppius and Sextus Manilius.

The senators, apprehensive about the state of the nation, held meetings every day, but spent them more in recriminations than in coming to decisions. They blamed the decemvirs for the murder of Siccius, Appius' appalling behaviour, and the disgrace of the armies in the field. It was decided that Valerius and Horatius should go to the Aventine, but they said they would do so only if the decemvirs put aside the insignia of their office, whose term had ended the year before. The decemvirs complained that they were being stripped of their rank; they would not lay down their office until the laws for which they had been elected had been enacted.

52. When Marcus Duilius, a former tribune, told the plebs that no progress could be made amid this continual wrangling, the plebs moved from the Aventine to the Sacred Mount, for Duilius maintained that nothing but the abandonment of the city would prompt the senators to deal with the situation; the Sacred Mount would be a reminder of the steadfast purpose of the plebs: they would come to realize that no harmonious resolution was possible without the restoration of the tribunes' power. They set out on the Via Nomentana, known in those days as the Via Ficulensis, and pitched camp on the Sacred Mount, following the restraint of their ancestors in violating nothing. Every able-bodied civilian followed the army, with wives and children accompanying them for a time, piteously asking what protection there could be for them in a city in which chastity and liberty counted for nothing.

There was a strange emptiness everywhere in Rome. Only a few elderly men moved about the forum, which appeared deserted once the senators had entered the senate-house. By now it was more than just Horatius and Valerius who gave vent to their feelings: 'What are you waiting for, senators? If the decemvirs persist in their obstinacy, will you allow everything to collapse and go up in smoke? What sort of power is it, decemvirs, that you are clinging to? Do you intend to issue laws to walls and buildings? Are you not ashamed that here in the forum your lictors virtually outnumber the other citizens? What will you do if the enemy should approach the city? What if the plebs return in arms when they find their secession has brought so little response? Do you want the end of your power to coincide with the collapse of your country? And yet either there must be plebeian tribunes or there can be no plebeians at all. We will be without patrician magistrates sooner than they will be without ones of their own. They wrested from our fathers a power that was new and untried, but now that they have fallen in love with it, they will assuredly never give it up—particularly when we have failed to moderate our own power in order than they might less feel the need of protection.' Assailed by these charges from every quarter and overcome by the consensus of the senators, the decemvirs said they would abide by whatever decision the senate should make. They would only say this, as both plea and warning: that they be protected from the animosity of the people, and their deaths should not accustom the plebeians to spilling the blood of senators.

53. Valerius and Horatius were then sent to negotiate the conditions on which the plebs would return and to secure a settlement; at the same time they were also instructed to shield the decemvirs from the anger and violence of the people. They set out and were received in the camp to the great delight of the plebs as the undoubted champions of liberty both at the start of the disturbance and now at its conclusion. For their services they were formally thanked on their arrival; Icilius acted as the spokesman of the multitude. And, when the envoys asked what the demands of the plebs were, it was he who negotiated the terms according to a pact reached before the envoys arrived, in which it was clear that their hopes rested more on an equitable settlement than on the use of force. The terms were these: that the tribunes' power and the right of appeal be restored, which had been the plebs' safeguards before the institution of the Decemvirate, and that there be no reprisals for having urged the soldiers or plebs to reclaim their liberty by seceding. Their only

harsh demand was for the punishment of the decemvirs, for they thought it fair that they be handed over, even threatening to burn them alive.

The envoys responded as follows: 'Those stipulations dictated by reason are so fair that they ought to have been granted even without asking; for you seek guarantees of liberty, not of licence to harm others. Your anger must be excused rather than indulged, for your hatred of cruelty has incited you to become cruel yourselves, and almost before winning your freedom you want to lord it over your adversaries. Will our country never be free from the violence of senators against plebeians or plebeians against senators? You need a shield rather than a sword. If an ordinary man enjoys equal rights and neither does nor suffers injury, that is enough and more for him. Even if there should be reason to fear you in the future, this will come after you have your magistrates and laws back again, when judicial decisions about our lives and fortunes will be in your hands. Then you will decide as each case comes before you; now it is enough that you have won back your liberty.'

54. When everyone agreed that Valerius and Horatius should act as they saw fit, they promised to return as soon as they had completed their mission. They left and, after they had set out the demands of the plebs before the senate, the other decemvirs made no objection, since there was no mention of their punishment, as they had expected there would be. Appius, harsh by nature and—given his great notoriety—prone to measure the hatred felt for him by the hatred he felt for others, declared, 'I am well aware of the fate that hangs over me. I see that our enemies will not attack us until they have the weapons in their hands. Their hatred will demand a blood offering. Still, I, too, will give up the Decemvirate.' The senate decreed that the decemvirs should step down from their office forthwith, that Quintus Furius, the pontifex maximus, should preside over the election of plebeian tribunes and that no reprisals be taken for the secession of the soldiers and plebs.

After these decrees had been issued and the senate dismissed, the decemvirs abdicated from office before the assembly to the great delight of everyone. The news was then relayed to the plebs. Those remaining in the city accompanied the envoys on their way. A second joyful crowd from the camp met the advancing throng. They congratulated one another for the re-establishment of liberty and harmony in the state. The envoys addressed the throng: 'May what is to happen prove favourable, fortunate, and happy for you and the republic. Return to your country, your household gods, your wives and children. But continue to show the same restraint in entering the city that you have shown hitherto; for you have violated no man's property despite the need of this great throng for so many basic necessities. Go to the Aventine, from which you set out; there, in that auspicious spot, where your liberty first began, you will elect tribunes of the plebs. The pontifex maximus will be there to preside over your meeting.'

All were swift to agree in approving everything. They picked up the standards and set out for Rome, their joy matching the joy of those who came to meet them. In arms they silently proceeded through the city to the Aventine. There the pontifex maximus immediately held the election. The tribunes of the plebs were chosen in this order: first of all, Lucius Verginius; then Lucius Icilius and Publius Numitorius, Verginia's maternal uncle,* the leaders of the secession; then Gaius Sicinius, the descendant of the man who, tradition says, was the first to be chosen tribune of the plebs on the Sacred Mount; and Marcus Duilius, who had distinguished himself as a tribune before the institution of the Decemvirate and had not failed the plebs in their fight against the decemvirs; next, more in hope of future promise than because of past accomplishments, were Marcus Titinius, Marcus Pomponius, Gaius Apronius, Appius Villius, and Gaius Oppius. As the first act of his tribunate Lucius Icilius immediately proposed to the plebs that there be no reprisals for the secession from the decemvirs, which was passed. At once Marcus Duilius carried a resolution for electing consuls with the right of appeal. All these acts took place in the Flaminian meadows, now called the Circus Flaminius, in a council of the plebeians.

55. An interrex presided over the election of Lucius Valerius and Marcus Horatius to the consulship, who entered office at once. Their consulship promoted popular measures that did not harm the senators but did provoke their displeasure, for they regarded any steps to safeguard the liberty of the plebs as a diminution of their power. First of all, since it was virtually an undecided point of law whether the senators were bound by decisions of the plebs, they carried a bill in the Centuriate assembly according to which measures passed by the plebs when voting by tribes were binding on all

the people, a law that proved to be a powerful weapon in tribunician legislation. They then not only revived another consular law on the right of appeal, the one and only bulwark of liberty, which had been flouted by the decemvirs, but added to its strength by passing a new bill that no one should declare elected any new magistrate without the right of appeal; whoever did such a thing would be rightfully and justly killed, for such a death should not be classed as a capital offence. Now that they had provided sufficient safeguards for the plebs through the right of appeal on the one hand and the help of the tribunes on the other, they turned to the tribunes themselves by reviving certain ceremonies whereby the person of the tribune was made sacrosanct: the ceremonies had not been observed for a long time, and indeed sacrosanctity itself had almost been forgotten. They made him inviolate in both religion and law by stipulating that anyone who harmed a tribune of the plebs, aedile, or any of the ten-man panel of judges* should be sacrificed to Jupiter and his worldly goods sold at the temple of Ceres, Liber, and Libera.

Legal experts say that this law does not make someone sacrosanct, but marks the person who harms any of these officials accursed; thus, an aedile can be arrested and imprisoned by higher magistrates, which may be illegal (for harm is being done to someone who should not have been harmed), but is still proof that an aedile is not held to be sacrosanct; on the other hand, the tribunes were made sacrosanct by an old oath of the plebs, when the office first originated.* Some have interpreted this Horatian law as applying in a similar way to consuls and praetors (the latter are elected under the same auspices as are the consuls); for the consul was called 'judge'. But this interpretation is refuted by the fact that in those days the consul was customarily styled 'praetor'; the title 'judge' came later.

Such were the consular laws. The practice also began under these same consuls of housing the senate's decrees with the aediles of the plebs in the temple of Ceres; these decrees had previously been subject to suppression or alteration at the whim of the consuls. Then Marcus Duillius, tribune of the plebs, proposed a bill, which the plebs passed, that whoever left the plebs without tribunes and whoever declared elected a magistrate without the right of appeal, should be scourged and beheaded. The patricians disliked, but did not oppose, all these measures because no single individual had yet suffered from any of their harsh provisions.

56. Now that tribunician power and plebeian liberty had been re-established, the tribunes judged the time both ripe and safe for attacking individual wrongdoers; they picked Verginius to bring the first accusation and Appius to be the first defendant. When on being indicted Appius entered the forum surrounded by the young patricians, the memory of his hateful tyranny came flooding back in everyone's mind on seeing him and his henchmen. Verginius then spoke: 'Speeches of eloquence were devised for doubtful cases; in this instance I will not waste your time by making a formal accusation of a man whose cruelty forced you to defend yourself with arms, nor will I allow him to add effrontery to his other crimes by making an exculpatory speech. I am going to do you the favour, Appius Claudius, of not discussing all those impious and wicked things you did over and over for two years on end. I will order your imprisonment on one charge only—unless you can convince a judge that you did not illegally award custody of a free woman to one who claimed her as his slave.'

Appius had no hope that the tribunes would help him or that the people's verdict would be in his favour. Nevertheless, he appealed to the tribunes and, as an attendant laid hands on him and none moved to intervene, he shouted, 'I appeal!' When this cry—the sole bastion of freedom—was heard coming from the same mouth that had lately pronounced against the very claim of freedom, silence fell. Then the people began to mutter to themselves: at last the gods were showing that they existed after all and were not indifferent to human affairs; punishment for arrogance and cruelty was coming late but sure; he who had taken away the right of appeal was now himself appealing; he who had trodden down all rights of the people was imploring the people's protection; he who had consigned a free person to slavery was now being hurried off to prison, sorely in need himself of the right of freedom.

In the midst of this murmuring Appius was heard imploring his fellow citizens for protection. He recalled the services of his ancestors to the republic at home and in war as well as his own ill-starred zeal for the Roman plebs, for whose sake he had incurred the anger of the senators by resigning his consulship in order to draw up legislation equitable to all; and finally there were the laws themselves, which were still standing as their author was being dragged off to prison. Furthermore, the good and bad points of his case would be put to the test when the opportunity to defend himself was granted; for the present, as a Roman citizen under indictment, he asked by virtue of the right belonging to all citizens permission to plead his case in a trial before the Roman people. He was not so afraid of hostility that he had no hope of the fairness and pity of his fellow citizens. But if he were to be imprisoned while under indictment, he once again appealed to the tribunes, warning them not to ape those whom they detested. And if the tribunes should confess they were bound by the same obligation of cancelling the right of appeal that they charged the decemvirs with having conspired to cancel, he still appealed to the people and begged for the protection of the consular and tribunician laws on the right of appeal passed in that very year. For what was the point of appeal if a man under indictment but not yet found guilty could not make it? If Appius Claudius could find no defence in the laws, what plebeian, what ordinary man in the street could find it? His case would show whether tyranny or liberty had been sanctioned by the new laws, and whether appeals to the tribunes and to the people against mistreatment by magistrates were real or mere words on paper.

57. In response Verginius declared that Appius Claudius alone was exempt from the laws and the norms of civilized behaviour among citizens and humans everywhere. He urged them to look up at his tribunal, that redoubt of malfeasance, where as decemvir in perpetuity he struck at the property, persons, and lives of the citizens, threatening everyone with beatings and execution, contemptuous of gods and men, surrounded by cut-throats rather than lictors; and when he turned from rapine and murder to lechery, while the Roman people looked on he tore a freeborn girl from the embrace of her father, as if she had been a captive in war, and made a present of her to a minion acting as his pimp. From that tribunal came a decree so savage, an award so unspeakable that he armed the father against his daughter; from that tribunal he had ordered to prison those lifting up the body of the dying girl—her betrothed and her grandfather—angered more by the frustration of his lust than by her death. And a prison had been built for him which he regularly referred to as the plebs' domicile. Verginius further declared that as often as Appius would cry 'I appeal', just as often would he challenge him to go before a judge and swear he had not awarded a free person to one who claimed her as a slave; if he refused to go, he

would order him to be imprisoned as a man condemned. And so
Appius was taken off to prison; no one objected, although the plebs
had severe misgivings, feeling that their liberty had somehow grown
too great in punishing such a man. The tribunes fixed a day for the
trial to begin.

In the meantime envoys from the Latins and Hernici arrived in
Rome to extend their congratulation on the concord between senators and plebeians, in honour of which they brought a gift of a
golden crown to be dedicated to Jupiter Optimus Maximus on the
Capitol; it did not weigh much, but reflected their lack of wealth, a
sign of piety rather than ostentation in their practice of religion.
These same envoys reported also that the Aequi and Volsci were
preparing for war on a grand scale. Accordingly, the consuls were
ordered to choose their spheres of operation by drawing lots. The
Sabines fell to Horatius, the Aequi to Valerius.* When they announced the levy for these wars, their popularity among the plebs
led not just the younger men to sign up, but a great number of older
volunteers as well, who had already satisfied their military obligations. The result was an army made stronger not only in numbers
but in the character of the soldiery, as the veterans mixed in with
the new recruits. Before they left the city they had the laws of the
decemvirs, known as the Twelve Tables, inscribed on bronze tablets, and set up in public. Some authorities say that the aediles
performed this task at the bidding of the tribunes.

58. Gaius Claudius, out of disgust with the crimes of the decemvirs,
and opposed more than anyone else to the arrogance of his brother's
son, had removed himself to Regillum, the ancestral home of the
Claudii. Now, advanced in age, he returned to defend in his hour of
need the man whose wickedness he had fled; clad in mourning
clothes and accompanied by kinsmen and clients he went about the
forum soliciting the support of individuals, begging them not to
brand the Claudian clan with infamy, not to think its members
deserving of chains and imprisonment. A man whom posterity would
hold in high esteem, legislator and father of Roman law, was lying
bound among thugs and night-prowling thieves. He urged them to
turn from anger to reflection and recognition, to accede to the pleas
of so many Claudii on behalf of one man rather than reject the
prayers of many out of hatred of just one. He, too, would make this
concession to the family and its honour, but would not be reconciled

with the man whom he now wished to help in his time of peril. Liberty had been recovered by courage; concord of the orders could be stabilized by clemency.

Some were moved more by his loyalty than by the case of the man for whom he was pleading. Verginius, on the other hand, begged that they pity him and his daughter, that they listen to the pleas not of the Claudian clan, fated to tyrannize over the plebs, but of those most closely connected to Verginia—three tribunes who had been elected to help the plebs and who now asked the plebs for their help and support. These tearful entreaties seemed to have a greater claim on justice. And so, with hope cut off and before the day of the trial, Appius took his own life.

Spurius Oppius, next in notoriety, was immediately fastened on by Publius Numitorius because he had been in the city when his colleague had unjustly adjudicated the case of Verginia. Oppius nevertheless incurred more hostility from the injuries he had done than from those he had failed to prevent. A witness came forward, a veteran who recounted his twenty-seven years of service and displayed eight special military decorations for all to see. He tore open his garment to reveal his back scarred from the decemvir's whips, challenging him to prove any wrongdoing on his part; if he did, he could vent his savagery as a private citizen by whipping him a second time. Oppius, too, was imprisoned, and ended his life before the day of the trial. The tribunes auctioned off the property of Claudius and Oppius. The other decemvirs left Rome for exile; their property was auctioned off as well. And Marcus Claudius, who had claimed Verginia, was put on trial and convicted, but when Verginius himself waived the death penalty, he was allowed to go into exile at Tibur. Thus the shade of Verginia, more fortunate in death than in life, moved from house to house in search of vengeance, and when all had been punished, found rest at last.

59. The senators were greatly apprehensive when they saw the tribunes wearing much the same expression as the decemvirs had. At this point Duilius, tribune of the plebs, put a salutary stop to the excesses of power by saying: 'Exercise of our liberty and punishment of our enemies have gone far enough. Accordingly, in what remains of the year I will not allow anyone to be brought up on charges or imprisoned. I do not want old, nearly forgotten wrongs to be raked up now that recent ones have been expiated by the punish-

ment of the decemvirs; the steadfast concern of both consuls in safeguarding your liberty guarantees that wrongdoing will be punished without the intervention of the tribunes.' This moderate policy of the tribune was the first step in relieving the senators of their fear, while it caused the growth of senatorial hostility to the consuls: they had been so completely devoted to the plebeian cause that it had taken a plebeian magistrate, not a patrician, to show concern for the safety and freedom of the senators; their enemies had become sated in punishing them before the consuls moved to block the licence of the people. Many also charged the senate with having acted irresolutely, since the patricians had backed the laws passed by the consuls; nor was there doubt that they had trimmed their sails during the storm that had beset the state.

60. After settling affairs in the city and putting the status of the plebs on a firm basis, the consuls went to take up their respective commands. Against the combined forces of the Aequi and the Volsci at Algidus Valerius deliberately refrained from engagement; if he had tried his luck he probably would have suffered a great defeat, given the morale of the Romans and her enemies after the ill-omened reverses under the decemvirs. He kept his troops in the camp, which he had pitched a mile from the enemy. Several times the latter moved into position in the area between the two camps ready for battle, and when they challenged the Romans to fight, not a Roman responded. Finally, tired from standing and waiting in vain for battle, and thinking that in effect the Romans had conceded victory, the Aequi and Volsci went off on plundering raids, some to the Hernici, others to the Latins. The troops left behind were sufficient to garrison the camp but not to fight a pitched battle.

When the consul realized this, it was now time for the enemy to be afraid; he drew up his troops in battle order and issued a challenge. When they refused battle because of awareness of their reduced strength, the Romans' spirit immediately lifted; they considered the fearful troops behind the rampart as good as beaten. After standing throughout the day ready for battle, they withdrew at nightfall. Full of hope, the Romans took rest and refreshment, while the enemy, discouraged and fearful, sent out messengers to recall the plunderers. Those near by returned, but those farther afield could not be found. At daybreak the Romans emerged from their camp intent on storming the rampart if the enemy refused to fight. And after a good part of the day had passed with no movement on the enemy's part, the consul ordered the standards forward; as the battleline got under way, the Aequi and Volsci became indignant to think that the rampart was protecting them, who had been the winners previously, rather than courage and arms. Accordingly, they took the initiative in demanding to fight, and their leaders assented. Part of their force had emerged from the camp gates while others were moving in good order to take their places in the ranks, when the Roman consul, before the enemy line could position itself in full force, advanced the standards. Moving against them, all of whom had not yet emerged, while those who had were not yet sufficiently deployed, as the fearful throng shifted about here and there looking to see where they and their fellows were and cowed by the battle-cry and the onrush, the Roman consul fell upon them. At first the enemy retreated, but after recovering their spirits, and as their leaders everywhere rebuked them for yielding to those they had beaten earlier, the fight began anew.

61. On the other front the consul bade the Romans remember that on that day they were above all fighting as free men on behalf of a free Rome and that their victory would be for themselves: they would not in their hour of triumph become the prey of the decemvirs. Their commander was not Appius, but the consul Valerius, descended from the liberators of the Roman people, and a liberator in his own right. He urged them to show that defeat in the earlier battles was due to the commanders, not the soldiers. It was shameful to show more courage fighting against citizens than foreign foes and to have greater fear of enslavement at home than at the hands of victorious enemies. In peacetime it had been only Verginia's purity that had put her in danger, only Appius' lust that had endangered her; but if the fortunes of war should so incline, everyone's child would be in danger from thousands of triumphant foes. Yet he would not utter an omen that neither Jupiter nor Father Mars would let happen to a city founded so auspiciously. He reminded them of the Aventine and Sacred Mount: where liberty had been won a few months before, there they should return with Rome's power undiminished. They should show that the nature of the Roman soldier was the same after the expulsion of the decemvirs as before their entry into office, and that with the establishment of equal rights the courage of the Roman people had not been impaired. After speaking

these words amid the standards of the infantry, he hurried to the cavalry. 'Come, young soldiers,' he said, 'surpass the infantry in courage as you surpass them in rank and privilege. The infantry is now sending the enemy into disarray at the first clash; urge on your horses and drive the enemy in their stricken state from the field. They will not withstand your attack; even now they are hanging back rather than moving against you.'

Spurring their horses on, they drove through the enemy ranks, already thrown into confusion by the onslaught of the infantry, and on breaking through the enemy lines, penetrated to the rear, while some of them circled around over unoccupied ground. They blocked most of the enemy from reaching their camp, as they took to their heels on every side, by riding past and frightening them away. The infantry, the consul himself, and the entire fighting force burst into the camp, and, after a great slaughter, the survivors fell into their hands, along with an even greater amount of booty.

The news of the battle reached not only the city but the other army in Sabine territory; in Rome it was celebrated with joy, in camp it fired the soldiers to achieve an equal victory. By sending his men out on raids and having them engage in minor skirmishes, Horatius had accustomed them to trust in him rather than remember the disgrace received under the command of the decemvirs; success in these lesser encounters had made them expect success in the major clash to come. But the Sabines were still fired by their victory in the previous year; they did not cease from issuing challenges and going on the offensive, asking why, like hit-and-run bandits, handfuls of men were frittering away the time by dashing back and forth—trying to fight a single war through a lot of trifling scuffles. Why didn't they confront them in a regular battle and let fortune decide the outcome once and for all?

62. The Romans were sufficiently fired up on their own, but indignation increased their fighting spirit: the other army would soon enter the city in victory, while they were subject to the insults of the enemy. When would they be a match for the enemy if not then? When the consul learned that the camp was full of such muttering, he called the soldiers together and addressed them: 'Men, I think you have heard how the fight went at Algidus. The army behaved as the army of a free people should; victory was won under the leadership of my colleague and through the courage of the soldiers. As for myself, what leadership and fighting spirit I will display will depend on you soldiers. It is possible both to prolong the war to our advantage and to finish it off quickly. If it is to be prolonged, I will continue as I have done in order that your hopes and ardour may increase; if you are fired up enough already and want the issue to be decided, come, raise here and now the battle-cry you will give in the field as a sign of strength and spirit.' After they raised the cry with boisterous enthusiasm, he prayed for success and declared he would go along with their wishes and would lead them into battle the next day. The rest of the day was spent preparing for the coming encounter.

The next day, as soon as the Sabines saw the Roman battleline being drawn up, they too, long since eager for battle, moved into position. The fight was between two confident forces, one buoyed up by long-continued military glory, the other by its new and unexpected victory. The Sabines enhanced their strength by strategic planning; for, while matching their battlelines with the Roman, they kept two thousand special troops in reserve, who were ordered to attack the Roman left wing in the heat of the battle. After nearly surrounding the wing and beginning to overpower it, the cavalry of the two Roman legions, about six hundred in number, leaped down from their horses and, as their men were retreating, flew to the fore, confronting the enemy and, by sharing in the danger, inspiring the infantry as well as making them feel ashamed: it was humiliating for the cavalry to be fighting their own and someone else's fight and for foot soldiers to be no match for horsemen fighting on foot.

63. And so they jumped into the fray that they had quit and headed for the spot from which they had begun their retreat. In a trice not only was the battle renewed, but the Sabine wing even began to waver. The cavalrymen, protected among the ranks of the infantry, remounted their horses and galloped to the other side of the field to announce their victory; at the same time they attacked an already stricken enemy, since the stronger wing of their force had been put to flight. No others showed greater courage in that battle. The consul provided for every contingency; he praised the brave and rebuked those who held back. The latter at once acted the part of brave men; shame spurred them as much as praise had the rest. The battle-cry was everywhere renewed: all threw themselves into routing the enemy, nor could Roman might be withstood. The Sabines

scattered in flight everywhere throughout the countryside, leaving their camp for the enemy to plunder. There it was not the possessions of Rome's allies, as at Algidus, that were recovered, but their own, lost to those who had devastated Roman territory.

With a double victory won in different battles on two fronts, the senate spitefully decreed only a single day of supplication* in the name of the consuls. On their own initiative the people in great numbers renewed the supplication for a second day, an act that, though disorganized, was performed by the populace at large with almost greater enthusiasm than on the first. The consuls had arranged to arrive in the city on these same two days; they called the senate into session on the Campus Martius, where, after they had reported on their achievements, the leaders of the senate complained that the meeting was being deliberately held in the midst of the soldiery to intimidate them. And so, to avoid giving grounds for further accusation, the consuls moved the meeting to the Flaminian meadows, where the temple of Apollo now is—even then it was known as Apollo's Precinct. There, after the senate voted overwhelmingly to deny the consuls a triumph, Lucius Icilius, tribune of the plebs, brought before the people the question as to whether the consuls should celebrate a triumph. Many stepped forward to argue against this, particularly Gaius Claudius, who in a vehement speech declared that the consuls wanted to triumph over the senate, not the enemy, and that they were seeking recompense for personal favours done the tribune, not recognition of their bravery. The people had never before awarded a triumph, he continued: discussion and decision about such an honour had always lain with the senate; not even the kings had infringed the power of Rome's highest order. The tribunes should not so extend their control to every aspect of government that no deliberation on public policy was permitted. The state would finally be free, the laws equal, if each order of the state retained its own rights and privileges. Other older senators voiced the same sentiments, but to no avail: the tribes unanimously voted in favour of the proposal. Then for the first time, without the sanction of the senate, a triumph was celebrated by order of the people.

64. This victory of the tribunes and plebs was nearly carried to dangerous excess by a conspiracy of the tribunes to have themselves re-elected and, so that their ambition might not be so conspicuous, to continue the consuls in office as well. They gave as their reason the united front presented by the senators, which had undermined plebeian rights by heaping indignities upon the consuls. What would happen if they attacked the new tribunes through consuls sympathetic to their cause, when the new laws were still in their infancy? For they could not always count on having a Valerius and a Horatius as consuls who would put the liberty of the plebs before their own interests.

But by an opportune stroke of luck the lot of presiding over the election fell to Marcus Duilius, a foresighted man who realized that continuation in office would provoke a hostile reaction. When he said that he would not recognize the candidacy of the incumbent tribunes, his colleagues fought back, urging him either to allow the tribes to vote as they wished or to surrender the post of presiding officer to one of them, who would hold the election in accordance with the law rather than the wishes of the senators. In the midst of this altercation, when Duilius summoned the consuls to his bench and asked what they intended to do about the consular elections, they replied they would elect new consuls. On finding he had popular supporters of an unpopular policy, he called a public meeting with them in attendance. When the consuls were asked in the people's presence what they would do if the Roman people, mindful of the liberty received from their hands and of their military achievements, should re-elect them consuls, they remained firm in their resolve.

And so Duilius, after praising the consuls for continuing to the end in being unlike the decemvirs, held the election. Five tribunes of the plebs were chosen, but because of the aggressive and undisguised politicking of the nine incumbent tribunes, none of the candidates won a majority of the tribes. He dismissed the assembly and thereafter did not convene it for electoral purposes. He said he had followed the law, which did not stipulate a particular number, only that the office not be vacant, and ordered that those elected co-opt their colleagues. He read out the formula of the statute, which went as follows: 'If I shall have asked for the election of ten tribunes of the plebs, if for any reason you shall have elected less than ten today, then let those whom these co-opt as their colleagues be lawful tribunes according to the same law as those are whom you shall have elected tribunes of the plebs today.' Duilius persevered to the very end in maintaining that the state could not have fifteen tribunes of the plebs; and so, having thwarted the ambition of his colleagues, he quit his office, approved by senators and plebeians alike.

65. In co-opting their colleagues the new tribunes won the good-will of the senators by actually selecting two patricians, who were also ex-consuls, Spurius Tarpeius and Aulus Aternius. Spurius Herminius and Titus Verginius Caelimontanus were elected consuls; they did not unduly favour either the senatorial or plebeian cause and enjoyed peace at home and abroad. Lucius Trebonius, tribune of the plebs, out of hostility to the senators declared that he had been deceitfully treated by them in co-opting the tribunes and had been betrayed by his colleagues. He brought forward a bill specifying that he who presided over the election of the tribunes of the plebs should continue until ten tribunes of the plebs were chosen. Trebonius spent his time in office attacking the senators, for which he received the cognomen Asper, meaning harsh.

Then Marcus Geganius Macerinus and Gaius Iulius became consuls. They calmed the strife between the tribunes and the young nobles without criticizing the tribunes' power, yet preserving the dignity of the senators. When a levy was decreed for a war planned against the Volsci and Aequi they kept the plebs from sedition by keeping the project on hold, affirming that all things abroad were tranquil during this time of domestic peace and that foreign foes took heart on beholding civil discord in Rome. The concern for peace also strengthened internal harmony. But the one order always sorely tested the self-control of the other, for the younger senators began to maltreat the quiescent plebs. When the tribunes tried to help the humbler folk, they at first had little effect; soon not even they themselves were inviolate, at least in their final months in office, when injury was done through cabals of the powerful and because all magistracies as a rule lose some of their effectiveness as the year draws to a close. At this juncture the plebs felt that the tribunes offered hope only if tribunes like Icilius were in office: in their eyes they had had for two years tribunes in name only. On the other side, the older senators thought their young members had been too aggressive, but preferred, if moderation was to go by the board, that they rather than their enemies prove the more militant.

So difficult is it to steer a moderate course in safeguarding freedom. Each man pretends to want equality but strives to better himself at the expense of his fellows; and in taking steps to prevent themselves feeling fear they make themselves feared, and, as if it were necessary either to inflict or to suffer wrong, the injuries we escape we visit upon others.

66. The next consuls were Titus Quinctius Capitolinus for the fourth time and Agrippa Furius. On entry into office they were faced with neither sedition at home nor war abroad, although both threatened. But soon civil strife could no longer be contained, as the tribunes and plebs attacked the senators by putting on trial one noble after another, which continually convulsed the assemblies in fresh disputes. These events acted on the Aequi and Volsci like a bugle call summoning them to arms, while their leaders, eager for plunder, argued that for two years now enlistment had not been possible because the plebs refused to obey the order: as a result, the Romans would not send out troops against them. Licence had led them to lose the habit of military service, they said; Romans no longer regarded Rome as a homeland in which all had a share; they had turned upon themselves the anger and hostility they once had shown to foreign enemies; this was their chance to crush the Roman wolves, who were attacking one another in blind fury. They combined their arms and first ravaged Latin territory; then, when no one appeared against them, warmongering euphoria brought them to the very walls of Rome. They plundered the area up to the Esquiline Gate, flaunting the devastation of Rome's territory by way of humiliating her. When no one retaliated they went back to Corbio, driving the livestock before them.

At this juncture Quinctius the consul called the people to an assembly. 67. He spoke, I am told, as follows: 'Although I am conscious of no wrongdoing, fellow citizens, it is with deep shame that I appear in your sight. To think you know, to think posterity will know, that in the fourth consulship of Titus Quinctius the Aequi and Volsci—not even a match for the Hernici a year or so ago—reached the walls of Rome in arms and suffered not a scratch! For a long time now life has been such that it has offered little hope, but if I had known that this year of all years was to bring a disgrace such as this I would have avoided it by exile or death, if there was no other escaping my office. And *this* is the upshot: if there had been real fighters at our gates my consulship would have witnessed the capture of Rome! My career was at its height, there was nothing more to live for; better to have died in my third consulship.

'Who was it for whom these most craven of enemies had such contempt—we consuls or you citizens? If we are to blame, remove the unworthy from office and, if this is not enough, penalize us as well; but if you are to blame, may no god or human punish your mistakes; may you only repent of them. Those enemies did not despise you for cowardice or feel confident in their own worth. No, beaten and put to flight so many times, stripped of their camp, deprived of their land, sent under the yoke, they know both themselves and you. What encouraged them was the conflict of the orders and the poison of this city, the struggles between the senators and plebeians, in which we failed to moderate our power and you your liberty, in which you had had enough of patrician magistrates and we of plebeian.

'Ye gods, what is it you want? You insisted on having tribunes of the plebs; in the interest of concord we allowed it. You set your hearts on having decemvirs; we permitted their election. You could put up with the decemvirs no longer; we forced them to resign. Even after they left office we watched as these most noble and honourable men suffered death and exile. You wanted to have the tribunes of the plebs back again and got your way, to elect consuls sympathetic to your cause; and although we saw it as unfair to the senate, we looked on as even our patrician magistracy was made a gift to you plebeians. Protection by the tribunes, the right of appeal to the people, plebeian resolutions binding on the senate, our privileges trampled down under the pretext of equality before the law— all this we have put up with and still put up with. What will it take to end the discord? When may we have a city united, a country belonging to all? We have shown ourselves calmer and more philosophical in defeat than you in your hour of victory. Isn't it enough that we must fear you? Against us the Aventine was seized, against us the Sacred Mount was occupied; we saw the enemy nearly capture the Esquiline, when no one lifted a finger to stop the Volsci as they mounted the ramparts. Yet it is against us that you show your bravery and brandish your weapons!

68. 'Come, adopt the same animosity you have shown in besieging the senate, making the forum a war ground and filling the prisons with the leading men of the state, to venture outside the Esquiline Gate, or, if you dare not even that, to look down from the walls on

your lands laid waste by fire and sword, on the livestock being driven off, on the buildings everywhere in flames. But, it might be argued, what we hold in common has taken the brunt of it: land burned over, the city besieged, victory in the hands of the enemy. Yet think for a moment. What of your personal possessions? Any moment now we will hear what losses each property owner has suffered. Where will you get the money to make up these losses? Will the tribunes restore and replace them? Let them rant and rave as much as you want, heap charge upon charge against our leaders, pass law after law, hold as many public meetings as you like—but none of you has ever returned from those meetings a whit richer, a whit better off. Who has brought back anything to wife and children from these meetings except animosities, hard feelings, and grudges against the government and its leaders? What is more, you always expect other people to extricate you from the unpleasant consequences of these things rather than being honest and blameless to begin with.

'In the old days, by god, we consuls were your commanders, not the tribunes; you served in the field, not the forum; your cry cowed the enemy in the battleline, not the senators of Rome in assembly; and with booty seized from enemy land you returned home to your household gods in triumph, bringing wealth and glory to your country and to each of you personally. But now you look on as the enemy walks off with your possessions. Go ahead, spend all your time attending meetings, live your lives in the forum; but the necessity of fighting a war, which you flee, is hot on your heels. You couldn't be bothered to march to the lands of the Aequi and Volsci; now the war is at your gates. If the enemy is not repulsed, he will soon be inside the city, he will mount to the citadel and the Capitol, he will pursue you into your very houses. A year ago the senate ordered an army to be levied and led to Algidus; but here we are, still sitting idly at home bickering among ourselves like a bunch of women, happy with our peaceful lives, not seeing that our idleness will quickly provoke a war on many fronts at once.

'I know what I am saying is not pleasant to hear. But even if my own nature did not prompt me to speak the truth rather than what you would like to hear, necessity does. Indeed, I would wish to please you, citizens, but your safety in my eyes is far more important, however you may regard me in the future. Man's nature is

such that he who speaks to the people in his own interest gets a
better reception than he who has nothing but the public good in
mind—unless perchance you think these contemptible, boot-licking
demagogues, who allow you to be neither in arms nor at peace, have
your interests at heart in goading and inciting you. Such agitation is
designed to promote their careers and to enrich themselves and,
because they realize they will count for nothing when the orders are
in harmony, they prefer to be leaders in a bad cause rather than in
none, the standard-bearers of upheaval and sedition. If you have at
last had your fill of such antics and want to return to the time-
honoured ways of your ancestors and yourselves, rather than embrace these new-fangled ones, do what you will with me if I do not
in a few days crush those who have ravaged our land, putting them
to flight and stripping them of their camp, if I do not shift from our
gates and walls to their cities this war that has you in the grip of
paralysis and fear.'

69. Seldom had a speech of a popular tribune been so warmly
received by the plebeians as this, delivered by the sternest of consuls. Even the young men, who were accustomed in such crises to
regard refusal of military service as a most potent weapon against
the senators, were ready to take up arms and go to war. The flight
of the country folk, those whose property had been ravaged, and the
wounded told of more frightful losses than those which lay before
their eyes; the entire city was filled with outrage.

When the senate was convened, all looked to Quinctius, regarding him as the only one capable of restoring Rome's greatness.
The leading senators said that his speech before the assembly
befitted consular authority, his many consulships and, in fact, his
whole life, filled as it had been with honours frequently given, and
more frequently deserved. Other consuls either had betrayed senatorial dignity through flattery of the plebs or had made the masses
more difficult to control by harshly defending the rights of their
order: Titus Quinctius had delivered a speech sensitive to the
high dignity of the senators, to the concord of the orders, and
particularly to the peril at hand. They begged him and his colleague to take control; they begged the tribunes to join the consuls
in a common effort to drive the war from the city and its walls and
to show the senators that the plebs were obedient at this moment
of national crisis; the country they all shared cried out to the

tribunes, imploring succour for lands ravaged and a city virtually under siege.

A levy was decreed and held, with everyone in agreement. The consuls in assembly declared that this was not the moment for hearing appeals and that all those of military age should present themselves at dawn the following morning on the Campus Martius: they would grant hearings to those who did not enlist once the war was over and would regard as deserters those who failed to make their case. The next day all the youth presented themselves. Each cohort chose its own centurions; two senators were put in charge of each cohort. We are told that all these steps were so quickly accomplished that the standards, issued from the treasury by the quaestors that very day and brought to the Campus, were carried out from the Campus by mid-morning and the new army, with a few cohorts of veteran soldiers following as volunteers, reached the tenth milestone. On the following day the enemy was sighted and the two camps pitched side by side at Corbio. On the third day, anger spurred on the Romans, while consciousness of guilt—since they had broken the peace so many times—as well as desperation spurred on the enemy; the battle was begun without delay.

70. Since there were two consuls with equal power in the Roman army, Agrippa ceded command to his colleague, a most salutary expedient in carrying out great enterprises. Quinctius, now commander-in-chief, handsomely repaid his colleague's willingness to take a subordinate position by sharing his plans and praises and by treating him as an equal, although he was not. Quinctius commanded the right wing of the battleline, Agrippa the left. A senior officer, Spurius Postumius Albus, was put in charge of the centre. They assigned Publius Sulpicius, another senior officer, to command the cavalry. The infantry on the right wing fought splendidly, though the Volsci resisted stoutly. Publius Sulpicius with his cavalry broke through the enemy's centre line. Although he could have returned directly to the main army, he thought it better to attack the enemy from the rear before they could reassemble the scattered troops; he would have quickly routed the enemy by his charge into their rear, as the infantry attacked from the front, had not the horsemen of the Volsci and Aequi kept him engaged for a time in a fight between the two cavalry forces. Sulpicius cried that this was not the time to hang back—they would be surrounded and cut off from the rest of the

army unless they put up a stiff fight from horseback; but, he said, it was not enough to rout the cavalry yet leave them unscathed: they must cut down horses and riders lest any return to the battle to renew the fight; those whose massed line of infantry had given way to the Roman onslaught would put up no resistance now. His words did not fall on deaf ears. In a concerted assault they defeated the entire cavalry, toppling many from their horses, stabbing horses and riders with their lances. This ended the cavalry battle. They then attacked the enemy infantry and, when it began to give way, sent a report to the consuls of their exploit.

The news raised the spirits of the conquering Romans and struck fear into the Aequi as they retreated. The rout began in the centre where the attacking cavalry had broken into the ranks; then the left wing began to give way under the assault led by Quinctius the consul; the right witnessed the greatest struggle. There Agrippa, stalwart and in the prime of life, seeing that the fighting was succeeding everywhere except where he was, grabbed the standards from the bearers and began to rush forward with them himself, even throwing some among the enemy in close array. His soldiers, fearing the disgrace of losing them, hurled themselves against the enemy. And so the Romans were winning on every front at once. News then came from Quinctius that he was victorious and was now threatening the enemy camp; he did not want to break into it before knowing whether the fight had been won on the left wing as well: if Agrippa had prevailed, he instructed him to join forces with himself so that the entire army might gain possession of the booty at the same moment. Agrippa came in victory to his victorious colleague at the enemy camp, each congratulating the other. There, after the few defenders had been quickly overcome, they burst through the defences without a fight; they then marched the army back, laden with a great deal of booty, among which were the possessions plundered from their lands.

I am informed that they did not ask for a triumph nor did the senate offer them one—nor is the reason reported why it was either rejected or not requested. My best guess after such a remove of time is as follows. The year before the consuls Valerius and Horatius had defeated the Sabines in addition to the Volsci and Aequi. In view of the fact that the senate denied them a triumph, Quinctius and Agrippa would have been loath to request one for an achievement half as

great, for, even if it had been granted, they would not have wanted
who they were to count for more than what they had accomplished.

71. This splendid victory over the enemy was spoiled by a judicial
decision of the Roman populace regarding allied territory. The
people of Aricia and Ardea each claimed a tract of disputed land and
had frequently gone to war over it; now, exhausted after many
defeats on both sides, they selected the Roman people to adjudicate
the matter. The magistrates allowed the envoys to plead their case
before an assembly of the people, and they did so with great vehemence.

After the testimony had been heard and it was time for the tribes
to be polled and the people to vote, Publius Scaptius, an aged plebeian, arose and said: 'If, consuls, I may be permitted to speak in the
interest of our country, it would be wrong of me to let the people
render a mistaken verdict in this case.' When the consuls said he
had no standing and could not be heard, he began shouting that the
interests of the nation were being flouted. They then ordered him to
be ejected, but he appealed to the tribunes. Since the tribunes almost invariably do not lead the multitude but are led by it, they
allowed Scaptius to address the people, who were eager to hear what
he had to say. He began by giving his age as 82 and stating that he
had done service in the disputed territory; he was not a young man
then, but already in his twentieth year of service when the battle at
Corioli took place.* And so, though he was bringing up a fact long
forgotten by others, he remembered it quite well himself: namely,
that the land in question had belonged to Corioli and that when
Corioli was captured it became the property of the Roman people by
right of war. He wondered how the people of Ardea and Aricia had
the face to hope to filch from the Roman people land that they had
never claimed before Corioli's fall, and then make the real owners
the judges of which of them owned it! He was near the end of his
days, he said; and even though he was old and only his voice was
left him, he could not bring himself to say nothing of the land's
rightful ownership—land that he long ago had helped to win for
Rome, doing his duty as a simple soldier. He strongly urged the
people not to ignore their own claim out of an over-nice regard for
scruples.

72. When the consuls perceived that Scaptius was being heard
not just in silence but even with sounds of approval, they called on

gods and men to witness a flagrant injustice in the making, and summoned the leading senators. In their company they went around to the tribes, imploring the people not to make an appalling decision even more appalling by setting the precedent of judges awarding disputed property to themselves; they conceded that a judge had the right to look out for his own interests, but what they would gain by awarding the land to themselves would never make up for the alienation of their injured allies, for a price cannot be put on the damage to one's reputation and honesty. Is this what the envoys would report at home, what would be on everyone's lips, what the allies and enemies would hear—to the dismay of the former, the delight of the latter? Did they suppose that Rome's neighbours would find the senile shyster Scaptius responsible? Scaptius would come up smelling like roses, while the Roman people would be branded as double-crossing thieves, fraudulent appropriators of other people's property. For what judge in a private case had ever awarded the object in dispute to himself? Even Scaptius, whose sense of shame had predeceased him, would not do this.

These were the arguments vehemently advanced by the consuls and senators; but greed and Scaptius, who had excited that greed, prevailed. The tribes voted that the land belonged to the Roman people. It is undeniable that the verdict would have been the same if the case had been tried in another court. In the present instance, however, the disgrace of the verdict was not mitigated by the merits of the case, nor were the people of Aricia and Ardea any more shocked or dismayed by it than the senators in Rome. The rest of the year was free of domestic and foreign trouble.

BOOK FOUR

1. Marcus Genucius and Gaius Curiatius were the next consuls. The year was fraught with difficulties both at home and abroad, for at its start the tribune of the plebs Gaius Canuleius introduced a bill allowing intermarriage between patricians and plebeians. This the senators believed would adulterate bloodlines and subvert the privileges their clans enjoyed.* Furthermore, the tribune had begun to bruit the idea that one of the consuls might be a plebeian, which prompted nine of them to join in introducing a bill giving the people the power to elect either plebeians or patricians to the consulship, as they wished. The senators believed that if this should succeed, control of the government would not only have to be shared with the dregs of society but would pass altogether from the hands of their leaders to the plebeians. The senate was therefore overjoyed at the news that the people of Ardea had revolted because of the territory that had been unjustly taken from them, that the Veientes were ravaging the Roman frontier, and that the Volsci and Aequi were voicing their unhappiness over the fortification of Verrugo; so strong was their preference even for an unsuccessful war over an ignominious peace. And so, exaggerating these reports even more, and to permit the uproar over so many wars to drown out the tribunes' proposals, they ordered that a levy be held and that preparations be made for an all-out war—and on an even greater scale, if that were possible, than the year before under the consul Titus Quinctius.

Gaius Canuleius then delivered a brief and defiant speech in the senate, saying that these terror tactics of the consuls would not deflect the plebs from their determination over the new laws and that as long as he was alive they would not hold a levy until the plebs should enact the bills proposed by himself and his colleagues. He then immediately summoned the plebs to an assembly.

2. One and the same moment saw the consuls inciting the senate against the tribune and the tribune inciting the people against the consuls. The latter declared that the tribunes were out of their minds; their reckless actions could no longer be tolerated; in fact, the situation had reached its limit; Rome had a greater war on its hands at home than abroad. What is more, the blame lay as much

with the senators as with the plebs, as much with the consuls as with the tribunes. Whatever activity is rewarded in a state invariably thrives the most: that is the key to producing excellent statesmen in peace, excellent fighters in war. At Rome the greatest reward went to political turmoil: each and all invariably held it in greatest honour. They should recall the majesty of the senate that their fathers had bequeathed to them and in what a weakened state it would be when they passed it on to their children*—while the plebs could boast that they had grown greater and more important. Therefore the limit had not really been reached, nor would it be as long as the leaders of sedition were honoured in proportion to sedition's success. Just look at what Gaius Canuleius was aiming at! Nothing less than the defilement of the clans, the confounding of public and private auspices, leaving nothing intact, nothing uncontaminated: in the end, with every distinction erased, a man would not know who he was or to what group he belonged. For what other effect would indiscriminate intermarriage have except to encourage the patricians and plebeians to mate like beasts in the wild? A person born from such a union would not know to what family he belonged or what his religious inheritance was. He would be half-patrician, half-plebeian, a creature at war with himself.

But it wasn't enough to confound all that was human and divine. Oh no, these demagogues were now preparing to mount an assault on the consulship! At first they had been content simply to talk about the possibility of one of the consuls becoming a plebeian; now they had actually introduced a bill enabling the plebeians to choose the consuls either from the patricians or the plebeians, as they wished. And their choice would no doubt fall on the most seditious of their number: the upshot would be men like Canuleius and Icilius occupying the highest office. The senate should pray to Jupiter Optimus Maximus not to allow the power that had once belonged to the kings to sink so low.* And they would sooner die a thousand deaths than allow such a disgrace to happen. They were certain that their ancestors, too, had they divined that by caving in to the plebeians completely they would not make them better disposed to themselves but, once they had won their first demands, would become even more intransigent in making others, each more outrageous than the last—had they known this, they would have resisted with all their might before submitting to the laws passed against them in the first secession. But by conceding in the matter of the tribunate they had opened the door to this second round of concessions. As long as tribunes of the plebs and senators existed in the same state there would be no end of the struggle. Either this order or that office must go—and, better late than never, they would have to take a stand against such outrageous and reckless demands. Could it really be that after breeding dissension at home and getting away with it—thereby inciting Rome's enemies to attack—they would forbid the state to arm and defend itself against the very ones they had incited? And that after virtually inviting Rome's enemies in, they would not permit an army to be enrolled against them, but that Canuleius would have the audacity to say in the senate that unless it recognized him as the victor and allowed his laws to be passed, he would forbid the enlistment of a single soldier? What else was this if not a threat to betray his country, a threat to allow it to be attacked and captured? What encouragement would this declaration give—not to the plebs at Rome but to the Volsci, Aequi, and Veientes? Wouldn't they expect that under Canuleius' leadership they would be able to mount to the Capitol and citadel? If the tribune had crushed the fighting spirit of the senators along with their power and privileges, the consuls were still prepared to take the lead in opposing the wrongdoing of the citizens before taking the field against the enemy.

3. At the very moment when these words were being spoken in the senate, Canuleius was delivering a speech in support of his laws and against the consuls: 'Fellow Romans, many times in the past I have been made painfully aware of how much the senators despise you, how unworthy they think you are to live in their company within the same city walls; but this feeling is especially strong now when I see their vehement attack upon the laws we have proposed. Yet what else can we do in response except to point out that we are their fellow citizens and, though not possessed of the same riches, yet live in the same country? By one bill we seek the right of intermarriage, which has customarily been granted to neighbours and foreigners; in fact, we have awarded citizenship, which is a greater thing than intermarriage, even to conquered enemies. By the other we propose nothing novel, but ask that a right belonging to the Roman people be reclaimed and reinstated: namely, that the people may bestow office on those it wishes.

'What has led them to confound heaven and earth? Why just now did they come so close to assaulting me in the senate, saying that they would not hesitate to lay hands on me and were perfectly willing to violate the sacrosanctity of a tribune? If the Roman people can freely elect whomever it wants as consul and if a plebeian who is worthy of holding the highest office is not prevented from holding it, will the city collapse? Is it the end of Rome's empire? Is it the same thing to raise the question of a plebeian becoming consul as it would be for a slave or freedman? Don't you realize what contempt they have for you? They would, if they could, take the very sunlight from you; they object to the fact that you breathe, you speak, you have the outward appearance of human beings. And—as god is my witness!—they maintain it is a violation of religion for a plebeian to become consul.

'Now, we may be an ignorant lot, we may not be versed in the intricacies of the calendar or in the secret lore of the priestly colleges;* but we do know what complete outsiders know: namely, that the consuls succeeded to the position the kings once held and they possess all the privileges and powers that the kings once enjoyed. Have you never heard that Numa Pompilius—not only not a patrician but not even a citizen of Rome—was summoned from Sabine territory and ruled at Rome at the bidding of the people and with the sanction of the senate? Or that later Lucius Tarquinius—not only not of Roman stock, but not even an Italian—the son of Demaratus of Corinth, who came here from Tarquinii to settle, was made king despite the fact that King Ancus' sons were still living? Or that his successor, Servius Tullius, born of a captive of Corniculum—with a nobody for a father and a slave for a mother—occupied the throne by virtue of his character and talent? I need not cite the case of Titus Tatius, a Sabine, with whom Romulus himself, father of his country, shared joint rule. In short, as long as no man of talent was excluded from the highest office on the grounds of family, Rome's power increased. And do they now reject a plebeian as consul, although our ancestors did not exclude foreigners as kings? Will they do so despite the fact that not even after the kings were expelled was the door shut to talent from outside? For it was after the expulsion of the kings that the Claudian clan came from Sabine territory and received not only citizenship but even admission to the patriciate. May a foreigner become a patrician and then be elected consul, while a citizen of Rome who happens to be a plebeian can have no hope of attaining to the highest office? Do we think it impossible for a brave and energetic man who has shown his worth in war and peace to be a plebeian—someone like Numa, Lucius Tarquinius, and Servius Tullius? Or, even if he should be such, will we deny him the reins of government, preferring to have as consuls men like the decemvirs—utter monsters, and every one a patrician—instead of those who were like the best of our kings, self-made men though they were?

4. 'But someone may say that since the expulsion of the kings no plebeian has been consul. This is no real argument. Do they mean *nothing* new should be tried? Yet when a nation is just beginning there are many things that have not been attempted. What reason can there be for not instituting something new that will benefit the state? In Romulus' reign there were as yet no pontiffs, no augurs; Numa Pompilius created them. The state had no census, no divisions by centuries and classes; Servius Tullius invented them. There was a time when there were no consuls; they came into being when the kings were expelled. The power of the dictator—even his title—were unknown; they began in the time of our fathers. There were no tribunes of the plebs, no aediles, no quaestors; it was decided that there should be. Within the last ten years we instituted decemvirs for drawing up the laws and then swept them from office. Who can doubt that in a city founded to last forever, and growing to a size we cannot now imagine, new commands, new priesthoods, new rights for groups and individuals will perforce come into being? The very prohibition of intermarriage between patricians and plebeians—was this not an innovation by the decemvirs a few years ago—one that set the worst kind of example, utterly demeaning to the plebs? Can there be any greater, any more blatant insult than to consider a part of the community unfit for intermarriage, as if they were polluted filth? That is equivalent to exile or banishment within the same city walls. They forbid us to share in ties of marriage and kinship because they do not wish to share their blood with us.

'And yet a great many of you nobles are not patrician by clan or bloodline but because you were co-opted into that body—some from Alba and the Sabines, others chosen by the kings or by vote of the people after the expulsion of the kings. Even supposing that this noble ancestry of yours would be polluted by intermarriage, have you not been able to keep it intact all along by contracting marriages in accordance with your personal wishes, by not marrying plebeian women yourselves and by forbidding your daughters and sisters to marry outside the patriciate? No plebeian would do violence to a patrician girl: such lechery is a patrician preserve. No one would force a man to enter on a marriage contract unwillingly. Yet actually to prohibit this by law, to remove any possibility of intermarriage between patricians and plebeians—this is nothing but a slap in the plebeians' face. Why don't you propose a law forbidding rich and poor to marry? At all times and in all places women have married men and husbands have taken wives in accordance with private agreements, but around this you have thrown the shackles of a most arrogant law, thereby destroying a community in which all share and creating two states out of one. Why not enact a law that no plebeian may live next to a patrician, walk down the same street, attend the same social functions, stand beside him in the same forum? What real difference is there if a patrician marries a plebeian wife or a plebeian a patrician? What right has been infringed? The children of course take the father's status. We have nothing to gain from the right of intermarriage with you except acknowledgement that we are human beings and your fellow countrymen; you have nothing at stake either—unless you find it a pleasure to insult and demean us.

5. 'Finally, does power ultimately rest with the Roman people or with you? When the kings were driven out did you become our masters or was liberty won equally for all? Should the Roman people be permitted to enact a law, if it wants, or, whenever a bill is proposed, will you retaliate by ordering troops to be enrolled? When I as tribune start to ask the tribes to begin voting, will one of you consuls immediately swear in the troops and lead them forth into camp, all the while threatening the plebs and their tribune? Haven't you already twice found out how ineffectual such threats are when the plebs are united in their determination?* No doubt you refrained from a fight because you had our best interest at heart! Might I suggest that there was no fight because the stronger side used greater restraint? And there will be no fight now, citizens. They will always test your resolve, but they will never risk a showdown of strength. And so I say to the consuls that the plebeians are ready to go to war now—it makes no difference whether the wars you talk of are real or fictitious—but only if you restore the right of intermarriage and at last make our country whole again, only if we

plebeians become one with you, only if we can join and unite with you in private ties that will make us relatives and kinsmen, only if the hope, the opportunity of holding office is granted to all who are brave and energetic, only if there is full partnership, equal participation in the running of our country, only—and this is the mark of equality before the law—if one may be both a citizen obedient to his elected officials and then in turn become one of those officials himself. If someone frustrates these hopes, you may warmonger as you will and talk one war after another into existence, but no one will enlist, no one will take up arms, no one will risk his life in the service of arrogant overlords who refuse a share in the offices of state or the right of marriage in private life.'

6. When the consuls had entered the assembly and set speeches had given way to wrangling, the tribune was told on asking why a plebeian should not be elected consul that no plebeian had the right to take the auspices and that the decemvirs had consequently forbidden intermarriage lest the auspices be confounded by those of questionable lineage—a reply that, while possibly true, was of no help in resolving the present dispute. Quite the contrary, for it was this remark that most caused the plebs to explode: they could not take the auspices because they were hateful in the eyes of the gods! But because they had a doughty tribune as their champion and were as determined as he in their fight, the senators in the end found themselves beaten; they allowed the law on intermarriage to pass, especially because they fancied that the tribunes now would either drop their fight to have plebeian consuls completely or would postpone it until after the war, and that the plebs, content in the meantime with the law on intermarriage, would be ready to answer the call to arms.

His victories over the senators won Canuleius much goodwill from the plebs, and this fired the other tribunes to continue the struggle: they fought for their bill with every resource at their disposal and so blocked the levy—though rumours of war were growing from day to day. The consuls, when they found it impossible to secure a resolution of the senate with the tribunes interposing their veto,* met privately with the senatorial leadership. It seemed as if victory must go either to the enemy or the citizens. Valerius and Horatius alone of the ex-consuls took no part in this discussion. Gaius Claudius proposed that the consuls use armed force against the tribunes, while the two Quinctii, Cincinnatus and Capitolinus, opposed the killing that would ensue and the violation of those whom they had recognized as sacrosanct by the agreement they had struck with the plebs. In the end the deliberations came down to this: that they should sanction election of military tribunes with consular power, to be selected from patricians and plebs alike, and that there be no change in how the consuls were elected. The tribunes and the plebs were content with this compromise.

The election of tribunes with consular power, three in number, was announced. Immediately anyone who had ever said or done anything smacking of sedition, especially former tribunes, donned the white togas of candidates and scurried about the forum soliciting the support of all they met; the result was that the patricians were reluctant to compete, first because they had little hope of being elected in face of plebeian hostility, and second because they thought it beneath them to have such people as colleagues. But in the end, yielding to the pressure put on them by their party leaders, they declared their candidacy in order not to seem to have tamely handed over the reins of government to others. The outcome of the election showed that men behave quite differently when they are struggling for freedom and dignity from when the fight is over and their judgement is unbiased. For every tribune elected was a patrician; the people were content that plebeians had been allowed to stand. Where might you find nowadays in a single man such self-restraint, fairness, and high-mindedness—qualities that then characterized the whole people?

7. In the 310th year from the founding of Rome military tribunes for the first time replaced the consuls as holders of the highest office.* Aulus Sempronius Atratinus, Lucius Atilius, and Titus Cluilius were elected, and during their tenure harmony at home produced peace abroad. Some authorities say that, because there was a war with Veii in addition to one with the Aequi and Volsci and to the defection of Ardea, two consuls were not sufficient to conduct operations on so many fronts at once; thus three military tribunes were elected (these sources do not mention the law that was promulgated concerning the election of plebeians as consuls). The military tribunes had the same power and insignia as the consuls. But the new magistracy got off to a shaky start because in the third month after entering office they resigned when the augurs decreed that their

election was like others in the past that had been rendered invalid by an irregularity, for prior to the voting Gaius Curiatius, who had presided, had improperly selected the area from which to take the auspices.*

When envoys from Ardea arrived in Rome to complain of the injury done to them, it was evident that, should their land be restored, they would remain friends and abide by their treaty. The senate replied that it could not rescind the people's decision; neither precedent nor right permitted it, to say nothing of their desire to preserve the concord of the orders: but if the people of Ardea were willing to bide their time and if they would let the senate see to the rectification of the wrong done to them, they would later be glad they had moderated their anger; furthermore, they should know that the senators had been as anxious originally that they not be mistreated as they were now that the mistreatment not be long-lasting. And so the envoys departed on cordial terms, saying that they would reopen the whole question at home.

Since the state had no supreme, or curule, magistrate, the patricians met and chose an interrex. A dispute as to whether consuls or military tribunes should be elected delayed a resolution for many days during the interregnum. The interrex and the senate supported the election of consuls, the plebeian tribunes and the plebs of military tribunes. The senators prevailed because the plebs saw no point in continuing the dispute: they were going to vote for patricians in either case. And the plebeian leaders preferred an election in which they were not candidates to one in which they would be embarrassed by rejection at the polls. The tribunes of the plebs did not push the dispute further either, as a favour to the senatorial leadership. Titus Quinctius Barbatus, the interrex, presided over the election as consuls of Lucius Papirius Mugillanus and Lucius Sempronius Atratinus. Under these consuls the treaty with Ardea was renewed, which is evidence that they were consuls in this year, although their names appear neither in early histories nor in the books of magistrates. I believe that because military tribunes began the year the names of these suffect consuls were omitted, as though the military tribunes were in office for the whole of the year. Licinius Macer vouches for the fact that the names of the consuls are preserved both in the treaty with Ardea and in the Linen Books stored in the temple of Juno Moneta.*

There was peace at home and abroad, despite threats from so many of Rome's neighbours.

8. This year, whether it had either military tribunes only or tribunes replaced by suffect consuls, was followed by one in which consuls were unquestionably the chief magistrates, Marcus Geganius Macerinus for the second time and Titus Quinctius Capitolinus for the fifth time. This same year saw the institution of the censorship, an office that began in a small way but grew to such importance that eventually to it fell complete control over morals and behaviour, the right to honour persons by enrolling them in the senate and in the centuries of knights or to dishonour them by expulsion, adjudication of disputes over boundaries between public and private property, and absolute control of state revenues.* The reason for its institution was that there had been no census for many years and one was urgently needed; moreover, the consuls could not do it since they were fully occupied with wars on many fronts at once. And so a motion was made in the senate that a new magistracy handle the onerous and quite unconsular task, and that it have its own secretarial staff, control over record-keeping, and the power to decide the rules according to which the census would be conducted. The new office was quite welcome to the senators because, though relatively unimportant, it was the prerogative of the patricians (they also thought, I imagine, that the wealth and social standing of its holders would add to its power and prestige over time, which in fact happened), while the tribunes looked on it as something more useful than prestigious (which it was at that moment); and so, not to create an unnecessary fuss over a minor issue, they let it go through without much objection. When the political leadership showed no interest in the office, the people elected Papirius and Sempronius to conduct the census, concerning whose consulship doubt was expressed a few pages back, in order that this office might compensate for their incomplete consulship. They were styled censors after the task they were assigned to complete.

9. While these things were going on in Rome, envoys came from Ardea imploring aid for a city on the verge of extinction. They were acting in the name of their ancient alliance and the treaty they had recently renewed. They were unable to enjoy the peace they had wisely kept with the Roman people in the midst of internal conflict—caused, it is said, by factional strife, which has been and will

be for most peoples more destructive than wars with foreign enemies, more destructive than famine, pestilence, or other national
disasters that men attribute to the wrath of the gods.

Two young men courted a beautiful plebeian girl. One of them,
himself a plebeian, relied on the approval of the girl's guardians,*
who were likewise plebeian; the other was a noble for whom the
only lure was the girl's beauty, and who was supported by his fellow
aristocrats. Such partisan sympathies made their way into the girl's
house as well; for her mother preferred the young noble because she
wanted as splendid a marriage as possible for her daughter, while
the girl's guardians succumbed to partisan feelings by favouring a
member of their own class. When the dispute could not be settled
within the home, it went to court. After the pleas of the mother and
the guardians had been heard, the magistrates decided in favour of
the mother's wishes in the matter of the marriage. But force proved
stronger; for the guardians, openly holding meetings in the forum
among men of their own party concerning this adverse judgement,
got a group of men together and kidnapped the girl from her mother's house. The aristocrats reacted even more strongly by arming
themselves in support of the young noble, outraged at being cheated
of his prize. A frightful battle ensued. Upon being worsted, the
plebs retreated in arms from the city and settled on a hilltop. But
their conduct was completely unlike that of the plebs of Rome, for
from this eminence they conducted raids on the lands belonging to
the aristocracy, ravaging them with fire and sword. They even collected a band of booty-hungry labourers and prepared to assault the
town, which hitherto had been untouched by any kind of violence.
The horrors of war in all its forms descended upon Ardea. The city
was infected, so to speak, with the madness of the two young men,
who sought a marriage of death through the overthrow of their city.

Neither side was content to rely on the weapons of war at home.
The aristocrats urged the Romans to come to the aid of the beleaguered city; the plebs appealed to the Volsci to join them in their
assault. The Volsci arrived first in Ardea, under the leadership of
the Aequan Cluilius,* and threw up a rampart before the walls.
When this was reported at Rome, the consul Marcus Geganius set
out at once with an army and, pitching camp three miles from the
enemy, ordered his men to take rest and refreshment, since the day
was drawing to a close. At the fourth watch he moved his troops

forward, and by sunrise the manœuvre was complete: the Volsci found that the Romans had hemmed them in more tightly than they had Ardea. In one spot the consul had managed to connect to Ardea's city wall, where his own men could pass in and out of the town.

10. The Volscian general, who up to then had fed his soldiers not with provisions prepared in advance but by food plundered day by day from the countryside, now suddenly found himself hemmed in by the Roman rampart and without supplies of any kind. He summoned the consul to meet with him, and said that if the Roman had come to lift the siege, he would march the Volsci off. The consul replied that it was for the conquered to accept terms, not make them, and that though it had been their choice to lay siege to allies of the Roman people, the Volsci did not have the option of choosing when they would depart. He ordered the commander to be handed over and their arms to be laid down as a confession of having been defeated and of their willingness to obey his commands; otherwise, whether they departed or stayed, he would be their determined foe and would return to Rome as victor over the Volsci rather than as bearer of a treacherous peace.

When the Volsci realized all hope had been cut off save the slight one of defeating the Romans in battle, they chose to fight despite everything being against them, including the ground itself, which was disadvantageous for battle and even more disadvantageous for flight. Cut down on all sides, they abandoned resistance and turned to entreaty. After their commander had been handed over and their arms surrendered, they were sent under the yoke and then dismissed with a single garment apiece, overwhelmed by disgrace and disaster. And when they stopped to rest not far from Tusculum, they paid the penalty for their previous attacks on the town: longstanding hatred led the inhabitants to slaughter them in their defenceless state: scarcely any survived to report the massacre. The Romans settled the tumultuous situation at Ardea by beheading the leaders of the sedition and giving their confiscated property to the public treasury. The inhabitants regarded this as a great service on the part of the Roman people, which atoned for their unjust decision earlier to award themselves Ardeate land; but to the senate it seemed more should be done to wipe out this sorry reminder of communal avarice.

The consul returned to the city in triumph, with Cluilius, the Volscian leader, led before his chariot and the spoils displayed that had been taken from the enemy sent under the yoke. The consul Quinctius in his civilian role equalled the glory of his military colleague—not an easy thing to do; for by dispensing justice equally to high and low he evinced such concern for concord and domestic peace that the senators regarded him as a strict consul and the plebs as quite kind-hearted. Against the tribunes he held his own more by force of character than contentiousness; five consulships administered in the same spirit and an entire lifetime lived as befitted a consular made the man almost as revered as the office.

And so there was no mention of electing military tribunes under such consuls as these; 11. The new consuls were Marcus Fabius Vibulanus and Postumus Aebutius Cornicen. They were aware of their predecessors' glorious achievements at home and abroad, particularly of the fact that the year had been so memorable in the eyes of allies and enemies because of Rome's great concern to come to the aid of Ardea in its hour of need. Stimulated by this record, the new consuls worked all the harder to wipe out from people's memories the notoriety of the unjust decision concerning Ardeate land; they did this by passing a decree of the senate that was designed to repopulate Ardea, which had lost most of its citizens in the domestic upheaval: the decree ordered that colonists be enrolled to act as a garrison against the Volsci. The decree was worded in this form and displayed for all to see, the aim being to conceal from the plebs and tribunes the fact that this was a first step toward rescinding the unjust decision; the plan was that, since there were far more eligible Rutulian colonists than Roman,* only the land appropriated by the unjust decision would be divided up and that none of it would be assigned to any Roman until all the Rutulian applicants had been given their plots. Thus the land returned to the Ardeates. A three-man board was elected for founding the colony at Ardea, Agrippa Menenius, Titus Cluilius Siculus, and Marcus Aebutius Helva. They offended the plebs because they had the unpopular task of assigning to allies land which the Roman people had judged belonged to themselves. And they displeased the senatorial leadership because they refused to show favouritism to anyone. When the tribunes ordered them to stand trial before the people, they avoided all harassment by settling down in the colony—an act that stood as a testament to their integrity and just dealing.

12. There was peace at home and abroad both in this year and the following, when Gaius Furius Pacilus and Marcus Papirius Crassus were consuls. The games were held this year that the decemvirs had vowed in accordance with a senatorial decree during the secession of the plebs from the senators. The tribune Poetelius failed in his effort to spark political discord; he had been re-elected tribune by running on a platform of land distribution to the plebs and the election of military tribunes. But the consuls refused to bring a motion before the senate concerning the land, and, although after a great struggle he prevailed in having the senate debate the question on whether to have consuls or tribunes, that body decided on consuls. The threats of the tribune to block the levy were ludicrous, since Rome was at peace with her neighbours: war was unnecessary, as were preparations for one.

After this tranquil year came the consulship of Proculus Geganius Macerinus and Lucius Menenius Lanatus, which was marked by many deaths and dangers: political unrest, famine, and the near imposition of tyranny's yoke, as men succumbed to the delights of free hand-outs. The only thing missing was a foreign war; had one been added to their other miseries, resistance could scarcely have been offered even with the help of all the gods. These calamities were ushered in by a severe famine caused perhaps by crop failure and perhaps through neglect, as men abandoned the countryside for the pleasures of the city and political assemblies (our sources report both explanations). The senators charged the plebs with laziness, while the tribunes of the plebs accused the consuls variously of double-dealing and dereliction of duty. Finally, at the prompting of the tribunes the plebs elected Lucius Minucius prefect of the grain supply, to which the senate made no objection. Time would show that Minucius' tenure in office was more successful in preserving liberty than in administering his duties, although in the end he deservedly gained both thanks and glory for alleviating the grain shortage. He saw to it that many delegations seeking grain were sent round to the neighbouring peoples over land and sea; but when they produced no result, save for a small amount from Etruria, he resorted to the following measures. In an effort to distribute what little was left more evenly, he forced people to divulge the amount of grain they had and to sell anything in excess of a month's supply; he deprived the slaves of part of their daily food; but this led him to level charges against the grain distributors, thereby exposing them to the anger of the people. Alas, this harsh proceeding did not alleviate the scarcity but only served to reveal how little food was really left. Many plebeians in despair could no longer prolong their lives in agony, but covered their heads and threw themselves into the Tiber.

13. Then Spurius Maelius, who was a member of the equestrian order* and a very wealthy man for those days, attempted to do something useful, but the means he used set an extremely bad precedent, and his motives were even worse. For he began to make free hand-outs of grain from stores he had bought in Etruria with his own money, using friends and clients as agents (which, I imagine, impeded the state's efforts to relieve the shortage). The prominence and influence he gained were greater than befitted a man in private life; the plebs were captivated by his generosity, and their goodwill and high hopes were guarantees of a sure consulship in the future.

Men can never have enough of fortune's favours, and so it was with him. He aimed at something greater, something illicit. Since even the consulship would have to be wrested from the unwilling senators, he began to think about kingship: only this would compensate for his manifold schemes and the sweat that would have to be put into the great struggle that loomed ahead. But the consular elections were imminent; he was balked, his plans not yet fully laid or developed. Elected consul was Titus Quinctius Capitolinus for the sixth time, a formidable adversary for one plotting revolution; his colleague was Agrippa Menenius, whose cognomen was Lanatus. Lucius Minucius was prefect of the grain supply, either because he had been re-elected or because he had been appointed for as long as the situation required. Our sources do not agree on the explanation except that in the Linen Books the name of the prefect is recorded for each year among the names of the magistrates.

It was Minucius who, while carrying out the same mission on behalf of the public that Maelius had undertaken as a private citizen, reported to the senate what he had discovered from the grain agents, who frequented both their houses. Weapons, he said, had been smuggled into Maelius' home and regular meetings had been held there, all of which pointed unequivocally to an attempt to usurp supreme power. The time had not yet been fixed, although everything else had been planned: the tribunes had been bribed to subvert the country's freedom, while the leaders of the mob had been assigned the parts they were to play. He had waited, he said, to lay the matter before the senate almost longer than was safe, for he had not wanted to vouch for anything uncertain or trivial.

After this announcement the senatorial leadership on every side railed at the consuls of the previous year for having allowed free hand-outs and meetings of the plebs in a private house to take place and at the new consuls for waiting for the prefect of the grain supply to lay such a momentous matter before the senate: a crisis like this cried out for a consul not only to bring it to light but to crush it. In reply Quinctius said the consuls were being undeservedly criticized: constrained by the laws on the right of appeal, which had been designed to weaken their office, they did not have the power to crush the conspiracy as its heinousness deserved, though they certainly had the will to do so. Rome needed now not just a brave man, but one who was also free and exempt from the constraints of the laws. He therefore would take it upon himself to name Lucius Quinctius Cincinnatus as dictator, whose will would be equal to his great power. Everyone supported this move, but Cincinnatus at first held back, asking what they were thinking of in placing him at his advanced age in the midst of such a great struggle. Then, when on all sides they declared that more good sense and courage coexisted in that aged spirit of his than in everyone else combined and heaped the praise he deserved upon him, and when the consul would not give way, Cincinnatus at last, after praying to the immortal gods that his old age not prove harmful or inglorious to the state in its hour of need, was named dictator by the consul. He himself then named Gaius Servilius Ahala as his master of the horse.

14. The next day, after setting up guard stations at various points, he entered the forum. The plebs, startled by this unexpected turn of events, fixed their attention on him, while Maelius and his supporters were conscious that the might of this great office was directed at them. Those who were not privy to the plot to set up a king wanted to know what calamity, what conflict had necessitated the naming of a dictator or why Cincinnatus, now over 80, had become head of state. Servilius, the master of the horse, was then sent by the dictator to Maelius: 'The dictator requires your presence,' he said. When

Maelius in fear asked why, Servilius said that he would have to defend himself and answer the charges brought by Minucius before the senate. Maelius stepped back among his band of supporters, and looking in every direction began to equivocate; but in the end, when the attendant on orders of the master of the horse tried to arrest him, he was pulled back by those standing around. He took to his heels, begging the Roman people to help him: he was being crushed by a conspiracy of the senators because of his generosity to the plebs. He begged them to help him in his extremity and not let him be slaughtered before their very eyes. As he was shouting these appeals Servilius Ahala caught up with him and cut him down. Covered with the blood of the slain man, and surrounded by a band of patrician youths, he returned to the dictator and reported that when Maelius had been summoned to appear before the dictator his own attendant had been repulsed and that Maelius had met the punishment he deserved in the very act of inciting the crowd, to which the dictator replied, 'Well done, Gaius Servilius! Our country has won back its freedom.'

15. He then ordered the multitude to assemble, which was in an uproar because people were at a loss as to what was going on. He declared that even if Maelius had been innocent of the charge of aiming at kingship, he had been rightly killed, since he had not answered the summons of the master of the horse to appear before the dictator. He himself had taken his seat to try the case, at whose conclusion Maelius would have suffered the fate his case merited. He had been plotting violence in order to avoid trial, when he had met a violent end. Nor should Maelius have been dealt with as a citizen. Here was a man born in a free country, enjoying its privileges and laws, a man who knew that from this city the kings had been driven out and that in the same year the sons of the king's sister, sired by the consul who was the liberator of his country, were beheaded by their father because they were plotting to restore the kings; here was a man who knew that from this city the consul Tarquinius Collatinus was bidden to resign his office and go into exile because his name was so hated; a city in which a few years later Spurius Cassius was executed for aiming to seize the throne; a city in which the decemvirs only recently had suffered loss of property, exile, and death for behaving with royal arrogance. In short, it was in *this* city that Spurius Maelius had conceived the hope of becom-

ing king. And what sort of a man was he? Now, even though nobility, high office, and great service entitle no man to aim at sole rule, members of the Claudian and Cassian families had nevertheless been emboldened to tempt the forbidden because of the distinction of their families: the consulships, decemvirates, and other high honours that fell to them and their families. But Spurius Maelius (for whom the plebeian tribunate was something to hope for, not expect)—this grain dealer with lots of money—flattered himself that he had bought the liberty of his fellow citizens for a few pounds of cheap wheat and thought that by tossing them some food he could entice a people victorious over all their foes to become his slaves. He fancied that a nation which could scarcely have stomached his becoming a senator would put up with him as king, invested with the power and insignia of the city's founder, Romulus, born of a god and received among the gods. His plot ought not to be considered a crime so much as a monstrosity. Yet his blood was not enough to expiate it: his house and the walls within which this mad scheme was hatched should be demolished, the tainted property he used to bribe his way to the throne sold at public auction. He would therefore order the quaestors to sell the property and put the proceeds in the public treasury.

16. He then ordered the immediate destruction of the house so that the site would be a reminder of the frustration of Maelius' wicked scheme. The levelled area was called the Aequimaelium. Lucius Minucius was honoured with a gilded ox outside the Trigemina Gate;* the plebs made no objection because he had distributed to them Maelius' grain at the rate of one copper coin per peck. I find in certain sources that this Minucius changed from being a patrician to a plebeian and that, having been co-opted as an eleventh tribune of the plebs, he calmed the tumult stirred up by the killing of Maelius. But it is scarcely credible that the senators would have allowed the number of tribunes to be increased, and that this innovation in particular would have involved a patrician and that thereafter the plebs did not hold on to it once it was in place, or at least did not try to do so. But most decisive is the fact that a law had been passed a few years before forbidding the tribunes to co-opt a colleague; this shows the inscription beside Minucius' death mask to have been false.*

Quintus Caecilius, Quintus Iunius, and Sextus Titinius were the

only tribunes who did not sponsor the law conferring honours on
Minucius and who had not stopped levelling charges against both
Minucius and Servilius before the plebs and complaining of the
undeserved death of Maelius. So they prevailed in having military
tribunes rather than consuls elected for the following year, confident
that by promising to avenge Maelius' murder and with six vacan-
cies—for this was the number that could be elected—even some
plebeians would be returned. The plebs, although they had been
upset by many different disturbances in the course of the year,
elected no more than three tribunes with consular power, among
them Lucius Quinctius, the son of Cincinnatus, whose unpopular
dictatorship had been used as a reason for sparking civil unrest.
Mamercus Aemilius, a man of the greatest distinction, was returned
first in the voting; Quinctius came next, followed by Lucius Iulius
in third place.

17. During the tenure of these magistrates Fidenae, a Roman
colony, defected to Lars Tolumnius, the king of Veii. They capped
their defection with a greater crime—killing on Tolumnius' orders
the Roman envoys Gaius Fulcinius, Cloelius Tullus, Spurius Nautius,
and Lucius Roscius who had come to inquire into the reason for
forswearing allegiance. Certain sources palliate the king's action by
claiming that when he had a lucky throw at dice and uttered something that might be construed as a command to murder, the people
of Fidenae took this as sufficient reason to kill them—which is quite
incredible; we are asked to believe that when the Fidenates, his new
allies, interrupted him to ask about a massacre that would violate the
law of nations, he could not get his mind off the game or that, if this
is what actually happened, they failed to consider the possibility that
his remark was a mistake. It is more probable that he wanted the
people of Fidenae to be so implicated in this monstrous deed that
reconciliation with the Romans would be beyond hope. Statues of
the envoys slain at Fidenae were placed at public expense on the
rostrum, or speakers' platform, in the forum.

A terrible struggle loomed with the peoples of Veii and Fidenae,
not just because they were Rome's neighbours but also because they
had started the war in such an appalling way. And so, with the plebs
and tribunes of that year quiescent out of concern for the national
welfare, there was no controversy over the election of consuls, who
were Marcus Geganius Macerinus for the third time and Lucius

Sergius Fidenas. I believe his cognomen came from the war he proceeded to wage; for he was the first to fight a successful battle with the Veian king on the near side of the Anio River. But it was not a bloodless victory: the grief for the lives lost was greater than the joy over the enemy's defeat; the senate ordered that a dictator be named, which is usual in emergencies—in this case Mamercus Aemilius. He picked as master of the horse his colleague of the year before when they had been tribunes of the soldiers with consular power, Lucius Quinctius Cincinnatus, a young man worthy of his great father. Included in the levy conducted by the consuls were veteran centurions with much experience in war as well as new recruits to make up the number of men lost in the last battle. The dictator ordered that Titus Quinctius Capitolinus and Marcus Fabius Vibulanus follow him as his lieutenants. The great power of the dictator and an incumbent equal to that power drove the enemy out of Roman territory and across the Anio. They occupied the hills between Fidenae and the Anio and fixed their camp there, nor did they venture into the plain below until the legions of the Falisci came to their aid. Only then was the Etruscan camp pitched before the walls of Fidenae. The Roman dictator, in turn, settled down not far from the confluence of the Tiber and Anio Rivers and there threw up a rampart in front where he was vulnerable to enemy attack.* The next day he drew up his battleline.

18. Opinions were split among the enemy. The Falisci, not liking military service far from home and quite self-confident, demanded battle; the men from Veii and Fidenae put more hope in dragging out the war. Tolumnius, although favouring the opinion of his own people but fearing the Falisci would not put up with distant campaigning, announced he would fight the next day. The dictator and the Romans were delighted, because the enemy had hitherto refused a fight; and on the next day, as the soldiers began muttering they would attack camp and city if the opportunity to fight was not given, soldiers from each camp marched out and formed their battlelines in the centre of the plain. The Veian army, having men to spare, sent around behind the mountains a contingent that was to attack the Roman camp as the battle was going on. The army of the three peoples was so drawn up that the Veientes were on the right wing, the Falisci held the left, while to the Fidenates belonged the centre. The dictator commanded the troops on the right wing facing

the Falisci, Quinctius Capitolinus the left opposite the Veientes; before the centre line the master of the horse with the cavalry took his place.

For a short time no one moved or spoke—the Etruscans not wanting to engage until they had to, the dictator looking back to Rome's citadel, waiting to receive from there a signal agreed on with the augurs, the moment consultation of the sacred birds proved favourable. As soon as he saw it, the battle-cry was raised and the cavalry sent against the enemy first; the infantry line followed in a furious onrush. Nowhere did the Etruscan legions withstand the Roman assault; the cavalry put up the greatest resistance, of whom by far the bravest was the king himself, who prolonged the struggle by riding up against the Romans as they rushed forward everywhere in loose pursuit.

19. There was at that time among the cavalrymen a tribune of the soldiers named Aulus Cornelius Cossus, a strikingly handsome man, equally strong and courageous, and proud of his birthright: from his ancestors he had received a glorious inheritance, to his descendants he left it in an even more splendid state. When he saw that wherever Tolumnius directed his attack the Roman squadrons became terrified, and when he realized from his royal attire that it was the king himself who was ranging over the whole battlefield, he cried, 'Is this the one who broke the treaty of man with man and violated the law of nations? If the gods will that anything sacred remains in the world, I shall soon offer him as a sacrificial victim to appease the spirits of the murdered envoys.' Digging in his spurs he bore down on the lone enemy with his lance lowered, striking him and toppling him from his horse. With the aid of his spear he at once vaulted from his horse to the ground. As the king tried to rise, he knocked him to the ground with the boss of his shield and transfixed him to the earth, stabbing him through again and again. He then stripped the spoils from the corpse of the king, cut off his head and, fixing it on a pike, paraded it around in victory to terrify the enemy. And so the enemy cavalry took to their heels, which alone had put the issue of the battle in doubt. The dictator pursued the fleeing legions and cut them down as they were driven toward their camp. Most of the Fidenates, who knew the terrain, fled into the mountains. Cossus crossed the Tiber with the cavalry into Veian territory and brought from there much booty to the city.

While the battle was going on, there was also a fight at the Roman camp against the division of troops sent there by Tolumnius, as mentioned before. Fabius Vibulanus first defended the rampart with a ring of fighters; then, while the enemy was intent on assaulting the rampart, he slipped out the right gate with some reserve veterans and suddenly fell on them. There were fewer casualties here among the panic-stricken enemy because there were not so many of them, but their fear as they fled was as great as had been that of their fellows in the main force.

20. Successful in every quarter, the dictator by a decree of the senate and at the bidding of the people returned in triumph to the city. But all eyes were fixed on Cossus during the triumph, as he carried the spoils of honour taken from the king; soldiers sang rough verses in which they compared him to Romulus. In a solemn ceremony he dedicated the spoils in the temple of Jupiter Feretrius, placing them next to the spoils of Romulus, who had been the only one up to that day to dedicate what are called the spoils of honour. Cossus had turned the attention of the citizens from the chariot of the dictator to himself, and was virtually the only one to enjoy the accolades of that crowded celebration. The dictator dedicated to Jupiter on the Capitol a golden crown a pound in weight at the order of the people and at public expense.

I have followed all earlier authorities in stating that Aulus Cornelius Cossus was military tribune when he dedicated the spoils of honour in the temple of Jupiter Feretrius, the second man to do so. And yet, aside from the fact that only spoils which one supreme commander strips from another supreme commander are properly regarded as spoils of honour and that we recognize no commander except the one under whose religious auspices a war is waged,* the inscription written on Cossus' spoils shows that both earlier historians and I are wrong about which office he held, and that Cossus won them in his capacity as consul. When I heard that Augustus Caesar, who founded and restored all our temples, including that of Jupiter Feretrius (which had collapsed from age), entered the temple and read the inscription written on the linen corselet, I thought it well-nigh sacrilegious to disqualify Caesar, who had refounded this very temple, as a witness to Cossus and his spoils. Each person can decide for himself how the mistake came about that the authorities date Aulus Cornelius' consulship ten years later (his colleague being Titus Quinctius Poenus), a mistake found in the oldest histories and in the books of magistrates, which, written on linen and stored in the temple of Juno Moneta, Licinius Macer repeatedly cites.* There is also an additional factor: this famous battle cannot be dated to that year because the three-year period around Aulus Cornelius' consulship saw no wars, but was marked by pestilence and famine—so much so that certain histories, like casualty lists, append only the names of the consuls. The third year after Cossus' consulship has him as a military tribune with consular power, as well as master of the horse, in which command he distinguished himself in a second cavalry battle. Conjecture is open to everyone, but it is pointless. For despite all the opinions that might be advanced, the fact remains that the winner of the fight wrote that he was Aulus Cornelius Cossus, consul: he had just placed the spoils in their sacred place and in doing so he was virtually face to face with Jupiter, to whom he had made his vow, and with Romulus; he would scarcely have falsified the inscription before such witnesses as these.*

21. In the consulship of Marcus Cornelius Maluginensis and Lucius Papirius Crassus armies were led into the territories of Veii and the Falisci. Captives and animals were brought back as booty. The enemy was encountered nowhere in the countryside nor was battle offered; yet their cities were not attacked because back in Rome a pestilence had begun. What is more, there was also an unsuccessful attempt to create a civil disturbance by the tribune of the plebs, Spurius Maelius, who, fancying the popularity of his name would help to get him a following, had brought an indictment against Minucius and had introduced a bill to sell off the property of Servilius Ahala at public auction. He claimed his namesake Maelius had been convicted on false charges brought by Minucius and charged Servilius with murdering a citizen without benefit of trial. These charges were in the eyes of the people more inconsequential than the one who had brought them, and they were more concerned about the growing pestilence, along with alarms and prodigies—particularly reports that houses in the countryside had collapsed from frequent earth tremors. A ceremony of supplication was conducted by the two men in charge of the Sibylline books, who dictated to the people the words to be said.

The following year, when Gaius Iulius for the second time and

Lucius Verginius were consuls, the plague worsened, which caused
such great devastation in the city and countryside that not only were
there no plundering raids beyond Rome's borders or no thought of
regular warfare by the senators or plebs, but the Fidenates—who at
first had stayed in the mountains or behind their city walls—actually invaded Roman territory in a plundering raid. Then, after joining up with the army of Veii (neither Rome's misfortunes nor the
entreaties of their allies could induce the Falisci to join them), the
two peoples crossed the Anio and took up a position not far from
the Colline Gate. The result was that there was as much panic in
the city as in the countryside. The consul Iulius stationed his forces
on the ramparts and walls, while the other consul Verginius consulted the senate in the temple of Quirinus. The senate decreed that
Quintus Servilius should be named dictator (some sources give his
cognomen as Priscus, others as Structus). There was a delay while
Verginius conferred with his colleague and then, after midnight
and with his permission, named the dictator, who in turn picked
Postumus Aebutius Helva as master of the horse.

22. The dictator ordered everyone to present himself at dawn
outside the Colline Gate. All those capable of bearing arms appeared, and the standards were brought from the treasury to the
dictator. This activity prompted the enemy to withdraw to higher
ground. The dictator went in pursuit, intending to fight, and not far
from Nomentum attacked and routed the Etruscan legions. He drove
them into the city of Fidenae, which he invested with a palisade.
But because the city was on a high and fortified site, capture by
scaling the walls was out of the question; in fact, even a siege would
be unavailing, since the inhabitants had not only enough grain for
their immediate needs, but had laid in beforehand a considerable
surplus. And so, having no hope of either storming the city or of
forcing its surrender, the dictator began to dig a tunnel up to the
citadel on the city's far side, where the defences were weak because
of its nearly impregnable position (the area was well known because
of its proximity to Rome). All the while he directed a frontal attack
at many places along the walls by using a quarter of his force at any
one time, each division succeeding another in a continuous assault
by day and night. Thus the enemy's attention was diverted from the
tunnel's construction, until, with the tunnel complete from camp to
the citadel, passage was opened up and, while the Etruscans were

preoccupied with sham alarms rather than real danger, a shout of the enemy above their heads revealed that the city was in Roman hands.

That year the censors Gaius Furius Paculus and Marcus Geganius Macerinus had a headquarters building constructed in the Campus Martius, and conducted the census of the people there for the first time.

23. I find in Licinius Macer's history that the same consuls were re-elected for the following year, Iulius for the third time and Verginius for the second. Valerius Antias and Quintus Tubero give the consuls as Marcus Manlius and Quintus Sulpicius. What is more, despite this egregious disagreement, both Tubero and Macer cite the Linen Books as their source. Neither hides the fact that the oldest authorities say that military tribunes were the chief magistrates this year. Licinius follows the Linen Books without hesitation; Tubero is uncertain of the truth. This is one of many aspects of that distant time that are shrouded in obscurity, which is where I shall leave the matter also.*

Etruria was greatly alarmed by the capture of Fidenae, for both the Veientes and Falisci were thoroughly frightened, the former because they feared the same fate, the latter because they were conscious of having joined Fidenae in the first conflict (although they had not given support when she revolted). Therefore, when the two states sent envoys around to the twelve nations to summon them to a meeting of all Etruria at the shrine of Voltumna, the senate, expecting a great conflict was in the offing, ordered that Mamercus Aemilius be named dictator for the second time. He in turn named Aulus Postumius Tubertus as his master of the horse. Their preparations for war were proportionally much greater: in the last conflict they had had but two peoples to confront, now they faced all of Etruria. 24. The sequel proved more peaceable than anyone had expected. Traders reported that aid was denied the Veientes, and that they were bidden to follow through by their own devices with a war they had begun on their own initiative and not, when things were going badly, to seek allies with whom they had not deigned to share their plans at the outset.

At this juncture the dictator, lest his appointment go for nothing now that he had no hope of achieving military glory, looked for some way to memorialize his dictatorship in the civilian sphere. He

lighted upon the censorship and made plans to weaken it, either
because he thought its power excessive or because he was offended
not so much by the prestige of the office as by its long duration. And
so, after convening an assembly, he said that the immortal gods had
undertaken to manage Rome's relations with her neighbours and to
make everything safe; he would do what needed doing here at home
by looking to safeguard the liberty of the Roman people. This could
best be preserved if great power was not of long duration and if
magistracies that could not be limited in their jurisdiction were at
least limited in the period of their tenure. Other offices were annual,
the censorship was for five years; it was a serious matter to live
beholden to the same people for such a long period, a great part of
a lifetime. He would introduce a law that the censorship last no
more than a year and a half. With great enthusiasm of the people he
carried the law the next day. 'Fellow citizens,' he said, 'I want you
to know by my actions how much long tenure in office displeases
me. I herewith abdicate the dictatorship.' And so, having laid down
his own office and having imposed a limit on another, he was escorted home with the thanks and great goodwill of the people. The
censors, angry that Mamercus had weakened this magistracy of the
Roman people, removed him from his tribe and, by increasing his
census rating eightfold, reduced him to the lowest rank of citizens.*
He is said to have borne this with great courage, looking to the cause
of the disgrace rather than the disgrace itself; and the senatorial
leadership, although they had not wished that power of the censorship to be weakened, are reported to have taken immediate offence
at this example of censorial ruthlessness, for each of them realized
that he would be subject to the power of the censors longer and
more frequently than he would ever be censor himself. In any event,
the people's outrage is said to have been so great that no one's
authority save that of Mamercus himself was able to save the censors from physical assault.

25. Through persistent opposition the tribunes of the plebs prevented the election of consuls and, when this nearly led to an interregnum, they finally prevailed in having military tribunes with
consular power elected. Their victory, however, went unrewarded:
no plebeian won. All those chosen were patricians, Marcus Fabius
Vibulanus, Marcus Folius, and Lucius Sergius Fidenas. A pestilence during the year gave respite from other concerns. A temple

was vowed to Apollo for the health of the people. The two men in charge of the Sibylline books consulted them and did many things to assuage the anger of the gods and ward off the plague from the populace. Nevertheless, there was great and indiscriminate loss of men and animals in the city and countryside. Fearful of a food shortage caused by the pestilence striking down the farmers, they sent to Etruria, the Pomptine district, and Cumae, and finally to Sicily, in search of grain. There was no mention of consular elections; all those elected military tribunes with consular power were patrician, Lucius Pinarius Mamercus, Lucius Furius Medullinus, and Spurius Postumius Albus. In this year the virulence of the disease slackened, while the grain previously imported averted any danger of a shortage. The Volsci and Aequi met to discuss the resumption of hostilities, as did the Etruscans at the shrine of Voltumna. There a decision was put off for a year and a decree was issued forbidding a meeting being held earlier, although the Veientes remonstrated in vain, saying that the same fate that saw the destruction of Fidenae now threatened Veii.

At Rome, in the meantime, the leaders of plebs, finding their long-cherished hope of attaining higher office frustrated so long as there was peace abroad, held a series of meetings in the houses of the tribunes of the plebs. There secret plans were hatched; they complained the plebs had so little regard for them that in all the years when military tribunes with consular power were being elected, no plebeian had been admitted to that office. Their ancestors had had great foresight in advising against opening up plebeian magistracies to patricians—otherwise the tribunes of the plebs would perforce have been patricians! The men of their own order looked on them as so much dirt; they were despised as much by the plebs as by the senators. Others among them excused the plebs and blamed the senators: by their power-hungry intrigues and scheming they had cut off the plebs from access to office; if the plebs could get a respite from their pleas and threats, if they could only catch their breath, they would have men of their own order in mind when casting their votes and, already having won the protection afforded by the tribunate, they would also lay claim to the highest magistracy.

To avert an unseemly scramble for office, it was decided the tribunes should promulgate a law that no candidate could appear in whitened clothing as a sign of seeking office.* Nowadays we might regard this as a trifling matter, one scarcely to be taken seriously, but in those days it sparked a great struggle among senators and plebeians. Still, the tribunes succeeded in passing the law, and it seemed that in their present irritation the plebs might well favour men of their own order. To thwart this possibility, the senate issued a decree that consular elections should be held. **26.** This was in response to reports by the Latins and Hernici of a great uprising on the part of the Aequi and Volsci. Titus Quinctius Cincinnatus, the son of Lucius (and who had the additional cognomen of Poenus), and Gaius Iulius Mento were elected consuls.

The horrors of war were now upon them. Their two enemies had sworn a sacred oath, which among them created the most binding commitment possible, to serve in the military,* and each sent forth powerful armies which met at Algidus, where the Aequi on one side and the Volsci on the other fortified their campsites and where their commanders were more intent than ever on making a strong entrenchment and drilling the troops. This news created greater alarm in Rome. The senate decided that a dictator should be named because these peoples, although often defeated, were renewing the war with a greater effort than at any time in the past. In addition, quite a few young Romans of military age had died from the pestilence. Above all else the perverse behaviour of the consuls—the discord between them and their arguments over every aspect of their plans— were the source of the gravest misgivings. Some sources say that these consuls were defeated in a battle at Algidus and that this was the reason for the naming of a dictator. But they do agree on the fact that, despite their disputes on other matters, on one issue they joined to oppose the will of the senate: not to name a dictator.

But as the reports from the field piled up, each more alarming than the last, and the consuls refused to submit to the authority of the senate, Quintus Servilius Priscus, who had served in the highest offices with distinction, declared, 'In this national crisis the senate calls on you tribunes of the plebs to force the consuls to name a dictator by virtue of your power.' On hearing this, the tribunes thought this was an opportunity to increase their power. After deliberating among themselves they issued a joint declaration that the consuls should obey the will of the senate; if they should go so far as to oppose the consensus of that distinguished body, they would order their imprisonment. The consuls preferred to be worsted by the tribunes than by the senate, declaring that their rights as supreme magistrates had been betrayed by the senate and put under the yoke of tribunician power—if consuls really could in any way be subject to a tribune's power or—and what worse fate could befall a citizen even in private life?—imprisoned! The two consuls could not even agree as to which of them should name the dictator, so the lot was used; it fell to Titus Quinctius, who named as dictator Aulus Postumius Tubertus, his father-in-law, the strictest of authoritarians. He in turn named Lucius Iulius as master of the horse. A levy and cessation of public business were decreed simultaneously and that throughout the city the only activity should be preparation for war. Scrutiny of those pleading exemptions from military service was postponed until after the war; and so even those whose status was in doubt were minded to report for duty. The Hernici and Latins were also ordered to furnish soldiers; each people was quick to obey the dictator.

27. All these activities went on at a furious pace. Gaius Iulius the consul was left to defend the city and Lucius Iulius, the master of the horse, to meet the sudden demands of war, so that those in camp might not be hindered by the want of anything they might need. The dictator, with Aulus Cornelius the pontifex maximus dictating the words, vowed the Great Games in face of the massive uprising,* and, setting out from the city after having divided the army with Quinctius the consul, reached the enemy. On seeing the two camps of the enemy with only a small space between them, they too fixed their campsites close to one another, the dictator's in the direction of Tusculum, the consul's of Lanuvium. Thus four armies and as many fortified camps occupied a large open area in whose centre there was scarcely room for minor sallies, much less for deploying a regular battleline on each side. Nor did they refrain from using their campsites as places from which to launch light-armed skirmishes, for the dictator was quite happy to let his men measure their strength against that of the enemy and anticipate their eventual victory by successes in these minor encounters.

The result was that the enemy, despairing of winning in a general engagement, attacked the camp of the consul by night, staking everything on this risky manœuvre. The sudden uproar roused not only the consul's watchmen and then the whole army, but awakened the dictator in his camp as well. In responding to the emergency the consul showed both courage and resourcefulness: he used some troops to reinforce the guard stations at the gates, others to ring the circumference of the rampart. In the dictator's camp, where there was less commotion, they were better able to mount a strategic response. Reinforcements under the lieutenant Spurius Postumius Albus were immediately dispatched to the consul's camp. The dictator himself took a small detachment by a short, roundabout route away from the centre of the commotion to a spot from which he could mount an unexpected attack on the enemy's rear. He left Quintus Sulpicius, a lieutenant, in charge of the camp and assigned command of the cavalry to Marcus Fabius, another lieutenant, whom he ordered to stay put until daybreak because of the confusion prevailing in the darkness. Everything that any other foresighted and energetic general would have done or commanded in such a situation, he duly did and commanded; but a splendid example of his extraordinary foresight and enterprise, one that does him no ordinary credit, was his bold decision to send Marcus Geganius with some crack cohorts to attack the enemy's camp. Reconnaissance had shown that over half of the troops had marched out of it some time before. The defenders that were left were thinking only of the danger elsewhere and were careless about their own situation, neglecting guards and outposts. He nearly captured the camp before the enemy realized they were under attack. A prearranged smoke signal told the dictator that the enemy camp had been taken; he ordered the news to be relayed to all quarters of the field.

28. As it grew light everything came into view. Fabius had attacked with the cavalry and the consul had broken out of his camp and fallen upon the now terrified enemy. In another part of the field the dictator had attacked the enemy's reserve force and those fighting in the rear ranks, driving on his infantry and cavalry in victory against the foe as they turned in every direction in response to the dissonant cries and sudden assaults. Surrounded, therefore, they would have been cut down to a man in the centre, paying the ultimate penalty for their revolt, had not the Volscian Vettius Messius, a man ennobled more by deeds than by birth, loudly upbraided his men as they milled about in a circle: 'Do you intend to present your throats here to the enemy's swords, undefended, unavenged? Why carry arms at all, why did you start the war in the first place? In

peacetime you run riot, in battle you move not a muscle. What hope do you have in standing here? Do you think that some god will appear and whisk you away? We must hew a path out of here with our swords. So come, follow where you see me taking the lead, and you will again see your homes, parents, wives and children. Armed men bar the way of armed men, not a city wall or rampart. You are their equal in courage and will be their superior because of necessity, which is the greatest and the ultimate weapon.'

They raised their battle-cry anew and followed him as he spoke these words and began to act on them; they drove a wedge into Postumius Albus' cohorts, and were beginning to push back Rome's victorious troops, until the dictator came to the rescue as his men started to give way. The outcome of the entire battle depended on what happened next. Success for the enemy hung on a single man, Messius. Many on each side were wounded, greater was the slaughter everywhere: now not even the Roman commanders went unscathed. Only Spurius Postumius, struck by a rock, left the battlefield, with a gaping head wound. But the dictator would not leave the seesaw battle, despite having been hit in the shoulder, nor would Fabius with his thigh nearly pinned to his horse, nor would the consul, although his arm had been torn away.

29. His onward rush carried Messius and an intrepid band of young fighters over the bodies of their slaughtered enemies to the camp of the Volsci, which had not yet been captured. The entire battle converged on this spot. The consul, pursuing those scattered in flight all the way to the rampart, attacked it and the camp within. On another side the dictator also moved up his forces. The siege was as spirited as the battle had been. Tradition says that the consul hurled a standard inside the rampart so that his soldiers might be all the keener in surmounting it and that in retrieving the standard they were the first inside. The dictator in turn, now that the rampart had been breached, had brought the battle into the camp itself. The enemy then began to surrender, throwing down their weapons on all sides; and with the camp and its defenders now in Roman hands, each of the enemy save for the senators were bound over to be sold as captives. That part of the booty the Latins and Hernici identified as theirs was returned to them; the rest the dictator auctioned off. After putting the consul in charge of the camp the dictator returned in triumph to the city and resigned his office.

Some sources say that Aulus Postumius beheaded his son because he deserted his post without permission when he saw a chance to display his prowess on the field: if true, a grim memorial of an outstanding dictatorship. But one is reluctant to believe this, nor is it obligatory, since opinions differ. One argument against it is the common phrase 'Manlian discipline'; we do not say 'Postumian'. Besides, the one first responsible for setting such an inhuman example would surely have been the first to be described as the notorious exemplar of cruelty. Moreover, Imperiosus, or Disciplinarian, was the cognomen given to Manlius; Postumius was branded with no such mark.*

The consul Gaius Iulius, instead of waiting to draw lots, dedicated the temple of Apollo in the absence of his colleague. On returning to the city and disbanding his army, Quinctius made no secret of his displeasure, even complaining about it in the senate, but to no effect.

In this year of great events occurred another that seemed at the time to have no relevance to Rome's history, for the Carthaginians, destined to be our fiercest foes, for the first time crossed with an army into Sicily in support of one side in the factional strife then rife on the island.

30. In the city the tribunes of the plebs agitated for the election of military tribunes with consular power, but they did not succeed. Elected consuls were Lucius Papirius Crassus and Lucius Iulius. When envoys from the Aequi asked the senate for a treaty, that body made the counter-proposal of unconditional surrender; a truce of eight years was the compromise. The Volscian nation, in addition to the disaster it had suffered at Algidus, fell into wrangling and internal strife between equally determined advocates of war and peace. For the moment the Romans found themselves at peace on every side. When one of the tribunes secretly alerted the consuls that the college of tribunes was getting ready to propose a law concerning the valuation of fines, an idea much in favour among the people, the consuls took the lead in proposing it and presided over its passage.

The next consuls were Lucius Sergius Fidenas for the second time and Hostus Lucretius Tricipitinus. Nothing of note occurred under these men. The following consuls were Aulus Cornelius Cossus and Titus Quinctius Poenus for the second time. The Veientes raided Roman territory. There was a rumour that certain young men from

Fidenae had participated in this raid, and investigation into the matter was assigned to Lucius Sergius, Quintus Servilius, and Mamercus Aemilius. Certain suspects were sent into exile at Ostia because it was not clear why they had absented themselves from Fidenae during the days in question. A number of colonists was added, and the land of those killed in the war assigned to them. Drought caused great suffering that year; not only was there no rainfall, but the natural sources of water within the earth were scarcely enough to supply the rivers that flowed year round. In some places the springs and streams dried up completely, causing animals to die of thirst; others died of mange, while contact with animals transmitted the disease to humans. At first it spread among the country folk and slaves; then it invaded the city. As men's bodies wasted away, their minds were affected as well, for all kinds of religious practices, many of them foreign, made their appearance as religious charlatans profited from preying on people's superstitious susceptibilities by introducing into their homes new religious practices. In the end the shame of such goings-on penetrated to the political leadership, as they beheld on every street and in every shrine foreign and outlandish rites of appeasement in seeking the peace of the gods. The aediles were then given the task of seeing to it that Roman gods alone should be worshipped and only in the traditional manner.

Revenge against Veii was put off to the following year when Gaius Servilius Ahala and Lucius Papirius Mugillanus were consuls. Religion again proved a stumbling-block to an immediate declaration of war and the dispatch of troops; the senate voted that the fetial priests should first be sent to demand reparations.* Recently there had been fighting at Nomentum and Fidenae with the Veientes, and instead of peace a truce was made, whose term had run out, although they had renewed hostilities even before its expiration. Nevertheless, the fetials were sent; but their words demanding reparations, delivered according to ancestral oath, were not heeded. A dispute then arose as to whether war should be declared by order of the people or whether a decree of the senate was enough. The tribunes won; they threatened to block the levy in order to make Quinctius the consul bring the question of war to a vote before the people. Every century voted for it. The plebs also carried the day by not having consuls elected for the coming year.

31. Four military tribunes with consular power were elected, Titus

Quinctius Poenus, consul the year before, Gaius Furius, Marcus
Postumius, and Aulus Cornelius Cossus. Of these, Cossus was put
in charge of the city, while the other three set out for Veii after
conducting a levy. These men proved how counter-productive a
divided command is in war. Each one followed his own counsels,
one preferring one course and another another, and in doing so they
enabled the enemy to capitalize on the situation; for the Veientes at
this advantageous moment attacked the disorganized battleline, as
some ordered the trumpet to sound the charge, others a retreat. The
nearby camp received the troops as they fled helter-skelter. The
disgrace was greater than the losses suffered. The state, unused to
defeat, was in shock. People cursed the tribunes and demanded a
dictator: on him the country depended. But again a religious obstacle stood in the way: a dictator could be named by no one save a
consul. But the augurs, when consulted, said that on this religious
point an exception could be made. Aulus Cornelius named Mamercus
Aemilius dictator and was himself the choice as master of the horse;
indeed, when the fortunes of Rome were in need of pre-eminent
worth, the earlier degradation of Mamercus by the censors did not
prevent a man from a family undeservedly stigmatized from being
put in control of the state.

The Veientes, elated by their success, sent envoys around to the
Etruscan peoples boasting that they had defeated three Roman commanders in a single battle. But when the league refused to become
involved, they attracted individual volunteers who hoped to share in
the booty. Only the people of Fidenae elected to renew hostilities
and, as if it were wrong to begin war without a crime, they first
stained their swords with the blood of the new colonists (as before
with the blood of the murdered envoys) and then joined the Veientes.
The leaders of the two peoples then consulted as to whether Veii or
Fidenae would be their headquarters. Fidenae seemed better posi-
tioned, and so the Veientes crossed the Tiber and settled there.

Rome was in a panic. The army, demoralized by its defeat, was
recalled from Veii and pitched camp outside the Colline Gate; armed
men were stationed on the walls, the forum was closed to public
business, and the shops were shuttered. Rome was more like a military camp than a civilian community. 32. At this point the dictator
sent heralds into the streets to summon the frightened populace to
an assembly. There he rebuked them for reacting in such extreme

fashion to the slightest shifts of fortune. This was a small set-back, due not to the courage of the enemy or the cowardice of the Roman army but to quarrelling among the commanders. Now they were petrified of Veii, defeated six times over, and of Fidenae, captured almost more often than attacked! Rome and her enemies were the same as they had been through the centuries; they possessed the same spirit, the same physical strength, the same weapons. He too was the same Mamercus Aemilius who as dictator had earlier defeated the combined forces of Veii, Fidenae, and the Falisci at Nomentum, and his master of the horse, Aulus Cornelius, would show the same prowess in battle as he had in the earlier war when as tribune of the soldiers he killed Lars Tolumnius, the king of Veii, in the sight of the two armies and brought the spoils of honour to the temple of Jupiter Feretrius. And so he urged them to take up their weapons, mindful of the triumphs, of the spoils, and of the victory they had enjoyed under his leadership—and equally mindful of the enemy: of the envoys criminally murdered contrary to the law of nations, of the massacre of the colonists at Fidenae in peacetime, of the broken truce, of this seventh abortive attempt to throw off their allegiance to Rome. As soon as their camp was pitched next to the enemy's, confidence would return and the joy the godless enemy felt over the disgrace of Rome's army would be cut short. Then the Roman people would realize how much better those men had served their country who named him dictator for the third time than those who had dishonoured his second dictatorship because he would not let the censors be autocrats without term.

Then, after making his vows to the gods, he set out and fixed his camp one and a half miles on the near side of Fidenae, with the mountains on his right and the Tiber on the left. He ordered Titus Quinctius Poenus, his lieutenant, to secure the mountains and without being detected to occupy a ridge to the enemy's rear. The next day the Etruscans, full of confidence from that earlier day when good luck had been more of a factor than good fighting, drew up their battleline. The dictator held back for a while, waiting for the scouts to report that Quinctius had reached the ridge near the citadel of Fidenae. When they did, he advanced his standards, drew up the infantry and led them against the enemy on the double. He told his master of the horse not to join the fight until ordered to do so: he would give a signal when he needed the cavalry's help; he urged

him to do his part at that moment, mindful of his combat with the
king, of his splendid offering, of Romulus and of Jupiter Feretrius.
The legions clashed in a mighty onrush. The Romans satisfied their
hatred with deeds and with words, calling the Fidenates traitors, the
Veientes brigands, reviling them because they were drenched with
the gore of the envoys they had so foully murdered, covered with
the blood of their new colonists, double-dealing allies, lily-livered
foes.

33. At their first clash the Romans had instantly repulsed the
enemy, but suddenly the gates of Fidenae opened and out rushed a
fresh fighting force in a tactic unheard of and unseen up to that
time. For a great throng carrying firebrands and burning torches
that lit up the whole scene came running out in a frenzy, and for a
moment this bizarre type of warfare terrified the Romans. The dictator responded by summoning his master of the horse and cavalry,
and then Quinctius from the mountains. He renewed the fight in
person by rushing up to his left wing which was retreating in fear
from the flames, where the scene resembled a firestorm more than a
battle. In a loud voice he cried, 'Will you let yourselves be smoked
out like a swarm of bees? Use your swords to put out the fire! But,
if we must fight not with weapons but with fire, I order each man to
intercept these firebrands and use them against the enemy. Come,
remember Rome's great name, remember the bravery of your ancestors and yourselves! Turn this conflagration upon Fidenae itself,
consume the city in its own flames, which you could not win over by
your acts of beneficence. The blood of your envoys and colonists
demand this, your lands laid waste demand it.'

The whole battleline acted on the dictator's command. Some firebrands were taken up from the ground where they had been thrown,
others wrenched away by force. Both sides fought fire with fire. The
master of the horse in his turn devised a new cavalry stratagem; he
ordered his men to release the horses' reins, while he himself, digging in his spurs, took the lead in charging into the centre of the
firestorm on his unbridled horse; the other horses became excited
and, free to gallop where they wanted, bore their riders into the
enemy's midst. Dust rose in the air and mingled with the smoke;
men and horses could see little in the gloom. At this the fighters
took fright, but not the horses; wherever the riders went they left
their opponents lying like so many toppled buildings. Then a cheer

from a new quarter was heard. As each side looked that way in surprise, the dictator cried that his lieutenant Quinctius had attacked the enemy from the rear. Another cheer went up and he plunged the standards forward even more fiercely.

And so the Etruscans found themselves being pressed by two different forces in two different battles, one in front, the other in their rear. They had no camp behind them to which to flee, while the mountains from which the enemy had just mounted this new attack afforded no protection either. The horses with slackened reins were carrying their riders in every direction. Most of the Veientes headed for the Tiber pell-mell, those Fidenates still surviving fled back to their city. flight carried the panic-stricken into the middle of the carnage. They were cut down on the banks; others were driven into the water and carried off by the current; even those who knew how to swim were weighed down by exhaustion, wounds, and panic. Only a few of that vast army got across. Another division of Veientes were carried past their camp into the city. The momentum drew the pursuing Romans in the same direction, particularly Quinctius and those who had recently descended with him from the mountains, the freshest for action because they had joined the fight only toward its end. 34. These troops, after bursting through the gates along with the enemy, rushed to the top of the walls and from the rampart gave the signal to their men that the city had been captured. When the dictator saw it (at that moment he was inside the enemy's abandoned camp), he realized his men wanted to scatter in search of booty, and, after telling them more could be expected in the city, he led them to its gates. Once inside the walls, he headed for the citadel, to which he saw the populace fleeing. The slaughter in the city was as great as on the battlefield until, throwing down their arms and asking for nothing save that he spare their lives, they surrendered to the dictator. The city and the camp were sacked. The next day each cavalryman and centurion received by lot one captive apiece, while those who had shown exceptional bravery received two.* The rest were sold off as prisoners of war. In triumph the dictator led his army back to Rome, victorious and enriched with booty, where he first bid the master of horse resign his office before doing so himself. Sixteen days before his country had been in the midst of a terrifying war; now, as he left office, it was at peace.

Certain historians record that there was a naval battle with the

Veientes at Fidenae, a feat as difficult to execute as it is to believe. Even now the river is not wide enough for one, and older writers say that in those days the channel was somewhat narrower—unless perchance these historians were aiming, as they sometimes do, to inflate the collision of a few boats in blocking the crossing of the river into a full-scale naval victory.*

35. The following year had military tribunes with consular power, Aulus Sempronius Atratinus, Lucius Quinctius Cincinnatus, Lucius Furius Medullinus, and Lucius Horatius Barbatus. A twenty-year truce was granted to Veii, and one for three years to the Aequi, although they had asked for a longer term; the city was also free from political unrest.

The following year, which was marked neither by war abroad nor unrest at home, was notable for the lavish celebration of the games vowed in the last war. The military tribunes put them on and neighbouring peoples attended. The tribunes with consular power were Appius Claudius Crassus, Spurius Naevius Rutilus, Lucius Sergius Fidenas, and Sextus Iulius Iulus. The spectacle was especially pleasing to the visitors because of the kind reception given them by their hosts, whose hospitality reflected community policy.

After the games the tribunes of the plebs held a series of fractious meetings in which they rebuked the multitude for being in awe of those they hated and for allowing themselves to live in unending subjection; they did not aspire to claim their share of the consulship and—even worse—they had no thought of themselves or their fellow plebeians when electing military tribunes, which was open to patricians and plebeians alike. They should cease therefore to wonder why no one agitated for the benefit of the plebs. Men work hard and endure danger in the expectation of honour and repayment; they tackle great projects if great rewards are forthcoming. It ought not to be expected or required of any tribune of the plebs that he rush blindly into combat at great danger to himself, and without reward, for he can be sure that the senators against whom he is struggling will be relentless and implacable in their fight against him and that the plebs on whose behalf he is fighting will not make the slightest gesture of appreciation. Men take great risks when they expect great rewards. No plebeian will despise himself when the plebs as a body cease to be despised. It was high time to ascertain through one or two test cases whether a plebeian is worthy of holding high office or whether the existence of a brave and energetic plebeian is a preternatural freak of nature. They had fought tooth and nail to make plebeians eligible for election as military tribunes with consular power. Men with outstanding records at home and abroad had been candidates; in the early years they had gone down to defeat, beaten black and blue, utter laughing stocks. In the end they ceased to expose themselves to insult. They really did not see why a law permitting something that would never happen should not be repealed. Surely it would be less shameful to accept inequality under the law than to be passed over as unworthy.

36. Speeches like this met with a ready reception, and some were inspired to stand for the military tribunate. Each promised to sponsor different measures to benefit the plebs if he got elected, such as dividing up public land, sending out colonies, and getting money for soldiers' pay by imposing a tax on the occupiers of public land. In response the military tribunes took advantage of an opportunity when, in the absence of the general population, the senators might be secretly instructed to return on a certain day and a decree be issued in the absence of the tribunes of the plebs: to wit, since the Volsci were reported to have entered Hernican territory on a plundering raid, the military tribunes should set out on a reconnaisance mission and that consular elections should be held. And so they set out, leaving Appius Claudius, son of the decemvir, as prefect of the city, an energetic youth who from earliest childhood had been brought up to hate the plebeians and their tribunes. The tribunes of the plebs found themselves unable to fight back either against the absent officials or against Appius, for the whole thing was a *fait accompli.** 37. Elected consuls were Gaius Sempronius Atratinus and Quintus Fabius Vibulanus.

An episode concerning non-Romans, but worthy of record, occurred in this year. Volturnum, an Etruscan city which is now Capua, was captured by the Samnites and named from their leader Capys (or, more likely, from the plain in which it is situated).* They seized it, moreover, at a time when the Etruscans were in a weakened condition from a previous war, and they had been accepted into a share of the city and its territory. But then, on a festal day, after the old inhabitants had dined heartily and fallen fast asleep, the new colonists rose up and massacred them by night.

To return to my story, the consuls I have named entered office on

13 December. Those sent to the area in question reported that a
Volscian war was brewing, as did envoys from the Latins and Hernici,
who affirmed that never before had the Volsci been more intent on
selecting commanders and in enlisting troops; in fact, they said, it
was a matter of common talk that they either would have to forget
warfare forever and accept the yoke of submission or would have to
match their adversaries with whom they were contending for supremacy in courage, endurance, and military prowess. These reports
were well-founded. But the senators not only did not take them
seriously enough, but Gaius Sempronius, who had received command of the war by lot and who was supremely confident that
fortune would see to it that Rome's past victories over this vanquished enemy would be repeated again this time, conducted all
his business in a rash and careless manner—so much so that more
Roman discipline was evident in the Volscian army than in the
Roman. And so fortune, as she often does, favoured the brave.

In the first battle, which Sempronius entered into without caution
or judgement, he failed to arrange for auxiliaries to reinforce his
main army or to position the cavalry suitably. The battle-cry was the
first indication of how the fight would go: the enemy's was louder
and more sustained, the Romans' ragged and uneven, growing fee-
bler each time it was repeated. And so the army's bungled war-cry
mirrored the fear in their hearts. This caused the enemy to charge
all the more aggressively, shields thrust forward and swords flashing. On the other side the crested helmets wavered, turning here
and there, faltering and uncertain, clustering together. At times the
standards held their ground but were abandoned as the fighters in
front fell back; at others they retired into their own maniples. As yet
there was neither outright flight or clear-cut victory. The Romans
were fighting defensively not offensively, while the Volsci, moving
their standards forward, bore down on the Roman line and saw
more of the enemy killed than in flight.

38. A general retreat began, as the consul Sempronius' rebuke
and encouragement proved equally futile; power and high office
counted for nothing. They would have soon been in full flight if
Sextus Tempanius, the leader of a ten-man cavalry squadron, had
not had the presence of mind to come to the rescue as the situation
worsened. At the top of his voice he told those cavalrymen who
wanted to save their country to jump down from their horses; and,

when the whole cavalry detachment responded as if a consul had issued the order, he cried, 'Unless this cohort uses its round shields to parry the enemy attack, Rome's supremacy is done for. My spear will be your standard. Follow it. Show Romans and Volsci that on horseback you are the equal of any cavalry, on foot of any infantry.' As they raised a cry of approval, he began his advance with spear held aloft. Wherever they went, they forced open a path, and those of their men they saw to be in the greatest difficulty they pushed forward to help with their small shields out-thrust. The fight was renewed in every place they went; there was no doubt that, if these few could have been everywhere at once, the enemy would have turned tail and run.

39. As resistance to them gave way on all sides, the Volscian commander signalled his men to open up a path for this new fighting force of the enemy with their circular shields so that their momentum would carry them to a place where they would be cut off from the main force. When this was done, they indeed found themselves blocked off, nor could they return by the way they had come, since the enemy had closed ranks and were densely packed together. On the other side, when those who had just saved the whole army had been completely lost to sight, the consul and the Roman legions were prepared for whatever fate might bring if only they could prevent the enemy from overwhelming these many brave men who were cut off.

The Volsci were now fighting in two directions at once. On one side they confronted the consuls and legions; on the other front they harried Tempanius and his horsemen, who repeatedly tried to break through to the main army, but without success. They then seized a hillock, protecting themselves in a circle, while inflicting casualties upon the enemy. The struggle continued to nightfall. The consul, too, did not let up in the fighting, but kept at the enemy as long as any daylight remained. Night separated them, with the outcome unresolved. Not knowing where they stood caused such fear in each camp that, abandoning the wounded and much of the baggage, the two armies withdrew to the nearest mountains, as if each had lost the battle. However, the Volsci continued to surround the hillock where Tempanius was for much of the night, but when they learned that their camp had been abandoned, thinking that their side had lost, they too fled into the darkness, each man for himself. Tempanius restrained his men until dawn because he feared an ambush. Then he himself went out with a few men to spy out the terrain, and when he found out from some Volscian wounded that their camp had been abandoned, he delightedly called his men down from the hillock and with them proceeded to the Roman camp. He found no one there—the whole place was deserted, the same unhappy spectacle as in the Volscian camp. And so, before the Volsci should realize their mistake and return, he took those wounded capable of travelling and, not knowing in what direction the consul had gone, proceeded to the city by the most direct route.

40. The news of the unsuccessful battle and the abandoned camp had already reached Rome, where grief over the cavalry was especially strong, expressed as much in official lamentation as by the men's families. In response to the alarm that filled the city the consul Fabius was stationing guardposts before the gates when the sight of the cavalry at a distance caused those who did not recognize them to panic. Soon, when their identity became known, the mood swung from fear to a joy so great that cries of thanksgiving for the cavalry's safe and victorious return spread throughout the city; from houses that had lately been plunged into grief the mourners streamed into the streets; trembling mothers and wives forgot decorum in their euphoria by rushing out to meet the approaching troops and, beside themselves with happiness, flung themselves into the arms of their loved ones.

The tribunes of the plebs saw this as an opportunity to revive the hostility against Marcus Postumius and Titus Quinctius, whom they had indicted for their defeat at Veii, by taking advantage of the present animosity felt for the consul Sempronius. And so, before the assembled people they declared that the state had been betrayed at Veii by its commanders and that, because they went unpunished, the army facing the Volsci had been betrayed by the consul, while these most galant cavalrymen had been left to die and the camp disgracefully abandoned. Then one of the tribunes, Gaius Iunius, ordered the cavalryman Tempanius to appear and, as he stood there, said, 'Sextus Tempanius, I put the following questions to you. Did the consul Gaius Sempronius in your opinion enter the battle at the right moment? Did he use back-up troops to reinforce the main army? Did he perform in any way as a good consul should? I ask also whether you, after the defeat of the Roman legions, took it upon yourself to have the cavalry dismount and renew the fight on foot. And, when you and your men were cut off from the main force, did the consul either come himself to your aid or send reinforcements? Further, on the following day did any reinforcements arrive or did you and the cohort force your way to the camp on your own initiative? I ask also whether the consul and the army were in the camp or whether you found it abandoned, along with the wounded. I charge you to answer these questions here and now, as your courage and honour demand, which alone have been Rome's salvation in this war. Finally, tell us where Gaius Sempronius and our legions are, tell us whether they abandoned you or you them; in a word, tell us whether we won or lost.'

41. In reply Tempanius is said to have made a speech that was rough-hewn yet impressive for a soldier, not cheapened by self-praise or capitalizing on the charges levelled against others. It was not, he said, for a soldier to evaluate the military expertise of his general, Gaius Sempronius; the Roman people had done that when they elected him consul. Nor was he the one to ask about good generalship or the skills of a consul, since estimates of these qualities required a great expert with a great brain to make. But he could relate what he had seen. Before being cut off from the main army he saw the consul fighting in the front line, giving encouragement and moving among the Roman standards and the missiles of the enemy. Later, when he could no longer see the main force, he still could tell from the noise and shouting that the battle continued to nightfall. Nor did he think that a rescue mission to the hillock which he occupied was possible, given the great number of the enemy. He did not know where the army was, but supposed that, just as the volatile situation had led him to seek safety for himself and his troops in a defensible place, so the consul had sought a more secure spot than the camp to safeguard the army. Nor did he think that the Volsci had fared any better than the Romans. Chance and darkness had spread confusion everywhere. Tradition says that at the end he asked for permission to leave, since he was exhausted from exertion and wounds, and that he was dismissed with great praise, as much for his temperate remarks as for his courage.

In the meantime the consul had reached the shrine of Quies on the road to Labici. There wagons and other means of transport were sent from the city to bring the army back, which was suffering from the effects of the battle and its night journey. A little later the consul entered the city, where he spent as much energy in giving Tempanius due praise as in exculpating himself. It was in an atmosphere of grief over the defeat and of anger at the commanders that Marcus Postumius, who as military tribune at Veii had acted in place of the consul, found himself on trial. He was convicted and fined ten thousand pieces of heavy bronze. His colleague Titus Quinctius, because as consul he had been successful against the Volsci under the auspices of the dictator Postumius Tubertus and again at Fidenae as a lieutenant of the other dictator Mamercus Aemilius, and because he shifted the entire responsibility for the disaster on to his convicted colleague, was acquitted by all the tribes. The memory of his revered father, Cincinnatus, is said to have helped him, as did Quinctius Capitolinus, now far on in years, who begged in suppliant fashion that they not make him, whose life was nearing its end, the one to report any grim news to Cincinnatus in the world below.

42. The plebs elected as tribunes in their absence Sextus Tempanius, Marcus Asellius, Titus Antistius, and Spurius Pullius, whom the cavalry, under Tempanius' urging, had also chosen to act as their centurions.* The senate, since the consulship was in bad odour because of the hatred felt for Sempronius, ordered that military tribunes with consular power be elected. Chosen were Lucius Manlius Capitolinus, Quintus Antonius Merenda, and Lucius Papirius Mugillanus. At the very start of the year Lucius Hortensius, tribune of the plebs, indicted Gaius Sempronius, consul the year before. In sight of the Roman people his four colleagues begged him not to prosecute their innocent general, in whom nothing could be faulted save bad luck. Hortensius became angry; this, he thought, was a test of his determination and that the defendant was counting not on the entreaties of the tribunes, which were a smokescreen, but on their veto power. And so, in words directed only at Sempronius, he asked where that well-known patrician rectitude was, where that reliance and confidence in his innocence was; before them a consular was hiding behind the tribunes' skirts. Then turning to his colleagues he said, 'As for you, if I choose to persist in the prosecution, what will you do? Do you intend to wrest from the people its right to decide, to subvert the power of the tribunate?' When they said in reply that the Roman people had absolute power over Sempronius and everyone else and that they neither wished nor were able to usurp the

people's right to sit in judgement; but if their pleas on behalf of their general, who was like a second father, were unsuccessful, they would don the dark clothing of suppliants and stand at his side.* Hortensius replied, 'The Roman plebs will not see its tribunes in mourning attire. I hereby drop the prosecution against Gaius Sempronius, since his command was such that it won him the great affection of the men under him.' Hortensius by being so receptive to their just entreaties pleased the plebs and senators alike, no less than did the four tribunes in showing their loyalty.

Good fortune ceased to favour the Aequi when they began to look upon the doubtful victory of the Volsci as their own. **43.** In the following year, in the consulship of Gnaeus Fabius Vibulanus and Titus Quinctius Capitolinus, son of Capitolinus, Fabius was assigned by lot to the command against them. But nothing memorable was achieved; for the Aequi put on a feeble show and then turned tail in disgraceful flight, which was no great victory for the consul. A triumph was consequently denied, but because he had partly compensated for the disgrace Sempronius had suffered, he was allowed to enter the city in an ovation.*

Although the war ended with less of a struggle than had been feared, the city unexpectedly passed from tranquillity to dissension in a series of sharp disputes between plebs and senators, which was initiated by disagreement over doubling the number of quaestors. The consuls proposed that in addition to the two urban quaestors two more be elected to serve the consuls in war. This received the senate's emphatic approval, but the tribunes of the plebs made a counter-proposal that some of the quaestors be plebeian—for up to that time they had been patricians. Both consuls and senators objected vigorously to this; then, as a concession they proposed that the people should have a free choice in electing the quaestors, just as they had in the case of the tribunes with consular power. But when this failed to win approval, they dropped the idea of increasing the number of quaestors altogether. Immediately following this, the tribunes proposed other politically divisive measures, among them one for an agrarian law. This agitation led the senate to favour the election of consuls rather than of tribunes, but a senatorial decree to that effect was vetoed by the tribunes. Then the state passed from consular rule to an interregnum; but even this provoked a great fuss—for the tribunes kept forbidding the patricians to assemble.

The greater part of the following year was taken up with struggles carried on by new tribunes of the plebs and a number of interreges, with the tribunes now preventing the patricians from assembling to choose an interrex, now forbidding the interrex to secure a senatorial decree to hold consular elections. In the end Lucius Papirius Mugillanus as interrex, in a rebuke of both senators and tribunes of the plebs, declared that the state, although abandoned and forgotten by men, was still standing, protected by the providence and care of the gods because of the truce with Veii and the pusillanimity of the Aequi. But if a real threat should arise in those quarters, was it then their wish that the state succumb because it had no patrician magistrate? That there be no army or no commander to enlist one? Or would they ward off a foreign war while in the midst of a civil one? If all these things should happen to coincide, Rome could scarcely avoid a crushing defeat—even though the gods were on their side. Why not compromise for the sake of concord, each side giving up a measure of its rightful claim, the senators by allowing the election of military tribunes instead of consuls, tribunes of the plebs by ceasing to forbid the citizens to elect in a free vote and without restrictions four quaestors from among plebeians and patricians?

44. First came the election of military tribunes with consular power: chosen were Lucius Quinctius Cincinnatus for the third time, Sextus Furius Medullinus for the second, Marcus Manlius, and Aulus Sempronius Atratinus, all patricians. With the last-named presiding, the election of quaestors was held; among the plebeian candidates were the son of Aulus Antistius, tribune of the plebs, and the brother of another plebeian tribune, Sextus Pollius.* But their power neither as magistrates nor at the polls was enough to overcome the nobility of those whose fathers and grandfathers had held the consulship. All the tribunes of the plebs were incensed, especially Pollius and Antistius, who were outraged at the defeat of their kinsmen. What sense could be made out of this, they asked. Despite their own services, despite the wrongs done them by the senatorial establishment, despite the natural impulse to exercise a privilege hitherto denied but now permitted, not a single plebeian quaestor had been elected, to say nothing of a military tribune. A father's plea for his son had gone for naught, as had that of a brother for a brother, both tribunes of the plebs, holders of a sacrosanct power that had been created to be the bulwark of liberty. Double-dealing had undoubtedly been involved: the wiles of Aulus Sempronius had played a greater role in this election than had his integrity. Their kinsmen had been defeated at the polls, they complained, because of his sharp practice. But because they could not attack Sempronius (whose innocence and incumbency in office protected him), they turned their wrath on Gaius Sempronius, Atratinus' paternal cousin, and, together with their colleague Marcus Canuleius, indicted him for the humiliation suffered in the Volscian war. These same tribunes next raised in the senate the issue of dividing up public land, a scheme that Gaius Sempronius had always vehemently opposed. They correctly foresaw that if he ceased his opposition the senators would be less inclined to support him in court or, if he persevered in his resistance up to the very day of trial, he would offend the plebs. He preferred to face the hostility and to defend the good of the state rather than himself, for he continued to oppose giving free hand-outs that would add to the popularity of the three tribunes, claiming that their aim was not to get land for the plebs but to stir up hostility against himself. What is more, he would also face the storm with a stout heart; the senate ought not to consider him or any other citizen of such importance that saving one man was worth harming the state at large. His determination continued undiminished. When the day came and he had pleaded his case, and despite his fellow senators having done everything they could to mollify the plebs, he was convicted and fined fifteen thousand pounds of bronze.

In the same year the Vestal Virgin Postumia was put on trial for unchastity. Although innocent of the charge, she came under suspicion because of dress more elegant and demeanour freer than befitted a Vestal. Her first trial resulted in a hung jury. At the second she was acquitted; the pontifex maximus, speaking on behalf of the pontifical college, ordered her to refrain from levity and to dress in a more religious and less studied manner. In the same year the Campanians captured Capua, a city then occupied by the Greeks.

The following year had as military tribunes with consular power Agrippa Menenius Lanatus, Publius Lucretius Tricipitinus, and Spurius Nautius Rutilus. 45. The year was notable for a terrible threat that, thanks to the good fortune of the Roman people, did not end in disaster. The slave population conspired to set fires in different parts of the city and, while the people were everywhere intent on saving their houses, to arm themselves and seize the citadel and Capitol. Jupiter thwarted this wicked plot and, when two of the slaves reported it to the authorities, the guilty were arrested and punished. Each informer was rewarded with ten thousand pieces of heavy bronze from the public treasury (then considered a princely sum), as well as with his freedom.

The Aequi then took steps to renew hostilities; moreover, it was reported at Rome on good authority that a new enemy had made common cause with the old: the state had become accustomed to war with the Aequi as an annual event, so to speak; now Labici had joined them. Envoys were sent to Labici to investigate, and when they brought back a two-edged report in which it appeared that preparations for war were not then under way but that peace would not last long, the people of Tusculum were asked to be on the alert for any fresh disturbance at Labici.

The next year had military tribunes with consular power: Lucius Sergius Fidenas, Marcus Papirius Mugillanus, and Gaius Servilius, son of Priscus, in whose dictatorship Fidenae had been captured. On their entrance into office, envoys arrived from Tusculum, who reported that the men of Labici had taken up arms and, together with the Aequi, had devastated their territory and had pitched camp at Algidus. War was then declared against Labici, and when a senatorial decree instructed two of the tribunes to set out for war and one to take charge of affairs at Rome, a dispute suddenly arose among the tribunes. Each claimed he was best for the command, and rejected the city as bringing no glory or honour. The senators were shocked at witnessing this unseemly dispute among the three tribunes. Quintus Servilius then said, 'Since no respect has been shown for this body or for the state, the power of a father will put a stop to this altercation of yours. My son will take charge of the city without drawing lots. I pray the other two will show more consideration and harmony campaigning in the field than they have in campaigning for the command.'

46. The decision was taken to hold a levy, but not from all segments of the population. Ten tribes were picked by lot; the two tribunes led the young men thus enrolled to war. The disputes that had begun between them in the city blazed up much more strongly in the camp because each continued to want the command wholly for himself. They agreed on nothing, each battled to defend his point of view; each insisted that he was right and thought his was the only command that counted. Their hearty detestation of one another continued until reproofs from their lieutenants brought them to agree that each would hold supreme command on alternate days. When this became known at Rome, Quintus Servilius, far on in years and of great experience, is said to have prayed to the immortal gods that discord between the tribunes not prove more harmful to the state than it had at Veii; and, as if defeat was sure to come, he urged his son to enrol soldiers and stockpile arms.

Nor was he a false prophet. For on a day when Lucius Sergius was supreme commander, the enemy in pretended fear retreated behind the rampart of their camp. The vain hope of storming the place drew Sergius to this unfavourable spot. The Aequi burst forth suddenly, driving the Romans down the sloping valley floor; many were caught and cut down, more because they were falling over one another than in full retreat. They remained in camp that day, but with difficulty; on the next, after the enemy had almost encircled them, they abandoned it by rushing in disgraceful flight through the gate on the far side. The commanders, their lieutenants, and the fighting force that stayed with the standards headed for Tusculum; others fanned out through the countryside and hastened by many routes to Rome, where they told of a defeat greater than had been the case. But men's anxiety was less because this outcome answered to their fears and because they had witnessed the steps that the military tribune had taken to meet just such an emergency. And after this official ordered the lesser magistrates to calm the confusion in the city, scouts were sent hastily to Tusculum, who reported that the commanders and army were there and that the enemy was still in their old camp. What gave them the most encouragement was the decree of the senate ordering that Quintus Servilius Priscus be named dictator, whose statesmanlike foresight the nation had come to know on many other occasions, but especially then in connection with the outcome of this war, for, in light of the discord among the tribunes, he alone had anticipated the defeat before it occurred. He chose as master of the horse the very one who had as military tribune named him dictator: his own son (this is what some say; others write that Servilius Ahala was master of the horse that year). He set out to war with a new army and, after having summoned those who were at Tusculum, he fixed his camp two miles away from the enemy.

47. It was now the Aequi's turn to behave in the face of success with the arrogance and negligence that had characterized the Roman commanders. And so at the very start of the battle, after sending in the cavalry and throwing the enemy soldiers stationed before the standards into confusion, the dictator ordered his own standards to advance immediately, even killing one of his own standard-bearers when he held back. So eager were the Romans to fight that the Aequi did not withstand their onslaught; beaten in the field, they ran pell-mell to their camp; its storming took a shorter time and less of a fight than had the battle. After the camp had been captured and sacked, the dictator permitted the soldiers to take plunder. The cavalry, which had pursued the enemy as they fled from the camp, reported that all the defeated Labicani and a great part of the Aequi had taken refuge in Labici. On the next day the army was led to the town, which was encircled, then captured by scaling ladders and sacked. The dictator returned to Rome with his victorious army and resigned his office eight days after having been appointed. Furthermore, before the tribunes of the plebs could stir up unrest by proposing a bill to divide up the land of Labici, a full senate seized the initiative by voting that a colony be established there. 1,500 colonists were sent from the city and received a little over an acre apiece.

Following the capture of Labici, military tribunes with consular power were elected: Agrippa Menenius Lanatus, Gaius Servilius Structus, and Publius Lucretius Tricipitinus (all for the second time), and Spurius Rutilius Crassus. For the next year they were Aulus Sempronius Atratinus for the third time, and Marcus Papirius Mugillanus and Spurius Nautius Rutilus for the second. These two years saw peace abroad, but at home unrest over agrarian legislation. 48. The rabble-rousers were Spurius Maecilius, tribune of the plebs for the fourth time, and Marcus Metilius, tribune for the third, both elected *in absentia*. They put forward a bill that land captured from enemies be divided up and allotted to individuals, a plebiscite that would have meant the confiscation of what constituted the wealth of a large part of the nobility—for, as was to be expected in the case of a city founded on foreign soil, there was virtually no public land that had not been won by force of arms, nor had the plebs ever acquired land that had been sold or assigned.* Thus, a terrible struggle loomed between plebs and senators.

The military tribunes, trying to find a plan to counter this scheme, consulted the senate and, in back-room conferences, the senatorial leadership. But nothing useful was proposed until Appius Claudius, grandson of the man who had been decemvir for drawing up the laws and the youngest member of the senatorial inner circle, is said to have laid before them an old family recipe for dealing with such a situation: his great-grandfather Appius Claudius had shown the senators that the one way to break a tribune's power was the veto of his colleagues.* New men* in politics, he continued, were easily brought to change their minds under the impress of their betters if the talk from time to time was about the problems of the day and not from a superior to an inferior. Their opinions depend on how well off they are: when they see colleagues taking the lead in this matter and winning all the plebs' goodwill, while none comes to them, they will scarcely be reluctant to embrace the cause of the senate, thereby gaining the favour of that body as a whole and of the senatorial leaders. This won everyone's approval, and Quintus Servilius Priscus took the lead in praising the young man for living up to his Claudian heritage. It was decided that each one present should entice whoever he could in the college of tribunes to cast his veto. The senate adjourned and its leaders began buttonholing the tribunes. They prevailed upon six of them to use their veto by persuading them through a mix of admonition and promises that this would win the goodwill of individual senators and of the senate as a whole.

On the next day the meeting of the senate went according to the following script. First, the subject was raised of the unrest that Maecilius and Metilius had caused and the terrible example they had set in proposing to give free hand-outs of land. Then one member of the senatorial inner circle after another arose to say he had no solution to propose himself except to ask for the tribunes' assistance: like a poor man in private life, the beleaguered nation fled for protection under their power, and it redounded to the credit of the tribunes and of the might of their office that the tribunate was as effective in resisting unprincipled colleagues as in harassing the senate and causing discord between the orders. Then all the senators began to speak at the same time, appealing to the tribunes from every quarter of the house. In the end, after silence had been called, those tribunes whom the senatorial leaders had earlier prevailed on to veto the bill promulgated by their colleagues indicated that they would do so, adding that the senate judged the measure would destroy the fabric of the state. The senate formally thanked those who cast their vetoes. The proposers of the bill called an assembly and in a vehement speech described their colleagues, among other things, as betrayers of the trust placed in them by the plebs and slaves of the consular establishment. They then gave up their proposal.

49. The following men were elected military tribunes with consular power for the next year: Publius Cornelius Cossus, Gaius Valerius Potitus, Quintus Quinctius Cincinnatus, and Gaius Fabius Vibulanus. Rome would have had two wars on her hands had not the religious superstition of the leading men at Veii put off one of them, for a flood of the Tiber devastated their landholdings, especially the farm buildings. At the same time their defeat three years before prevented the Aequi from coming to the rescue of Bolae, one of their towns. Bolae had raided the neighbouring territory of Labici and waged war against the new colonists. They expected that all the Aequi would come to their defence for this outrage, but when this did not materialize, they lost both town and territory in a war scarcely worth describing, involving as it did a siege and one small battle. The tribune of the plebs Lucius Decius tried to pass a bill to send colonists to Bolae, as in the case of Labici, but this came to nothing because of a veto by his colleagues, who indicated that they would allow only those plebiscites that were in accord with the will of the senate.

In the following year, when Gnaeus Cornelius Cossus, Lucius Valerius Potitus, Quintus Fabius Vibulanus for the second time, and Marcus Postumius Regillensis were military tribunes with consular power, the Aequi recaptured Bolae and sent reinforcements and colonists of their own. The war against the Aequi was assigned to Postumius, a man of perverse character, which was more in evidence after the victory than during the campaign. After energetically enrolling troops and leading them to Bolae, he broke the spirit of the Aequi in a series of skirmishes before finally breaking into the town. He then turned his attack from the enemy to his fellow citizens, for although in the course of the siege he promised the booty to the soldiers, once the town was captured he reneged. I am inclined to think that this was the cause of the army's anger rather than that, in a city recently plundered and newly colonized, there was less booty than the tribune had led them to expect.

He added to their anger when he was later summoned by his colleagues to return to the city because of tribunician unrest. For in a public meeting conducted by Marcus Sextius, tribune of the plebs, who in proposing an agrarian bill said that he would also introduce one to send colonists to Bolae, since it was only right that the town and its territory should belong to those who had taken it by force of arms, Postumius made the following stupid, almost insane, remark: 'If my soldiers don't quiet down, I'll have them flogged.' These words shocked the senators when they heard of them as much as those in the audience. In the past, Sextius as tribune of the plebs, who was a combative and forceful speaker, had discovered that more than any of his political opponents Postumius made himself an easy target because of his arrogant nature and intemperate tongue. He would goad and snipe at him in order to get him to make invidious remarks hurtful both to himself and to the senatorial order as a whole and what it stood for, and he would draw none of the military tribunes into debate more often than he did Postumius. On this particular occasion, following Postumius' brutal and heartless remark, he said, 'Did you hear this man threaten to flog his soldiers as if they were his slaves? And yet, despite this, will you continue to regard this monster as worthier of high office than those who send you out as colonists where you will have your own land and community, who find places for you to settle in your old age, who fight for your well-being against cruel and arrogant opponents such as this man? You may wonder why so few champion your cause. What rewards might they hope from you? The offices you give your opponents rather than to the defenders of the Roman people? You groaned just now on hearing what this man said. But it meant nothing. If you were to cast your votes at this very moment, you would still prefer this man who threatened to flog you to those who want to see you established on your own land, in your own homes, with your own fortunes.'

50. Once report of what Postumius had said reached the soldiers in camp their indignation became much greater: was this thief, who had cheated them of the booty, actually threatening to flog his soldiers? The upshot was that when their grumbling came into the open and the quaestor Publius Sextius thought the disturbance could be put down by the same strong-arm tactics that had provoked it, he sent a lictor to one of the jeering soldiers; this caused an outcry and a brawl, in the course of which Sextius was struck by a rock and rushed away from the mob, as the one who had hit him shouted that the quaestor had got what the commander had threatened his soldiers with. Postumius was called to the site of the fracas, where he made everything worse by his harsh interrogation and ruthless punishments. Finally, as his rage continued out of control and people were rushing to the screams of those whom he had ordered to be killed beneath a wicker frame piled with rocks,* he jumped down from his tribunal to confront those trying to stop the executions. His lictors and centurions waded into the crowd to disperse it, pushing and shoving everywhere; this provoked such outrage that the military tribune was stoned to death by his own army.

After this appalling act had been reported at Rome, the tribunes of the plebs vetoed the military tribunes when they tried to create a senatorial commission of inquiry into their colleague's death. But this dispute became tangled in another struggle, sparked by the apprehension of the senate that fear and anger at this inquiry would lead the plebs to elect military tribunes from their own ranks. And so they strove with all their might to have consuls elected. When the tribunes of the plebs would not allow the passing of the senatorial decree and vetoed the holding of consular elections, the state reverted to an interregnum. 51. Victory then lay with the senators. With Quintus Fabius Vibulanus as interrex presiding over the elections, Aulus Cornelius Cossus and Lucius Furius Medullinus were returned as consuls.

At the start of their consulship the senate passed a resolution that the tribunes should propose to the people at the first possible moment the establishment of a commission of inquiry into Postumius' death and that the plebs should put whomever they liked in charge of it. The plebs, with the agreement of all the people, entrusted the consuls with the task. Yet, although they proceeded with extreme fairness and forbearance (only a few were to be punished, and these were widely believed to have then committed suicide), the plebs still bitterly resented it: for years on end measures that would conduce to their welfare had come to nothing, while in the interim a law to crush and kill them had been swiftly passed and had been carried out with utmost rigour. This would have been the ideal moment, now that the mutiny had been suppressed, to divide up the territory of Bolae in order to assuage their anger, which, if done, would have lessened their desire for an agrarian law, whose aim was to oust those senators from the public land they had wrongfully occupied. As it was, this very conviction of having been mistreated continued to rankle: the nobility was not only stubbornly holding on to the public land it had seized by force, but would not even divide up among the plebs land from the enemy—land that would soon be appropriated by only a few, as had always happened.

That same year the consul Furius led his legions against the Volsci, who were ravaging Hernican territory; but when he failed to encounter them, he captured Ferentinum, where a great many of the Volsci had gone. There was less booty than had been expected because the Volsci, having little hope of defending the place, took what they could and left the town by night; the next day the practically deserted place was captured. It and its territory were given as a gift to the Hernici.

52. Following this year, which had been quiet because of the moderation of the tribunes, came the year when Lucius Icilius was tribune of the plebs, in the consulship of Quintus Fabius Ambustus and Gaius Furius Pacilus. At the very start of the year, as if it was the allotted task of his name and family, he stirred up unrest by promulgating agrarian laws. But a pestilence fell upon the state, more threatening than destructive, which diverted attention from the forum and political struggles to the home and care of the sick, and which is considered to have been less harmful than political upheaval would have been. After having escaped with few deaths in proportion to the large numbers who fell ill, the state in the following year, when Marcus Papirius Atratinus and Gaius Nautius Rutilus were consuls, experienced a shortage of food, as often happens, because of the neglect of agriculture. Hunger would now have been harder to bear than pestilence had not the shortage been alleviated by sending envoys round to all the peoples living near the Etruscan sea and along the Tiber to buy grain. The envoys were haughtily refused purchases by the Samnites at Capua and Cumae, but received kind assistance from the tyrants of Sicily. Most of the food was brought down the Tiber because of the eager co-operation of

Etruria. The extent of the sickness was revealed when the consuls searched for men to act as envoys: there were so few fit senators that only one could be found for each delegation, the other two slots being supplied by men of the equestrian class. But when these concerns abated, all those troubles that regularly afflicted the state returned: discord at home and war abroad.

53. In the consulship of Manius Aemilius and Gaius Valerius Potitus the Aequi were preparing for war, while the Volsci, although not participating as a matter of public policy, joined the force as paid volunteers. When this news was reported—for they had already descended on Latin and Hernican territory—Marcus Menenius, tribune of the plebs and sponsor of the agrarian bill, blocked the consul Valerius from holding the levy; any who did not want to serve refused to take the oath, relying on the tribune's protection. At this juncture came the sudden report that the citadel of Carventum had been seized by the enemy. This humiliation not only provided the senators with the means for stirring up hostility against Menenius but gave the other tribunes, who had agreed earlier to veto the agrarian bill, a more justifiable reason for opposing their colleague.

And so for a long time the dispute continued: the consuls called on gods and men to bear witness that the blame for any reverse or humiliation from the enemy, whether already inflicted or yet to come, would rest with Menenius, who was blocking the levy, while Menenius thundered in reply that if those illegal occupiers of public land would give up their claims, he was prepared to cease his opposition to the recruitment. The nine tribunes then interposed, stopping the dispute by issuing a decree on behalf of the college: they would come to the aid of the consul Gaius Valerius if in holding the levy and in the face of their colleague's veto he punished or used other forms of coercion in dealing with those refusing military service. When, armed with this decree, the consul had rope thrown around the necks of those who were appealing to the tribune, the rest out of fear took the oath.

The army was led to Carventum's citadel and, although soldiers and commander heartily disliked one another, it vigorously attacked those guarding the citadel, driving them out and capturing it; the fact that some of the defenders had been carelessly allowed to slip out on a plundering raid created a good opportunity to attack. There was quite a lot of booty from their continual plundering raids, all of which had been collected for safety in this spot. The consul ordered the quaestors to auction it off and to put the proceeds in the treasury, saying that the army would not share in the booty as long as it refused military service. The plebs' and soldiers' anger against the consul increased. And so, when by a decree of the senate he entered the city in an ovation, the soldiers used their licence to sing crude, impromptu verses, some that pilloried the consul, others that praised Menenius, while at every mention of the tribune's name the people vied with the soldiers in applauding and praising him. The anxiety the senators felt in the situation was greater than the licence the soldiers used against the consul, which by now was a virtual custom, and, as if Menenius would surely win if he was a candidate for the office of military tribune, the senators precluded that possibility by holding consular elections.

54. Elected consuls were Gnaeus Cornelius Cossus and Lucius Furius Medullinus for the second time. On no other occasion were the plebs more upset at not having elections for military tribunes. They showed their displeasure by striking back when electing quaestors: for the first time plebeian quaestors were returned, such that out of four, only one patrician, Caeso Fabius Ambustus, was elected, whereas three plebeians, Quintus Silius, Publius Aelius, and Gaius Papius were preferred to young scions from Rome's most distinguished houses. The Icilii, I find, encouraged the people to indulge in such independent voting; coming as they did from a family that was firmly opposed to the senatorial establishment, three were elected tribunes of the plebs that year by proposing a platform full of many sweeping measures to a people who were most eager for them and by threatening not to lift a finger on their behalf unless at least in the coming election of quaestors—which alone the senate had opened to plebeians and patricians—they screwed up their courage to do that which they had long wished for and which the law sanctioned.

The plebs reckoned this a glorious victory, and regarded the winning of the quaestorship not as an end in itself but as a springboard for new men to reach the consulship and win a triumph. The senators, on the other hand, were indignant not that the offices were being shared but as if they had lost them; they affirmed that under these conditions they would not raise children to be shut out of offices held by their ancestors and to see those occupying places of

preferment that were theirs; nothing was left to them save to sacrifice on behalf of the people as Salian priests and other religious
functionaries, powerless and without authority.* With feelings of
both parties running high, the plebs took courage in having three
men from such a celebrated family as champions of the popular
cause; the senators, believing that the election of the quaestors,
where a free choice between patrician and plebeian was open to the
people, would provide a pattern for everything to come, pushed for
consular elections, which were not yet open to all. The Icilii in
response declared that military tribunes ought to be elected and that
the plebs deserved their share of honours at last.

55. Yet at the moment the consuls were engaged in no activity
that the tribunes might block, thereby wresting from them what
they wanted. But then a surprising opportunity opened up: the
Volsci and Aequi had moved beyond their borders to plunder the
land of the Latins and Hernici. When the consuls began to hold a
levy for the war in accord with a decree of the senate, the tribunes
vigorously opposed it, declaring that this was a heaven-sent opportunity for themselves and the plebs. There were three of them, each
full of energy and, by this point in Rome's history, of good family,
considering they were plebeians. Two took on the task of keeping
the consuls under continuous surveillance, one on one, while the
third harangued the plebs, mixing restraint with incitement. Hence
the consuls could not hold the levy, nor the tribunes have the elections they were seeking. At a point when the plebeians were getting
the upper hand came the news that, when the soldiers who had been
left to garrison the citadel at Carventum had slipped out on a plundering raid, the Aequi stormed it after killing the few who had been
left behind to guard the place, as well as others as they were hurrying back to the citadel and still others as they ranged over the
countryside. This blow to the nation boosted the tribunes' agenda
still further. Despite being begged to desist in their opposition to
the war and despite the resulting odium for not yielding in this
national crisis, their refusal brought victory: a senatorial decree ordered the election of military tribunes, but with the specific proviso
that tribunes of the plebs of that year would be ineligible to stand
for that office or for re-election. The senate was clearly stigmatizing
the Icilii, who, they charged, were seeking the consulship as a reward for a rabble-rousing tribunate. The levy and other prepara-

tions for war were then begun with agreement of all the orders. Authorities disagree on whether both consuls set out to the citadel of Carventum or whether one remained behind to hold the elections; the following points on which they do agree seem assured: there was a retreat from Carventum after a long and unsuccessful siege, Verrugo in Volscian territory was taken back by the same army, and the territories of both the Aequi and Volsci were widely devastated, producing a great deal of plunder.

56. At Rome the plebs' victory in having the sort of election they wanted was counterbalanced by the results: contrary to everyone's expectation, three patricians became military tribunes with consular power, Gaius Iulius Iulus, Publius Cornelius Cossus, and Gaius Servilius Ahala. The patricians, it is said, used trickery in the elections, a charge that the Icilii brought against them at the time: by getting many unworthy candidates to run along with the worthy, the presence of these conspicuously base individuals turned the people away from the plebeians as a whole.

News then arrived that the Volsci and Aequi were gathering to wage all-out war, whether in hope because they had retained their hold on the citadel at Carventum or out of anger at losing the garrison at Verrugo; that the people of Antium were chiefly responsible and that their envoys had gone around to the peoples of each nation to rebuke them for inaction because they merely watched from behind their walls as the Romans ranged over their land and ravaged it the year before and as their garrison at Verrugo was overwhelmed; soon not only armies would be sent into their territories but colonies as well; and the Romans were not just keeping what they had divided up among themselves, but had even captured Ferentinum from them and made the Hernici a present of it. As the envoys came to each people and inflamed them with such talk, a good number of young soldiers were enrolled. Thus those of military age from all the peoples gathered at Antium and, having pitched camp there, awaited the enemy.

When this report reached Rome it caused a greater uproar than the situation warranted. The senate at once ordered that a dictator be named, the last resort in a desperate crisis. Tradition says that Iulius and Cornelius were greatly offended and that the situation caused strong feelings on all sides. When the senatorial leaders got nowhere in complaining that the military tribunes were not abiding by the senate's will, they resorted in the end to an appeal to the tribunes of the plebs, reminding them that previously the consuls also had been constrained by their power in a similar crisis. The tribunes of the plebs were delighted at the discord among the senators. There was no use in appealing to them, they said, since they were scarcely citizens and less than human in their eyes; if high office were ever open to them and the nation's government became something to be shared, only then would they see to it that magisterial presumption would not make senatorial decrees go for naught. In the meantime, having cast off all respect for laws and magistrates, the patricians would have to wield the tribunes' power for themselves.*

57. This dispute held everyone's attention at a most unsuitable moment, since a great war was at hand. For a long time Iulius and Cornelius took turns complaining of the injustice of depriving them, who were quite fit to assume command of the war, of the office bestowed on them by the people. At this point Servilius Ahala, the third military tribune, said he had held his peace all the while, not because he had no opinion to give—for what good citizen regarded his own interests as separate from those of the nation?—but because he preferred that his colleagues yield to the senate's authority of their own free will rather than allow the senate to beg the tribunes' help against them. Then, too, if the situation had allowed it, he would willingly have given them time to retreat from the overly obstinate position they had taken. But since the necessities of war do not wait upon man's deliberation, the nation took precedence in his eyes over accommodation to his colleagues. If the senate's decision remained unchanged, he would name a dictator in the night to come; should anyone veto the senate's decision, he would be content to abide by its authority. After winning by this action the praise and thanks he deserved from every quarter, he named Publius Cornelius dictator and was in turn chosen by him as master of the horse. Those who compared him with his colleagues saw in him an example of how favour and preferment sometimes come more readily to those who do not seek them.

The war was not noteworthy. The enemy was cut down at Antium in a single battle, and an easy one at that; the victorious army devastated Volscian territory. A fortress at the Fucine Lake was stormed and its three thousand defenders taken captive, while the rest of the Volsci were driven within their walls, leaving the land undefended. The dictator, after waging a war that put nothing to the test save good fortune, returned to the city crowned with greater success than glory, and resigned his office. The military tribunes, making no mention of consular elections (because, I suppose, they were angry at the appointment of the dictator), announced elections for military tribunes. At this the senators were faced with a far more serious concern, for they realized their cause had been betrayed by those of their own faction. And so, just as the year before they had made all the plebeian candidates disliked, even the worthy, by encouraging the unworthy to stand as well, so now, by having the most distinguished and influential senatorial leaders declare their candidacy, they retained their hold on all the positions, in order that there be no opening for any plebeian. Four were elected, all having been previous incumbents of the office: Lucius Furius Medullinus, Gaius Valerius Potitus, Gnaeus Fabius Vibulanus, and Gaius Servilius Ahala, the last re-elected after holding the office the year before, because of the recent popularity of his extraordinary moderation and for his other virtues as well.

58. In that year, because the truce with the people of Veii had run out, demands for restitution were initiated through envoys and the fetial priests.* When they arrived at the border they were met by a delegation from Veii. They asked that they not proceed to their city before they themselves had approached the senate in Rome. Since the Veientes were suffering from internal discord, the request that restitution not be sought was granted; it was against senatorial policy to take advantage of the troubles of others. And as for the Volsci, Rome suffered a disaster in the loss of the garrison at Verrugo. Timing here was critical: help could have been given to those under siege by the Volsci if it had been hurried up, but in fact the reinforcements arrived only after the garrison had been slaughtered and the Volsci had dispersed in search of booty, and at that point they were defeated. Responsibility for the delay rested no more with the senate than with the tribunes, who, because it was reported the garrison was resisting with all its might, failed to realize that there is a limit to human endurance, however courageous. But those brave soldiers did nevertheless not go unavenged, either while alive or in death.

In the following year, when Publius and Gnaeus Cornelius Cossus,

Gnaeus Fabius Ambustus, and Lucius Valerius Potitus were military tribunes with consular power, war with Veii broke out because of the arrogant response of the Veian senate to the envoys sent to claim restitution: they were told that if they did not speedily clear out of Veii and her territory, they would get the same treatment that Lars Tolumnius had given them. The senators reacted in anger, decreeing that as soon as possible the military tribunes should bring before the people a bill to declare war on Veii. On first hearing of its promulgation, the young men of military age complained that the war was not yet over with the Volsci: recently two garrisons had perished, the camp retained at peril; no year passed without a pitched battle and, as if they did not have enough on their hands already, a new war was in the making with a neighbouring people which was very powerful and which would rouse all of Etruria against them.

These spontaneous complaints were further exacerbated by the tribunes of the plebs, who repeatedly asserted that the plebs' greatest war was with the senators; they were being deliberately exposed to the hardships of military service and slaughter at the hands of the enemy; they had been exiled far from the city so that they might have no respite at home, where, mindful of liberty and colonies, they might concentrate on questions like public land or the free exercise of their votes. The tribunes canvassed the veterans individually, counting up the number of years each had served and of his wounds and scars, asking if there was any place left on the body to receive a fresh wound, and what more each could be expected to give to the state beyond the shedding of his blood. And so by bringing up these complaints at times in conversation and at times in public meetings, they made the plebs reluctant to undertake the war. The result was that the vote on the law was put off, since the hostility it aroused made rejection as good as certain.

59. In the meantime it was decided that the military tribunes should lead the army into Volscian territory; only Gnaeus Cornelius was left in Rome. The other three, after it became clear that the Volsci had nowhere pitched camp and would not engage them in battle, moved off each in a different direction, and devastated Volscian territory. Valerius headed for Antium, Cornelius for Ecetrae; wherever they went, they plundered buildings and fields far and wide, in order to divide the forces of the Volsci. Fabius did no plundering, but moved against Anxur, which was their chief goal, to besiege it.

Anxur, which is now Terracinae, was situated on a hill that sloped down to the marshes. From this direction Fabius began his assault. Four cohorts were sent round with Gaius Servilius Ahala to a hill overlooking the city; his men took it and from this higher elevation, which was not garrisoned, assaulted the walls with great shouting and commotion. Those who were guarding the lower city opposite Fabius were stunned by the uproar, which allowed scaling ladders to be moved up. Soon the enemy was everywhere upon them, and for a long time there was a pitiless slaughter of both those fleeing and those resisting, whether armed or unarmed. And so the vanquished were forced to fight back because there was no hope in surrender. Then came the sudden order that no one should be hurt save those in arms, which caused all those still surviving to drop their weapons voluntarily, of whom up to two and a half thousand were captured alive.

Fabius kept his soldiers from the rest of the booty until his colleagues should come up, saying that the capture of Anxur was effected by the other armies as well, since they had diverted the rest of the Volsci from defence of the town. When they arrived, the three armies plundered the city, which was full of wealth accumulated over many years. This indulgence of the commanders was the first step in reconciling the plebs with the senators. Next, in the most well-timed act of beneficence imaginable of the political leaders to the plebs, the senate, without any prompting on the part of the plebeians or their tribunes, decreed that henceforth soldiers should be paid from public funds, whereas up to that time each soldier served at his own expense.

60. Tradition says the plebs never welcomed anything with greater delight; flocking to the senate-house, they grasped the hands of the senators as they left, affirming that they were rightly styled fathers* and that hereafter no man, as long as he had breath in his body would spare life or limb in defence of so munificent a fatherland. While this generous act would help bolster their family finances, at least for the duration of their military obligation to the state, what made their joy even greater and their thankfulness more heartfelt was the fact that it had been voluntarily offered, never having been part of the programme of the plebeian tribunes or requested directly by themselves.

The tribunes of the plebs, who alone did not share in the general happiness and concord of the orders, affirmed that this would not redound to the credit of the senate as a whole or to the plebs' prosperity as much as they supposed: the proposal seemed better now than it would when actually implemented. For where would the funds come from, if not from the people? The senators were therefore being generous with other people's money and, even if everyone else should accept this, those whose military service was behind them would not put up with others serving under better conditions than they themselves had experienced, or, having paid for their own years of service, with now being obliged to pay for others as well. Some of the plebs were impressed by these arguments; in the end, after imposition of tribute had been announced, the tribunes went so far as to proclaim that they would come to the aid of anyone who did not contribute to the military chest.

The senators unwaveringly continued on the excellent course they had begun. They were the first to pay the tribute, and because there was as yet no silver coinage, some of them brought heavy bronze to the treasury in their wagons in a calculated and effective gesture. After the senate had paid its tax in punctilious conformity to the worth of each member, as established by the census, those plebeian leaders who were on friendly terms with the nobles began by pre-arrangement to make their contributions also. When ordinary plebeians saw that these men were praised by the senators and were regarded by men of military age as good citizens, they suddenly spurned the aid of the tribunes and began to rival one another in their eagerness to contribute.

And so the declaration of war on Veii was passed, and new military tribunes with consular power led an army composed mostly of volunteers to Veii. **61.** These tribunes were Titus Quinctius Capitolinus, Quintus Quinctius Cincinnatus, Gaius Iulius for the second time, Aulus Manlius, Lucius Furius Medullinus for the third time, and Manius Aemilius Mamercus. These men were the first to invest Veii. At the beginning of the siege a well-attended meeting of the Etruscans held at the shrine of Voltumna failed to agree on whether the whole nation should join in a war to defend Veii.

This siege went more slowly in the following year, when some of the tribunes and part of the army were called away to fight the Volsci. This year had as military tribunes with consular power Gaius Valerius Potitus for the third time, Manius Sergius Fidenas, Publius

Cornelius Maluginensis, Gnaeus Cornelius Cossus, Caeso Fabius Ambustus, and Spurius Nautius Rutilus for the second time. There was a pitched battle with the Volsci at a place between Ferentinum and Ecetra; the victory went to the Romans. Then the tribunes started to besiege Artena, a Volscian town. During an attempt of the enemy penned up in the city to break out, the Romans seized the opportunity to force their way in. They captured everything save the citadel, a naturally defensible site to which a squadron of armed men had withdrawn. In the city below many a man was cut down or captured. Then the siege of the citadel began, but it could not be captured by force, since its defenders were sufficient for the size of the place, nor did the Romans place hope in surrender, because all the town's food had been stored in the citadel before the city's capture. The Romans would have despaired of success and withdrawn had not a slave betrayed the citadel. He let the soldiers in at a spot where the approach was steep, and they seized the place. When the senators had been cut down, the rest of the crowd, overcome by sudden fear, surrendered unconditionally. The city and citadel of Artena were destroyed and the legions led back from Volscian territory. Now all Rome's power was concentrated at Veii. The man who betrayed Artena was given his liberty and the wealth of two families as a reward; the name he took was Servius Romanus. Some authorities consider Artena to have belonged to Veii rather than the Volsci. The fact that there was a city of the same name between Caere and Veii caused the mistake; but the kings of Rome destroyed this place, and it belonged to the Caerites, not the Veientes. There was another town of the same name in Volscian territory, whose destruction I have just described.

BOOK FIVE

1. With peace prevailing on other fronts, Rome and Veii faced one another in arms, harbouring such anger and hatred that defeat would surely mean the extinction of one of them. Each held elections markedly different from the other. The Romans increased the number of military tribunes with consular power; eight were chosen, a higher number than ever before: Manius Aemilius Mamercus for the second time, Lucius Valerius Potitus for the third, Appius Claudius Crassus, Marcus Quinctilius Varus, Lucius Iulius Iulus, Marcus Postumius, Marcus Furius Camillus, and Marcus Postumius Albinus. The people of Veii, on the other hand, weary of the annual competition for office, which had led to rioting from time to time, elected a king. This offended the peoples of Etruria, who disliked monarchy as much as they did the king personally. He had previously made himself hateful to the Etruscans because of his wealth and arrogance when he peremptorily broke up the solemn religious festival that it was sacrilegious to interrupt: angry that another man had been preferred to himself as priest by a vote of the twelve peoples, he abruptly withdrew his performers (most were his slaves) when the celebration was midway through. Thus the Etruscans, who are more completely devoted to religion than any other people and pride themselves on their skill in divine worship, decreed that aid be denied Veii as long it was under a monarch. No mention of this was made at Veii out of fear of the king, who reacted to such negative news by holding the messenger to be the instigator of insurrection, not the source of idle talk. Although word reached Rome that conditions were quiet in Etruria, it was also reported that Veii was a subject of discussion in all the meetings held there; accordingly, Rome built her fortifications on two fronts at once, some facing the city to stop the inhabitants from breaking out, others looking north toward Etruria to prevent any help arriving from that direction.

2. Since the Roman commanders thought a siege rather than an assault offered greater hope for success, they began to construct a winter camp, which was something new in the Roman military, and their plan was to continue hostilities throughout the winter. The tribunes back in Rome had not had an excuse for stirring up politi-

cal unrest for some time, but when they learned of this, they jumped at their chance. In a hurriedly called public meeting they inflamed their plebeian audience: so *this* was the reason for paying the soldiers! They had known all along that the sop their enemies had thrown them had been dipped in poison. The liberty of the plebs had been sold off. Soldiers had been subject to indefinite detention, exiled from city and nation. Not even with the change of season and the onset of winter would they see their homes and look to their affairs. What did they think the reason was for requiring soldiers to serve without term? Nothing less than this: to frustrate efforts to improve the lot of the plebs by rendering powerless their one source of strength, the large number of young men liable to military service as they met in assembly. What is more, they were subject to far harsher harassment and oppression than the people of Veii. The latter were spending the winter under their own roofs, in a city protected by stout walls and a naturally defensible site, while the Roman soldier, toiling and struggling, covered with snow and frost, was holding out under canvas, not allowed to lay aside his arms even in wintertime when all conflicts by land and sea are in abeyance. The kings had not imposed this degree of slavery upon the Roman plebs; neither had the arrogance of the consuls, even before the creation of the tribunician power; nor had the absolute power of the dictator or the oppression of the decemvirs. But the military tribunes had: they made the soldiers serve year-round, lording it like tyrants over the Roman plebs. What would they do if they became consuls or dictators, who had made this lesser form of consular power so savage and harsh? Yet the plebs had only themselves to blame. There were eight military tribunes and not one was a plebeian. In time past the patricians had regularly filled the three places available each year after heated electioneering; now they were proceeding to retain their hold on the office by fielding a team of eight! And even in this mob no plebeian had a place, who, if nothing else, might remind his colleagues that those serving in the army were not slaves but free men and fellow citizens, and that at least in winter they ought to return to hearth and home, and for a bit of time see again parents, children, and wives, exercise their freedom, and elect magistrates.

As they harangued the audience with these and similar arguments, Appius Claudius stepped forward, a formidable adversary who had been left in the city by his colleagues to suppress tribunician agitation. From his youth he had been schooled in the conflicts with the plebeians, and a few years before, as I noted some pages back,* he had advocated nullifying the tribunes' power through the veto of their colleagues. 3. He, then, a talented and practised speaker, delivered an oration of the following kind.

'If there was ever any doubt, fellow citizens, whether the tribunes of the plebs have always been political agitators in your interest or their own, this year has emphatically given the answer. I am happy that at last your long-standing misconception is at an end, and congratulate both you and, because of you, our country, particularly since this misconception has been removed at a time when your affairs are in such a flourishing state. Is there anyone who doubts that the tribunes of the plebs were never as offended and upset by wrongs done to you—if there really have ever been any—as by the beneficent gift of the senators to the plebs of pay for military service? What else do you think those men used to fear, or today want to destroy, if not the concord of the orders, which in their eyes most undermines their power? Ye gods, they are like quack physicians looking for work, who always want the state to be suffering some affliction that you will call them in to cure. Are you tribunes the champions or the enemies of the plebs? Are you the prosecutors or defenders of our soldiers? Unless perhaps you come right out and say 'Whatever the senators do we don't like, and it makes no difference whether it benefits the plebs or hurts them'—in this behaving like masters who forbid their slaves to have anything to do with strangers and correspondingly think it right that no one have contact with their slaves for good or ill; in this you are just like them, when you forbid the senators from having any dealings with the plebs, lest we encourage them by obliging and generous gestures and cause them to attend to what we say and to obey us. If you have any feeling for human kind—to say nothing of your fellow citizens—shouldn't you be on our side, wholeheartedly encouraging the kindness of the senators and the complaisance of the plebs? If this harmony continues unimpaired, who would not venture to affirm that soon our realm will be greater than any of our neighbours?

4. 'I shall argue shortly that my colleagues' decision not to bring the army back from Veii with the war unfinished was not only expedient but necessary. I now want to speak about the actual con-

ditions of military service. If I were giving this speech to the camp instead of to you I am confident that the soldiers would judge my words to be fair. And even if I could not come up with any arguments of my own, I would be content simply with those my adversaries advanced. They say that the recent decision to pay the soldiers was wrong because none has ever been given. How then can they now object to the principle of imposing new obligations upon those who have received new benefits? Labour is never without recompense, and recompense is scarcely ever paid without labour. Work and pleasure, dissimilar in nature, are yet paired with one another in a sort of natural association. Previously a soldier was unhappy that he laboured for the state at his own expense, but he was glad for part of the year to farm his land, from which he produced enough to support himself and his family at home and while serving his country. Now he is happy that the state helps out and he is delighted to be paid. He should therefore think it fair for him to be absent a little longer from home and property now that he is not burdened by heavy expenses. Suppose the state should ask him to make a reckoning. Would it be right to say, "Since you receive a yearly salary, you should give a year's work. Or do you think it fair to receive a whole year's pay for a half-year's service?" I am reluctant to dwell on this topic, citizens. For this is the way one should speak when addressing mercenaries. But I prefer to deal with you as with fellow citizens, and think it fair that you deal with me as you would with your country.

'Either the war should not have been undertaken at all, or it should be waged as befits the dignity of the Roman people and be finished at the first possible moment. Moreover, it will be finished if we press our siege hard, if we do not leave before our goal has been fully attained with the capture of Veii. By heaven, if nothing else does, the shame of failure should have made us persevere. Once, long ago, the whole of Greece besieged a city for ten years for the sake of one woman. How far from home were they? How many lands and seas lay between? Yet we are reluctant to endure a siege for one year, at a place less than twenty miles away, practically within sight of the city.

'Ah, but the cause of the war is trifling: we have no justifiable grievances that would constrain us to persevere! Seven times they renewed hostilities and have never kept their word in peace. Over and over they have ravaged our lands. They forced the fidenates to defect from us and killed our colonists there. They were the agents of the foul murder of our envoys. They aimed at rousing all of Etruria against us, and even today continue to try. They were close to assaulting the envoys we sent to demand satisfaction. **5**. Should a war be waged against such people with forbearance and in fits and starts? If hatred that is fully justified does not move us, will not even the following considerations do so? The city is hedged about by extensive fortifications which keep the enemy within the walls; he no longer farms his land, and what was under cultivation before has suffered the ravages of war. If we recall our army, who could doubt that he would invade our territory, not only to take revenge but also out of necessity, since he would have to rob others of what he had lost? You tribunes urge us to withdraw. If we do, we will not postpone the war but face it within our own borders.

'Now let us consider what concerns our soldiers most immediately, whom the good tribunes wanted to deprive of their pay and whose best interests they now want to champion. What precisely is at issue? Veii is completely encircled by a rampart and a ditch; each took an enormous amount of effort to build. Our soldiers also constructed guard stations—a few at first, but a great many when the army was increased. They also built earthworks facing not just inward toward the city but outward toward Etruria, to block any help that might come from there. And what of the towers, moveable sheds, protecting screens, and other apparatus used in the siege of cities?* After so much effort has been expended and the end of our toil is at last in sight, do you think these constructions should be abandoned, only to have to sweat through the rebuilding of every one of them from scratch next summer? How much less effort it will take simply to keep what we have, to press on, to persevere and to finish the fight! For it will certainly not take long, provided we carry on unremittingly and do not delay the outcome by stopping and restarting.

'I have been speaking of the loss of time and effort. But what of the danger? Surely the ongoing discussions in Etruria about sending aid to Veii forbid us to forget the peril we risk by spinning out the war. Right now they are angry and hostile and say they won't send any; as far as they are concerned, Veii is ours to take. But who can guarantee that their attitude will remain the same if the war goes on?

If you withdraw now, Veii will send out greater and more frequent appeals, and what offends the Etruscans, the election of a king at Veii, could be changed with time either by the will of the state, in order thereby to win the support of Etruria, or by the decision of the king himself, unwilling to let his rule affect adversely the well-being of the citizens.

'Review now the many prohibitive consequences of withdrawal: loss of the works built with so much effort, the imminent devastation of our lands, a war with Etruria as she rallies to the defence of Veii. This is what you advocate, tribunes. You are no different from someone who gratifies a sick man's desire for food and drink, thereby prolonging his illness and perhaps making recovery impossible, when a strict regimen would enable him quickly to regain his health.

6. 'By heaven, even if it were not an issue in this war, surely it is absolutely essential to military discipline in the future that our soldiers become accustomed not just to enjoying the fruits of a victory in hand but, if it is slow in coming, bearing up despite fatigue and awaiting the fulfilment of their hopes, however delayed, and, if the war is not finished at summer's end, remaining throughout the winter and not, like the birds of summer, scurrying for shelter and sanctuary as soon as autumn is upon them. I need hardly remind you that the passion and pleasure of hunting plunge men through frost and snow into woods and mountains. Will we not adopt in the constraints of war that same willingness to endure hardship that we bring to sport and pleasure? Do we think the bodies of our soldiers are so fragile, their spirits so irresolute, that they can't last through one winter in camp away from home? That they are like sailors who fight only in season and when the weather is fine, unable to tolerate heat or cold? They would certainly blush if anyone charged them with such things. They would insist that they were fighters in body and spirit, able to wage war in both winter and summer; that the tribunes were not elected to be patrons of sissies and pacifists; and that their ancestors, they well remembered, had not created the tribunate amid the comforts of hearth and home.*

'What is worthy of your soldiers' courage and worthy of the name of Rome is this: not to think just of Veii and this war, but to establish a reputation that will live on to affect other wars and other peoples. Or do you fancy it makes little difference whether our neighbours, in judging the people of Rome, conclude that if one of

their cities can withstand a Roman attack for a brief time, it would
have nothing to fear, or whether our name inspires such terror that
neither the fatigue of a long siege nor the storms of winter can make
a Roman army quit the siege of a city and that Rome recognizes no
other end to a war than victory and conducts hostilities as much by
perseverance as by brute force? Perseverance is necessary in all types
of warfare but especially so in the siege of cities, a great many of
which, impregnable because of their siting and fortifications, time
itself overcomes through famine and thirst and takes it captive—just
as you will capture Veii, provided the tribunes of the plebs do not
come to the aid of the enemy and Veii finds in Rome the help that
they are begging for in vain from Etruria.

'In fact, could Veii wish for anything better than to see Rome rent
by dissension, which then would spread like some contagion to the
camp? Our enemy acts upon the orders given him, so much so that
neither the pressure of the siege nor aversion to monarchy has caused
him to lift a finger in protest. The aid denied him by Etruria has not
made his spirits waver, and whoever advocates disobedience will die
on the spot: no one will say to him with impunity the things that are
said to you. A Roman soldier who abandons the standards or leaves
his post is punished by being clubbed to death; yet those who advocate abandoning the standards and quitting the camp are heard not
by one or two soldiers but by whole armies in open assembly—so
much so that no matter what a tribune of the plebs advocates,
whether it be betrayal of our country or dissolution of the state, you,
my fellow citizens, are accustomed to hear him out and, intoxicated
by the tribune's power, to let him get away with every sort of
villainy. It only remains for everything they have said to be repeated
in the camp and in the presence of the soldiers, thereby corrupting
the army and encouraging disobedience to the commanders. In short,
freedom at Rome has come down to this: freedom to scorn the
senate, magistrates, and laws, freedom to flout tradition and the
institutions of our ancestors, freedom to subvert military discipline.'

7. Appius showed that he was as adept as the tribunes of the
plebs in haranguing the people. Then an occurrence from a most
unexpected quarter decided the dispute. News of a disaster at Veii
gave the victory to Appius and his side, while at the same time
strengthening the concord of the orders and making men even more
determined to carry on the siege of Veii. For after the rampart with

its palisade had been raised against the city but before the protective sheds had been fixed to the walls (with greater care being given to constructing the works by day than safeguarding them at night), the city gate suddenly opened and a great crowd, most carrying torches, discharged their firebrands; in a single hour the palisade and sheds had burned up, both of which had taken a long time to build; many a man perished in the flames or was put to the sword as he vainly tried to extinguish the fire.

When this was reported at Rome everyone was sick at heart; the senate was concerned and fearful that both city and camp would be in the grip of political turmoil and that the tribunes of the plebs would exult over their country's defeat, as if they had been responsible for it. But all at once those belonging to the order of knights or equestrians, but to whom horses had not been given by the state,* after first conferring among themselves, asked permission to address the senate. When this was granted, they pledged to serve in the cavalry using their own horses. They were warmly thanked and, when word of their offer spread through the forum and city, the plebs straightway flocked to the senate house, declaring themselves members of the infantry order and promising to serve their country as foot soldiers extraordinary,* whether the senate wished to march them out to Veii or to some other place; if to Veii, they pledged not to return until the enemy's city was in their hands. At these words the senators were almost beside themselves with joy, for they did not instruct the magistrates to praise the plebeians as they had in the case of the knights, nor did they summon the crowd into the senate-house to listen to a formal speech of thanks nor stay within doors of the building, but, standing on the top steps, each senator signified by words and gestures to the crowd assembled below the nation's delight, calling Rome a city blessed, invincible and eternal because of this marvellous co-operation, praising the knights and the plebs, calling it a red-letter day in Rome's history, and confessing that what had just been done surpassed the goodwill and generosity of the senate. Senators and plebeians vied in shedding tears of happiness; then, after the senators had been called back into session, a decree was passed instructing the military tribunes to call a meeting and formally thank the infantry and cavalry and to say that the senate would remember their patriotism, and that, further, all those who promised to serve as volunteers should receive pay. A fixed sum was also marked for the cavalry. This was the first occasion on which the cavalry served using their own horses. The volunteer army was led to Veii and not only rebuilt the constructions that had been destroyed but even began new ones. Supplies were conveyed from the city with greater care than before lest an army so deserving should be in want of anything.

8. The following year had as military tribunes with consular power Gaius Servilius Ahala for the third time, Quintus Servilius, Lucius Verginius, Quintus Sulpicius, Aulus Manlius for the third time, and Manius Sergius for the second. During their tenure, while everyone was concerned with the war against Veii, the garrisoning of Anxur was neglected because of furloughs granted to the soldiers and through the indiscriminate admittance of Volscian traders; when the sentries at the gates were suddenly overpowered, the place was captured. Relatively few soldiers perished because, except for those who were sick, everyone was out in the countryside and neighbouring cities trafficking in goods like so many sutlers.

Nor did things go any better at Veii, where the state had concentrated all its efforts; for the Roman commanders had more animosity for one another than for the enemy, while the scope of the war widened with the sudden involvement of the Capenates and Falisci. These two Etruscan peoples had bound themselves by oaths, after sending envoys back and forth between themselves, and then unexpectedly sent their armies in Veii's defence. They were her closest neighbours and believed that if she were defeated they would be the next to succumb in a war with Rome, while the Falisci had the additional motive of having already taken part in the earlier war with Fidenae. By chance they attacked the encampment commanded by the military tribune Manius Sergius and caused great panic because the Romans believed all of Etruria had left their cities and had come to Veii's defence in massed array. And the people inside Veii were spurred to act by the same belief. Thus the Roman encampment was faced with a fight on two fronts; rallying together, they moved the standards now in one direction and now in another, but these efforts were not sufficient to keep the Veientes penned up within the encircling fortifications nor to keep those fortifications from being attacked or to protect themselves from the enemy on the outside. Their one hope was that help would come from the main camp and that some legions would confront the Capenates and Falisci, while others would prevent the townspeople from breaking out. But Verginius was in command of the camp, and he and Sergius detested one another. When Verginius learned that most of the forts were under attack, that the earthworks had been breached, and that the enemy was pouring in from both directions, he held his soldiers under arms, saying that his colleague would send to him if he needed help. Verginius' callousness was matched by Sergius' obstinacy, who, lest he seem to have asked help from a personal enemy, preferred to be worsted by the foe than win through a fellow citizen. For a long time the soldiers were cut down in the middle; finally, abandoning the fortifications, a handful headed for the main camp, the greatest number (including Sergius himself) for Rome. There, when he put all the blame on his colleague, the decision was taken to summon Verginius from the camp and to put lieutenants in charge during his absence.

The situation was then discussed in the senate, which became the scene for mutual recriminations between the two military tribunes. A few had the nation's interest at heart; most favoured one man or the other, each influenced by personal feelings and partiality. 9. The leaders of the senate proposed that, whether the disaster was due to the fault or to the bad luck of the commanders, the nation ought not to wait to hold elections at the usual time but should choose new military tribunes at once, to take office on 1 October. As the senate was proceeding to vote on the measure, the rest of the military tribunes made no objection, but Sergius and Verginius, whose tenure in office was plainly responsible for the senate's unhappiness, asked to be spared such a disgrace, and then vetoed the senatorial decree, declaring that they would not leave office before 13 December, the regular date for the change to new magistrates. In the midst of this the tribunes of the plebs, who had unwillingly held their tongues when men were acting in harmony and the state was prospering, suddenly burst into harsh threats: unless the military tribunes submitted to the will of the senate they would order their imprisonment. Then Gaius Servilius Ahala, one of the military tribunes, said, 'As for you and your threats, I would very much like to conduct an experiment to find out whether the cowardice of you plebeian tribunes is as great as the illegality of what you threaten. Ah, but it is wrong to go against the will of the senate. So stop trying to make matters worse in the midst of our troubles. As for my colleagues, they will either abide by the senate's decision or, if they balk, I will name a dictator at once, who will force them from office.' All the senators approved his remarks. They were delighted to have found another weapon, more powerful than the tribunes' blustering threats, to bend magistrates to their will. And so, bowing to the general consensus, they held elections for military tribunes who would enter office on 1 October, and resigned from office before that day.

10. The next year saw many events at home and abroad, when the following were military tribunes with consular power: Lucius Valerius Potitus for the fourth time, Marcus Furius Camillus for the second, Manius Aemilius Mamercus for the third, Gnaeus Cornelius Cossus for the second, Caeso Fabius Ambustus, and Lucius Iulius Iulus. War was waged on multiple fronts at the same time: against Veii, Capena, and Falerii as well as at Anxur, where there was an effort to wrest it from Volscian control; at Rome there were troubles over both the levy and collection of tribute, as well as a dispute concerning the co-option of plebeian tribunes, and no slight disturbance over the trials of the two tribunes who had lately held consular power.

The military tribunes first took on the task of recruitment, not only enrolling the junior men but requiring that the seniors serve in the force protecting the city. But the increase in the number of soldiers necessitated an increase in expenditure to pay them. Tribute was being collected for this purpose, but those remaining at home proved unwilling contributors, since in defending the city they had to discharge obligations both to the military and to the state. These obligations, considerable in themselves, were made to seem more onerous in the fractious meetings held by the tribunes of the plebs, who argued that the senators had instituted military pay so that they might crush some of the plebs by military service, the rest by taxation. One war was already being dragged out into a third year and had been deliberately mismanaged so that it would go on longer. A single enlistment had provided soldiers for four wars at once, for which boys and old men were being hauled away. Military duty went on in summer and winter alike, with no break for the unhappy plebs; and, as if this were not enough, new taxes had been imposed, so that when they finally dragged bodies exhausted by toil, wounds, and old age back to their homes, they found their land unworked from their long absence and that what little money was left from their military earnings had to go to pay the tribute—like a loan that must be repaid at exorbitant interest.

What with the levy, the tribute, and other more important matters that weighed on their minds, they were unable to elect the full number of plebeian tribunes. There followed a fight to co-opt patricians for the open spots. When this failed, they still manœuvred to get around the law by having Gaius Lacerius and Marcus Acutius co-opted as tribunes of the plebs, who unquestionably owed their positions to the power of the patricians. 11. By chance Gnaeus Trebonius was tribune of the plebs that year and, in his defence of the Trebonian law, he was seen to be fulfilling a duty incumbent on his name and family.* He charged that what certain senators had wanted and what, despite an initial set-back, they had succeeded in getting through the military tribunes had been accomplished by patrician deceit and the criminal collusion of his colleagues—loudly protesting that the Trebonian law had been subverted and that the tribunes of the plebs had been co-opted not by the vote of the people but at the bidding of the patricians: things had deteriorated to the point that either patricians or their stooges must now be accounted plebeian tribunes, while the sacred laws were flouted and tribunician power wrenched from their hands.

Feelings were running high not just against the senators but against the plebeian tribunes, both those who had been co-opted and those who had done the co-opting. At this point three members of the college, Publius Curiatius, Marcus Metilius, and Marcus Minucius, afraid for themselves, attacked Sergius and Verginius, military tribunes of the year before; they thereby diverted the anger and hostility the plebs felt for themselves to these two. The tribunes declared that those weighed down by the levy, tribute, long military service and the length of the war, those outraged by the defeat at Veii, those whose homes were in mourning for dead sons, brothers, and kin—to them had been given (thanks to the tribunes) the right and power of making the two guilty ones pay for the humiliation of the state and their private grief. Responsibility for all these evils lay with Sergius and Verginius. And this, they said, formed the basis of the prosecution as much as of the defence! For each of the two guilty parties said the other was responsible, Verginius accusing Sergius of running away, Sergius accusing Verginius of treachery. All this, they

continued, was so lunatic that what happened was more likely the
result of mutual agreement and patrician collusion. For in order to
drag out the war they had previously given the Veientes the opportunity to burn down the fortifications, and now they had betrayed
the army and surrendered the Roman camp to the Falisci. All this
was aimed at keeping the young soldiers at Veii so they would grow
old there, and at preventing the tribunes from bringing proposals
to the people concerning land and other matters of benefit to the
plebs, and from engaging in a full political programme before all the
people and combating patrician cabals. The senate and the Roman
people, and then their own colleagues, had already given their verdicts on the defendants, for the senate decreed that they should be
removed from office, their colleagues forced them to quit when they
refused to do so out of fear that a dictator would be named, while
the Roman people elected military tribunes to take office not on 13
December, the regular date, but at once, on 1 October, because the
nation could not go on any longer with these men in office. And yet,
already crushed and condemned by so many verdicts, they now
appeared for their trial before the people believing that they had
made amends and paid a sufficient penalty by having retired into
private life two months early, not understanding that this was not a
punishment, but to prevent them from doing further harm. In fact,
their colleagues were also forced from office, who were certainly
innocent of any wrongdoing. They urged their fellow Romans to
recall their feelings on hearing of the recent defeat and on seeing the
soldiers, wounded, fearful and in flight, pouring in through the
gates and pointing the accusing finger not at fortune or any of the
gods, but at these very commanders. They felt sure that there was
no one in the present assembly who on that day had not cursed and
reviled Lucius Verginius and Manius Sergius—their persons, their
houses, their fortunes. It made no sense for them not to use their
power against these men, for they were entitled to do so and
honour-bound to do so, while the culprits were the men on whom
they had called down the wrath of heaven. The gods themselves
never lay hands on the guilty; they are content to hand the sword
of vengeance to those who have been wronged.

12. Fired up by these speeches, the plebs condemned each man to
pay ten thousand pieces of heavy bronze, as Sergius got nowhere in
blaming bad luck and Mars, who can take both sides in war, while

Verginius begged that he not suffer greater misfortune at home than he had in the field. The people's anger against these men pushed into the background thoughts of the cooptation of the tribunes and the circumvention of the Trebonian law.

The victorious tribunes promulgated an agrarian bill to give the plebs an immediate reward for their verdict in the trial. They also forbade tribute to be collected, there being so many armies to pay, whose success to date consisted in no resolution one way or the other in any of the wars then being waged. For at Veii the camp that had been lost was recovered and strengthened with forts and guard stations; the military tribunes Manius Aemilius and Caeso Fabius were in charge there. Marcus Furius, facing the Falisci, and Gnaeus Cornelius in the territory of Capena encountered none of their enemies outside the walls; booty was taken, the farmhouses and crops burned over; their towns were not attacked or besieged. As for the Volsci, after their territory had been ravaged, Anxur was unsuccessfully attacked, situated as it was on a lofty site; after force proved unavailing, a siege was begun with rampart and ditch. The command against the Volsci was in the hands of Valerius Potitus. Such was the situation in the field.

But greater energy was put into creating political turmoil in the city than in waging war abroad; and thus tribute could not be collected because of the tribunes nor pay sent to the commanders, although the soldiers kept demanding their money; the contagion of civil unrest came close to infecting the camp as well. Amid the hostility of the plebs toward the senators, the tribunes of the plebs said that this was the time to put liberty on a secure footing by taking the highest office away from the likes of Sergius and Verginius and giving it to brave and energetic plebeians. Yet the electorate asserted its right by electing only one plebeian as military tribune with consular power, Publius Licinius Calvus: all the rest were patricians, Publius Manlius, Lucius Titinius, Publius Maelius, Lucius Furius Medullinus, and Lucius Publilius Volscus.* The plebs as a whole were amazed that they had won such a great prize, not just the individual who had been elected, a man who had held no offices before, having sat in the senate for many years and now quite old. Nor is it clear what special merit he had to become the first plebeian elected to this new office. Some believe he owed his elevation to his kinsman Gnaeus Cornelius, who had been military tribune the year

before and had given triple pay to the knights;* others think it was
because he gave a timely speech on the concord of the orders, which
found favour with both senators and plebs. The tribunes of the
plebs, rejoicing at this victory, dropped their opposition to the tribute, which had been the greatest obstacle to running the state. People
contributed promptly and the proceeds were sent to the army.

13. Anxur in Volscian territory was quickly retaken when on a
festal day the sentry posts were poorly manned. The year was notable for a cold and snowy winter, so much so that roads were blocked
and the Tiber became impassable for boats. The food supply was
not a problem because stores had been laid up in advance. And
because Publius Licinius had conducted himself in office as unas-
sumingly as he had entered into it (the joy of the plebs at this being
greater than the unhappiness of the senators), the plebs conceived
the desire to vote for members of their own class for military tribunes. Marcus Veturius was the only patrician candidate to win a
place; the rest were plebeian, chosen military tribunes with consular
power by nearly all the centuries in the Centuriate assembly: Marcus
Pomponius, Gnaeus Duillius, Volero Publilius, Gnaeus Genucius,
and Lucius Atilius.

The harsh winter was followed by an oppressive summer, pesti-
lential to all animal life and caused either by the extreme and rapid
change in the weather or for some other reason. When the cause of
the incurable plague could not be found and no end was in sight, the
senate decreed that the Sibylline books should be consulted.* The
two-man board in charge of sacred rites thereupon placated the
following deities in an eight-day ceremony called the lectisternium,
the first ever held in Rome: Apollo and Latona, Hercules and Diana,
Mercury and Neptune; three couches were set out and a banquet
served, as lavish as could be provided in those days.* The rite was
also celebrated in private homes. Tradition says that throughout the
city the doors of the houses were thrown open and that everywhere
acquaintances and strangers without distinction were invited to par-
take of all the goods set out for their enjoyment. Even personal
enemies were addressed in a kind and friendly way and people
refrained from quarrelling and lawsuits. Those in fetters were released from their bonds; it was then considered an affront to the
gods to put back in chains those who had been the recipients of the
gods' help.

Meanwhile at Veii the Romans had many things to fear at once when three wars were concentrated into one. For, as had happened earlier, the Capenates and Falisci suddenly came to Veii's help by surrounding the Roman siegeworks; a battle on two fronts ensued against these three armies. The memory of Sergius' and Verginius' convictions contributed more than anything to Rome's victory. Accordingly, troops sallied forth from the main camp (from which in the previous battle help had been withheld) and, taking a short route, came up from behind the Capenates and attacked them as they were facing the Roman palisade. When the fight began, the Falisci took fright as well: an opportune sally from the camp drove them back in fear. The victors then pursued those they had repulsed and slaughtered a great many. A little later they by chance became easy targets as they wandered about; the Romans sent to devastate the land of Capena wiped out these survivors of the battle. As for the Veientes, many fled back toward the city and were cut down before the gates, while those inside, fearful that the Romans would burst in at the same time, closed the doors upon the last of their own men and shut them out.

14. Such were the events of this year. The time for the election of military tribunes was at hand, which concerned the senators almost more than the war, inasmuch as they realized the highest office had not only been shared, but virtually lost to them. Accordingly, they agreed ahead of time to field a slate consisting of their most distinguished members, believing that the voters would be reluctant to prefer others to such men as these. But taking no chances and acting as if they all were candidates, they tried to involve both gods and men in the process by declaring that the elections of the last two years were proof of divine displeasure: the intolerable winter of the year before last had been like a divine warning, and in the year just past that warning had been translated into fact; the pestilence that had fallen on city and countryside was no doubt due to the anger of the gods, who, the books of fate said, must be placated if the pestilence were to be averted; in the electoral assemblies that had been convened under the auspices of the gods the results had displeased them; the office had been vulgarized and the distinctions among the clans erased. Aside from the distinction of the candidates, the electorate was also impressed by the religious argument; so they chose all patricians as military tribunes with consular power, chiefly the

most illustrious candidates: Lucius Valerius Potitus for the fifth
time, Marcus Valerius Maximus, Marcus Furius Camillus for the
second time, Lucius Furius Medullinus for the third, Quintus
Servilius Fidenas for the second, and Quintus Sulpicius Camerinus
for the second. Under these tribunes nothing memorable was achieved
at Veii; their entire effort went into plundering raids. The two most
successful commanders, Potitus at Falerii and Camillus at Capena,
brought back huge amounts of booty, leaving nothing untouched
that fire or sword could destroy.

15. In the meantime numerous prodigies were reported, in which
the senate put little belief and hence set aside because only individuals had vouched for them and because, with the Etruscans as enemies, there were no haruspices who might avert these omens through
sacrifice.* But one caused special concern: the rising to an unwonted
level of the waters of the lake set in the forest of Alba, without any
rain having fallen from the sky or for any other reason that would
exempt it from being regarded as supernatural. Envoys were dispatched to the oracle at Delphi to ascertain what the gods meant by
this prodigy.

But the fates presented Rome with an interpreter closer to home,
a certain elderly man of Veii who, amid the jibes hurled between the
Roman and Etruscan sentries, prophesied in the manner of an inspired seer that Rome would never capture Veii until the water was
let out from the Alban lake. At first what he said was disregarded as
a random taunt, but when it continued to be a subject of discussion,
one of the Roman sentries asked the Veian closest to him (there had
developed an interchange between the two sides owing to the length
of the war) who the man was who had made this riddling utterance.
The Roman, who was a man of religious sensibility, on learning the
old man was a haruspex, coaxed him to confer with him privately, if
he could spare the time, about averting an omen that affected him
personally. When the two, unarmed and unafraid, had gone some
distance from their respective lines, the Roman, who was young and
strong, seized the feeble old man as everyone looked on and carried
him to his side amid the frustrated roars of protest from the Etruscans.
The man was first brought to the Roman commander, who in turn
sent him to the senate in Rome. When the senators asked what he
meant about the Alban lake, he replied that the gods had undoubtedly been angry with the Veian people on the day in which they had

prompted him to reveal the fall of his country that the fates had in store. Accordingly, he could not recant the prophecy he had uttered while divinely inspired as if it had not been spoken—possibly he would have committed a religious sin as much by being silent about what the immortal gods wanted known as by revealing what ought to have been concealed. So it had been written in the books of fate, so it had come down in Etruscan lore, that whenever the Alban waters had risen to a great height, the Romans would prevail over Veii provided they properly drained away the water. Unless this happened the gods would not abandon the walls of Veii. He then explained the prescribed ritual for causing the water to flow out. But the senators thought the man's authority and trustworthiness was suspect, and so decreed that they should await the return of the envoys with the response of the Pythian priestess at Delphi.

16. Before the envoys returned from Delphi or expiatory rites were found for the Alban prodigy, new military tribunes with consular power entered office: Lucius Iulius Iulus, Lucius Furius Medullinus for the fourth time, Lucius Sergius Fidenas, Aulus Postumius Regillensis, Publius Cornelius Maluginensis, and Aulus Manlius. In that year the people of Tarquinii joined the ranks of Rome's enemies. Many wars were going on simultaneously: against the Volsci at Anxur, where the garrison was under siege, against the Aequi at Labici, who were attacking the Roman colony, and against the Veientes, Falisci, and Capenates. When the people of Tarquinii saw that Rome was occupied with these wars and that the situation within her walls was just as worrisome because of the struggles between the senators and plebs, they thought that this was an opportunity to strike a blow of their own. So they sent a light-armed force into Roman territory on a plundering raid: for the Romans either would look the other way and not retaliate (so as not to burden themselves with yet another war), or would come after them with a small force of insufficient strength. Rome was more indignant than worried by the plundering raid of the Tarquinienses; so she did not put great effort in her response nor delay it for long. Aulus Postumius and Lucius Iulius were unable to hold a proper levy—for they were prevented by the tribunes of the plebs; but marching out with what was virtually a band of volunteers that they had cajoled into joining them, they ducked through Caeretan territory by following cross-country tracks,* and crushed the Tarquinienses as they were returning from pillaging, laden with booty. They killed many a man, captured all that they were carrying, and returned to Rome with the spoils taken from Roman territory. A space of two days was given to the owners to claim their property; on the third the part unclaimed (much of it belonged to the enemy himself) was sold at auction and the proceeds divided up among the soldiers.

The other wars, particularly the one with Veii, had been brought to no conclusion. At this point the Romans, despairing of success by human effort, were looking to the fates and the gods, when the envoys returned from Delphi, bringing with them a response that agreed with the prophecy of the captive seer: 'Roman, let not the waters of Alba remain in the lake, let them not flow seaward in a stream of their own making, but send them forth, irrigating the land, quenching them through many, wide-separated rivulets. Then boldly press your attack on the enemy walls, knowing that victory has been vouchsafed you by the fates, which are herein revealed, over this city you have long besieged. At battle's end you must bring in victory a splendid gift to my temple and must repeat in ancestral fashion those sacred rites of your country that you have failed to carry through.'

17. The captive seer then began to be regarded with awe, and the military tribunes Cornelius and Postumius took steps to involve him in the expiatory rites of the Alban prodigy and in placating the gods according to correct religious procedure. In addition, the exact cause was finally found for the god's charge that religious rites had been neglected or a solemn ceremony interrupted: namely, that the magistrates, having been faultily elected, had announced the date for the Latin festival and the sacrifice on the Alban Mount improperly:* the sole way to expiate these transgressions was for the military tribunes to resign from office, the auspices be taken afresh, and an interregnum begun. A decree of the senate ordered that these steps be taken. There were then three successive interreges: Lucius Valerius, Quintus Servilius Fidenas, and Marcus Furius Camillus. In the meantime there was no respite from political wrangling, as the tribunes of the plebs vetoed all elections until there was a prior agreement that the majority of military tribunes be plebeian.

While these things were going on, the people of Etruria met at the shrine of Voltumna. When the Capenates and Falisci demanded that all Etruria should join in a communal effort to raise the siege of

Veii, they were told that a negative response to such a request had been given previously:* they should not ask for help in such a great enterprise from those they had not consulted at the outset; moreover, their current situation necessitated a negative response, for in that part of Etruria a new and unfamiliar people had arrived on the scene, the Gauls, with whom there was neither an assured peace nor open hostilities. Nevertheless, they would make this concession to their blood, their name, and the dangers currently threatening their bloodkin: they would make no move to prevent any of their young men who wanted to fight as volunteers from doing so. In Rome rumour said that the number of the enemy was great, in consequence of which internal discord began to dissipate, as tends to happen in face of the common danger.

18. The senators were not displeased when the centuries that had been picked by lot to vote first selected Publius Licinius Calvus as military tribune, although he had not sought the post, a man of proven moderation in his earlier tenure of the post, though now quite old. It was clear all his colleagues of that same year would be reelected as well, Lucius Titinius, Publius Maenius, Gnaeus Genucius, and Lucius Atilius.* After the tribes had voted but before the results were formally announced, the interrex gave permission to Publius Licinius Calvus to speak: 'I see by your choices for the year to come you were thinking of our former magistracy and were seeking an omen of concord,* something especially to be desired at the present time. Even though my colleagues you elected are the same men—in fact even better now from their experience in office—you can see I am not the same, but a shadow of what I once was—Publius Licinius in name only. Bodily strength is on the decline, sight and hearing are impaired, memory fails and the mind's sharpness is blunted. But look upon this young man,' he said, embracing his son. 'He is the mirror image of the one whom you elected earlier as the first military tribune from the plebs. In presenting him to the nation, I declare that he was raised in accordance with my principles and will stand in for me, and I ask, fellow citizens, that you bestow the office you have given me without my asking to the man before you, who does seek to fill it, and in consideration of my entreaties on his behalf.' The father was granted his request, and his son Publius Licinius was announced as having been elected military tribune with consular power along with those mentioned above.

The military tribunes Titinius and Genucius set out against the Falisci and Capenates but, while waging the war with greater *élan* than caution, fell into an ambush. Genucius paid for his rashness by an honourable death, falling before the standards in the front ranks. Titinius made a stand on the top of a rise of ground where he assembled the thoroughly frightened soldiers; but he did not venture to engage the enemy on level ground. More disgrace than loss of life had occurred, although it came close to turning into a major defeat; yet it generated all kinds of rumours, which caused panic not just in Rome, but also in the camp at Veii. There the soldiers were with difficulty prevented from fleeing when the rumours spread through the camp that the commanders and army had been slain and that the victorious Capenates and Falisci, and all the soldiers in Etruria, were not far off. At Rome people believed the situation was even more chaotic: that the camp at Veii was already under attack, that some enemy forces were already headed for the city prepared to attack. People rushed out onto the walls, while the matrons, whom fear for the nation had brought forth from their homes, supplicated the gods, asking that if the sacred rites had been correctly repeated, if the prodigies properly expiated, they ward off destruction from the houses, temples, and walls of Rome and turn the panic upon Veii.

19. The games and the Latin festival had now been repeated, the water now let from the Alban lake into the land below, and the fates began their assault upon Veii. Then a leader fated to destroy that city and save his country, Marcus Furius Camillus, was appointed dictator, naming Publius Cornelius Scipio in turn as master of the horse. Everything suddenly changed with the change of commander: men's hopes were different, their spirits different—even the fortune of Rome herself seemed to have been transformed. As his first step he punished according to military code those who had fled in panic from Veii, showing that it was not the enemy the soldiers had most to fear. Then, having fixed a day for enlistment, he used the interval to make a personal trip to Veii to raise the soldiers' morale. From there he returned to Rome to enrol the new army, from which no one pleaded to be excused. Even young foreigners from the Latin and Hernici promised their help and came to join him. After thanking them before the senate and completing all essential preparations for the war, the dictator vowed, in accordance with a decree of the

senate, to celebrate the Great Games after Veii had been captured
and to rebuild and dedicate the temple to Mater Matuta, which had
previously been dedicated by the king Servius Tullius.*

Setting out with his army from the city, which looked to the
outcome with greater suspense than confidence, he first engaged the
Falisci and Capenates in the territory of Nepe. Good fortune, as she
usually does, followed upon thorough planning and strategy. Camillus
not only routed the enemy in battle but drove them from their camp
as well, getting possession of much booty, of which the largest part
was turned over to the quaestor, the little that was left to the soldiers. From there the army was led to Veii, where the forts were
built so as to cluster even more tightly together; to construct them
he employed the soldiers who previously had been used to making
rash forays against the enemy between the city walls and Roman
rampart; he ordered them henceforth to engage in no fighting unless
he so commanded. Of all the army's constructions by far the greatest and most laborious was a tunnel that was dug from the camp up
to Veii's citadel. To avoid carrying on the project by fits and starts
and exhausting the same group of underground diggers, he divided
the workers into six shifts, one to take over from another in rotation
over a period of six hours. There was no let-up by day or night until
the tunnel had reached the citadel.

20. When the dictator saw that victory was now in his grasp, that
a very wealthy city was on the point of capture and that the plunder
would be greater than in all of Rome's previous wars put together,
he was afraid that in distributing the booty tight-fistedness would
make the soldiers angry or prodigality create resentment among the
senators. So he dispatched a letter to the senate, saying that by the
goodwill of the immortal gods, his own leadership, and soldiers'
tenacity the Roman people would at any moment have Veii in its
power. What did they think should be done about the booty? Two
opinions divided the senate. One was by the aged Publius Licinius,
who tradition says was the first his son called on to speak; he proposed that a proclamation be made to the effect that whoever wanted
to share in the booty should go to the camp at Veii. The other was
by Appius Claudius, who argued that such liberality was unprecedented, extravagant, unfair, and ill-advised. Should the senate decide that it was against religion to put money captured from the
enemy into a treasury depleted by the wars, it was his opinion that

it be designated as a fund from which to pay the soldiers, thereby easing the burden on the plebs of paying tribute. Every household would benefit equally from such a boon and it would keep the predatory hands of the idle urban mob from grabbing the prizes won by Rome's gallant fighters, since it usually happens that those who seek to share in toil and danger hang back when seeking to profit from it. Licinius replied that this revenue would forever be the source of suspicion and hatred, the cause of charges made before the plebs, which in turn would engender political turmoil and revolutionary laws. It was therefore preferable to mollify the plebs by this boon, to succour those ground down and squeezed dry by the payment of tribute over so many years, and to enable those whom this long war had virtually brought to the threshold of old age to enjoy immediately the booty realized in that war. People would be more thankful and happier if each man could return home with what he had personally taken from the enemy rather than if he had got many times its value by the determination of someone else. The dictator himself would escape resentment and the charges that would arise from that resentment, for this was the reason he had left the matter in the hands of the senate; that body should now in turn leave it to the people, whereby each man would have what the chances of war brought to hand. It seemed safer to the senate to select the course of action that would increase the senate's popularity. Accordingly, it issued a decree that those who wanted to share in the booty should set out for the dictator's camp at Veii.

21. A huge mob set out and filled the camp. After the dictator had taken the auspices he came forward and ordered his soldiers to take up arms. He then made this prayer: 'Under your guidance, Pythian Apollo, and quickened by your divine power, I go now to destroy the city of Veii, and I vow a tenth of the booty to you. And at the same time I beseech you, Queen Juno, who are for the present patron divinity of Veii, to follow us in victory to Rome, now our home and soon to be yours, where a temple worthy of your majesty will await to receive you.' After finishing this prayer, he attacked the city on all sides, using the huge number of men at his disposal, in an effort to disguise the peril from the tunnel, which grew greater with every passing moment. The Veientes, unaware that they had by now been given up as lost by their own seers and by the oracles from across the sea, unaware that the gods had been invited to share in

the booty and still others had been called forth from their city
through vows of the enemy to house them in a new temple in his
own land, not knowing that this day was their last nor having the
slightest inkling that a tunnel had undermined their walls and the
citadel was filling up with the enemy at that very moment, rushed
out on the walls in arms, each man for himself, wondering why the
Romans, who had not moved from their sentry posts for many days
were now heedlessly attacking the walls as if suddenly struck mad.

At this point in the tale, the following episode is told: while the
king of Veii was sacrificing, a remark of a seer to the effect that
victory would lay with him who cut up the entrails of the victim was
heard by the soldiers in the tunnel, who then burst through, snatched
up the entrails and brought them to the dictator. Now, in matters so
ancient, I am satisfied to accept as true what has the appearance of
truth. But this story has more of the miracle-working one sees on
the stage than credibility and is not worth my taking the trouble to
affirm or refute.*

The tunnel, which was full of picked soldiers, suddenly disgorged
these armed men into the temple of Juno on the citadel of Veii.
Some rushed to attack the enemy on the walls from behind, others
tore back the bolts of the gates, still others set afire the buildings
from whose rooftops women and children were throwing down stones
and tiles. The entire city was filled with cries of menace and panic,
intermingled with the wailing of women and children. In an instant
the enemy was everywhere in Veii: those in arms were hurled down
all along the circuit of walls and the gates thrown open, while of the
Romans outside some rushed in, others moved up scaling ladders to
the now deserted walls. Fighting went on everywhere until, after a
great slaughter, resistance began to fade; at this point the dictator
ordered a herald to proclaim that the unarmed were to be spared.
This ended the bloodshed. As the unarmed began to give themselves up, the dictator permitted the soldiers to scatter for booty.
When he saw that the plunder brought before him was considerably
greater in amount and value than he had hoped or anticipated, he is
said to have raised his hands to heaven and prayed that, if the good
fortune of himself and the Roman people seemed excessive to god
or man, it might be in his power to allay such resentment with the
least harm to himself personally and to the Roman public at large.
There is also a tradition that as he turned in making his prayer he

fell, and that those who speculated after the event about what this portended said it anticipated the conviction of Camillus himself and then the capture and devastation of Rome, which occurred a few years later.

The day was spent in slaughtering the enemy and plundering the great riches of Veii. **22.** The next day the dictator sold off the free inhabitants as prisoners of war. Even though this was the only money to be put in the public treasury, the plebs resented it. They gave credit for getting the booty they took home with them not to the commander, who had referred to the senate a matter that was his to decide in order to gain backing for his own tight-fistedness, or to the senate, but to the Licinian family, whose son had brought the matter before the senate and whose father had proposed the most popular motion.

After the things belonging to men had been carried from Veii, they began the removal of the dedications to the gods and of the gods themselves, acting more like worshippers than despoilers. For a select group of young men picked from the army as a whole, who had been assigned to transport Queen Juno to Rome, having ritually bathed and clothed in white, entered her temple in awe, at first hesitantly stretching forth their hands in reverence, because in Etruscan ritual only a priest from a particular clan was accustomed to touch her statue. Then a certain soldier, either divinely inspired or as a young man's joke, asked 'Would you like to go to Rome, Juno?' At this his companions exclaimed that the goddess had nodded yes; then, to conclude the scene, came this addition: she was heard to say that she was willing. In any event, tradition affirms that she was moved from her place with little effort, being light and easy to carry, as if she were moving with them, and that she was brought without harm to the Aventine to dwell forever, where the vows of the dictator Camillus had summoned her, and where later the same man dedicated the temple to her that he had vowed.

Such was the fall of Veii, the wealthiest city of the Etruscan nation. Proof of her might can be seen in her very overthrow: for ten summers and winters she endured a continuous siege, she inflicted somewhat more damage than she received, and, in the end, even when fate was working her ruin, she was taken by a stratagem and not by force.

23. When the news of Veii's fall was announced at Rome, even though the people had expiated the prodigies and taken account of the Pythian oracle's responses, and on the human level had made the best possible choice in Marcus Furius as commander-in-chief, still, because they had been fighting for so many years with mixed results and had suffered numerous reverses, they were filled with immense joy as if from something unhoped for, and, even before the senate could issue its decree, all the temples were crowded with the matrons of the city giving thanks to the gods. The senate decreed a public thanksgiving for four days, more than for any previous war. Moreover, when the dictator arrived, all ranks of society thronged to greet him in numbers as no man had been honoured before, and his triumph was celebrated on a scale far grander than was customary. He was particularly conspicuous as he entered the city riding on a chariot drawn by white horses, which seemed to place him on a level too high for a citizen or a mortal. People thought it a religious transgression for the dictator to put himself on a footing with Jupiter and the Sun in using these horses:* this was the sole but overriding reason why they were more impressed than pleased by the triumph. Then he contracted for the building of Queen Juno's temple on the Aventine and dedicated another to Mater Matuta; after discharging these religious and secular duties, he resigned the dictatorship.

A debate thereupon began about the gift to Apollo. When Camillus said he had vowed a tenth part of the booty and the pontiffs declared that the people were under a religious obligation to pay it, it was not easy to see how they could get the people to return the booty so that a tenth part of it could be taken for religious use. In the end they fell back on what seemed the most workable plan: whoever wished to release himself and his house from this religious obligation should make a personal estimate of the booty's value and deposit a tenth part in the public treasury, so that from it an offering made of gold might be made, worthy of the greatness of the temple and the power of the god, and as befitted the dignity of the Roman people. Raising funds in this way further alienated the plebs' feeling toward Camillus. While this was going on envoys from the Volsci and Aequi arrived to treat for peace, which was granted, more to give the state a breathing spell after such a long and exhausting war than because those making the request were deserving.

24. The year following the capture of Veii had six military trib-

unes with consular power: two named Publius Cornelius, Cossus and Scipio, Marcus Valerius Maximus for the second time, Caeso Fabius Ambustus also for the second time, Lucius Furius Medullinus for the fourth, and Quintus Servilius for the third. The Cornelii received by lot the war against the Falisci, Valerius and Servilius the one against Capena. They did not attack or besiege the enemy cities, but ravaged the land and brought back agricultural booty; no fruit-bearing trees and no crops were left standing in the countryside. This disaster brought the people of Capena to heel; peace was granted when they asked for it. War continued against the Falisci.

At Rome in the meantime political unrest continued in different forms. In an effort to allay it there had been a vote to found a colony among the Volsci, for which three thousand Roman citizens were enrolled, and a three-man board created for the purpose had assigned each man three and seven-tenths acres apiece.* A movement began to reject such largess. People thought they had been thrown a sop to divert them from a greater prize: for why had the plebs been banished among the Volsci when the splendid city of Veii and its land were next door? The latter's territory was more extensive than that of Rome, and they exalted the city over Rome, pointing to its site, its great extent, its buildings and neighbourhoods, both public and private. This was in fact the beginning of the well-known proposal to move to Veii, which was even more widely discussed after Rome's capture by the Gauls. What is more, they proposed that Veii be populated partly by plebeians and partly by senators, saying that the Roman people could inhabit two cities in a single commonwealth. The political leadership was so opposed to these ideas that they affirmed they would rather die in the sight of the Roman people than to let such a proposal come to a vote: there was already dissension enough in one city: what would it be like in two? Should one expect a man to prefer a conquered city to his own country, the conqueror, and to permit Veii after its capture to enjoy greater prosperity than when it was safe and sound? Finally, the citizens might, if they chose, leave their fatherland behind, but no force in the world would ever make *them* abandon their fatherland and citizens, or to follow Titus Sicinius to Veii as its founder (for he was the plebeian tribune who proposed the measure), abandoning the deified Romulus, son of a god, father and founder of the city of Rome. 25. During this heated and acrimonious debate (for the senators had attracted some of the plebeian tribunes to their side), the plebs stayed their hands for no other reason than that whenever an uproar arose as the signal to start a riot, the leaders of the senate would present themselves to the mob, bidding it to attack, strike down, and kill them. While the plebs held back from doing violence to these aged and eminent statesmen, shame also blunted their anger in making any further such attempts.

Camillus harangued the people repeatedly throughout the city: it was no wonder that the state had gone mad, when, obligated by a vow, it considered the fulfilment of that obligation as the least of its priorities. He would say nothing of the method of contribution, although it really amounted more to a pittance than a tenth, as each man released himself personally from an obligation while freeing the state as a whole. But his conscience would not let him be silent on the way this tenth was calculated: namely, that the booty in question consisted only of moveable property; there was no consideration of the city and its territory, which were also included in the vow.

The senate viewed the dispute as problematic and so referred it to the pontiffs, who, after interviewing Camillus, decided that a tenth of what had belonged to the people of Veii before the vow was made and had come into the power of the Roman people after the vow, was sacred to Apollo. Thus the city and its territory were part of the estimate. Funds were taken from the treasury and the military tribunes with consular power were directed to purchase gold with this amount. When the money proved insufficient, the matrons met to consult on the matter and as a body promised the gold to the military tribunes; they then brought all their personal jewellery to the treasury. This was as pleasing as anything ever was to the senate. Tradition says that because of the matrons' generosity they were rewarded with permission to use a carriage in connection with religious rites and games as well as wagons on holy and working days.* When the gold received from individuals had been weighed and the amount of moneys owed was deemed paid, the decision was taken to fashion a golden bowl to be deposited in Delphi as a gift to Apollo.

The moment the people were relieved of their religious obligation, the tribunes of the plebs renewed political unrest. They incited the multitude against all the leading men, and above all against Camillus: in making the booty from Veii public property and sacred, he had reduced its value to nothing. They inveighed fiercely against their opponents when they were absent, but in their presence, when they actually appeared before the angry crowd, they held their tongues. And when they realized the issue would carry over into the next year, the people re-elected the same tribunes who had proposed the bill to move to Veii, while the senators likewise suborned those who would veto it. Thus most of the same plebeian tribunes were re-elected.

26. In the election of military tribunes the senators succeeded after a strenuous effort in having Marcus Furius Camillus returned. They said that they wanted a commander in readiness to fight Rome's wars, but they were really seeking someone to oppose tribunician give-away programmes. Elected military tribunes along with Camillus were Lucius Furius Medullinus for the sixth time, Gaius Aemilius, Lucius Valerius Publicola, Spurius Postumius, and Publius Cornelius for the second time.

At the start of the year the tribunes of the plebs made no move until Marcus Furius Camillus had set out against the Falisci, to whom this war had been entrusted. In putting off their designs, they lost momentum, while Camillus, whom they feared most as an opponent, increased his reputation in fighting the Falisci. For when the enemy initially stayed behind their walls, thinking this the safest course, Camillus devastated their land and burned their farm buildings, which forced them to come out of the city. But fear prevented them from going very far; they fixed their camp about a mile from the town, relying solely on the safety afforded by the difficulty of approach over rough and broken terrain, some access roads being narrow, others up steep inclines. Camillus, however, using a captive from the locale as his guide, broke camp late at night and by dawn showed himself occupying an elevated and more commanding position. The Romans, using a workforce of three divisions, began to fortify the site; the rest of the army stood ready for battle. When the enemy tried to stop these efforts, he worsted them and put them to flight. The Falisci were thereupon filled with such great fear that they fled past their own camp, which was closer, and headed for the city. Many were cut down and wounded before they rushed through the gates in panic; their camp was captured. When the booty was given to the quaestors, the soldiers became very angry but, cowed by their commander's severity, they both hated and admired his worth. Then began a siege of the city and the construction of siegeworks; from time to time as opportunity offered the towns-people attacked the Roman sentry posts and small fights broke out. As time went on success inclined to neither side; in fact, the be-sieged had more food and other supplies from stores collected beforehand than did the besiegers. It seemed that the war might last as long as the one at Veii, had not fortune presented the Roman commander at once with an opportunity to demonstrate his ac-knowledged worth as a military man and with an early victory.

27. There was a custom among the Falisci for young boys to have the same man as their teacher and companion,* and also for a large number of children to be entrusted to the care of a single individual, which still exists in present-day Greece. A man who was seen to excel in learning was chosen, as is usually the case, to instruct the offspring of the leading citizens. In peacetime it had been his habit to bring the children outside the city for games and exercise, a custom he continued even in wartime, sometimes taking them a shorter distance from the gate, sometimes longer. One day he saw his chance: by telling stories and engaging them in play, he strayed further away than usual, ultimately bringing them to the outposts of the enemy and from there to Camillus at his headquarters. There he capped this monstrous deed with a more monstrous boast: he had delivered Falerii into the Romans' hands by putting these children in their power, for their parents were the heads of government there. On hearing this, Camillus made the following reply: 'A villain yourself, you have come with a villainous gift to a people and a commander unlike yourself. We are not allied with the Falisci by any pact that man has made but by a law of nature existing now and always, which has formed a common bond between us. There are laws in warfare, as there are in peace, and we have learned to follow them with as much justice as with bravery. The weapons we hold will not be used against these children, who are spared even when cities are captured, but against men who are themselves in arms and who, neither harmed nor hurt by us, attacked the Roman camp at Veii. You have defeated the Faliscans in the only way you could— by unheard-of treachery. I shall defeat them in the Roman way—by courage, siegeworks, and arms, as I did at Veii.'

Stripped and with his hands tied behind his back, he was given by Camillus to the children to be returned to Falerii; he gave them switches with which to whip the traitor as they drove him back to

the city. The people at first rushed to catch sight of the spectacle;
then the magistrates convened the senate to discuss the strange turn
of events. Such a change of heart came over the Falisci that the
entire population, who in their savage hatred and anger had a short
time before practically preferred the destruction of Veii to the peace
granted Capena, now demanded peace. Rome's fair dealing and
the commander's just behaviour were lauded in forum and senate-
house; with everyone in agreement, envoys set out to Camillus
in camp and from there, with Camillus' permission, to the senate
in Rome in order to effect the surrender of Falerii. Introduced into
the senate, they are said to have spoken as follows: 'Senators, defeated by you and your commander in a victory that neither god
nor man can grudge, we surrender ourselves to you, in the belief
that we will do better living under your rule than our own laws.
Nothing could do greater credit to a victor. The conclusion of this
war teaches mankind two salutary lessons: you preferred fair dealing
rather than taking advantage of the victory offered you, while we,
under the stimulus of this fair dealing, have presented you with that
victory. We are in your power: our gates are open; send those who
will take arms, hostages, and the city itself. You will not regret our
fidelity nor we your rule.' Thanks were given to Camillus both by
the enemy and by the citizens. The Falisci were ordered to supply
money to pay the soldiers for the year, so that the Roman people
would not be subject to tribute. After peace had been granted, the
army was brought back to Rome.

28. Because Camillus had overcome the enemy with justice and
honour, his return to the city was greeted with much greater praise
than when white horses had pulled his chariot through the city in
the celebration of his triumph. Although he made no mention of his
vow, the senate's respect for his reticence was such that he was
immediately released from it. The envoys chosen to take the golden
bowl as a gift to Apollo in Delphi were Lucius Valerius, Lucius
Sergius, and Aulus Manlius. They set out in a single warship, but
were captured not far from the Sicilian strait by pirates from Lipara
and taken to their city. This island nation customarily divided up
booty that had been seized as if privateering were a state-run enterprise. By chance a certain Timasitheus was the highest magistrate
that year, a man more like the Romans than his own people. His
respect for the status of the envoys, their gift, the god to whom it

was being sent, and the reason for sending it filled the people, who usually model themselves on their rulers, with a similar attachment to proper religious feeling. He entertained the envoys as guest-friends, gave them an escort of ships for their journey to Delphi, and brought them back safely to Rome. The senate issued a decree making him a guest-friend and presented him with gifts from the nation.

In the same year fighting against the Aequi was carried on with mixed success, so much so that neither the armies nor the people back in Rome could decide whether they had won or lost. The Roman commanders were the military tribunes Gaius Aemilius and Spurius Postumius. At first they acted jointly; then, when the enemy had been routed, it was decided Aemilius should garrison Verrugo, while Postumius should devastate its territory. As the latter was leaving the scene of a successful engagement in a disorganized and negligent manner, the Aequi attacked, threw them into a panic, and drove them into the nearest hills. From there fear even spread to the other force at Verrugo. After gathering his men in a safe spot, Postumius called them together and upbraided them for being afraid and running away, saying that they had been put to flight by an enemy notorious for spinelessness and turning tail. The whole army cried out that he was right in what he said, admitting its disgrace but promising to set things right, and asserting that the enemy's elation would not be long-lived. They demanded he lead them at once to the enemy camp (it could be seen in the plain below) and said that if they did not capture it before nightfall he could punish them in any way he liked. After praising them, he gave orders that they take food and rest and be ready at the fourth watch.

Meanwhile, the enemy, to prevent the Romans from fleeing by night from the hill they occupied, had cut them off from the road that led to Verrugo. Battle was joined before the sun rose—yet the moon shone all night, and visibility was as good as if it had been daytime. But the uproar reached Verrugo, where it was believed the Roman camp was under attack; so terror-stricken were the troops that, although Aemilius tried to hold them back and pleaded with them, they fled in disorganized groups to Tusculum. From there the rumour reached Rome that Postumius and his army had been wiped out. When daylight revealed that their fear of being ambushed by a widely pursuing enemy was baseless, Postumius rode past the battleline, reminding his men of their promises; he filled them with such enthusiasm that from that point on the Aequi could not withstand their assault. Then came the slaughter of those fleeing, which, as happens when soldiers act more in anger than with valour, wiped the enemy out. A laurelled letter from Postumius reached Rome, still in a baseless panic because of the grim report from Tusculum, saying that victory lay with the Roman people and that the army of the Aequi had been destroyed.

29. Because the plebeian tribunes continued to agitate for their bill to migrate to Veii, the plebs aimed to re-elect the bill's sponsors and the senators to retain in office those who would veto it. But the plebs prevailed; the senators avenged their loss by decreeing that consuls be elected, a magistracy hateful to the plebs. And so after a lapse of fifteen years consuls entered office; they were Lucius Lucretius Flavus and Servius Sulpicius Camerinus. At the start of the year there was no tribune willing to cast his veto; so the tribunes of the plebs combined in an effort to pass the law, while the consuls resisted with equal vigour in opposing it.

At this juncture, as the entire state was absorbed in this one issue, the Aequi took by storm Vitellia,* a Roman colony in their territory. Most of the colonists fled in safety to Rome because the capture of the town by treachery at night-time permitted escape through the far side of the city. The consul Lucius Lucretius was chosen to deal with the situation. He set out with his army and defeated the enemy in a pitched battle, but returned to Rome in victory to be confronted by a considerably greater fight. An indictment was brought against Aulus Verginius and Quintus Pomponius, tribunes in the last two years, whom the senators felt they must unite to defend in order to preserve the honour of their body; for no charge concerning their personal conduct or the conduct of their magistracy was brought except that, to please the senators, they had vetoed the tribunes' bill. Nevertheless, plebeian anger prevailed over senatorial influence, and a terrible precedent was set when the innocent men were fined ten thousand pounds of heavy bronze apiece. This outraged the senators. Camillus openly charged the plebs with wrongdoing, for in turning against their own by rendering this misguided verdict they failed to understand they had subverted the tribunician veto and that with the overthrow of the veto they had destroyed the tribunes' power; for they were deceived in expecting that the senators would put up with a tribunate that had run amok. If tribunician excess could not be curbed through tribunician help, the senators would discover another weapon. He also berated the consuls because without protest they had permitted those tribunes who had followed the senate's will to be disappointed in the expectation that the state would protect them.

By haranguing the people in this fashion, he increased their hostility with each passing day. 30. Nor did he refrain from urging the senate to oppose the law. On the day it was to be voted on, he said, their only thought on entering the forum should be that this was a fight for their altars and hearths, for the temples of the gods, for the very soil that had given them birth. As for himself, if in this fight for his country it were right for him to be concerned with his own glory, it would be a fine thing indeed if the city he had captured were to be filled with people, if every day he could enjoy a reminder of his own glory and have the city featured in his triumph before his very eyes,* if everyone walked in the footsteps of his fame. But he thought it wrong that a city deserted and abandoned by the immortal gods should be repopulated, that the Roman people should dwell on captive soil and exchange their victorious fatherland for a city defeated.

These exhortations roused the leading men to action; senators, old and young, entered the forum in a body as the law was to be voted on. They then scattered, each going to his own tribe, buttonholing fellow members and launching into a tearful entreaty not to abandon their country for which they and their fathers had fought with such bravery and success; they pointed to the Capitol, the temple of Vesta, and the other temples of the gods round about, and begged them not to drive the Roman people from their native soil and tutelary deities into the land of the enemy as exiles and expatriates, and so bring it about that it would have been better for Veii not to have been captured if this meant Rome would not be abandoned. Because they were using entreaties rather than force and in these entreaties frequently mentioned the gods, most people's religious feelings were touched, and the bill was rejected by one more tribe than those who voted for it. This victory so delighted the senators that on the next day, when the consuls brought the matter before them, they issued a decree that the lands of Veii be divided among the plebs in parcels of seven acres apiece, not just to the heads of families but to every male child in each household, their aim being to encourage the rearing of children.

31. The plebs were won over by this distribution of land and put up no resistance to holding consular elections. Chosen consuls were Lucius Valerius Potitus and Marcus Manlius, who later received the cognomen Capitolinus. These consuls celebrated the Great Games that the dictator Marcus Furius had vowed in the war with Veii. In the same year the temple of Queen Juno, vowed by this same dictator in this same war, was dedicated, and tradition says the ceremony was attended with great enthusiasm by the married women.

A minor war was fought against the Aequi at Algidus, for the enemy scattered in flight almost before battle was joined. A triumph was decreed to Valerius because he had shown greater persistence in slaughtering them as they fled; Manlius was allowed to enter the city in an ovation.* In the same year a new war broke out with the people of Volsinii;* but troops could not be mustered because of famine and pestilence in Roman territory from excessive heat and lack of rain. Accordingly, the Volsinienses, joined by the Sapienates and arrogantly confident, even invaded the Roman countryside; war was then voted against the two peoples.

Gaius Iulius, the censor, died; in his place Marcus Cornelius was chosen, which later was viewed as a religious transgression because Rome was captured in this *lustrum*.* Thereafter no censor who died in office has ever been replaced. The consuls, moreover, were stricken by the sickness, and it was decided that the auspices be renewed through an interregnum.* And so, after the consuls resigned their office in accordance with a decree of the senate, Marcus Furius Camillus was made interrex; he was succeeded first by Publius Cornelius Scipio and then by Lucius Valerius Potitus. The latter presided over the election of six military tribunes with consular power, the aim being that if even some should fall ill, the state would still have enough magistrates at the helm.

32. The following entered office on 1 July: Lucius Lucretius, Servius Sulpicius, Marcus Aemilius, Lucius Furius Medullinus for the seventh time, Agrippa Furius, and Gaius Aemilius for the second. Of these, the war against Volsinii fell to Lucius Lucretius and Gaius Aemilius, that against the Sapienates to Agrippa Furius and Servius Sulpicius. The first conflict was with Volsinii. A huge number of the enemy took part, but the war was not difficult to fight. The battleline gave way at the first clash; eight thousand armed men were put to flight and cut off by the cavalry; they then laid down

their arms and surrendered unconditionally. When the Sapienates heard of the result they did not venture to engage in battle, but stayed behind their walls under arms. The Romans gathered booty everywhere in the territory of the Sapienates and Volsinii because no one opposed them; finally, with Volsinii exhausted from the war, a twenty-year truce was granted the city on the condition that it return the property it had taken from Roman territory and furnish the army's pay for that year.

In that same year Marcus Caedicius, a plebeian, reported to the tribunes that in New Street, where the shrine now stands above the temple of Vesta,* he had heard in the dead of night a voice that was more than human; it bade him tell the magistrates that the Gauls were coming. This warning was disregarded, as happens when the author is of humble status, and also because the Gauls were a people who were far off and therefore quite unknown. Not only were the warnings of the gods disregarded, as destiny began to run her course, but the only human that could save the city, Marcus Furius, was driven out. For he was indicted by Lucius Apuleius, tribune of the plebs, because of the way he had handled the booty at Veii. In these same days he had also lost a young son and, when he summoned to his house his clients and tribe members, who constituted a sizeable portion of the plebs, and asked what their feelings were in the matter, they told him that they would contribute as much as needed to pay his fine, but could not vote to acquit him. So he went into exile, but not before he prayed to the immortal gods that, if they judged him innocent of the injustice that had befallen him, they make his ungrateful country want him back at the first opportunity. In his absence he was fined fifteen thousand pounds of heavy bronze.

33. After Rome had expelled the one citizen whose presence would, if anything in this life is certain, have prevented her capture, and with the fateful disaster bearing down upon the city, envoys from Clusium came seeking aid against the Gauls. Tradition says that these peoples, attracted by the produce and especially by the wine, which was an indulgence then new to them, had crossed the Alps and had taken over lands previously occupied by the Etruscans; that Arruns of Clusium had exported wine into Gaul with the express purpose of encouraging them to come, in anger that Lucumo, whose guardian he was, had committed adultery with his wife and knowing that Lucumo was a most influential young man whom he could not

punish without outside help; and that Arruns was the one who led
them over the Alps and exhorted them to attack Clusium. Now I do
not dispute that Arruns or some other man from Clusium brought
the Gauls to that city. But historians are in general agreement that
the Gauls who fought at Clusium were not the first to cross the
Alps. Indeed, the Gauls had come into Italy two hundred years
before they attacked Clusium and before they captured Rome, nor
were the people of Clusium the first Etruscans the Gallic armies
attacked, for they had fought many times before with those who
lived between the Apennines and the Alps.

Prior to Roman rule the power of the Etruscans extended far over
land and sea. The names given to the upper and lower seas that
surround Italy like an island are proof of how powerful they were,
for the peoples of Italy call one the Tuscan Sea from the nation as
a whole, the other the Atriatic from Atria, an Etruscan colony, while
the Greeks call them the Tyrrhenian and Adriatic. And they populated the lands adjacent to both seas, founding twelve cities in each
area, first settling the one on the near side of the Apennines facing
the lower sea and later the one on the far side of the Apennines,
sending out as many colonies as there were mother cities; these
colonies occupied the entire area across the Po with the exception of
the Veneti, who inhabit a corner of the Adriatic. They were undoubtedly also the founders of the Alpine peoples, especially the
Raeti, whose location subsequently made them quite uncivilized,
retaining nothing save their language, although that too became
debased.

34. This is what we are told about the crossing of the Gauls into
Italy: during the reign of Tarquinius Priscus at Rome, the chief
power among the Celts, whose country comprises a third of Gaul,
lay with the Bituriges, who used to supply the Celtic nation with its
king. At that time his name was Ambigatus, pre-eminent for courage and the blessings of good fortune in private life and as a public
figure. The population was so large and the soil so fertile that it
scarcely seemed possible to keep such large numbers under control.
When Ambigatus grew old and wished to unburden his kingdom of
so many people, he announced that he would send forth Bellovesus
and Segovesus, the adventurous sons of his sister, to settle in those
lands the gods gave them by augury; they were instructed to take as
many men as they liked so that none might withstand their coming.

To Segovesus the Hercynian forests then fell by lot;* to Bellovesus the gods gave the more promising road to Italy. He took the surplus population of the Celtic tribes: from the Bituriges, Arverni, Senones, Aedui, Amboni, Carnutes, and Aulerci.* Setting out with a great force of infantry and cavalry he came to the Tricastini. There the Alps confronted him. I do not wonder that they appeared impassable, since no one had as yet crossed them, as far back as memory goes, unless one chooses to believe in the fables concerning Hercules' exploits. The high mountains held the Gauls back, penned up, so to speak, and they looked for a route that would lead over the summits that touched the sky to another world beyond. A religious scruple also restrained them, when they heard that strangers seeking a place to settle were under attack by the tribe of the Salvi. These were the people of Massilia, who had come by ship from Phocaea.* This the Gauls thought an omen of their own aspirations, and so they gave help in order that the Massiliotes might, without interference by the Salvi, fortify the site they had first occupied on landing.

They themselves then passed through the Taurini and crossed the passes of the Julian Alps. After defeating the Etruscans in battle not far from the Ticinus River and on hearing that the land which they now occupied belonged to the Insubres, the same name as a tribe in the territory of the Aedui, they took this as an omen and founded a city, naming it Mediolanium.* 35. Then another band consisting of Cenomani, under the leadership of Elitovius, using the same pass as their predecessors and with the encouragement of Bellovesus, crossed the Alps and occupied the sites where the cities of Brixia and Verona now stand. The Libui were the next settlers, followed by the Salvi, in the territory around the Ticinus River near the ancient people of the Laevi Ligures. Then came the Boii and Lingones, who crossed over the Poenine Pass.* By this time, holding everything between the Po and the Alps, they crossed the Po by rafts, driving out not only the Etruscans but even the Umbri, but stopping on the far side of the Apennines. The Senones were the latest to arrive, settling in the territory between the Utens and Aesis rivers.* I find it was this tribe that came to Clusium and then to Rome, but it is uncertain whether they were alone or were helped by all the Gallic peoples of the Cisalpine region.

The people of Clusium were thoroughly frightened by the new war they faced, particularly the large numbers of the foe, their strange appearance, and the kind of weapons they used—and they had heard of the frequent defeats suffered by the Etruscans living on both sides of the Po. And so, although they enjoyed no right of alliance or friendship with the Romans (except that they had not defended their kinsmen at Veii against the Romans), they sent envoys to Rome to seek help from the senate. They received no direct aid, but three envoys, the sons of Marcus Fabius Ambustus, were dispatched, who were instructed to urge the Gauls in the name of the senate and the Roman people not to attack the allies and friends of the Roman people, by whom they had not been injured; further, the Romans would be bound to come to their defence if the situation required; but it seemed better not to resort to arms, if this was possible, and as a new people to make the acquaintance of the Gauls in peace rather than in war.

36. It would have been a peaceable embassy had not the bellicose envoys behaved more like Gauls than Romans. After delivering their message in a meeting of the Gauls, they received the following response: although they were now learning of Rome for the first time, they were yet ready to believe that those whom the people of Clusium had called on in their hour of need were brave men; and because the Romans preferred to defend their allies against themselves by sending an embassy than resorting to arms, they would assuredly not reject the peace that was offered—provided that the people of Clusium ceded a part of their territory to the Gauls, who were in need of land, which the people of Clusium possessed in greater quantity than they could cultivate. Otherwise a peaceful solution was not possible. Furthermore, they wished to receive a response while the Romans were present and, should the land be denied them, they would fight in the presence of these same Romans, who could then report back how much the Gauls surpassed all other mortals in martial prowess. When the Romans asked what right they had to demand land belonging to others or to threaten war, and what business the Gauls had in Etruria in the first place, they received the menacing reply that right consisted in the weapons they carried and that all things belonged to those who had the courage to use them. And so, with feelings running high on both sides, they rushed to arms and battle was joined.

There the envoys took up arms, contrary to the law of nations, and the fates began to bring down ruin on the city of Rome. Nor could what they did escape notice, since three of the noblest and bravest young Romans were fighting in the front ranks of the Etruscans, so conspicuous was the valour of the strangers. What is more, Quintus Fabius, riding far forward of the battleline, killed the Gallic commander by stabbing his lance through his side as he was charging ferociously into the very standards of the Etruscans. The Gauls recognized him as he gathered the spoils, and word was passed from one end of the battleline to the other that the envoy was the one responsible. Their anger against Clusium vanished; sounding the trumpet for retreat, they turned their menace upon the Romans. Some thought they should march on Rome at once, but the older men persuaded them first to dispatch envoys to complain of the injuries and demand that the Fabii be bound over to them, in accordance with the law of nations. After the Gallic envoys had set forth their complaints as instructed, the senators viewed what the Fabii had done with disapproval and thought the barbarians' demands were just, but favouritism kept them from issuing a decree embodying their true sentiments in opposition to men of such great nobility and influence. And so, in order that the blame for a possible defeat in a war with the Gauls not lay with themselves, they referred the decision concerning the Gauls' demands to the people, among whom wealth and popularity had so much more effect that those whose punishment they were asked to decide were elected military tribunes with consular power for the coming year. When the Gallic envoys heard this, they reacted with justifiable anger. Openly threatening war, they returned to their own people. Elected military tribunes along with the three Fabii were Quintus Sulpicius Longus, Quintus Servilius for the fourth time, and Publius Cornelius Maluginensis.

37. In face of the looming catastrophe—so completely does fortune blind us mortals when she wants to remove all obstacles to her growing power—the state that against Fidenae, Veii, and other nearby peoples named in many a crisis a dictator as a last resource looked on this occasion to no extraordinary command or safeguard, although they were facing an enemy hitherto unseen and unheard-of—one that had stirred up war from the ocean and the ends of the earth. The tribunes whose reckless behaviour had ignited the war were the heads of state; in conducting the levy they were no more thorough than if this had been an ordinary conflict, even making

light of the rumoured gravity of the danger. In the meantime the
Gauls, after hearing that those who had violated man's unwritten
laws had been honoured by election to office and their embassy
mocked, and beside themselves with anger (to which the Gauls are
uncontrollably prone), immediately pulled up their standards and
surged forward in a rapid order. In response to the tumult caused by
their swift advance, terrified cities rushed to arms and the countryfolk
fled, but the Gauls signified by their shouting wherever they went
that their destination was Rome, their cavalry and infantry taking up
a vast expanse, as they spread out far and wide. Even though their
approach was known through rumours and reported by messengers
from Clusium and other places, Rome was thunderstruck by the
swiftness with which they moved, which is shown both by the haste
in mustering the army, as if it were meeting a spur-of-the-moment
emergency, and the difficulty of getting any further than the eleventh milestone, where the Allia, a river descending steeply from the
mountains above Crustumerium, joins the Tiber not far from the
main road. The enemy filled the entire place, in front and on every
side, all the while making horrifying sounds, with menacing chants
and all kinds of noise, for the Gauls by nature are fond of such
empty bravado.

38. There the military tribunes drew up the battleline without
first fixing their camp, without building a rampart behind which
they might find refuge, paying no heed to the gods much less to the
mortals they faced, and without taking the auspices or offering sacrifice. They extended the two wings to prevent being surrounded by
the huge number of the enemy, but were none the less unable to
match their front line with that of the enemy, even though extending the wings caused the centre to be weak and difficult to hold
together. On their right was a slight rise of ground, where they
decided to station some reserve forces, which proved to be the place
where the fear and flight began and which was the sole refuge for
those who fled. For Brennus, the Gallic chieftain, fearing a stratagem, especially in view of the paucity of the enemy, and suspecting
that the high ground had been occupied for just this purpose and
that as the Gauls were making a frontal attack on the Roman legions
the reserves would attack his rear and flank, moved against these
forces in order to drive them from their position, having no doubt
that his numerically superior army would have an easy victory on

level ground. And so the barbarians were blessed not only by fortune but also by foresighted leadership.

On the other side no one behaved like a Roman, not the commanders, not the troops. Fear and flight filled their hearts, together with such utter thoughtlessness that most of them fled to the enemy city of Veii, although the Tiber stood in their way, rather than taking the direct route to Rome, to their wives and children. For a brief time the reserves found protection in their position; as for the rest of the army, as soon as the Gauls' battle-cry was heard those nearest on the flanks and those furthest away at the rear ran from this enemy they had barely seen, without even trying to fight or to raise a battle-cry of their own, without having suffered a scratch or having even been touched. Men were not killed as they fought, but from behind as they struggled through their own men who were blocking their flight. A great slaughter took place along the bank of the Tiber, where the entire left wing had fled after throwing down their arms, and many were swallowed up in the swirling waters, not knowing how to swim or too weak to make the attempt, weighed down by their breastplates and other protective gear. Yet most fled safely to Veii, from where they failed to send men to Rome to defend the city or even news of their defeat. All those on the right wing, who were furthest from the river and closer to the mountains, headed for Rome, where they rushed to the citadel without even bothering to close the city gates behind them.

39. Their sudden victory seemed to the Gauls like a miracle, virtually paralysing them. At first they stood rooted in shock, as if not comprehending what had happened; their next fear was that this was a trap; they then turned to gathering the spoils of the slain and piled up the arms in heaps, as is their custom; at last, with the enemy nowhere in sight, the army moved forward and reached Rome a little before sunset. When the cavalry that had been sent ahead to reconnoitre reported that the gates had not been closed, no sentinels were stationed before the gates, and no armed men were to be seen on the walls, they regarded this as another miracle, much like the first, and were brought up short. Fearful of the darkness and not knowing the layout of the city, they settled down between Rome and the Anio River, after sending scouts around the walls and the other gates to find out what the enemy was doing to meet this desperate crisis.

Those in the city, because most of the army had found refuge in Veii rather than in Rome, believed that only those who had fled to the city had survived. All the living and dead were mourned alike, and virtually the whole city was filled with the sounds of lamentation. Private grief was then swallowed up in fear for the nation when they learned that the enemy was at hand; soon the howls and cacophonous cries of the barbarians as they moved in groups around the walls were heard. Throughout the whole time apprehension held them in its grip, and lasted until the sun rose the next day, so much so that they expected to be attacked at any moment: at the Gauls' first approach, when they reached the city—otherwise they would have remained at the Allia; then at sunset, because little daylight remained—surely they would attack before it grew dark; then in the darkness itself—Rome's panic would be greater under the cover of night. Finally, with dawn approaching they were beside themselves with fear, and close upon this fear came what they were dreading: the enemy's standards were seen moving through the gates.

Yet a complete change had come over the city during the night and in the course of the following day: the Romans were not the same as those who had fled in such panic at the Allia. For when they saw no hope of defending the city with the small force on hand, they took the following decisions: the young fighters with their wives and children were to retire to the citadel and Capitol, where food and weapons had been gathered, and from this fortified place they were to defend gods and men, and the very existence of Rome; the flamen and priestesses of Vesta were to take the sacred objects of the nation far from the carnage and the flames, and the cults of the gods were not to be abandoned as long as any survived to perform them. If the citadel and the Capitol, where the gods resided, if the senate, which guided the ship of state, if the youth of military age survived the ruin that threatened the rest of the city, the loss of most of the older people would be bearable, for they would perish in any event, should they remain in the city. And in order to make the mass of plebeians endure their fate with greater equanimity, those seniors who had celebrated triumphs and those who had held the consulship proclaimed they would die along with them and that they, who could not bear arms or defend their country, would not be a burden to those in arms by depriving them of the sustenance they needed to carry on.

40. So did the elders console one another as death approached. Then, turning to the young fighters, they escorted them to the Capitol and citadel, exhorting them to remember that in their hands lay whatever fortune was left the city, victorious in all her wars for three hundred and sixty years. As those upon whom rested all hopes and resource departed from those who had determined not to survive the city's capture, their plight and the sight of it were pitiable indeed, and when the women rushed back and forth in tears, turning now to one group and now the other, asking husbands and sons to what fate they were abandoning them, the final stroke of human misery was realized. Yet when a great many of them followed their relatives into the citadel, no one stood in their way or called out, because it was inhumane to cast out these non-fighters, however much it might have helped the besieged. Another large group consisting mostly of plebeians poured out of the city as if in a continuous stream, because such a small hill could not hold them all and because of the scarcity of food. They made for the Janiculum hill, from which some scattered through the countryside, others to neighbouring cities. There was no one to lead them and no concerted plan, each following his own hopes and his own counsels, having despaired of aid from the state.

Meanwhile the flamen Quirinalis and the Vestal Virgins, with no thought for their personal affairs, debated what they would have to leave behind, for they had not the strength to carry everything, or what hiding place would prove the safest; in the end they decided the best plan was to put them underground, stored in jars in the shrine next to the house of the flamen Quirinalis, where now it is sacrilege to spit. They divided up the remainder among themselves and took the road over the bridge of wooden piles that leads to the Janiculum.* Lucius Albinius, a plebeian, saw them as they began their ascent. He was moving along in a wagon with his wife and children, part of the crowd of non-combatants leaving the city. Preserving even at this moment the respect owed to the gods on the one hand and to men on the other, he regarded it as a sin for the priests of his country to be on foot, carrying the sacred relics of the Roman people, while he and his family were seen riding in their cart. He ordered his wife and children to step down and, putting the virgins and the sacred objects in the wagon, he brought them to Caere, where the priestesses were destined to go.

41. At Rome meanwhile, after everything possible under the circumstances had been done for the defence of the citadel, the throng of elders returned to their homes and awaited the enemy's coming, resolved to die. Those who had held curule magistracies,* wishing to end their days wearing the insignia of their former fortunes, honours, and merit, seated themselves on chairs inlaid with ivory placed in the centre of their homes, clad in their most august raiment, worn when they had escorted the images of the gods in solemn procession or when celebrating a triumph. Some writers affirm that, with Marcus Folius the pontifex maximus dictating the formula, they swore to sacrifice their lives to save their country and the citizens of Rome.*

The Gauls had not been under the pressures of war during the night just ended nor had they at any time been engaged in a battle whose outcome was in doubt, while at present they had no need to use force or violence in taking the city. They entered Rome through the open Colline Gate, neither in anger nor keyed up for battle, and on reaching the forum their eyes looked to the surrounding temples of the gods and to the citadel, which alone seemed prepared to oppose them. They departed the forum after leaving a small protective force in case of attack from the citadel or Capitol, and scattered in search of booty. They met no one in the streets. Some plunged in a body into the nearest buildings, others continued to places far off, as if there they would find houses as yet untouched and full of plunder. But the very solitude made them uneasy; wary of falling into a trap as they wandered about, they returned to the forum and the places near by, and grouped together. There, on finding the houses of the plebeians bolted and the doors of the nobles flung wide, they were almost more hesitant to enter those that were open than those that barred their way. Indeed, they gazed as in veneration at the beings seated in the vestibules of their homes, for their attire and bearing surpassed those of mortal men, and in majesty of countenance and gravity of expression they were most like to deities. They approached them as if they were statues and as they stood there Papirius, one of the elders, is said, when a Gaul touched his beard (all wore full beards in those days), to have struck him with his ivory staff. The Gauls were enraged and a massacre began; the rest were cut down where they sat. After killing the leading statesmen no one was spared. The houses were ransacked, emptied, set afire.

42. The fire on the first day did not, however, spread far or wide, which is unusual in a captured city. Perhaps not everyone was bent on destroying the city, or perhaps the Gallic leaders had fixed on a policy of starting selected fires to frighten the besieged into surrendering out of concern for their personal property and of not burning all the buildings so that what remained could be used as a bargaining tool to bring their enemies to heel. As the Romans looked down from the citadel and beheld their city filled with the enemy and all the streets busy with their comings and goings, and as successive disasters appeared now in one quarter, now in another, they were unable not just to think through what was going on but even to hold their wits together from the assault on their eyes and ears. On every side came the uproar made by the enemy, the cries of women and children, the crackling of the flames, the crash of falling buildings. Appalled and distracted, their minds, heads, and eyes turned in all directions, as if fortune had placed them there to witness the spectacle of their dying country and had left them to fight not for anything they owned but for their lives alone. More to be pitied than any of those who have suffered siege in the past, they were cut off from their country and saw all that they possessed in the hands of the enemy.

The night that followed this terrible day proved equally agonizing. Dawn succeeded unquiet night and no moment went by in which some new disaster was not before their eyes. Yet, though afflicted and weighed down by great misfortune, they were not so crushed that, even if everything they saw was levelled by fire and collapsing in ruin, they were unprepared to defend the Capitol courageously, however small it was, however ill-provided, the sole remaining bastion of liberty. In the end, as if inured to the evils that were piling up day after day, they no longer thought or cared about what they owned, looking to the weapons and swords in their right hands as representing their only remaining hope.

43. The Gauls, too, who for the past few days had been waging a fruitless war upon the buildings of the city, when they saw that nothing was left amid the burned-out ruins save an enemy in arms, and that he had not been cowed at all by the destruction they had wrought and was not about to surrender without fighting, decided to make an all-out effort to capture the citadel in a direct assault. At first light, on a given signal, the forum was filled with the assembled horde, and after giving their war-cry and raising their shields over their heads, they began to ascend in close formation. The Romans reacted without rashness, without fear. They reinforced the guardposts at all the approaches, and wherever they saw the enemy's standards being directed, there they concentrated their forces, allowing the enemy to move ever upward unopposed, because the higher up the steep incline they got, the easier they could be repulsed. When the Gauls were about half-way up, the Romans counter-attacked and, as they rushed down from their higher position, their very momentum routed the Gauls, tumbling them to their deaths down the cliff. Thereafter the enemy never made an attempt to mount a direct assault, either in groups or all together. And so, giving up hope of taking the place by frontal attack, they got ready to mount a siege. Up to that time they had given no thought to one; moreover, what foodstuffs had been in the city the fire had destroyed, while all the produce in the countryside had been quickly gathered during this time and taken to Veii. Accordingly, they divided their army, one part to plunder peoples near by, the other to besiege the citadel, with those ravaging the countryside supplying the food for the besiegers.

As the Gauls set out from the city, Fortune herself brought them to Ardea to learn first-hand the nature of Roman valour. Camillus was in exile there, saddened more by the fortune that had befallen his native city than by his own, but feeling old and useless, railing against gods and men, indignant, and wondering where those men were who had captured Veii and Falerii under his command, men whose courage had always surpassed their luck. Suddenly came the news that the Gallic army was approaching and that the people of Ardea had gathered in fear to decide how to respond. Hitherto he had not attended their meetings, but now, like one divinely inspired, he entered the assembly and spoke as follows. **44.** 'Men of Ardea, old friends in the past and now my fellow citizens—for so your kindness and my hapless fortune would have it—let none of you think that I stand here before you unmindful of my status; but the present situation and the danger that faces us all requires each man to help in whatever way he can in this fearful crisis. And when might I demonstrate my appreciation for the great kindness you have shown me, if I hold back now? How else might I be of use to you, if not in war? Because of this ability I stood secure in my native city until, undefeated in war, I was driven out in peacetime by ungrateful citizens. Yet, men of Ardea, fortune has given you the opportunity to show your thanks to the Roman people for the great services they have done you, which you yourselves remember—for those conscious of their debts need no chiding—as well as the opportunity to win renown in defeating a common enemy, who approaches in undisciplined force. This is a people to whom nature has given big bodies and much bravado—both unreliable: every time they fight the terror they cause is greater than their real strength. Rome's capture is proof of this. They seized a city whose gates were open. From the citadel and Capitol a small group drove them back. Now, tired of the siege they mounted, they have wandered off to pillage the countryside. They stuff themselves with food and gulp down wine and, when darkness falls, lie down like cattle everywhere along the river banks, taking no steps to protect themselves, posting no guards or sentinels, even more careless than usual because of their successes. If you want to defend these walls, if you do not want everything here to fall into the hands of the Gauls, I urge you to take up your weapons at the first watch, to follow me in force as we go forth—not to battle but to butchery. If I do not give them to you like so many lambs for the slaughter, I am ready to suffer the same fate at Ardea that I did in Rome.'

45. Friend and foe alike considered no contemporary the equal of Camillus in warfare. After the assembly had broken up, they took rest and refreshment, ready to move the instant the signal was given. When it came, they presented themselves before Camillus at the gates. Darkness had descended and it was quiet, and not far from the city they found, as Camillus had predicted, the Gallic camp unguarded and everywhere in disarray. They raised a great cry and burst in. They met no resistance, the slaughter was indiscriminate. The unarmed Gauls were cut down as they slept. But those on the edges of the camp jumped up in panic from where they had bedded down, not knowing what the nature of the attack was or where it was coming from. They fled helter-skelter, some in ignorance running straight toward the enemy. Flight carried a great many to the territory of Antium, where the townspeople sallied forth and cut them off.

In the territory of Veii there was a similar massacre—this time of Etruscans, who were so far from taking pity on Rome, their neigh-

bour for nearly four hundred years and now crushed by an enemy
hitherto unseen and unheard-of, that they raided Roman territory
during this time and, laden with booty, were even contemplating an
attack on Veii and the garrison there, Rome's last hope. The Roman
soldiers had seen them moving through the countryside and then,
gathering into a line of march, driving the cattle they had taken
before them, and they saw their camp being pitched not far from
Veii. At first they felt sorry for themselves, then came resentment,
then anger: were even the Etruscans, whom they had saved from
fighting the Gauls by turning the war upon themselves, aiming to
mock them by capitalizing on their misfortunes? They came close to
losing self-control and staging an immediate attack, but, held back
by the centurion Quintus Caedicius, whom they had chosen as their
commander, they settled down until nightfall. They only lacked a
leader equal to Camillus; in all else events transpired in the same
order and with the same success. In addition, using captives as
guides who had survived the night massacre, they moved against
another band of Etruscans at the Salt Works,* where they surprised
them the following night, creating even greater carnage; they then
returned to Veii, rejoicing in their double victory.

46. At Rome meanwhile the siege was for the most part without
incident and all was quiet, for neither side was inclined to act, while
the Gauls' only concern was to let no one slip past their sentries.
Then suddenly a young Roman drew on himself the admiration of
citizens and enemies alike. It was a regular custom for the Fabian
clan to offer sacrifice on the Quirinal hill. To perform it Gaius
Fabius Dorsuo, with his toga girt up in Gabine fashion* and carrying the implements for sacrifice in his hands, descended from the
Capitol and strode through the midst of the enemy sentries, unmoved by shouts or threats. After reaching the Quirinal he performed the entire ceremony in traditional fashion and then returned
the way he had come, maintaining the same composure of countenance and gait, for he had placed his confidence in the favour of the
gods, whose worship he had not forgotten even under the threat of
death. The Gauls allowed him to rejoin his men on the Capitol
either because they were overawed by this amazing act of courage or
because they, too, were sensible to the claims of religion, for as a
people they are scrupulous in this regard.

At Veii meanwhile not only had morale improved, but numbers

and strength also. It was there that Romans had gravitated who had been wandering about the countryside after the defeat at the Allia or the capture of the city; in addition, volunteers from Latium poured in, wanting to get their share of the booty. The time now seemed ripe to reclaim their country and wrest it from enemy hands; but, though strong, they had no one to lead them. The place itself was a reminder of Camillus, and many of the soldiers who had served under his auspices and successful leadership were present. Moreover, Caedicius declared he would not wait for god or man to put an end to his command, but, mindful of his status, would himself ask for the appointment of a commander-in-chief. It was unanimously agreed that Camillus should be summoned from Ardea, but only after first receiving the blessing of the senate in Rome—so great was the respect for proper procedure, so sensitive were they to the niceties of the situation when their own situation was well-nigh hopeless.

Yet the messenger would have to pass through the enemy sentries at great peril to himself. For this a gallant young man, Pontius Cominius, volunteered his services: buoyed on a strip of cork, he floated down the Tiber to the city. There he landed as close to the Capitol as he could and, climbing up the steep cliff (which was therefore not guarded by the enemy), he gained the top of the hill and, conducted to the magistrates, reported the charge given him by the army. After the senate decreed that the Curiate assembly* should proceed to recall Camillus by order of the people and he then be named dictator at once and that the soldiers should have the commander they wished, he departed, using the same route, and hastened with his message to Veii. Envoys were dispatched to Camillus at Ardea and escorted him immediately to Veii—although I would prefer to think he did not leave Ardea until he had heard the law had actually been passed, for he could not return to Roman territory without the permission of the people nor possess the auspices to lead the army without having been named dictator. The curiate law was accordingly passed, and he was named dictator in his absence.

47. While these things were going on at Veii, at Rome in the meantime the citadel and Capitol were in great peril. For the Gauls, after finding traces left by the messenger from Veii, or perhaps discovering for themselves that the cliff above the shrine of Carmentis could be scaled, sent out on a starry night an unarmed man to

explore the way first, and then, passing up weapons to one another where the going was rough, supported by those below and pushing up others in turn or pulling up their fellows from above as the going required, they emerged on the summit in such silence that not only did the guards fail to hear them, but the dogs as well, animals quick to respond to sounds in the night. But the geese sacred to Juno heard them, which had been untouched despite the severe shortage of food. And this proved Rome's salvation. For Marcus Manlius, consul three years before and an outstanding soldier, was alerted by their honking and the beating of their wings. He snatched up his weapons and called his fellows to arms. Striding forward, as the others held back in alarm, he struck a Gaul standing on the summit with the boss of his shield and pushed him over the precipice, the downward fall toppling those closest. Manlius then cut down others, who let go their weapons in terror and clung desperately to the rocks with their hands. Then other Romans grouped together and drove back the enemy, hurling javelins and stones, whereat the Gallic force collapsed utterly and plunged down headlong.

After the uproar had subsided, the rest of the night was spent quietly, or at least as quietly as possible for people still in turmoil, even though the danger had now passed. At dawn the trumpet called the soldiers to assemble before the tribunes, who proceeded to reward bravery and punish cowardice. First, Manlius was praised for his courage and given rewards not only by the military tribunes but also by the soldiers acting together, for each one brought to his house (it was on the citadel) a half-pound of spelt and a cup of wine—a small thing in the telling, but a great proof of the high regard in which he was held, given the scarcity, when each man deprived himself of sustenance he needed to keep body and soul together and gave it by way of honour to one man. Next, the guards who had been stationed at the point where the enemy had appeared on the citadel were ordered to stand forth, and, when Quintus Sulpicius, the military tribune, declared he would punish every one of them according to the harsh code of the military, he changed his mind when the assembled soldiers united in loudly accusing a single sentry; so he spared the others and, to everyone's approval, ordered the culprit, whose guilt was manifest, thrown from the precipice. Thereafter sentries on each side were more alert, both among the Gauls, on learning that messengers were moving back and forth between Veii and Rome, and among the Romans, mindful of the peril they had faced in the night.

48. But of all the evils that afflicted the two sides in the siege and the war, famine was the greatest. The Gauls were stricken with pestilence as well, for their camp lay between the hills in a place scorched by the flames and choked with heat, which the slightest breath of wind filled up with ash and dust. As a people they are accustomed to damp and cold, and are therefore quite intolerant of such conditions; now they had not just fallen victim to stifling heat, but were dying from disease that spread among them as if through a herd of cattle. Not having the energy to bury the dead individually, they heaped up the bodies indiscriminately and cremated them, giving the name Gallic Pyres to the site. They then struck a truce with the Romans, and soldiers on both sides began talking back and forth with the permission of their commanders. When the Gauls kept repeatedly pointing to the Romans' starved state and the consequent necessity of surrendering, those on the Capitol are said to have rained down bread on the enemy guardposts to conceal their plight.

But there came a time when the famine could no longer be disguised or further endured. And so, while the dictator was holding a levy of his own at Ardea (having ordered his master of the horse Lucius Valerius to fetch the army from Veii) and was making preparations and exercising the troops with the aim of enabling them to oppose the enemy on equal terms, the army on the Capitol in the meantime, exhausted from standing guard day and night, having surmounted every misfortune save starvation, which alone nature would not let them overcome, looking day after day for help from the dictator, and, in the end, as both hope and food failed them, seeing the guards staggering to their posts, their wasted bodies barely able to support the weight of their arms—the army finally bade the authorities negotiate surrender or ransom on whatever terms they could, the Gauls having made no secret that they could be persuaded to lift the siege for no very great price. Then the senate convened and the military tribunes were told to treat for peace. A meeting between the military tribune Quintus Sulpicius and Brennus the Gallic chieftain followed. They fixed on an amount: a thousand pounds of gold was the price put on the nation that was destined to rule the world. To this utterly demeaning transaction insult was added when, after the Gauls used dishonest weights and the tribune protested, Brennus tossed his sword on the scale, uttering words intolerable to Roman ears, 'Woe to the vanquished!'

49. But god and man forbade the Romans be a ransomed people. For by some chance, before the unspeakable business could be carried through, when the gold had not yet been completely weighed out owing to the dispute, the dictator intervened, and ordered the gold taken away and the Gauls removed. When they balked and said they had made an agreement, he informed them that no agreement was valid that had been made without his order by a magistrate of lesser authority after he had been named dictator; and he told the Gauls to make ready for battle. He ordered his men to pile up their backpacks in a heap, to take up arms, and to recover their country by iron instead of gold, having before their eyes the shrines of the gods, their wives and children, the soil of their country ravaged by the evils of war, and all those things that duty enjoined them to defend, reclaim, and avenge. He then drew up his battleline, as the terrain permitted, on ground uneven by nature and in a city half in ruins, and made provision for everything that good generalship could plan or devise for the benefit of his men.

The Gauls were alarmed by this unexpected turn of events; they seized their weapons and attacked the Romans more in anger than good judgement. But now Fortune had reversed her course, now the favour of the gods and man's intelligence were on Rome's side. And so at the first clash the rout of the Gauls was accomplished with as little effort as they themselves had expended in their victory at the Allia. Then in a more regular battle at the eighth milestone on the road to Gabii, where they had gone after taking flight, they were defeated for a second time under the leadership and auspices of the same Camillus. The slaughter was total: their camp was captured and not even a messenger survived to report the disaster. The dictator, after taking back his country from the enemy, returned to the city in triumph, in which his soldiers, in rough, extemporaneous verse, deservedly called him Romulus, parent of his country and the city's second founder.

There is no question that the country he had saved in war he now saved again in peace, by preventing the scheme to migrate to Veii, which the tribunes advocated more strongly after the burning of the city and which the plebs of themselves were disposed to favour.

This was the reason why he did not resign the dictatorship after his triumph, for the senate begged him not to leave the state in such an unsettled condition. **50**. His first act, as a man of great religious sensibility, was to bring before the senate matters pertaining to the immortal gods. The following decree was the result: all shrines should be rebuilt, marked with boundary stones and purified because they had been in enemy hands; the method of purification was to be sought in the Sibylline books by the two men in charge of them; the people of Caere should be made the guest-friends of the city because they had housed the sacred objects of the Roman people and their priests and, owing to their kindness, the worship due the immortal gods had not been interrupted; the Capitoline Games should be instituted because Jupiter Optimus Maximus had protected his temple and the citadel of the Roman people at a terrifying time, and to celebrate these games Marcus Furius the dictator was to form a board selected from among those who lived on the Capitol and citadel. Then a proposal was made to expiate the omen of the nocturnal voice that was heard to foretell the Gallic attack before it happened but had been disregarded, and the order was given to build a temple to Aius Locutius, the Speaking Voice, on New Street. Because people could not remember what gold had been recovered from the Gauls and what had been taken from different temples in the confusion and stored in the shrine of Jupiter, they were at a loss how to put it back; accordingly, the senate decreed that all of it was sacred and should be placed beneath Jupiter's throne. Even before this happened, when the state did not have enough gold to pay the Gauls the full amount agreed upon, religious feeling had been shown when the matrons supplied the deficit in order to leave gold that was sacred untouched. Now they were thanked, and given in addition the right to have a customary speech of praise delivered at their funerals, as in the case of men. Only after these steps had been taken that pertained to the gods and that fell under the senate's purview, did he reply to the tribunes of the plebs, who in one meeting after another had been urging their constituents to move to Veii, a city ready and waiting to receive them, and to abandon their ruined country. Camillus entered one of these meetings, accompanied by the entire senate, and delivered the following speech.

51. 'So hateful to me are these conflicts with the plebeian tribunes, citizens, that throughout my unhappy exile at Ardea my one consolation was the thought that I was far removed from this strife, and that precisely because of it I would never return—not even if you called me back repeatedly by decrees of the senate and votes of the people. But now your altered fortune, not a change of heart, has forced my return, since at issue is whether our country is to continue in this place, not whether I am to live in our country. And I would now make no move and would gladly hold my tongue, if this present dispute were not also a fight for our country; but to fail her at this juncture, so long as a spark of life remains, would be in the eyes of others an affront to honour, in the eyes of Camillus an affront to heaven also. For why are we trying to win the city back, why did we wrest it from enemy hands when they had it under siege, if we voluntarily abandon what we have recovered? Not long ago, with the Gauls victorious and the whole city in their power, gods and the men of Rome nevertheless held out on the Capitol and citadel. Now, with Romans victorious and the city retaken, will even the citadel and Capitol be abandoned? Will good fortune devastate the city more completely than did our misfortune?

'Even if the religious practices that were established when this city was founded and have been handed down by our forebears meant nothing to us, still, the power of the gods has been so clearly revealed in Rome's affairs in these past days that mankind, I believe, will never again disregard any aspect of their worship. If you review in your minds the successes and failures of recent years, you will find that everything the gods favoured turned out well, everything they opposed did not. Take the war with Veii first. Think of the time and effort it took! And think, too, of the fact that it did not end before the gods advised us to let the waters from the Alban lake. And what of the disaster we have just experienced? Did it not occur only after we had disregarded the voice from heaven warning of the Gauls' coming? After our envoys violated the law of nations, after we failed to punish them because of this same disregard of religion? The conclusion is inescapable. The penalty we paid to gods and men in suffering defeat, capture, and ransom is so great that we stand today as an object lesson to the entire world.

'Yet then, in our darkest hour, we remembered the gods. We fled to them on the Capitol, to the home of Jupiter Optimus Maximus; amid the loss of our personal possessions, we buried some sacred objects in the earth, others we took from the enemy's sight and carried them to cities near by. Though abandoned by gods and men we still did not forsake the gods' worship. They therefore gave us back our country, gave us back victory, gave us back the honour we long enjoyed in warfare but had lost, and upon enemies who in blind avarice had broken their word and the truce in weighing out the gold, they brought panic, flight, and death.

52. 'Seeing such telling evidence of what happens when the power of heaven is honoured and when it is slighted, do you realize, citizens, how great a sin we are about to commit now, having barely survived the shipwreck of our former guilt and calamity? Our city owed its foundation to augury and to the auspices taken then. There is no place in it that is not filled with religious associations and divine power. There are as many days fixed for religious ceremonies as there are places in which they are performed. Do you intend, men of Rome, to abandon all the gods of the state and all those we worship privately? How does this compare with what that outstanding young man Gaius Fabius did during the recent siege? He excited the wonder no less of the Gauls than of you when, quitting the citadel, he strode through Gallic spears and performed the rites of the Fabian clan on the Quirinal hill. Is it your pleasure that the sacred rites of families not be interrupted even in wartime, while the state religion and the gods of Rome are abandoned in peace? That our nation's pontiffs and flamens be more derelict in their public duties than a private person practising the rites of his clan?

'Possibly someone might say that either we will perform these ceremonies at Veii or we will send our priests here to perform them. But neither can be done while maintaining their sacral integrity. I need not enumerate all the holy rites by type and all the gods. The feast of Jupiter will suffice. His couch* cannot be set up in any other place than the Capitol, can it? And I do not need to mention the everlasting flame of Vesta and the image which is housed in her temple as guarantor of Rome's empire.* What of your shields, Mars Gradivus, and you, father Quirinus?* Citizens, do you intend to abandon and profane all these holy things that are coeval with the city, some even antedating its founding?

'Look now at the difference between us and our ancestors. They handed down certain religious ceremonies that we are obligated to perform on the Alban Mount and at Lavinium. If it was wrong for rituals to be moved from enemy cities to us here in Rome, how can

we move them to the enemy city of Veii without committing sacrilege? Come, think how often ceremonies are repeated because some
step in ancestral ritual has been omitted through negligence or accident. Not so long ago, in consequence of the prodigy of the Alban
lake, what else turned our fortunes around when the war was going
badly at Veii if not the repetition of sacred rites and the renewal of
the auspices? But then we acted like men mindful of their ancient
religious inheritance when we brought to Rome foreign deities and
introduced new ones. Queen Juno was recently carried to the Aventine
from Veii. Remember the enthusiasm of the married women, the
great throng of people who celebrated her dedication! We ordered a
temple to Aius Locutius be built because of the voice from heaven
that was heard in New Street. At the senate's direction we added the
Capitoline Games to the others we regularly hold and created a new
board to oversee them. What point was there in making such inno-
vations if we were about to leave Rome along with the Gauls, if our
occupation of the Capitol through so many months of siege was not
voluntary, but because fear of the enemy kept us there?

'We speak of rites and of temples, but what of our priests? Doesn't
it occur to you how great the sacrilege would be? There is only one
place for the Vestals, and nothing save the capture of the city has
ever moved them from it. It is a sin for our priest of Jupiter, the
flamen Dialis, to spend a single night outside the city.* Do you
intend to have our priests of Rome transmogrified into priests of
Veii? Will your Vestals desert you, Vesta? Will the flamen by living
on foreign soil bring down, night after night, a crushing burden of
sin upon himself and the nation?

'And what of the other things whose performance depends on
taking the auspices, most of which take place within the city's sacred
boundary? How can we consign them to such oblivion, to such
neglect? The Comitia Curiata, which concerns our military, the
Comitia Centuriata, in which you elect consuls and military tribunes—where can they be convened, after the auspices have been
taken, except in the places they are customarily held? Will we trans-
fer these things to Veii? Or will the people at great inconvenience
come back here to elect them, to a place forsaken by gods and men?

53. 'Aside from the fact that everything has been polluted and no
act of atonement can set it right, someone might say it is quite
apparent that our present predicament requires us to quit a city

wasted by fire and lying in ruins, to move to Veii where everything
is intact, and not to burden our indigent plebs by having to rebuild
here. That this argument is more specious than real is, I think,
apparent to you, citizens, even if I were not to mention it, for you
remember that even before the Gauls' arrival, when the city was safe
and sound, when the public and private buildings were intact, this
same proposal to move to Veii was discussed. What is more, I want
you tribunes to realize how much your thinking differs from mine.
You maintain that even if it was unnecessary then, it is necessary
now, while I, on the contrary—do not be surprised until you understand my meaning— am convinced that even if it was right to consider moving while Rome was still untouched, we must not abandon
her now that she is in ruins. Previously, the reason for migrating
was our victory in capturing Veii, a glorious thing for us and our
descendants; now it is a source of shame and humiliation, but something that the Gauls can glory in. For we will be seen not as having
left as victors, but to have lost our country after being defeated; it
will be said we had no choice, that we were forced to abandon our
tutelary deities, to go into exile, to flee the place we could not
defend after the rout at the Allia, the capture of the city, and the
siege of the Capitol. Will Romans be seen as incapable of rebuilding
a city that the Gauls were able to demolish? If they should come
again with a new force—for everyone agrees that their numbers are
scarcely to be believed—if they should decide to settle in this city
which they captured, must not one expect that you would permit it?
Or suppose it was not the Gauls but your old enemies, the Aequi or
Volsci, who chose to migrate to Rome—would you want them to be
citizens of Rome, you of Veii? Or do you prefer this to be a place
where you are not rather than a city where the enemy is? Frankly, I
cannot conceive of anything more disgraceful. Are you prepared to
put up with such outrage, such humiliation, because you are loath to
rebuild?

'If in the whole city no finer, no grander dwelling could be built
than the hut of our founder,* isn't it better to live in huts like
shepherds and peasants amid our tutelary deities and the things
sacred to us than to go *en masse* into exile? Our ancestors, who were
refugees and shepherds, quickly built this city in a place where there
was nothing except forests and marshes. Are we loath to rebuild the
structures that have burned, while the Capitol and citadel remain

untouched, while the temples of the gods still stand? In face of a conflagration that has affected us all, shall we refuse to do together what each of us would have done if his own house had burned down?

54. 'But that is not all. If accident or arson should cause a fire to break out in Veii, and if, as can happen, the wind spreads the flames, destroying a great part of the city, will we look to Fidenae or Gabii, or to some other city, where we can take up residence? Does our native soil, does mother earth, as we call her, have so little hold on us that love of country is love for the buildings and timbers placed upon her? Let me now make a confession, even though I find it more painful to mention the wrong you did me than the suffering I endured. All the time I was in exile, whenever I thought of my country, I beheld in my mind's eye everything that surrounds us here at this moment: the hills and plains, the Tiber, the familiar earth and sky, which saw my birth and upbringing. It is my fervent wish, citizens, that love for this place will so fill your hearts that you will remain where you are, and that you will not, if you do leave, be wracked by longing, homesick for your native soil. Gods and men chose this place to found a city for excellent reasons: these health-giving hills, the river near to hand that conveys provisions from places inland and up which goods from abroad are brought, the sea conveniently close by, but not so near that we are exposed to danger from foreign fleets—the very heart of Italy, a place uniquely fitted to promote the growth of our city. The size itself of a city so new is proof. Rome is now in its three-hundreth-and-sixty-fifth year, citizens.* For a long time you have waged wars against peoples far older, and all the while, not to enumerate the cities one by one, not the numerous strongholds of the Volsci combined with the Aequi, not the armies and navies of all of Etruria, spanning the breadth of Italy from sea to sea, have been your equal in war. In view of the success you have enjoyed here, what reason, in heaven's name, could there be for trying some other place—for though your valour may accompany you, the good fortune that attends this site assuredly cannot.

'You see the Capitol before you, where once the unearthing of a human head was taken as a sign that this spot marked what would be the centre of empire and head of the world. Here, when the Capitol was cleared of buildings, the gods of Youth and of Boundaries, Iuventas and Terminus, would not allow themselves to be moved, to the great joy of your ancestors.* Here is Vesta's fire, here the shields of Mars fell from the sky, here, if you remain, all the gods in heaven will shower their blessings upon you.'

55. Camillus' speech is said to have moved them greatly, especially when he spoke of religion, but a fortuitous remark decided the question. During a meeting of the senate, held shortly thereafter to discuss the matter in the building built by King Hostilius,* a cohort of soldiers returning from sentry duty chanced to be marching through the forum. When they reached the place of assembly, the centurion called out, 'Standard-bearer, plant the standard; we will do best to remain here.' When the senators heard what he had said they came out of their chamber crying that they accepted the omen, while the plebs crowded around, voicing their agreement. The proposed law was then rejected by the voters.

Rebuilding began haphazardly all over the city. Roof tiles were supplied at public expense, while those who pledged to finish construction within a year were allowed to take wood and stone from wherever they could find them. The haste with which they worked resulted in an irregular street plan, as they built over empty areas without attention to the exact boundaries between their own and others' property. This is the reason why the old sewer system, which originally followed its course through public land, now runs in many places under private dwellings, and the result is a city that resembles one built piecemeal rather than laid out according to a master plan.

EXPLANATORY NOTES

BOOK ONE

5 *Aeneas and Antenor . . . Helen*: Homer represents the aged Antenor as urging the return of Helen (*Iliad*), but not Aeneas (whose descendants, however, Poseidon prophesies will rule over the Trojans: *Iliad* 20.203).

The spot . . . Veneti: this was the location of Livy's native city Patavium (modern Padua); Livy assumes his readers know that Antenor founded Patavium.

Laurentine territory: a district in Latium some fifteen miles south of Rome.

7 *Indiges*: 'an obscure term which must mean "divine ancestor"' (Ogilvie).

Ascanius . . . founder: Virgil in the *Aeneid* follows the tradition that Ascanius was the son of Creusa. Julius Caesar and his adoptive son Augustus belonged to the Julian family.

Silvius . . . ruler: the Alban king list that follows was devised in the later Republic to bridge the gap of over 400 years between the fall of Troy and the founding of Rome (traditional dates: 1184 and 753 BC). Some early writers had simply made Romulus the son or grandson of Aeneas.

Ancient Latins: or *Prisci Latini*, were so designated to distinguish them from later Latin colonies whose populations were not necessarily ethnically Latin in origin but who enjoyed the same juridical rights as had the earlier colonies.

8 *Vestal*: the Vestal Virgins, six in number in historical times, worshipped Vesta, goddess of the communal hearth of the state. They were never to let the sacred fire in the temple go out, and were to remain virgin during their priesthood (the penalty for unchastity was entombment alive).

'She-wolf' . . . originated: lupa, she-wolf, also means prostitute in Latin.

9 *Lupercal*: in the Lupercalia naked youths ran through the Forum, hitting bystanders with strips of goatskin. The meaning of the ceremony has been much disputed by both ancients and moderns.

11 *Geryon*: the slaying of Geryon, a triple-bodied (or triple-headed) monster in Spain, was the tenth of Hercules' twelve labours.

Evander: in myth Evander was variously viewed as a minor deity, a mortal of divine parentage, or having a wholly human genealogy. The Hellenic origin of the stories surrounding him is shown in his Greek name, which means 'good man' (whereas Cacus means 'bad man').

Sibyl: this is the Sibyl of Cumae in south Italy, made famous in the sixth book of Virgil's *Aeneid*, in which she is Aeneas' guide to the Underworld. Her prophecies were gathered at Rome into the Sibylline books, which were consulted only at the command of the senate by a special priestly college.

12 *The Potitii . . . branch*: at 9.29 Livy recounts the story. The censor Appius Claudius Caecus in 312 BC sanctioned this change in religious practice; tradition claimed that in retaliation the gods not only wiped out the family of the Pinarii but caused Appius to go blind (*caecus* means blind in Latin).

lictors: attendants of the higher Republican magistrates; they carried the fasces, a bundle of rods encasing a double-headed axe, the former symbolizing the power of scourging, the latter of decapitation.

the curule chair and the toga praetexta: the curule chair, inlaid with ivory, was used by the higher magistrates of the Republic; the purple-bordered toga praetexta was worn by magistrates and children.

14 *games . . . horses*: the Consualia honoured Consus, god of the granary or storehouse; when horse-races were added to the festival, the festival became identified with Neptune (Greek Poseidon), the god of horses.

'To Thalassius!' . . . weddings today: this anecdote is one of many that were advanced to explain the mysterious cry *Talassio* at Roman weddings.

15 *a new title*: Livy apparently derives Feretrius from *ferculum* or *feretrum*, the wooden frame on which the 'spoils of honour' (*spolia opima*) were hung.

16 *twice . . . rare indeed*: won by Aulus Cornelius Cossus in 437 BC (see 4.20) and Marcus Claudius Marcellus in 222 BC.

religious duties: without actually identifying Tarpeia as a Vestal Virgin, Livy depicts her as such (to make her treachery more pronounced). The Vestals drew water daily from the spring of the Camenae outside the Porta Capena.

18 *Lacus Curtius*: this cavity in the forum was regarded as an entrance to the underworld; Romans threw coins into it annually for good luck.

19 *three centuries . . . uncertain*: a century was a military unit of theoretically 100 men. The names of these centuries were also the names of the three original tribes (each consisting of ten *curiae*), although Livy does not identify them specifically as tribes. The *curiae* and the three tribes were doubtless later Etruscan inventions that were anachronistically carried back to the earliest days of the city (the names of the three centuries derive from Etruscan gentile names). One of the *curiae* was called Rapta: 'the abducted maiden'.

Fidenae: an Etruscan city some five miles north of Rome on the left bank of the Tiber, the same side on which Rome was situated.

20 *Veii*: a large Etruscan city some twelve miles north of Rome.

21 *Romulus' divinity*: the deified Romulus was regularly identified with the god Quirinus in later cult (cf. 5.2).

23 *(today . . . in advance)*: this change was enacted by the Publilian law of 339 BC.

Pythagoras . . . Croton: Numa reigned *c*.700 BC, whereas Pythagoras came to south Italy *c*.530 BC. The reign of Servius Tullius, who was succeeded by Tarquinius Superbus, ended in 535, according to traditional dating.

24 *the temple of Janus . . . sea*: the First Punic War ended in 241 BC; Titus Manlius was consul in 235 (the consul of 241 was Aulus Manlius). Augustus defeated his rivals Antony and Cleopatra at Actium in 31 BC, closing the gates of Janus in 29; he received the title Augustus on 16 January 27 BC. He closed the gates a second time in 25 after his campaign in Spain. It follows that this passage was written between 27 and 25. The Argiletum was a district just north of the forum.

25 *intercalary months . . . started*: Livy seems here to attribute to Numa the invention of a nineteen-year intercalary cycle (the Romans counted inclusively), devised by Meton, a Greek astronomer of the fifth century BC.

flamen Dialis, or priest of Jupiter: the flamen Dialis was hedged about with a great many taboos, such as not being able to be absent from Rome for a single night (cf. 5.52) or to look upon the sight of blood. A flamen was a priest of a particular deity, a pontiff (below, same para.) of religious matters in general.

ancilia: tradition said that one shield had fallen from heaven and that eleven duplicates were made to reduce the chances of the original being stolen. The figure-eight shape of the shields is very ancient, known from Homer and various Cretan and Mycenaean monuments.

26 *Camenae*: probably water deities in origin, they were sometimes identified with the Muses in Greek mythology and with poetry in particular.

Argei: there were twenty-seven shrines of the Argei distributed throughout the four regions of the city. On 24 May twenty-seven rush puppets called Argei were thrown into the Tiber by the Vestal Virgins, the significance of which is obscure.

29 *The fetial priest*: the fetials were a priestly college in charge of declaring war (see ch. 32) and making treaties. Each mission required two of them, one to bring a clump of grass with earth attached (hence he carried a piece of Roman soil with him wherever he went), the other (the *pater patratus*: 'one who is made a father') to act as the surrogate father of the Roman people as a whole.

32 *high treason*: *perduellio*; evidently because Horatia was a traitor in mourning for an enemy of the state, and her brother, rather than awaiting due process of the law, took that process into his own hands.

legal powers as a father against his son: the head of a Roman family had complete power (*patria potestas*) over all its members, including the power of life and death.

33 *Horatian Spears*: *Pila Horatia* was taken in antiquity to mean either 'the

Horatian column' or 'the Horatian spears'. If the latter is the older interpretation, it would seem to belong to that version of the story in which the Horatii were from Alba.

34 *twelve Salian priests . . . Panic*: this is a second group of Salian priests (the first is mentioned in ch. 20). There is no other indication of there being shrines at Rome to Pallor and Panic (*Pallor* and *Pavor*); the motif seems to have been borrowed from Homer (*Iliad* 11.37).

37 *Curia Hostilia . . . generation*: the Curia Hostilia was burned to the ground in 52 BC, chosen by the mob as the pyre for the murdered Publius Clodius. It was rebuilt, but razed in 44 BC to make way for a new senate-house on a different site, the Curia Julia. Cf. also 5.55 and the note to p. 341.

40 *Aequiculi*: another name for the Aequi, a tribe next mentioned in ch. 53. Aequiculi comes from the false etymology *aequum colere* 'to cultivate equity'. Ogilvie's excellent notes on this chapter show clearly that the formulas recorded here are not genuinely old, but derive from antiquarian reconstructions of the second century BC.

pater patratus: compare the fetial formula for striking a treaty described in ch. 24.

44 *knights*: or *equites*; in the later Republic just below the senators on the social scale ('the equestrian order'). Originally they were cavalrymen in the army, but later allied contingents took over this duty. The picture Livy gives here is especially anachronistic, since the knights were not given special seating in the Circus until 67 BC.

45 *Ramnes*: an alternate spelling of Ramnenses (ch. 13).

48 *slave*: the story may have originated from the fact that the name Servius is suggestive of the Latin word for slave, *seruus*.

51 *classes and centuries . . . in the following way*: the system outlined in what follows essentially describes the Roman army at an early stage of its existence, with several latter changes to account for the fact that the army also became, in effect, a voting assembly of the people as a whole (the Comitia Centuriata). Juniors were 17 to 45 years in age, seniors 46 to 60. The system of rating by asses (an *as* was a bronze coin by weight) cannot go back beyond 269 BC, when the Romans issued their first coins.

three of which . . . inaugurated: that is, Ramnenses, Titienses, and Luceres. See chs. 13 and 36.

52 *right to vote*: in historical times no Roman assembly operated on the principle of one man, one vote; rather they used unit voting, the unit being the century for the Comitia Centuriata (there were 193 centuries) and the tribe for the Comitia Tributa (there were 35 tribes). Unit voting gave disproportionate weight to the wealthy, the elderly, and rural landowners.

One should not be surprised . . . Servius Tullius: Livy's meaning is not at all clear. Tribes were a division of the people originally based on place of residence (a second popular assembly of the people, the Comitia Tributa, was based on these tribes). Livy seems to be referring to a time after 241 BC (the year in which the last and thirty-fifth tribe was created) when some type of co-ordination between tribes and centuries in the Comitia Centuriata was made.

52 *'tribute'*: *tributum* was a tax intermittently levied to meet the cost of wars.

Campus Martius: it lay outside the *pomerium*; the army could not enter the city in arms save to celebrate a triumph.

Fabius Pictor: Rome's first historian, a senator and ambassador to Delphi in 216 BC, who wrote his work in Greek.

54 *son*: Servius' reign of forty-four years clearly precludes Tarquin being a young man at this point.

58 *Proud*: the common rendering of *Superbus*; but the word more properly means arrogant or overbearing.

capital charges: that is, charges affecting a man's civil personality or status (*caput*), including life, citizenship, and place in the community.

64 *Terminus*: a *terminus* was a boundary stone in which a divine force (*numen*) was believed to reside. The god Terminus therefore represented all boundary stones on Roman land.

Fabius . . . Piso: Lucius Calpurnius Piso Frugi, consul 133 and censor 120, was an early historian who wrote in Latin; Fabius Pictor, Rome's first historian, wrote in Greek (hence the sum is reckoned in Greek talents).

65 *renovations . . . original constructions*: this is Ogilvie's interpretation; *haec noua magnificentia* might equally refer to the magnificence of the city in general rather than to the Circus and Cloaca Maxima specifically.

snake: the snake portends the death of someone, since the souls of the dead were commonly believed to be reincarnated into snakes.

Brutus: in Latin *brutus* means stupid.

BOOK TWO

71 *fasces*: they symbolized the power of higher magistrates (see 1.8 and the note to p. 12). Twelve lictors carrying the fasces had accompanied the kings; in the Republic the twelve fasces alternated between the two consuls on a monthly basis.

72 *senators*: in the early books Livy regularly denotes senators and patricians by the word *patres*, 'fathers', because in these years the two terms were virtually if not exactly synonymous. In governmental contexts I have most often translated *patres* as senators; in contexts that emphasize the struggle between the patricians and plebeians I have occasionally translated *patres* as patricians.

75 *temples and porticoes*: the Tiber island contained temples to Aesculapius and other gods. The embankments were built to suggest the shape of a

ship floating in the river.

76 *uindicta*: this was a formal legal ceremony before a magistrate (a praetor in later times) in which the manumittor touched the slave and asserted his freedom, which claim the praetor then ratified. The origin and exact meaning of the word *uindicta* is disputed.

77 *returned to Rome in triumph*: this is the first triumph under the Republic recorded by Livy. The triumph, granted by the senate, was a procession of a victorious general through the city to the Capitol, where he sacrificed and gave thanks to Jupiter. He was dressed as Jupiter, having also a laurel branch, sceptre, and crown, with his face painted red. Captives and booty were displayed in the procession; his soldiers followed, crying 'Io triumphe', intermingling praises and coarse verses about him.

79 *appeal . . . magistrates*: no magistrate could put a citizen to death or pronounce a sentence affecting his civil status without the citizen having the right to appeal the decision to the people as a whole. Compare ch. 18 and the note to p. 89.

a man . . . sacrificial victim to the gods: a man who attempted to make himself king became *sacer*, a religious outcast liable to be killed by anyone with impunity.

80 *Cumae*: the oldest Greek settlement on the Italian mainland, situated a short distance from modern Naples (which was one of its colonies). See also chs. 14 and 35.

84 *maiming of his right hand*: Scaeuola means left-handed.

86 *the next consuls*: Livy omits the year 507 BC. See Ogilvie's note in his Commentary and Livy's own comment in ch. 21; cf. also ch. 39 and the note to p. 111.

87 *clients*: a client was a free man who entrusted himself to the protection of a more powerful and richer man and sometimes received support in the form of money or food. In return the client assisted his patron in his private and public life and paid him respect, especially by greeting him at his home in the morning.

Pometia and Cora: Livy repeats the capture of Cora and Pometia in ch. 22, some eight years later; the doublet, one of a number in the *Ab Urbe Condita*, is doubtless due to a change of source that had different dating. See, for example, his complaints in the next chapter and in ch. 21 on discrepancies among his sources.

88 *a dictator*: the dictator superseded the consuls, who were subordinate to him and could, if he chose, play no role in the state. His term was for a maximum of six months. Because they were appointed to meet emergencies (usually military) dictators took pride in resigning as soon as they had solved the emergency.

89 *master of the horse*: that is, captain of the cavalry, subordinate to the dictator and appointed by him.

axes carried before him: twenty-four lictors carrying the axes within the fasces preceded the dictator even in the city, where his power to use them was absolute. The consuls were obliged to remove the axes from the fasces when inside the city, where a sentence of execution could be appealed to the people (*prouocatio*). In the field the right of appeal did not exist.

91 *the Saturnalia instituted as a holiday*: the Saturnalia was celebrated on 17 December, but was later extended to as many as seven days; a carnival spirit prevailed, gifts were exchanged, while slaves were given the liberty to speak and act as they liked.

93 *debt*: a man was called *nexus*, 'bound, tied', who borrowed money at interest; if he failed to pay he was bound to render personal service to the creditor, presumably until he had discharged his debt. The creditor could treat the man like a slave, even putting him in chains.

97 *temple of Mercury . . . pontiff*: Mercury was the patron of the market place, commerce, and trade.

98 *appealed*: on the right of appeal, or *prouocatio*, see ch. 8 and the note to p. 79.

102 *By sending in the cavalry . . . ineffective*: Livy's meaning is not very clear. Ogilvie believes that in withdrawing troops from the line to make it deeper the Volscians created gaps through which the cavalry penetrated.

104 *sacrosanct magistrates*: a person who laid hands on a tribune was considered *sacer*: i.e. he could be killed as a sacrifice to the gods with impunity by anyone. See also ch. 8 and the note to p. 79.

107 *tribunes . . . live or die*: Livy represents Coriolanus as being indicted by the tribunes before the popular assembly, a procedure that did not actually develop until the third century BC.

clients: on clients see ch. 16 and the note to p. 87. Clients were plebeians, but not all plebeians were clients.

108 *A repetition . . . at Rome*: any religious ceremony in which a flaw or interruption occurred had to be repeated from its inception, even if it were a ceremony of many days' duration.

'the lead dancer': that is, the slave. The games began with dancers at the head of a religious procession.

111 *Spurius Nautius and Sextus Furius were now the consuls*: Livy omits the years 490 and 489 BC (cf. Dionysius of Halicarnassus, *Roman Antiquities* 7.68, 8.1).

114 *his father . . . CASSIUS' PROPERTY*: the father, or *paterfamilias*, had the right of life and death over those in his power. Although by strict law he was the owner of all that those in his power possessed, it was customary to permit a son (and slaves) to enjoy money they acquired as if it were their own.

115 *Vestal Virgin . . . punishment*: the penalty was entombment alive.

116 *the Aequi*: in the next chapter Livy refers to Fabius' campaign against the Veientes as being against the Aequi, apparently out of carelessness rather than because he has switched to another source that told a different version of events.

117 *thwart the rest*: that is, to veto the actions of one or all of his colleagues.

124 *the Carmental Gate . . . outpost*: the Porta Carmentalis was traditionally connected with bad luck. The Cremera was a small tributary of the Tiber some six miles north of Rome.

125 *they passed beyond . . . path*: reading *insidias . . . superassent*; Ogilvie less well emends the manuscripts to *praesidia . . . superassent*, evidently understanding *superassent* to mean 'overcome (a detachment of troops)'.

the temple of Hope: an ancient shrine on the Esquiline hill, on the far side of Rome from the Tiber and Janiculum.

127 *capital charge . . . two thousand asses*: on capital charges in Rome, see 1.49 and the note to p. 58. Livy's meaning here is not very clear; apparently the tribunes dropped the capital charge and convicted Menenius of a lesser offence.

129 *the laws . . . no protection whatever*: compare ch. 33 and the note to p. 104.

131 *tribunes . . . clients*: Livy fails to tell us how the tribunes were elected up to this time: probably in an unofficial assembly of the plebs (*concilium plebis*) which the lex Publilia transformed into the tribal assembly (*comitia tributa*: cf. ch. 58). Clients had the right to vote, but Livy does not explain why their votes would count for little in the Tribal Assembly, whereas they had before.

son of Appius . . . detested by them: see ch. 27.

The tribunes . . . blocking the law: Ogilvie punctuates differently, taking 'on the following day' (*postero die*) with the next clause.

'Go, Quirites, if it seems best to you': in this phrase, spoken by the magistrate as an assembly was preparing to vote, the word *discedo* signifies 'go join your voting unit' (e.g. century or tribe). Cf. 3.11.

134 *previously decorated soldiers*: these were soldiers who had been previously awarded double rations or double pay for their valour (*duplicarii*).

135 *the struggle of the orders*: that is, between plebeians and the senatorial order.

opponent of the law . . . consul: the chief aim of the law would be to distribute public land (*ager publicus*: i.e. land taken from an enemy) among the poorer citizens; but wealthier men had occupied some or all of it and treated it as their own. This motif, which runs throughout Livy's account of early Roman history, seems to be an anachronism, a throwback from conditions of the third and second centuries BC. Its inception is narrated in ch. 41.

137 *the third watch*: the night was divided into four equal watches.

BOOK THREE

140 *fixed a permanent camp in Latin territory*: that is, he did not select a
different campsite at the end of a day's activities, as was usual for armies
on the move during a campaign.

141 *exceptional appointment*: instead of having the consul draw lots for his
field of operation (*prouincia*), the senate assigned it (= *extra ordinem*).

142 *a cessation of public business voted*: during a *iustitium* all courts were closed
and all public business suspended.

the lustrum was closed by Quinctius: on the 'closing of the *lustrum*' see
1.44.

143 *a resolution . . . 'should see to it that the state suffer no harm'*: this, the so-
called *senatus consultum ultimum*, was first passed in 121 BC and has been
here retrojected into Rome's earliest days.

145 *Valerius Antias . . . thirty*: Valerius Antias, an annalist of the first century
BC, wrote a history that covered at least 75 books. Livy usually cites him
to disagree, accusing him variously of lack of diligence (39.43), exaggeration (32.6), and outright lying (26.49). Nevertheless, Livy continued
to use him, even as a main source (38.50, 55). Antias was fond of citing
precise and inflated battle figures. Those in ch. 8 doubtless derive from
him.

start of the year: the beginning of the secular or calendar year varied
widely in the early Republic. The date was fixed at 15 March in 222 BC,
at 1 January in 153. The religious year began on 1 March.

146 *aediles . . . power*: probably an anachronism; the aediles had not yet become regular magistrates. In later times they were in charge of the
maintenance of the city, the food supply, and certain religious celebra-
tions. Compare ch. 55 and the note to p. 197.

147 *the curio maximus, Servius Sulpicius*: this official was head of the association of thirty *curiae*, or city wards, which Livy earlier (1.13) had attributed to the creation of Romulus.

interregnum . . . consuls: on the interregnum see 1.17, which occurred in
the Republic when the consuls had died, resigned, or had not yet been
elected. The interrex, a senator and patrician, would propose two names
for the assembly to ratify. If they rejected the names, succeeding interreges would propose new names until approval was secured.

149 *five men . . . power*: ten years later (chs. 31ff.) Livy records the creation
of the Decemvirate, ten men 'with consular power to write up the laws'
(resulting in the famous Twelve Tables). Here he records the proposed
creation of five men 'for writing up laws concerning consular power',
which seems to be a distorted anticipation of what is to come, and one
difficult to explain.

150 *ouatio*: ovation; a kind of lesser triumph awarded by the senate for
bloodless victories, or those over enemies who were less formidable or of
low status (as over slaves or pirates). Political jealousies, however, often

determined whether the senate awarded a triumph or ovation.

Sibylline books: see 1.7, 5.13, and the notes to pp. 11 and 296.

154 *tribunes ... rescue*: the tribunes here protect the individual rights of a patrician, although strictly they were representatives only of the plebeians.

157 *the tutelary deities of our country*: that is, the Dioscuri, Castor and Pollux, who were sometimes styled Di Penates Publici. Valerius refers to them again below, along with *penates priuati*, the tutelary gods of individual Roman households.

158 *dictator of Tusculum*: the chief magistrate in Tusculum (fifteen miles from Rome) and in some other Latin towns was styled a dictator.

159 *punished ... free or slave*: that is, free men were beheaded, slaves crucified.

163 *disregard his vote*: the consuls could refuse to accept the name of candidates for election. The appeal to Claudius is made on the assumption that he would be the one presiding at the coming consular election.

religious law ... death of the consul: on the closing of the *lustrum* (a ceremony of purification) see 1.44.

provinces: *prouincia* in Latin means a special function or task assigned to a magistrate. Much later it also came to denote a territory outside Italy administered by a governor sent from Rome.

165 *older writers*: presumably Livy refers to early historians such as Calpurnius Piso Frugi (see 1.55 and note to p. 64).

168 *master of the horse*: on this office, see 2.18 and the note to p. 89.

twelve stakes with which to build a palisade: each soldier normally carried three or four stakes, which were fixed on the camp's rampart. The unusually high number here probably reflects Cincinnatus' plan to besiege the besiegers by encircling them (ch. 28).

170 *abdicated the dictatorship ... six months*: since a dictator was appointed to meet a specific emergency (usually military, sometimes religious), it was a point of pride to resign as soon as possible to show how swiftly he had solved the crisis.

171 *each class*: reference is to the five propertied classes, whose establishment Livy had described in 1.42–3.

173 *other sacred laws ... abrogated*: Livy refers especially to the law establishing the sacrosanctity of the tribunes: see 2.33.

174 *And while enjoying ... absolute fairness*: the Latin of this sentence is obscure; the translation is only approximate.

177 *there was no point in removing the axes ... appeal*: when a consul entered the city, the axe would be removed from the bundle of rods to signify that he no longer had the power to execute someone summarily and that citizens had the right to appeal his decisions to the people. See 2.18 and the note to p. 89.

180 *king . . . title of those performing sacrifices*: Livy refers to the 'king of sacrifices', the *rex sacrificulus* or *rex sacrorum*. See 2.2.

  a single king: reading *tunc uno* or *uno tandem* for the meaningless *tum eodem* of the manuscripts.

181 *assemble to name an interrex*: on this procedure see ch. 8 and the note to p. 147.

182 *What is more . . . to be prejudged*: the text is corrupt; the translation, following Ogilvie, gives only approximate sense.

  house divide on this proposal . . . point: after the senators had given their opinions on the question the presiding magistrate had put before them, the magistrate chose one for the senate to vote on. They voted yes or no by walking to different sides of the senate chamber.

185 *free status . . . flout the law*: one of the Twelve Tables (which Appius of course had helped to frame) provided that when a man's freedom was in question, he should be presumed free until the court could decide. As Ogilvie notes, this was analogous to the presumption of innocence in modern law.

188 *in rags of mourning . . . women*: suppliants and defendants at Rome regularly appeared in the worn, shabby garments of mourning as a sign of their plight and to elicit sympathy.

196 *Verginia's maternal uncle*: in chs. 45 and 57 Numitorius is styled her grandfather (*auus*); here he is her *auunculus*. This, among other discrepancies in this passage, probably indicates a change of source.

197 *aedile . . . panel of judges*: the aediles (cf. ch. 6 and note to p. 146) were in origin the overseers of the plebeian temple of Ceres on the Aventine. What the ten-man panel of judges was is unclear; it may be identified with the later ten-man board for adjudicating questions of freedom and slavery (*decemuiri stlitibus iudicandis*).

  Legal experts . . . originated: the distinction is between the person who is protected from violation (*sacrosanctus*) and the one who commits such a violation (*sacer*). On the latter, see 2.33 and notes to pp. 79 and 104.

200 *Sabines . . . Valerius*: Livy writes very obscurely here. The Sabine war evidently refers to the threat mentioned in ch. 51 (cf. ch. 61), while the Aequi and Volsci have joined forces in a second war (ch. 60).

206 *supplication*: a *supplicatio* was a solemn thanksgiving during which the temples were open and the cult statues were placed on couches to receive the people's prayers. Originally it was celebrated in time of pestilence, later for military victory.

215 *when the battle at Corioli took place*: see 2.33. Corioli was captured in 493 BC; the year is now 446.

BOOK FOUR

217 *intermarriage between patricians and plebeians . . . enjoyed*: intermarriage had been specifically forbidden in the Twelve Tables. The patricians

were organized by clans (*gentes*), each with religious observances (*sacra*) peculiar to it (cf. 5.52). At 10.23 a patrician girl who married a plebeian was excluded from rites (in this case Pudicitia) that were the prerogative of the patricians. Even Canuleius concedes in ch. 4 that 'the children take the father's status'. The patricians claimed the sole right to take the auspices (*auspicia*): that is, to be the mediators between gods and humans. Since little public business could be conducted without taking the auspices, it followed that only they could hold the highest public offices.

218 *in what a weakened state ... to their children*: the text is corrupt at this point, although the general sense is clear.

the power that had once belonged to the kings to sink so low: in theory the absolute power of the kings had devolved upon the two consuls. See ch. 3 and 2.1.

220 *versed in the intricacies of the calendar ... priestly colleges*: until 304 BC (see Livy 9.4) the calendar (*fasti*) was kept secret. The character of each day determined whether one could engage in public or private business, or none at all. The *commentarii pontificum* were procedural handbooks of the pontiffs that regulated such questions as legitimacy and inheritance.

222 *already twice found out ... in their determination?*: the reference is to the two secessions of the plebs, the first in 494 BC (2.31–3), the second in 449 (3.50–4).

223 *impossible to secure a resolution ... veto*: this is the earliest instance of a tribune vetoing a resolution of the senate, and is probably an anachronism.

224 *In the 310th year ... highest office*: military tribunes with consular power were elected fifty-one times between 444 and 367 BC, consuls twenty-two times. Note, however, that L. Atilius came from a plebeian family (cf. 5.13).

225 *the area from which to take the auspices*: on the selection of such an augural site see also 1.6 and 3.20.

Licinius Macer ... Juno Moneta: Licinius Macer was a historian of the first century BC, tribune of the plebs in 73, praetor in 68 or 67; he was convicted of extortion in 66 and committed suicide. His history was partial to the plebeian cause and to the achievements of his own family. The Linen Books (*Libri Lintei*) contained lists of magistrates (see chs. 20 and 23 also); the temple of Juno Moneta on the Capitol was not built until 344 BC (Livy 7.28). Suffect consuls were those elected after the start of the year when the chief magistrates had died, left office or, as here, had their election declared invalid.

226 *institution of the censorship ... state revenues*: all citizens had to declare the worth of their property to the censors, who then drew up the lists of the orders (*ordines*), based on wealth, with the senators and the knights holding the first two ranks. But anyone could be struck from the list for questionable or immoral behaviour. Moreover, the censors let out all state contracts to persons who would bid for the right to carry them out

(building or repair of temples and the collection of taxes are examples); those chosen were styled publicans (*publicani*): i.e. private individuals who had contracted to carry out public business.

227 *the approval of the girl's guardians*: the law of Ardea is understood to be the same as that of Rome. Every woman was under the legal control of either her father or, if he were dead (as in this case), of one or more male guardians (*tutores*), whose chief purpose was to see that heritable property did not pass out of the father's side of the family. The wishes of the legal guardians would be presumed to have greater weight here. The mother must also be presumed to be under the legal control either of her father or of one or more guardians.

the Aequan Cluilius: unless Aequus is a unique first name (*praenomen*), we have here the anomaly of an Aequan commander of a Volscian force. Note 3.25, where the Aequi are commanded by a Cloelius (= Cluilius).

229 *more eligible Rutulian colonists than Roman*: the Rutuli were the inhabitants of the land surrounding Ardea. Cf. 1.2.

231 *member of the equestrian order*: Livy evidently means he was a (plebeian) member of one of the eighteen centuries of cavalrymen or knights (*equites*); cf. 1.43.

234 *a gilded ox outside the Trigemina Gate*: probably an ox with gilded horns, which was meant to be sacrificed, although Livy's meaning is uncertain. All other sources speak of a statue of Minucius atop a column.

inscription beside Minucius' death mask . . . false: Livy evidently refers to the Trebonian Law of 448 BC (see 3.65). Noble families regularly made death masks of their distinguished members and displayed them in the atria of their houses along with inscriptions outlining the highlights of each man's career. These inscriptions were sometimes falsified to enhance the family's reputation (see 8.40).

236 *there threw up a rampart . . . enemy attack*: the Latin is corrupt here; I have followed Ogilvie's interpretation of the passage in his *Commentary*.

238 *supreme commander . . . under whose religious auspices a war is waged*: that is, only a consul or dictator could be regarded as a supreme commander (*dux*) in this period. Even military tribunes with consular power do not seem to have fought under their own auspices, much less ordinary military tribunes.

239 *the oldest histories . . . Licinius Macer repeatedly cites*: on the Linen Books, or *Libri Lintei*, and Licinius Macer, see ch. 7 and the note to p. 225. Livy's text actually reads *septimo anno* (seventh year), which has been emended to *decimo* (tenth): i.e. 428 BC (see ch. 30) rather than 431 BC (counting inclusively: the present year is 437). But 'seventh' may be what Livy wrote, out of carelessness.

I have followed all earlier authorities . . . such witnesses as these: this paragraph was almost certainly a later insertion into the text (in ch. 32 Livy once again calls Cossus a military tribune). The question of whether an officer other than a supreme commander could claim the spoils of honour was a sensitive topic for Augustus, who in 29 BC (shortly before this was written) denied for just this reason the request of Marcus Licinius Crassus to dedicate the spoils he took from the chieftain of the Bastarnae, whom he had killed in personal combat (Dio Cassius 51.24). See the discussion in the Introduction.

241 *This is one of many aspects . . . I shall leave the matter also*: this is a striking example of Livy's approach to history: he relies on his written authorities, but will not consult the Linen Books himself to determine whether Tubero or Macer was correct (or neither). On Macer, see ch. 7 and the note to p. 225, and ch. 20; on Antias see 3.5 and the note to p. 145.

242 *removed him from his tribe . . . lowest rank of citizens*: those of the lowest rank were termed *aerarii*. When the censors removed Mamercus from his tribe, he lost the right to vote; when they increased the amount of his assessment, Mamercus was liable to higher taxes.

244 *no candidate could appear in whitened clothing as a sign of seeking office*: *candidatus* literally means 'dressed in whitened clothing'.

sworn a sacred oath . . . to serve in the military: this *lex sacrata* declared that anyone who failed to report for military duty was a sacrificial forfeit to the gods (*sacer*): i.e. liable to be killed by anyone with impunity.

245 *vowed the Great Games . . . massive uprising*: that is, the vow was to give the games (a celebration in honour of the gods) in the event of Rome's success. The Great (= Roman) Games were at this period not annual, as they were in later times, but votive: i.e. vowed for specific occasions (cf. 2.36).

248 *Some sources say . . . no such mark*: at 8.7 Livy recounts the more famous story of Manlius Imperiosus' execution of his son for similarly disobeying orders on the battlefield.

249 *fetial priests . . . reparations*: on the fetial priests see 1.32.

253 *each cavalryman and centurion . . . two*: it was assumed that the ordinary soldier would secure his own booty.

254 *Certain historians . . . a full-scale naval victory*: it is to Livy's credit that he suspects exaggeration and invention on the part of some of his sources. But this instance may reflect the misinterpretation of a genuine notice deriving ultimately from the *Annales Maximi* (see Introduction). *Classis* in Livy's day meant fleet, whereas in early Latin it denoted property owners qualified for military service, and then by extension the army itself. So the notice *classe pugnatum* would have meant that the army fought at Fidenae, not that there was a naval battle.

255 *In response the military tribunes . . . a fait accompli*: Livy is so condensed here that it is difficult to know exactly what is going on and why: e.g. why most of the population should be absent or how the tribunes of the

plebs could be kept in the dark; presumably Appius Claudius presided over the consular elections.

255 *Capua . . . Capys (or, more likely, from the plain in which it is situated)*: apparently deriving Capua from the Latin *campus*, plain or field. The general area was known as Campania, the inhabitants as *Campani*.

260 *the cavalry . . . centurions*: this refers to the episode of the cavalry fighting as infantry in chs. 38–9; centurions were infantry officers.

261 *they would don the dark clothing of suppliants and stand at his side*: on defendants and their supporters appearing in mourning attire, see 3.47 and the note to p. 188.

enter the city in an ovation: on this lesser form of a triumph, see 3.10 and the note to p. 150.

262 *Aulus Antistius . . . Sextus Pollius*: these names may be manuscript errors; the reference seems to be to Titus Antistius and Spurius Pullius of ch. 42. The difference might also be due to a change of source by Livy.

267 *nor had the plebs ever . . . sold or assigned*: the text is corrupt. The translation follows Ogilvie's substitution of *unquam* for *praeterquam*.

his great-grandfather Appius Claudius . . . the veto of his colleagues: actually his great-great-grandfather; see 2.44.

New men: or *noui homines* was a phrase used in the later Republic to describe men whose ancestors had never held a curule magistracy, such as the consulship; compare ch. 54.

270 *killed beneath a wicker frame piled with rocks*: for this type of punishment see 1.51.

274 *as Salian priests . . . without authority*: on the Salian priests see 1.20.

276 *having cast off . . . power for themselves*: the text is corrupt here and the general sense somewhat doubtful.

277 *fetial priests*: on the fetial priests see 1.32.

279 *senators . . . rightly styled fathers*: Livy regularly calls the senators *patres*, or fathers. See 1.8.

BOOK FIVE

284 *as I noted some pages back*: see 4.48.

286 *towers . . . siege of cities*: wooden sheds, or penthouses (*uineae*), with sloping roofs, were fixed against the walls to protect the siege workers from enemy missiles. The moveable screens (*testudines*) similarly protected siege engines and the like.

287 *their ancestors . . . amid the comforts of hearth and home*: this is evidently a reference to the secession to the Sacred Mount, described in 2.32–33.

289 *the order of knights . . . the state*: on the establishment of the centuries of knights (*equites*), see 1.43.

members of the infantry order . . . foot soldiers extraordinary: there was no actual infantry order (*pedestris ordo*); Livy puns when he has the plebs promise to fight as 'soldiers extraordinary': i.e. outside the regular ranks (*extra ordinem*).

293 *the Trebonian law . . . his name and family*: on the Trebonian law, see 3.65.

295 *electing only one plebeian . . . Volscus*: in fact, only Manlius and Furius were patricians.

296 *Some believe . . . triple pay to the knights*: Livy calls Cornelius the *frater* of Licinius, which might signify an adoptive brother, a half-brother, or a cousin. Yet Cornelius was not military tribune when the cavalry's pay was increased, according to Livy's account in ch. 7.

the Senate decreed the Sibylline books should be consulted: for earlier consultations of these books, written in hexameter verse and believed to have originated with the famous Sibyl at Cumae, see 3.10 and 4.25. The oracles were not consulted to divine the future but to learn how the anger of the gods might be appeased.

placated the following deities . . . as lavish as could be provided in those days: in a lectisternium selected gods were presented with a sacrificial feast. Tables laden with food were set before the couches, each of which had the images of two gods placed on it in a reclining position.

298 *haruspices who might avert these omens through sacrifice*: haruspices were Etruscan religious experts summoned by the senate in religious emergencies involving either interpreting the entrails of sacrificial victims, lightning strokes, or, as here, omens and prodigies. Private persons might also consult them (cf. 1.56).

299 *through Caeretan territory by following cross-country tracks*: Rome enjoyed in this period close relations with Caere, an Etruscan city thirty miles north of Rome (Veii lay roughly midway between Rome and Caere). Cf. chs. 40 and 50.

300 *religious rites . . . improperly*: faultily elected officials (i.e. religious flaws occurred) could not properly engage in religious activities. The Latin festival on the Alban Mount, in honour of Jupiter Latiaris, was participated in by many of the surrounding Latin communities. Livy represents Rome as in charge of the proceedings, which she was at a later time, but not at this early date.

301 *a negative response . . . previously*: see ch. 1.

all his colleagues . . . Atilius: yet this list of five is, with the exception of Licinius himself, wholly at variance with the list of six given in ch. 12. A change of source is probably responsible. Note that Livy does not acknowledge the discrepancy, much less try to grapple with it.

before the results . . . an omen of concord: the centuries of the Centuriate assembly that were first to vote were picked by lot; the results were announced to the centuries yet to vote, and they were considered an omen of divine favour.

303 *the temple to Mater Matuta . . . Tullius*: Mater Matuta was an ancient Italic goddess of fertility.

305 *this story . . . affirm or refute*: Livy makes the same disclaimer, using some of the same language, in his Preface.

307 *drawn by white horses . . . these horses*: a chariot drawn by four white horses was associated especially with Jupiter and the Sun (Sol); Romulus was said to have used them, as did Julius Caesar in Livy's lifetime. The triumphator was traditionally dressed as Jupiter and proceeded to Jupiter's temple on the Capitol to give thanks for his victory.

308 *three and seven-tenths acres apiece*: the Roman acre (*iugerum*) was about two-thirds of an English acre.

309 *permission to use a carriage . . . days*: wheeled vehicles were ordinarily prohibited in the city during daylight hours.

311 *the same man as their teacher and companion*: in early Rome children were educated at home by their parents or attended a common school (cf. 3.44). For the latter they were accompanied by a slave who acted as an escort and protector, not as a teacher. The Greek system described here, combining the two functions into one (the *paedagogus*), came into vogue in Rome in the second century BC.

314 *Vitellia*: probably the same as Vetelia (2.39).

315 *a reminder . . . before his very eyes*: the reference is to the pictures or models of conquered cities that were carried in triumphal processions.

316 *an ovation*: on the *ouatio* see 3.10 and the note to p. 150.

Volsinii: an Etruscan city some sixty-five miles north of Rome (modern Bolsena).

lustrum: the (usually) five-year period between censorships. See 1.44, 3.3, and 3.22.

interregnum: on the interregnum see 1.17, 3.8 and the note to p. 147.

317 *the shrine . . . temple of Vesta*: the reference is to the shrine of Aius Locutius ('the Speaking Voice'); see ch. 50.

319 *the Hercynian forests . . . by lot*: this was the upland area of south Germany and included the Black Forest.

the Bituriges . . . Aulerci: the names of many of these tribes survive in modern-day France: e.g. Bourges, Auvergne, Sens, Chartres.

Phocaea: a Greek city in Ionia, on the Aegean coast of what is now modern Turkey. Massilia is modern Marseilles (founded *c*.600 BC).

Mediolanium: modern Milan.

the Poenine Pass: the Great St Bernard Pass.

the Utens and Aesis rivers: these rivers encompassed roughly the land between modern Ravenna and Sinigaglia on the Adriatic Sea.

325 *the bridge of wooden piles . . . the Janiculum*: this bridge was the *pons sublicius*, whose original construction Livy describes in 1.33.

326 *curule magistracies*: in this early period curule magistrates (i.e. higher magistrates entitled to use the curule chair of wood and ivory: cf. 1.8) included dictators, consuls, censors, and the two curule aediles; praetors, a later creation, were also curule.

sacrifice their lives . . . Rome: this sacrifice, called *deuotio*, was a ceremony in which a man swore on oath to forfeit his life to the gods in order that he might divert their anger from the people to himself. At 8.9 Livy gives the complete formula when narrating the *deuotio* of Decius Mus.

330 *the Salt Works*: or Salinae; they were on the outskirts of Rome.

in Gabine fashion: the phrase *Gabino cinctu* refers to wearing the toga so that both arms were exposed and free; it was used during certain religious ceremonies, and presumably was introduced from the nearby town of Gabii (cf. 1.54 and ch. 49).

331 *the Curiate assembly*: the most ancient of Roman assemblies, consisting of the thirty *curiae* or city wards (see 1.13); it ratified the supreme command of those elected in the Centuriate assembly and also acted in certain matters in which religious questions were involved, such as wills and adoptions. In the late Republic the assembly existed only in fossilized form, each *curia* being represented by a lictor.

337 *feast of Jupiter . . . couch*: the image of Jupiter was placed on a couch (*puluinar*) and food laid before it. Cf. the lectisternium, ch. 13.

the image . . . empire: the statue (the Palladium) was of an armed goddess, said to have been brought from Troy; it was housed in the shrine of the Vestals, where only they and the pontifex maximus could look upon it and worship it.

shields . . . Quirinus: on the shields (*ancilia*) see 1.20 and the note to p. 25. Camillus refers to them again at the end of his speech (ch. 54). Quirinus was often identified with the deified Romulus.

338 *the flamen Dialis . . . outside the city*: see 1.20 and the note to p. 25.

339 *the hut of our founder*: the hut of Romulus was carefully preserved and periodically renewed. The post holes of the one on the Palatine hill are still visible today.

340 *Rome . . . citizens*: 365 is a mystical number, a period made up of as many years as a year is of days. In ch. 40 he says it is the 360th year, which he may simply intend as a round number.

341 *the unearthing . . . ancestors*: on the unearthing of the head and the temple of Terminus, see 1.55 (where, however, Livy does not mention Iuventas).

in the building . . . Hostilius: on the Curia Hostilia, see 1.30 and the note to p. 37. It probably burned during the Gallic Sack; archaeologists have found evidence of fire damage dating to the early fourth century in the area where the Curia stood. The Comitium, or place of public assembly, was in front of the Curia.

INDEX

cos. = consul; mil. trib. = military tribune with consular power; tr. pl. = tribune of the plebs. Within families names are listed by praenomen rather than cognomen. All dates are BC.

The Oxford World's Classics Website

www.worldsclassics.co.uk

- Browse the full range of Oxford World's Classics online

- Sign up for our monthly e-alert to receive information on new titles

- Read extracts from the Introductions

- Listen to our editors and translators talk about the world's greatest literature with our Oxford World's Classics audio guides

- Join the conversation, follow us on Twitter at OWC_Oxford

- Teachers and lecturers can order inspection copies quickly and simply via our website

www.worldsclassics.co.uk

American Literature

British and Irish Literature

Children's Literature

Classics and Ancient Literature

Colonial Literature

Eastern Literature

European Literature

Gothic Literature

History

Medieval Literature

Oxford English Drama

Poetry

Philosophy

Politics

Religion

The Oxford Shakespeare

A complete list of Oxford World's Classics, including Authors in Context, Oxford English Drama, and the Oxford Shakespeare, is available in the UK from the Marketing Services Department, Oxford University Press, Great Clarendon Street, Oxford OX2 6DP, or visit the website at www.oup.com/uk/worldsclassics.

In the USA, visit www.oup.com/us/owc for a complete title list.

Oxford World's Classics are available from all good bookshops. In case of difficulty, customers in the UK should contact Oxford University Press Bookshop, 116 High Street, Oxford OX1 4BR.

A SELECTION OF OXFORD WORLD'S CLASSICS

THOMAS AQUINAS	Selected Philosophical Writings
GEORGE BERKELEY	Principles of Human Knowledge and Three Dialogues
EDMUND BURKE	A Philosophical Enquiry into the Origin of Our Ideas of the Sublime and Beautiful Reflections on the Revolution in France
THOMAS CARLYLE	The French Revolution
CONFUCIUS	The Analects
FRIEDRICH ENGELS	The Condition of the Working Class in England
JAMES GEORGE FRAZER	The Golden Bough
THOMAS HOBBES	Human Nature and De Corpore Politico Leviathan
JOHN HUME	Dialogues Concerning Natural Religion and The Natural History of Religion Selected Essays
THOMAS MALTHUS	An Essay on the Principle of Population
KARL MARX	Capital The Communist Manifesto
J. S. MILL	On Liberty and Other Essays Principles of Economy and Chapters on Socialism
FRIEDRICH NIETZSCHE	On the Genealogy of Morals Twilight of the Idols
THOMAS PAINE	Rights of Man, Common Sense, and Other Political Writings
JEAN-JACQUES ROUSSEAU	Discourse on Political Economy and The Social Contract Discourse on the Origin of Inequality
SIMA QIAN	Historical Records
ADAM SMITH	An Inquiry into the Nature and Causes of the Wealth of Nations
MARY WOLLSTONECRAFT	Political Writings